Wagner and Tolkien:
Mythmakers

Renée Vink

Wagner and Tolkien:
Mythmakers

2012

Cormarë Series No. 25

Series Editors: Peter Buchs • Thomas Honegger • Andrew Moglestue • Johanna Schön

Editor responsible for this volume: Andrew Moglestue

Library of Congress Cataloging-in-Publication Data

Vink, Renée:
Wagner and Tolkien: Mythmakers
ISBN 978-3-905703-25-2

Subject headings:
Tolkien, J.R.R. (John Ronald Reuel), 1892-1973
Wagner, Richard, 1813-1883
The Lord of the Rings
Der Ring

Cormarë Series No. 25

First published 2012

© Walking Tree Publishers, Zurich and Jena, 2012

All rights reserved. No portion of this book may be reproduced, by any process or technique, without the express written consent of the publisher

Cover illustration *The Ravens of Wotan* (1911) by Arthur Rackham

Set in Adobe Garamond Pro and Shannon by Walking Tree Publishers
Printed by Lightning Source in the United Kingdom and United States

BOARD OF ADVISORS

ACADEMIC ADVISORS

Douglas A. Anderson (independent scholar)

Dieter Bachmann (Universität Zürich)

Patrick Curry (independent scholar)

Michael D.C. Drout (Wheaton College)

Vincent Ferré (Université de Paris 13)

Thomas Fornet-Ponse (Rheinische Friedrich-Wilhelms-Universität Bonn)

Verlyn Flieger (University of Maryland)

Christopher Garbowski (University of Lublin, Poland)

Mark T. Hooker (Indiana University)

Andrew James Johnston (Freie Universität Berlin)

Rainer Nagel (Johannes Gutenberg-Universität Mainz)

Helmut W. Pesch (independent scholar)

Tom Shippey (University of Winchester)

Allan Turner (Friedrich-Schiller-Universität Jena)

Frank Weinreich (independent scholar)

GENERAL READERS

Johan Boots

Jean Chausse

Friedhelm Schneidewind

Patrick Van den hole

Johan Vanhecke (Letterenhuis, Antwerp)

To my mother
Willemina Maria (Wil) Rijsdijk

Series Editor's Preface

It is hardly possible to explore the works of Tolkien and Wagner without at some point suspecting the presence of echoes and parallels. Yet attempts to understand these often founder when confronted with Tolkien's own much-quoted assesment that all similarity ends with the roundness of the rings (a statement, that as we shall see, may well be misunderstood). So is there or is there not any connection that goes beyond the common sources that both authors drew upon?

Despite the many decades since the publication of *The Hobbit*, *The Lord of the Rings* and Tolkien's various posthumous works (and indeed the 15 years that Walking Tree Publishers can now look back upon) it is remarkable that the connection between Wagner and Tolkien has so far attracted so little attention. It was all the more surprising when not one but two major studies were presented to us almost simultaneously. Obviously the time was right for this topic. The different focus and high quality of the two works convinced us to publish them both. Christopher MacLachlan's *Tolkien and Wagner: the Ring and Der Ring* was released earlier this year, and is now joined by the present monography.

Special thanks are due to all who supported its production, especially Madline Seiler, Stefanie Busch and Johanna Schön.

In the name of Walking Tree Publishers I wish you enjoyable and stimulating reading.

Andrew Moglestue
Zurich, June 2012

Contents

Introduction

The Master and the Professor - Wagner and Tolkien   xiii

Part One, Two Round Rings

Chapter 1, A Conspiracy Unmasked?   3

1.1. A Ring of Power   3
1.2. Two round rings   4
1.3. How well did Tolkien know Wagner?   9

Chapter 2, Searching for Sources   15

2.1. A list of similarities   15
2.2. 'Faint and disparate echoes'   29
2.3. Common sources   31

Chapter 3, What has it got in its pocketses?   39

3.1. No   39
    Birzer 39 / Bratman 42 / Spear 43 / Müller 43 / Scott Rohan 46
    Ridpath 49
3.2. Yes   49
    Hillard 49 / Shippey 50 / Haymes 57 / Bayreuth and sundry 57
    Ross, Kasper, and sex 59 / The racism card, Schwartz & Arvidsson 60
    Hate-speak 69
3.3. Deliberately   71
    Hall 71 / O'Donoghue 72 / Spengler 73 / 'Thief Tolkien' 75

Chapter 4, Other Approaches — 81

4.1. The evils of power — 81
Werner 81 / Luke, and Ross again 82 / What power? 83
Views of evil 87 / Fear of the end 90

4.2. A poisoned imagination? — 91
Chism and the poisoned sources 91 / From myth to history 97

Chapter 5, Conclusion — 105

Part Two, Myths, Fairy Tales and Endings

Chapter 6, Romanticism and Mythmaking — 113

6.1. Introduction — 113
6.2. National myths — 115
Tolkien in England 116 / Wagner in Germany 120
6.3. Modern myth — 126

Chapter 7, Nature and its Defilement — 131

Chapter 8, A World too Much? Fantasy versus (Stage) Drama — 135

8.1. Myth and drama — 135
Dramatic narrative 136 / Faërian drama 137
Visual representation 141
8.2. Fantasy drama — 144
8.3. Music, words and the invisible stage — 147

Chapter 9, Tragedy, Elegy, Eucatastrophe — 153

9.1. Tragedy versus comedy — 153
9.2. Revolution versus restoration — 154
9.3. The end of myth — 155
9.4. The end of the world? — 157

Chapter 10, Conclusion — 163

Contents

Part Three, The Amateur and the Professional

Chapter 11, Sources and Resources   171

11.1. Pure and adulterated northernness   171
11.2. Sigurd versus Siegfried   178

Chapter 12, Language   185

12.1. Words, grammar and syntax   185
    Tolkien's archaisms 185 / Attack and defence 188
    Wagner's archaisms 190 / Wordplay 193 / Philological jests 196
    Kennings 198
12.2. Alliterations   200
    Stave rhyme rediscovered 200 / Some technicalities 200
    Wagner's verse 202 / Tolkien's development 211
    Rhythm and patterns 216
12.3. Proverbiality   218

Chapter 13, Narrative Elements   223

13.1. The Ring and the Legend – correspondences   223
    Introduction 223 / From the beginning to Ragnarök 223 / Baldr 226
    The solar hero and the Saviour 228 / Odin and Wotan 235
13.2. The Ring and the Legend – differences   239
    Assorted differences 239 / Characteristic choices 242
    Half-brother and full brothers 244
13.3. Solving a conundrum: The ring at the core   245
    The sources 245 / The botched tradition 249 / The ring of fire 253
    Did they do it? 256

Chapter 14, Conclusion   265

Afterword   271

Bibliography   273
Index of fiction   289
General index   295

About the Author

Renée Vink was born in Amsterdam and studied Scandinavian languages at the Universities of Leiden (The Netherlands) and Göteborg (Sweden). She has been working as a translator from Swedish, Norwegian, Danish, English and German into Dutch since the 1980s, translating among other things the poetry in Tolkien's *The Legend of Sigurd and Gudrún*. Being a long-time Tolkien fan and scholar, she has also published a number of articles in various Tolkien-related magazines from 1982 onwards. Her other main interest is the work of Richard Wagner.

Introduction

The Master and the Professor - Wagner and Tolkien

Ever since the publication in the 1950s of J.R.R. Tolkien's The Lord of the Rings, people have noticed similarities between this work and another one in which an evil ring of power plays a major role: Richard Wagner's four part opera cycle Der Ring des Nibelungen (The Ring of the Nibelung). At first, comparisons between the two occurred sporadically in newspaper articles, journals of various kinds and the odd anthology of Tolkien-centered essays. After the rise of the Internet, especially in the wake of Peter Jackson's cinematic adaptation of Tolkien's epic, their number increased dramatically. Many web forums mention Tolkien and Wagner in close proximity. The number of articles and essays on the subject published this century, either on paper or on the Internet, already dwarfs the number written between 1955, when the final part of *The Lord of the Rings* appeared, and 2000, the year before the first film hit the screens.

Lovers of Tolkien's work, fans and scholars alike, often react to this by attempting to banish the German composer from the English author's premises. As Wagner (1813 - 1883) preceded Tolkien (1892 - 1973) by three quarters of a century, many who discover similarities between the two ring stories assume that Tolkien must have been influenced by Wagner, that his epic is therefore derivative, or even that he is a plagiarist. Tolkien fans often react to this by dismissing even the slightest suggestion that Wagner's work could have left its mark on Tolkien's. Their main arguments are 1) that any similarities existing between the two result from the fact that both drew from the same Icelandic sources, and that 2) Tolkien thoroughly disliked Wagner's Ring and rejected the comparison. To prove this they quote his reply to a letter from the Swedish translator of The Lord of the Rings, who claimed the two rings to be identical: 'Both rings were round, and there the resemblance ceases.'

Most champions defending Tolkien's independence from Wagner leave it at that. But some, quoting one of his biographers, add that Tolkien held Wagner's interpretation of the source material in contempt. As a philologist, they argue, he must have deplored Wagner's distortion of the old myths and stories from the Scandinavian North - those same stories that were so dear to him, that he could read in the original language and that he taught at Oxford University. They point out that Wagner was a dilettante who had to make do with translations and did not respect the integrity of the old texts. Why this negative judgement would preclude any influence by Wagner remains unexplained, though.

One cannot entirely avoid the impression that such dismissals do not only spring from a genuine desire to defend a beloved author against the accusation of theft, but also from an active dislike of the other party. Wagner, the opportunistic anti-Semite with his dubious morality, has always been a controversial figure, but never more so than since the Second World War, in which the Nazis used his work as propaganda material in the service of a horrible and abhorred ideology - something to which it lent itself a little too well. Even today, Wagner's operas still have not been entirely decontaminated and the question is whether they ever will. For a great many Tolkien-fans, the association with this suspect composer is unwanted, especially as people have accused Tolkien's own works of showing fascist and racist tendencies.

For others, some Tolkien enthusiasts and scholars among them, the arguments against the comparison do not hold water. They realise at least that denying something does not make it go away, and that an author is not always the best judge of his own work. They try to take an objective look at the matter and usually end up admitting – if they do not begin by doing so – that there are similarities between the two Rings which do not spring from the Icelandic source material. They then tend to mitigate this conclusion by claiming that it is the overall result that matters, that Tolkien does something original with the elements he has borrowed, that there are things he does better than Wagner, that his ethics surpass those found in the Ring des Nibelungen and even that he was a good Christian whereas Wagner was an anarchist and a fiend. Others, who are equally fond of both, are just happy to point out any correspondences they have found. One or two move beyond this and address new and interesting aspects of the matter.

Introduction

One category of Tolkien lovers acts according to the maxim that attack is the best defence. Of course there are similarities, they say. Tolkien deliberately used Wagner's work, precisely because Wagner had so badly distorted the elements he had ripped from the old Icelandic stories. His aim was to wrest them from Wagner's stranglehold, to pull them from under the shadow of Nazism and fascism and to recreate the proper Northern atmosphere in which they could be themselves again. If these Tolkien fans are truly bold, they claim he was successful in doing so: today, Tolkien's *The Lord of the Rings* is the more popular of the two. In short, J.R.R. Tolkien is the Anti-Wagner Triumphant. Given the number of opera house websites that flash Tolkien's Ring to draw attention to Wagner's, they may have a point - or do they?

Staunch Wagnerians laugh at this, if they are aware of it. Which is usually not the case, as studying Tolkien fandom is not foremost on their agendas and they rarely feel they have to (dis)prove anything concerning Tolkien. Nevertheless some of them spend a thought or two on the similarities between the two Rings. They consider it a given that Tolkien borrowed at least his Ruling Ring from Wagner, and usually that settles it. Most of those who say a little more tend to give the English professor short shrift. The least damning verdict is that his work is charming but shallow: 'Wagner light'. Others call it immature, claim that the characters lack development and consider the absence of sexuality a blemish. On the whole, they do not take Tolkien nearly as seriously as they take Wagner.

In the spring of 2009, the subject 'Wagner and Tolkien' presented itself in a new light when Tolkien's *The Legend of Sigurd and Gudrun* was published. The longer of the two lays in this volume, written during the early 1930s, tells largely the same story as Wagner's Ring cycle. Christopher Tolkien, who wrote the commentary to his father's poems, even mentions Wagner in his foreword, but only to inform the readers why he does not mention him in the rest of the book. He may have attempted to create distance between Wagner's Ring and his father's lays, but this cat was going to come out of the bag regardless. Whatever is the case, that Tolkien composed his own version of the tale of Siegfried and Brünnhilde - or Sigurd and Brynhild - was in itself enough of an incentive to revisit the subject.

At the time the Legend appeared, no book-length comparison between Wagner's work and Tolkien's existed, and the analyses published until then did not cover all bases. This study is an attempt to fill this lacuna. Usually in such comparisons the casualty is Wagner's music. In this study I will take it into consideration on occasion, though as I am no musical theorist, my observations will of necessity remain limited both in quantity and in quality.

The first part will offer a survey of the publications written on the subject until now, and of the positions their authors take in what is for the most part a controversy between pure Tolkienists and people who like both Wagner and Tolkien, with the odd Wagnerian showing up every now and then. I will use these analyses and opinions to add my own comments and theories. That the comparison between the two famous ring works will take up a large part of this survey is inevitable, but other aspects will also be addressed.

Both Wagner and Tolkien were capable and successful mythmakers who underpinned their own creations with theoretical writings and whose mythmaking had a national aspect to it. For both, death, immortality and the need to accept the finiteness of human existence were fundamental themes. They took a keen interest in nature, endangered by the economical and industrial developments of their times. Though one was a dramatist and the other preferred fairy stories, Tolkien had a good sense of drama and for a dramatic work, Wagner's Ring has remarkably strong narrative strains. This correspondence is also borne out by the conclusions of their major works: while the ending of LR is eucatastrophic but not unambiguously happy, the ending of the Ring cycle is by no means as purely tragic as one would think at first sight.

In the third part some more technical aspects of the Wagner-Tolkien relationship will be addressed. It has been suggested that as a professional philologist, Tolkien deplored the success of a work that in his eyes played havoc with the integrity of its medieval source texts – the work, moreover, of an amateur without firsthand knowledge of these texts. I will argue that the popularity of Wagner's Ring with the general public contributed to and perhaps inspired Tolkien's desire to recreate the story of Sigurd the Dragonslayer in a manner more faithful to the originals. Further, I will try to assess the differences between his philological professionalism and Wagner's amateurism by comparing the linguistic, stylistic and poetic aspects of Wagner's Ring cycle with those of Tolkien's Arda writings and his Legend. Their use of Germanic alliterative metre will receive special attention. A survey of some important similarities and differences between the treatment of the Dragonslayer tale in the Legend and in the Ring, with the mystery surrounding Sigurd's/Siegfried's treatment of the (ex) valkyrie Brynhild/Brünnhilde serving as a case study, will conclude the comparison between the two mythmakers.

Prior knowledge of Wagner's Ring and Tolkien's fictional works will be assumed; therefore no summaries will be given.

Acknowledgements

My warm thanks go to the people who each in their own way contributed to the creation of this book by giving good advice, pointing me to interesting articles and other information, challenging my assumptions, checking my facts and quotes, correcting my English and providing encouragement. In alphabetical order, they are: Pamina Fernandez Camacho (Cádiz), Walter Gelaudemans (Hook of Holland), Thomas Honegger (Jena), Inger Mees (Copenhagen), Frank Wasmus (The Hague) and Sjoerd van der Weide (Tilburg).

Part One

Two Round Rings

Chapter 1

A Conspiracy Unmasked?

1.1. A Ring of Power

'The New Lay of the Völsungs', the first of the two epic poems in Tolkien's posthumous *The Legend of Sigurd and Gudrún*, unmistakably tells the same story as Wagner's opera cycle *Der Ring des Nibelungen*. Both used an ancient, somewhat convoluted tale from Norse myth and saga. When Tom Shippey reviewed the new Tolkien publication for the *Times Literary Supplement*, the headline, taken from the body of the review text, was a triumphant 'Tolkien Out-Wagners Wagner'.

Shippey staked the claim that Tolkien's poem offered a solution to a *Königsproblem*, a major conundrum of Germanic philology, that had baffled Wagner. What was the matter with the ring cursed by the dwarf Andvari and later found by Sigurd in the dragon's hoard that made Brynhild demand Sigurd's death? The *Poetic Edda* might have told us, except there is a gap of eight pages in the Codex Regius, the main surviving manuscript. The three Icelandic prose versions of the story and the Middle-High German *Nibelungenlied* all contradict each other. Wagner tried to disentangle the knot, but did not entirely succeed. Tolkien did, or so Shippey says.[1]

The question whether Shippey is right will be addressed in the second part of this book; that is not the point here. The question is: why would anyone want Tolkien to have out-Wagnered Wagner badly enough to raise such a conclusion like a victorious banner over a captured castle? The answer involves a magic ring of power.

---

1 When Hans-Ulrich Möhring's German translation of *The Legend* appeared in 2010, reviewer Wieland Freund of the German newspaper, *Die Welt*, denied that Tolkien had out-Wagnered or 'over-Wagnered', as it was translated, calling the claim a bit *gehässig* (spiteful). In fact, Tolkien had 'under-Wagnered' Wagner, having dug deeper for sources. Unfortunately for Freund, this is not the case: they mostly use the same sources.

1.2. Two round rings

The first person known to have compared Tolkien's One Ring with Wagner's Ring of the Nibelung was Rayner Unwin, the son of Tolkien's publisher Stanley Unwin. According to Carpenter's biography he did so because the division of *The Lord of the Rings* into separate sections made Frodo's ring resemble that of the Nibelung (206). The first to compare the two works in a written text seems to have been William Blisset in an article called 'The Despots of the Rings' (1959); he did not rule out any direct influences. Many followed. And the suggestion that Tolkien borrowed from Wagner does not stop at a perceived influence of one ring on the other. 'Henceforth I shall remain a derivative Wagnerian hero', proclaims the character Túrin Turambar in a parody on *The Children of Húrin* in *The Guardian* of April 24, 2007. But generally, the focus remains on the two rings.

'Both Rings were round, and there the resemblance ceases', was Tolkien's terse reaction to the comparison. Or so many say, from Tom Shippey to the secondary school student in the town of Wunsiedel, Germany, who brought up the matter in an essay about Tolkien's *The Lord of the Rings*. In Internet forum discussions this quote is frequently used to enlighten participants who wonder if Tolkien was influenced by Wagner, often with the intention of smothering further discussion of the subject. Other suggestions for sources of inspiration for Tolkien's Ring epic rarely meet with the – sometimes vehement – denial that follows the merest mention of Wagner's operatic cycle. Many attempts to discuss the matter peter out after a few posts. 'J.R.R. Tolkien's fans have long maintained a certain conspiracy of silence concerning Wagner', as Alex Ross wrote in a column in the *New Yorker* in 2003. *The Tolkien Encyclopaedia* promptly proves him right by not giving Wagner's *Ring* an entry. *The Keys of Middle-earth* lists all kinds of sources for *The Hobbit* and *The Lord of the Rings*, from Plato's works to G.K. Chesterton's (Lee & Solopova, 11f). Wagner, however, merely receives a footnote in which his *Ring* is said to have 'similarities with Tolkien's story' (Lee & Solopova, 111). The biographies published after Carpenter's generally ignore him.[2]

---

[2] The exception is White's biography, generally considered to be quite flawed.

If Tolkien students take the quote about the two round rings for granted and refrain from further investigation, this can lead to serious errors. In a study of Tolkien's Northern sources that otherwise contains many valid points, Gloriana St. Clair claims that 'Andvari's ring, which occurs in the story line of *Völsunga saga*, *Nibelungenlied*, and Wagner's *Ring of the Nibelung* is a dull, inane bauble compared with the power and brooding malevolence of Tolkien's One Ring' (St. Clair, V, 2). But Andvari plays no role either in the *Nibelungenlied* or in Wagner's work, while 'power and brooding malevolence' apply perfectly well to the ring forged and cursed by Alberich. The author obviously ought to have checked her facts more thoroughly. This is the most glaring example, but it stands for many others. Too long, Tolkien scholars and fans alike have been prone to comment on the matter of the two rings without knowing the *Ring* cycle sufficiently well. Fortunately this seems to be changing, as more and more people from the Wagnerian side are joining the discussion.

It is understandable that people who love Tolkien's work want to reject allegations of plagiarism and lack of originality. Bradley Birzer remarks that since the first comparisons in the 1950s, many critics have used Wagner's *Ring* against Tolkien. In those rare cases in which Tolkien is called to Wagner's defence, he seems to draw the short end. Rejecting accusations of coarseness, shallowness, silliness, confused thinking and cheap emotionality leveled at Wagner's 'second-rate myth' full of 'overblown bombast', philosophers Philip Kitcher and Richard Schacht write:

> We agree with a celebrated Oxford professor of Anglo-Saxon who inverted the standard opinion of *Beowulf* by suggesting that the critics were focusing, wrongly, on the poem's historical episodes while ignoring the monsters at its heart. That professor, J.R.R. Tolkien, went on to defend his claims about the power of myth by creating one of his own – indeed an elaborate narrative with a cast of dwarves and monsters, with plenty of magic and even with a Ring of Power at its center. (Kitcher & Schacht, 5)

But then the authors rain on the Tolkien fan parade by adding that his book does 'not deserve the serious attention and reflection lavished on the *Ring*' (6).

Still, however undesirable a connection between the creator of the hobbits and Hitler's favourite composer (an honour Wagner shared with Franz Léhar) may be to some, it keeps popping up. Attempts to stifle the debate by blunt denial will only be counterproductive and draw more attention to the controversy. If Tolkien was influenced by Wagner, this does not automatically mean that he aped either the Incomparable Master, or the Despicable Proto-Nazi. It is virtually impossible for any reader not to be influenced by other people's texts. But even deliberate echoes do not make a work derivative. The importance of artistic originality – a notion that originated in the Romantic age, as the medievalist Tolkien knew very well – is overrated. In this age of intertextuality and interrelatedness it ought to be possible to address the relation Wagner-Tolkien without building barricades or digging trenches.

Ross overstated his point, though: a fair number of Tolkien scholars have addressed the matter over the years. Like the fans on the forums, not a few among them also assume that the statement about the round rings is Tolkien's first and last word on the matter. They either proceed to discuss something else or, albeit hesitantly and often implicitly, they suggest that Tolkien was self-delusional and/or obscuring the truth. Others simply ignore the statement. Only a few take a closer look at the context in which Tolkien actually made it.

Yet it is worth doing so. The statement was first published in Humphrey Carpenter's biography of 1977: 'The comparison of his Ring with the *Nibelungenlied* and Wagner always annoyed Tolkien; he once said: "Both rings were round and there the resemblance ceased"'[3] (206). Readers of the biography had to take this on faith until *The Letters of J.R.R. Tolkien* appeared in 1981. There, the statement in question is found in Letter nr. 230, dated 8 June 1961 and addressed to Allen & Unwin. In this letter Tolkien fumes about the introduction to the Swedish translation of *The Lord of the Rings*, both by Åke Ohlmarks. Ohlmarks was a sloppy and conceited man (the latter qualification was Tolkien's own, *Letters*, 263) and his translation full of errors; in 1977 he was not allowed to translate *The Silmarillion*.[4] His unauthorised introduction to *LR* is, in Tolkien's words, full of 'presumptuous impertinence' (*Letters*, 305).

---

3 Carpenter's quote has the past tense, though Tolkien used the present tense.
4 After an unfortunate incident with a member of a Swedish Tolkien Society Ohlmarks struck back and wrote *Tolkien och den svarta magin* in which he accused Tolkien himself, his family and all Tolkien societies of Satanism and Nazism. This book contains a prime example of his sloppiness: the English occultist Aleister Crowley becomes 'Allister Prowley'.
In 1992 Erik Anderson made a new translation of LR, consulting several Swedish Tolkien scholars to avoid mistakes of the Ohlmarks kind.

Tolkien is not amused, and when Sauron is said to represent the Soviet dictator Stalin he even becomes angry. Among other offences, Ohlmarks has concocted a ring story of his own, to which Tolkien adds his comments (Ohlmarks's text in italics):

> *The Ring is in a certain way 'der Nibelungen Ring'* ...
>
> Both rings were round, and there the resemblance ceases.
>
> *... which was originally forged by Volund the master-smith, and then by way of Vittka-Andvare passed through the hands of the mighty asar [Æsir] into the possession of Hreidmar and the dragon, after the dragon's fall coming to Sigurd the dragonslayer, after his murder by treacherous conspirators coming to the Burgundians, after their death in Atle's snake-pit coming to the Huns, then to the sons of Jonaker, to the Gothic tyrant Ermanrik, etc.*
>
> Thank heaven for the *etc*. I began to fear that it would turn up in my pocket. Evidently Dr. O thinks that it is in his. But what is the point of all this? Those who know something about the Old Norse side of the 'Nibelung' traditions (mainly referred to since the name-forms used are Norse) will think this a farrago of nonsense; those who do not, will hardly be interested. But perhaps they are also meant to conclude that Dr. O also has *mästerskap*.[5] It has nothing whatsoever to do with *The Lord of the Rings*. (Letters, 306f)

No one halfway familiar with the *Ring des Nibelungen* will recognise Ohlmarks's description as a summary of Wagner's tetralogy, which has a markedly different cast carrying German or Germanised names. Wagner's ring itself also has a rather different history than the one given above. Moreover, Tolkien clearly assumes Ohlmarks is rambling about the Norse traditions rather than about their 19th-century adaptation and transformation by Wagner, or about the Middle-High German *Nibelungenlied*, to which the summary is equally inapplicable. What he balks at is the suggestion that his ring has anything to do with this pseudo-scholarly rubbish.

It is easy to guess why Carpenter interpreted the sentence about the two round rings the way he did. He probably focused on the name Nibelungen, which automatically, and not surprisingly, must have triggered connotations with Wagner. Also, he seems to have taken Wagner's work for an adaptation of the *Nibelungenlied*. But he cannot have been too familiar with either, or with the Icelandic tales, or he would have recognised Ohlmarks's nonsense

---

5 Swedish for 'mastery' (Tolkien's note).

for what it was. In short, the passage in the biography is inaccurate and therefore misleading.

This misrepresentation could be one of the reasons, along with Hitler's admiration and Wagner's own controversiality, why most Tolkien biographers and encyclopedias do not mention the composer or dismiss him as cursorily as Carpenter did. As Edward Haymes puts it, they 'have been complicit in covering up any real connection' (Haymes 2004). Of the scholars, only Ellison (15) and Bratman (166, n. 4) note that Tolkien was not referring to Wagner in his letter.

Could the writer of the pseudo-scholarly nonsense actually have been thinking of Wagner's cycle when he wrote 'der Nibelungen Ring'? To Ohlmarks, the differences between the old poems and sagas on the one hand and Wagner's adaptation of them on the other may have seemed inconsequential, like the fact that the title of Wagner's tetralogy is *Der Ring des Nibelungen* (singular) not '*der Nibelungen Ring*' (plural). Tolkien's German was good enough to know the difference, but he had the evidence of Ohlmarks's sloppy thinking right under his nose, so the possibility that his translator had the German composer in mind must have occurred to him. If it did, he evidently decided to let this sleeping dragon lie. As a matter of fact, he had an excellent reason to avoid the name Wagner after World War II, which lay less than twenty years in the past.

Tom Shippey believes that Tolkien made the statement as a 'response to a dumbed-down (but frequently repeated) opinion, to the effect that "Tolkien got it all from *The Ring of the Nibelung*"' (Shippey 2007, 97). One wonders how frequently this could have been repeated prior to 1960, when Ohlmarks wrote his farrago of nonsense – years ahead of the explosion of personal opinions called the Internet. No inventory of early reviews mentioning Wagner's *Ring* has ever been made, while the reviews that managed to acquire either fame or notoriety remain silent about it. That C.S. Lewis and W.H. Auden, both Wagner-lovers, do not mention the Ring in their reviews is interesting: did they have private reasons to know the comparison irked Tolkien? Was it bandied about in Oxford in the mid-fifties?

In the end, the vehemence of Tolkien's reaction to Ohlmarks remains suspicious, as though a monster of Wagnerian proportions is lurking beneath the surface after all. If that is the case, it had best be caught and displayed for readers to make their own assessment.

1.3. How well did Tolkien know Wagner?

Did Tolkien have anything to say about Wagner at all? In *Letters*, the name is conspicuous by its absence. Carpenter's biography contains one other reference to Wagner. In the summer of 1911, Tolkien and a number of his school friends formed a group called the Tea Club, which evolved into the 'Tea Club, Barrovian Society' (TCBS). At meetings of this club, Tolkien

> delighted his friends with recitations from *Beowulf*, the *Pearl*, and *Sir Gawain and the Green Knight*, and recounted horrific episodes from the Norse *Völsungasaga* with a passing jibe at Wagner whose interpretation of the myths he held in contempt. (Carpenter, 193)

His source, Carpenter tells us in an appendix to his biography was Christopher Wiseman (275), the only one among Tolkien's TCBS friends to have survived the First World War. Assuming that Wiseman's recollections and Carpenter's rendition of them are correct, this means that Tolkien at the age of 19 did not think much of Wagner.

The music critic and fantasy author Michael Scott Rohan assumes that Tolkien uttered his jibes before he knew enough Old Norse to read Wagner's source texts in the original and must have used the *Völsunga saga* translation of Morris and Mágnusson (1888). In that case he must have done so before early 1911, when he read a paper about Norse sagas at school, illustrating it with quotes from the original medieval texts (Scull & Hammond, 23). According to the Swedish Anglicist Arne Zettersten, who frequently visited Tolkien in the 1960s and early 1970s and got to know him well, he had indeed started to read Icelandic sagas in the original during his school years (Zettersten, 243).

The work of William Morris was a main influence on Tolkien, who later explicitly acknowledged his debt to *The House of the Wolfings* (1889) and *The Roots of the Mountains* (1890) (*Letters*, 303), while *The Hobbit* was arguably influenced by the journals Morris wrote during his visits to Iceland in 1871 and 1873 (Burns, 74-92). Morris also wrote the epic poem *The Story of Sigurd the Volsung and the Fall of the Nibelungs*, a retelling of the *Völsunga saga* in rhymed verse. Although he shared Wagner's interest in the subject matter, he never attended any performances of the *Ring*, and in the 'Introduction' to his complete works he is reported to have said that it was

> nothing short of desecration to bring such a tremendous and world-wide subject under the gaslight of an opera: the most rococo and degraded form of art - the idea of a sandy haired German tenor tweedledeeing over the unspeakable woes of Sigurd, which even the simplest words are not typical enough to express. (Morris, viii)

As Morris's complete works appeared in 1911, one wonders if Tolkien at some point read this introduction and applauded Morris's sentiments.[6]

On the whole it is remarkable that he should have written and said so very little about Wagner's work. But based on what is there, it looks as though Tolkien did not really feel like commenting on that other long *Ring*-story.

Was he acquainted with the *Ring* music? From the 1860s until at least the First World War, Wagner was a veritable hype, not just in Germany but practically all over the western world. People not only attended performances of his music dramas, they also studied his ideas about art, society and religion; many learned German to be able to read his works in the original. He became the subject of a personality cult during his own lifetime, a veritable Wagnerolatry (Magee, 29). Over ten thousand books and articles about Wagner had appeared before the composer's death in 1883. For decades 'Wagnerism' was a cultural and political movement. His writings on art inspired French (Baudelaire, Verlaine – who wrote a sonnet on *Parsifal* – and Mallarmé) and Russian (Aleksandr Blok) symbolism and was hailed by Christians, socialists and occultists alike as an

---

6 Decades before Morris wrote this, Wagner had also come to consider the opera of his time the most rococo and degraded of arts, to such a degree that he rejected even the word opera itself as a designation for his own works (until he resurrected it years later). Mainly for this reason he set out to change it fundamentally. The *Ring* cycle is one of the results of this endeavour and it is a pity Morris never gave it the benefit of the doubt; few words are less applicable to Siegfried's singing than 'tweedledeeing' (if one insists on using a pejorative, 'bellowing' would be more suitable). Possibly he considered Wagner a rival: *The Story of Sigurd the Volsung* appeared in 1876, the year when the *Ring of the Nibelung* was first performed in Bayreuth, at a time when Wagner's sun was rising in England and Morris was more or less eclipsed. In her thesis Jane Ennis considers Morris's work to be an anti-*Ring*.

antidote against scientific materialism and the excesses of the modern industrial society. Wagner influenced many composers of his own generation and almost all major composers of the two generations following his own (the exception being Strawinsky); Shostakovich even wanted to write a Russian equivalent of the *Ring* cycle. It was mainly due to Wagner that opera changed from a form of entertainment just one step above vaudeville to a serious form of art. He also deeply influenced Nietzsche and through him several important 20th century philosophers. Thomas Mann remained an ambivalent Wagnerian all his life. Wagner was a favourite of the French painters Degas, Cézanne and Gauguin and the American painter Whistler.

In Great Britain Wagner began to acquire popularity in the 1850s; in 1855 he visited England, where he gave a number of concerts and was invited for an audience with Queen Victoria and Prince Albert. His popularity grew; in 1873 and 1888 two successive Wagner Societies were founded. Writers, poets and artists like G.B. Shaw, Swinburne, Yeats, Wilde, Conrad, Bulwer-Lytton, Beardsley and Rackham admired Wagner[7] and his influence is also found in the earlier works of Joyce – who did not like him much –, Woolf, D. H. Lawrence – who wrote a Wagnerian novel in 1912, *The Trespasser* – E.M. Forster and T.S. Eliot, all at most a decade older than Tolkien.[8] Wagner operas were staged frequently in Britain from 1870 onwards; the year 1888 alone saw performances of *Tristan und Isolde*, the entire *Ring* and *Die Meistersinger*.

While it is not known that Tolkien attended any opera performances during his early years, he may have heard piano adaptations of Wagner's music, or excerpts performed during concerts, which would mean he was at least somewhat familiar with the music.[9] That he was well-acquainted with the entire *Ring* cycle is unlikely, though. The quality of recorded music was still insufficient to provide a proper impression of such a richly orchestrated work; the first complete

---

7 George Bernard Shaw's treatise *The Perfect Wagnerite*, became a classic; Arthur Rackhams illustrations to the *Ring* Cycle are still popular today.
8 W.H. Auden, younger than Tolkien and among his first admirers, came to Wagnerism later in life and ended up calling him 'perhaps the greatest genius that ever lived' (quoted by B. Magee, 48).
9 However, when Alex Ross jokingly writes: 'Admit it, J.R.R., you used to run around brandishing a walking stick and singing "Nothung! Nothung!" like every other besotted Oxford lad' this sounds more like a youthful C.S. Lewis, who became a Wagner fan before he ever heard the music and was more likely to brandish sword-like objects than Tolkien was. In the German version of Ross's article, the 'admit it' suddenly becomes a reference to witnesses who had allegedy 'seen' young Tolkien acting as described. Whether this deserves the qualification 'gained in translation' is dubious.

recording of it dates from the late 1950s, after the invention of the LP. So his youthful contempt of the *Ring* was most likely aimed at the libretto – form, content or both – written by Wagner himself.

It is tempting to dismiss this contempt for Wagner's version of the story as the hasty judgement of an overbearing young student feeling at ease among friends. At the time, Tolkien was probably unaware of the fact that it had never been Wagner's intention to create a faithful stage adaptation of any of the old sagas and poems that he used as ingredients for his *Ring* and that, consequently, such criticism completely missed the point. Yet, given his passion for the genuine article, for the ancient texts themselves in the form in which they had been handed down to posterity, it is doubtful whether he would have revised his judgement if he had been aware of it.

As Tolkien put it many years later, in 1955, he was 'not dramatic or operatic in taste'. He preferred Fantasy to Drama (Scull & Hammond 467; *On Fairy-stories* § 70-74). No wonder he thought little of Wagner's adaptation of the Norse myths and sagas. Not only had Wagner changed the originals, his work was meant for the stage; for a time, he even insisted that his theatrical works be called dramas instead of operas. Without the music the libretti are even less than stage plays, though. In 1853 Wagner published the texts of his *Ring* in a private edition for his friends. They seem to have liked them, which was probably the reason behind the public printing of 1863, but after he started composing *Das Rheingold* (The Rhinegold) he could no longer bear to look at the poems without the music. Opinions differ as to the literary merits of these libretti. Many, even people who love the music, are disdainful of them, others have a better opinion of them. The *Ring* libretti are commonly considered Wagner's best poetry. In 2009 the German theatre and opera director Sven-Eric Bechtolf recorded the entire text of the cycle on CD after discovering that listeners could tolerate long stretches of it surprisingly well.

Did Tolkien eventually hear the entire *Ring*? What little we know, is that early in 1934 he and the two Lewis brothers regularly met in Oxford to study and discuss the texts of the *Ring* operas in preparation for a planned attendance to the complete cycle at Covent Garden. Nothing came of this particular plan, as the seats were never booked. However, Tolkien's daughter Priscilla remembers her father attending at the performance of a *Ring* opera, probably *Siegfried*, together with C.S. Lewis; according to her they were among the few who did not wear full evening dress. That Tolkien went to Wagner performances more than once was confirmed in the BBC TV interview 'Tolkien in Oxford' of March 30, 1968 (Scull & Hammond, 616; Rosebury, 132).

Official sources have nothing more to report, but there is some additional information regarding Tolkien's possible appreciation of Wagner's music. According to a student of Lewis's, Derek Brewer, there was a rumour that Lewis and Tolkien annually attended the full *Ring* cycle in London (mentioned by Birzer). And on 18 March 2008 'Captain Bingo' wrote at the Internet forum *LotRplaza*: 'In one of the recordings made at the Church House bookshop in 1977 to launch *The Silmarillion*, Priscilla Tolkien mentioned that her father's favourite composers were Sibelius & Wagner.'[10] Bingo indeed – if the Captain's memory does not deceive him.

Tolkien's preference for Sibelius is corroborated by two separate issues of *Amon Hen*, the bulletin of the Tolkien Society. No. 208 contains an interview with the Irish politician and early defender of *The Lord of the Rings* (1962) Christopher Fettes, who stated that Sibelius was Tolkien's favourite composer. When a reader enquired how he knew this, Fettes replied in *Amon Hen* 210: 'I had tea with Tolkien one afternoon in about 1965 and asked who was his favourite composer. He immediately answered: "Sibelius."' This is no great surprise: the Finnish composer was profoundly inspired by the *Kalevala*, the national epic of Finland, a work Tolkien loved and admired to the extent that he tried to read it in the original language. Finnish in its turn strongly influenced the structure of his invented language Quenya. One of Sibelius's *Kalevala*-inspired works is the symphonic poem *Kullervo*. The story of Kullervo and his sister Aino became a source of inspiration for *The Children of Húrin*.

Now Sibelius admired Wagner, and several of his early works, *Kullervo* among them, are clearly inspired by the German composer. Add to this that Tolkien loved the broodingly mysterious *Freischütz*, an opera by Wagner's immediate

---

10 http://www.lotrplaza.com: Forum 'Tolkien the Man', thread 'Sibelius', 2nd post, dated March 17, 2008, retr. date 2-10-2011. Unfortunately, I have not been able to listen to the recording mentioned by Captain Bingo.

forerunner Carl Maria von Weber – yet another of Tolkien's favourite composers (Scull & Hammond, 617)[11] – and it seems safe to say that he must indeed have appreciated Wagner's music, to say the least. Circumstantial though the evidence may be, there is quite a lot of it. Whether he maintained his youthful criticism of the libretti after making his acquaintance with the music remains conjecture, but he would by no means have been the only one to love the music but little else about Wagner. One thing, is clear, though: Tolkien had a more than passing knowledge of Wagner's *Ring*.

---

11 Wagner, too, was a great admirer of Weber, and his first operas have often been compared to *Der Freischütz*.

Chapter 2

Searching for Sources

2.1. A list of similarities

What similarities are the people who compare Tolkien and Wagner actually talking about? In 1969, Lin Carter was the first to draw up a list in his book *Tolkien, a Look Behind The Lord of the Rings* (136ff). Like most others after him, he included *The Hobbit* in the comparison: the One Ring first occurs there. In a modified and rearranged form this list contains:

1. A dragon guarding a treasure, slain by a hero.

- In *Der Ring des Nibelungen* the giant Fafner, having acquired Alberich's treasure (including the ring and the Tarnhelm), changes into a dragon and withdraws to a cave with the treasure. Much later Siegfried kills him with his sword.
- In *The Hobbit* the dragon Smaug lies on the Dwarven treasures inside the Lonely Mountain. Later, Bard the Bowman shoots him with an arrow.

2. A magical ring of gold that bestows power upon the bearer, but carries a curse: it brings death and moral decay and completely corrupts the wicked little dwarf who once possessed it. Though Carter omits to mention this, the ring is forged with the specific purpose of gaining absolute power and enslaving others.

- Alberich forges a ring to achieve world domination,[12] enslaving others with the help of gold. When Wotan, wanting its power for himself, takes it by force Alberich curses it: '*Wer ihn besitzt, den sehre die Sorge, und wer ihn nicht hat, den nage der Neid*' (may care consume whoever possesses it and envy eat

---

[12] This property of the ring was taken from an object in the *Nibelungenlied*, a 'wishing rod' that conveys world power and forms part of the treasure of the Nibelungs that Siegfried acquires. It is mentioned once and plays no role in the story; Wagner merged it with the ring that plays a major part in the Norse versions of the story, *Andvaranaut*, the 'jewel of Andvari'.

whoever has it not). He describes 'the master of the Ring as the slave of the Ring', *Des Ringes Herr als des Ringes Knecht*. This refers to the fact that the ring determines the life of everyone who possesses or desires it. The curse causes the death of many. Those who have or desire it commit evil. It even corrupts Siegfried, the free hero, who lies under oath after having ripped it from Brünnhilde's finger (Kitcher & Schacht, 172-173). Alberich himself becomes totally evil in his attempt to get it back.

- Sauron forges the One Ring to achieve world domination, enslaving others by control of the will. Those who possess it slowly grow addicted to it until even the thought of losing it becomes torture. The desire for it leads to all kinds of evil and even corrupts a noble man like Denethor, Steward of Gondor. The Ring itself causes many deaths; the last to die is Gollum, who possessed it for centuries and is totally perverted by it in the end. One major difference between the One Ring and the Ring of the Nibelung, however, is that the One Ring has a will of its own and tries to return to its Maker, Sauron, often by betraying its bearer.

Another thing Carter does not mention is that this Ring of Power does not just grant world domination regardless of who wears it. In Wagner's work, it is only in *Das Rheingold* that we see the true power of Alberich's ring at work. Fafner is not interested in dominating the world, Siegfried has no idea about its properties and when Brünnhilde tries to use it to ward off her assailant, it does not work: for her it is a token of love and in the *Ring* cycle love and the lust for power are mutually exclusive. Tolkien's One Ring only grants power according to the stature of its bearer: Gollum does not achieve anything with it, while Frodo cannot rule the Ringwraiths even though he possesses the master ring. Generally, Wagner's concept of the Ring as an instrument of power remains vaguer than Tolkien's, but on the other hand so many of Tolkien's characters withstand its lure[13] that the writers of the *Lord of the Rings* film script considered it necessary to have Faramir give in to it for a while, which he does not do in the book. Both rings are above all ploys to move the story forward.

---

13 In this respect, Fëanor's silmarils bear more resemblance to Alberich's ring.

3. Two relatives quarrelling about the ring, of which one kills the other.
- After having acquired the treasure the Giant Fasolt claims the ring because in return he has given up Freia, the goddess of love and youth. Alberich's curse immediately manifests itself: Fasolt is killed by his brother, Fafner, who covets the ring as well.
- When Déagol finds the ring in the Great River, his cousin Sméagol demands it as a birthday present. However, Déagol refuses to give it to him and Sméagol promptly kills him.

4. A talisman of invisibility connected with the ring.
- In Wagner's work, the ring comes with the Tarnhelm, forged by Alberich's brother Mime. This device will give the wearer any shape he wishes or render him invisible. It is used only once for this last purpose, though: in *Das Rheingold* 3 Alberich makes himself invisible to terrorise Mime. After that, it is only used for shape-changing.
- Tolkien's One Ring renders the wearer invisible, like the Nine Rings for Mortal Men. It is used often for this purpose in the beginning of the story; in the later stages it becomes too dangerous.

Tolkien's *The Silmarillion* has a dwarf-forged helm with magical properties, the Dragon-helm of Dor-lómin, but this does not grant invisibility. In *The Lord of the Rings* we find the Old English cognate of the word Tarnhelm, Dernhelm, as the name of the disguised Éowyn. Making the instrument of invisibility a helmet was Wagner's idea: the *Nibelungenlied* has a Tarn*kappe*, a cloak (cf. Middle High German 'cappa', which means 'cloak', though many modern renditions depict it as a kind of cap or helmet). It is possible that Tolkien introduced the name Dernhelm as a Wagnerian allusion. If so, Tolkien inverts Wagner by associating a woman's disguise with an object used as a disguise *against* a woman in the *Ring*.

Another possible source of inspiration for the invisibility of Tolkien's ring would be the *Ring of Gyges*, a tale Plato tells in his *Republic*. It introduces an invisibility ring to raise the question whether a man would remain moral if he did not have to fear the consequences of his actions. This touches on a point that both Tolkien and Wagner make by combining power and invisibility: power is at its most dangerous and pernicious when it is not visibly present but works behind the scenes, remaining a constant threat.

5. A broken sword being reforged.
- In *Siegfried*, the shards of Siegmund's sword Nothung are ground into fragments and recast by his son Siegfried, because Mime is unable to do it. The new sword is also called Nothung.
- The Elven smiths of Rivendell reforge Elendil's broken sword, Narsil, for Elendil's heir, and it receives a new name: Andúril.

Since the publication of Carter's book, many have added to the list. These are the additions I consider relevant (similarities not accounted for in footnotes have been noticed by more than one reader):

6. Many acquire the ring by stealing or robbing it.
- Wotan robs the ring from Alberich and Fafner from Fasolt, murdering him. Siegfried kills Fafner and finds it in his cave; later he pulls it forcibly from Brünnhilde's finger. The evil Hagen tries to take it from Siegfried's finger after he has killed him, but fails to do so.
- Isildur takes the One Ring from Sauron's finger, Sméagol murders Déagol for it, Bilbo cheats Gollum to keep it and Gollum bites it from Frodo's finger before falling to his doom with it.

7. One of the owners of the ring hides in a cave for a long time, doing nothing (much) with it.
- Fafner in the *Ring*. He does not do anything with it, except guarding it jealously.
- Sméagol-Gollum in *The Lord of the Rings*. He occasionally uses the ring to hunt or spy on the orcs but has no idea what more it can do.

8. Two characters play a riddle game.
- The Wanderer and Mime in *Siegfried*.
- Bilbo and Gollum in *The Hobbit*.

9. The ring betrays its bearer.
- It betrays Alberich by allowing Wotan and Loge to rob him, and Fasolt, Fafner and Siegfried by getting them slain. It betrays Brünnhilde when she

tries to use it against the fake Gunther (Siegfried in disguise). Gunther and Hagen are killed in the attempt to take it.
- It betrays Isildur by slipping from his finger and getting him shot while he tries to escape the orcs, Gollum by getting lost under the mountains and Frodo by overcoming him and having him claim it, and by letting Gollum bite it from his finger – though this turns out a good thing. It betrays Denethor and Boromir by bringing them under its spell – in the case of Denethor from afar.

10. A hero receives information from a talking bird.
- Siegfried from the *Waldvogel* (Forest Bird) in *Siegfried*.
- Bard from the thrush in *The Hobbit*.

11. The wish for eternal youth/the prolongation of life.[14]
- The gods (with the exception of Loge) and the giants in the *Ring* cycle; most of them want/need Freia for her apples of eternal youth.
- Many mortals in Tolkien's works, including the nine Mortal Men who became the Ringwraiths.

11a. Mortality and death must be accepted (Ellison 1988, 17f).
- Brünnhilde must come to terms with the fact that she has become a mortal woman, while Wotan has to learn to accept his own end.
- In Tolkien's work this theme is more prominently present in *The Silmarillion*, and particularly in the 'Akallabêth', the story of the Downfall of Númenor. In this story fear of death and envy of the immortal Elves and Valar leads to the rebellion of the Númenoreans and the destruction of their island. The theme also plays a primary role in the 'Athrabeth Finrod ah Andreth' (*Morgoth's Ring*, 304-366). Here an immortal Elf, Aegnor, and a mortal maiden, Andreth, fall in love but are never united. Aegnor's brother Finrod maintains it is only for the best, but the embittered Andreth disagrees.

One of Wagner's strong points is that he clearly shows Brünnhilde's initial dismay on realising what it means to become mortal, to acquire a mortal coil. Tolkien, who has different views of what happens when a deathless person acquires the

---

14 In Wagner, this applies to the Rhinegold in general, in Tolkien to all the 'great Rings', but that it is present as a motif in both ring stories seems remarkable, especially given the importance of the theme of mortality and death in both works.

capacity to die, does not address this aspect in the main body of his *Ring* text. However, in Appendix A, 'Part of the Tale of Aragorn and Arwen', he hints at the darker side of becoming mortal by having Arwen realise that if mortality is 'the gift of the One to Men, it is bitter to receive.'

11b. An immortal woman becomes mortal.
- Brünnhilde in *Die Walküre* (The Valkyrie).
- Arwen in Appendix A of *The Lord of the Rings* and her foremother Lúthien Tinúviel in *The Lay of Leithian*, (*Lays of Beleriand*, 151-372), retold in *The Silmarillion*. Unlike Brünnhilde, both give up their immortality of their own free will.

An immortal woman becoming mortal is an important motif in Tolkien's works, but interestingly, it also occurs more than once in Wagner, from an early stage onward. When he was twenty years of age, he wrote an opera called *Die Feen* (The Fairies), based on a tale by Carlo Gozzi. In it, the fairy Ada willingly enters into a marriage with the mortal Arindal,[15] though she will lose her immortality if he fails a test set by her father, the Fairy King and she refuses to give him up. They remain together for eight years and have two children, but then he asks a forbidden question and is thrown out of the fairy realm. But Ada loves him too much to give him up and does indeed relinquish her immortality for him. After many trials and tribulations, during which Arindal proves himself worthy of Ada after all, the lovers are reunited. The fairy king restores her immortality and also grants it to her husband.

This early work, never performed during Wagner's own lifetime, is rather unoriginal and superficial from a musical point of view. The immortality theme returned in *Der Fliegende Holländer* (The Flying Dutchman) and much later in *Parsifal*. There, life without end is seen as a curse and the accursed man wishes for death; in the case of Amfortas in *Parsifal* this desire is caused by an incurable, painful wound.

---

15 Mentioned by MacLachlan: A fairy woman marrying a mortal is also the subject of a now forgotten opera based on an Irish myth, *The Immortal Hour* (1914) by composer Rutland Boughton (1878-1960). The music combines Celtic folk elements with Wagnerian Leitmotif techniques. The opera, which does not end happily for the mortal, was performed 376 times in London in 1922-23 but Tolkien does not mention it anywhere (which does not necessarily mean he did not know it).

The motif of an immortal woman losing her immortality first explored in *Die Feen* apparently held enough appeal for Wagner to reuse it in *Die Walküre*. In this later work he does not reverse the effect, turning a love story into a tragedy of betrayal and murder instead, though in the end a freely chosen death leads to redemption.

Tolkien went from a love story in which the idea of relinquishing immortality never even arises ('The Fall of Gondolin', the first version of the Idril and Tuor story in *Book of Lost Tales*) via a story in which giving it up leads to a qualified happy ending for the lovers (Beren and Lúthien), to a tale in which the loss of immortality ends in bitterness for the woman who has become mortal (Aragorn and Arwen).

What both have in common, is that the immortal maiden loses her immortality for the sake of love. Brünnhilde incurs Wotan's wrath by trying to save Siegmund, deeply moved as she is by his steadfast love for Sieglinde. Her own love for her father Wotan also influences her actions, as she knows it is his deepest wish that Siegmund shall live. Tolkien's immortal maidens Lúthien and Arwen both give up their immortality out of romantic love for mortal men: Beren and Aragorn.

As Brünnhilde willingly dies a sacrificial death in the end, here becoming mortal is a partial parallel to the incarnation of Christ. The closest parallel in Tolkien is Gandalf, a divine spirit who assumes a destructible body and who sacrifices himself for the other members of the Fellowship.

12. Loss of primeval innocence and restoration of harmony in the end.
- After Alberich's theft of the gold, the world of the naïve Rhinedaughters loses its state of innocence. Harmony is restored when the ring returns to the Rhine in the end, but at a price: many have died, the gods have gone under and Brünnhilde has had to sacrifice herself.
- The Shire, the world of the naïve hobbits, loses its innocence when Saruman subjects it to his greed. Harmony is restored when Saruman is vanquished, but at a price. People have died, and Frodo has had to sacrifice earthly happiness for the greater good of Middle-earth.

13. Nature is defiled (Ellison 1988, 17) and theft of a primeval source of light plunges the world into darkness.[16]
- With the gold, Alberich robs the Rhine of light, leaving its waters dark and gloomy. Wotan cuts a branch from the World Ash to turn it into his spear of Law, causing the Ash to wither.
- Mordor is a desolate waste full of war machinery. Saruman cuts down trees to create a war industry of his own. In *The Silmarillion* Morgoth poisons the waters of Beleriand and turns the green plain of Ard-Galen into a waste land. *The Silmarillion* has two shining trees, Laurelin and Telperion, that wither and die when the huge spider Ungoliant sucks the light out of them.

13a. A symbolical tree is dying or dead:
- the World Ash starts to die after Wotan has broken off a branch to use for a spear.
- the White Tree of Gondor withered after the line of Elendil failed. The Two Trees of Valinor do not survive the attack by Morgoth and Ungoliant.

Tolkien combines the violation of these two trees with the extinguishing of the light; in Wagner's *Ring* these are separate, though related occurrences. Both series of events involve the violation of Nature in the pursuit of power. In Tolkien's works, this often takes the form of cutting down trees. Saruman has many trees felled in the forests around Isengard, and later also the Party Tree in the Shire. After Sauron has infiltrated Númenor, he orders the White Tree in the courts of Armenelos, Nimloth, to be cut down. The only tree cut down in Wagner's work is the withered World Ash; this provides the firewood for the conflagration of Walhall.

The huge difference between the two is, that in Tolkien's works the trees that wither or are cut down usually survive in the form of a sapling or another offshoot which acquires new significance: the Sun is the last fruit of Laurelin, the Moon the last flower of Telperion. The last fruit of Nimloth, stolen by Isildur before the tree's destruction, becomes the White Tree of Minas Tirith. This tree withers, but Aragorn finds a sapling which is planted at the spot of

---

16 Also mentioned by Ellison, and independently by Hein van Eekert in his radio-introduction to the 2009 performance of *Das Rheingold* in the Dutch town of Enschede.

its dead predecessor. The hobbits' Party Tree is replaced by a mallorn, the seed of which was a present from Galadriel to Sam Gamgee. There is no renewal, however, for the tree-herds, the Ents. The Entwives have disappeared, and they do not return.

As Wagner does not indicate that the World Ash is in any way replaced by a new tree, the differences on this point are at least as great as the similarities.

14. One or more characters – spirits of nature – who engage in singing 'nonsense' verses are, or would be, untrustworthy guardians of the gold/the One Ring.
- The Rhinemaidens sing 'Wagalaweia wallala weialaweia' etc., after which their song slowly evolves into known language (German).[17] They carelessly tell Alberich the secret of the power resident in the Rhinegold, after which he is able to steal it.
- Tom Bombadil inserts a 'Hey dol! Merry dol! A ring a dong dillo!' into the song that introduces him. In the Council of Elrond Gandalf states that Bombadil would make an unsafe guardian of the ring, as he would most likely forget it or throw it away.

14a. Tolkien and Wagner entertained similar, conservative ideas about the relation of sound and sense in language, though based on different convictions.
- In his treatise *Oper und Drama* (Opera and Drama) Wagner proposes that while Man lived in harmony with nature and grasped it on an emotional level, 'he kept inventing language roots which were characteristic for the objects and their relations' (1852, II, VI).[18] This capacity atrophied when Man gradually turned his back to nature and language lost its instinctive understanding of its own roots. This resulted in their mutilation and atrophiation, which he deplored.
- Contrary to the default view in modern linguistics that the relation between sound and sense is arbitrary,[19] Tolkien believed that this had not always been so. Once upon a time, a name reflected the nature of the thing named. Our

---

17 Wagner developed these 'words' from the term *heilawac*, 'holy wave' which he found in Grimm.
18 German: 'erfand er auch noch Sprachwurzeln, die den Gegenständen und ihren Beziehungen characteristisch entsprachen.'
19 Formulated as the distinction between signifier and signified in Ferdinand de Saussure's *Course de Linguistique Générale* of 1916. Most linguists take this position. See Ross Smith's study *Inside Language*, especially pp. 50-68, for an in-depth discussion of Tolkien's views on linguistic aesthetics.

words (*logoi*) are rooted in God's Word (*Logos*), and the separation of a word's form and its meaning resulted from the Fall of Mankind. In several of his letters, in the poem *Mythopoeia* and in his lecture 'A Secret Vice', in which he uses terms like 'phonetic fitness' and speaks of 'the fitting of notion to oral symbol' ('Secret Vice', 204, 206),[20] he alludes to this belief, and it is the main principle behind his invented languages. One character we see giving things their proper name is Tom Bombadil.

14b. The Tolkien character who uses primal language is married to a river-daughter, while the creatures who use primal language in Wagner's *Ring* are the daughters of the river Rhine. Moreover, Tom Bombadil's wife is named *Gold*berry. It is tempting to see Tolkien's introduction of a river-daughter with gold in her name as a little joke on Wagner. Unlike the Rhine-daughters Goldberry, though playful, is not frivolous – and she does not make fun of dwarf-sized characters but takes them seriously and treats them well.

15. A mysterious, bearded figure walks around in a cloak and a wide-brimmed hat.
- The Wanderer (who is really Wotan) in *Siegfried*.
- Both the good wizard Gandalf and the evil Saruman in *The Lord of the Rings*.

16. To prevent the evil maker of the ring from laying hands on it again, it must be returned to the element from which it came, its shape being symbolic for its cyclical life:
- the waters of the Rhine in Wagner
- the fires of Mount Doom in Tolkien.

17. A central character gives the ring away of his own free will.[21]
- Siegfried in the *Ring*.
- Sam, and to a lesser degree Bilbo, in *The Lord of the Rings*.

18. Self-immolation on a pyre by one of the characters.
- Brünnhilde in *Götterdämmerung* (The Twilight of the Gods)

---

20 The title of the lecture shows that he was aware of being on thin ice, from a professional point of view, so he cloaked his ideas in the guise of a personal hobby. He even coined a Quenya word for phonetic fitness, *lamatyavë*, meaning 'individual pleasure in the sounds and forms of words'. (*Morgoth's Ring*, 215.)
21 According to Haymes 2009 this is Bilbo, but Sam Gamgee seems a better candidate, as Bilbo needed Gandalf's prompting.

- Denethor in *The Return of the King*.

The difference is that in Brünnhilde's case this is a sacrifice, made to purify the cursed ring, and a good thing. Denethor commits suicide, a bad thing.

19. A warlike young woman who ceases being a shieldmaiden, first noted by Bradley (116).
- Brünnhilde in *Die Walküre*.
- Éowyn in *The Return of the King*.

Also, both disobey an order: Brünnhilde attempts to give victory to Siegmund, who is ordained to die, Éowyn does not stay at home as she is being told, but joins the army of the Rohirrim. Her action is rather more successful than Brünnhilde's, and unlike her Wagnerian counterpart she gives up arms of her own free will.

20. An evil character grasps or tries to grasp the ring at the end but perishes in a cataclysmic event by the same element to which the ring has been returned.
- At the conclusion of *Götterdämmerung*, the river Rhine floods its banks and washes over Brünnhilde's pyre, sweeping the ring along. When Hagen dives in to grasp it before it can disappear, the Rhinemaidens grab him and pull him into the depths, where he drowns. The waves swallow the ring.
- In the second book of *The Return of the King*, after Frodo has claimed the One Ring for himself, Gollum leaps at him, bites off his finger with the ring on it. He starts dancing but falls into the fires of Mount Doom, where he perishes together with the One Ring. This brings down the Dark Lord and his realm of evil.

21. When the ring is destroyed, corrupted power is overthrown.
- At the end of the *Ring* cycle, Walhall burns with all its denizens.
- The Dark Lord Sauron is vanquished when the One Ring is destroyed.

22. The (Light-)Elves disappear from the world, which is left for Men to make a fresh start.

- *Götterdämmerung* ends with the burning of Walhall and the destruction of the Gods – also called the 'Licht-Alben',[22] the Light Elves. Mankind remains to create a better world.
- At the end of *The Lord of the Rings*, the remaining Light-Elves and the wanderer Gandalf leave Middle-earth, taking ship to the Undying Lands of Valinor. The Fourth Age will be an age of Men.

By bringing Tolkien's other works (with the exception of *The Legend of Sigurd and Gudrún*, which will be dealt with separately) into play, the list can be expanded a little further still:

23. The world is born from music and history from disharmony.

- Wagner's entire *Ring* world grows out of a single, long held E-flat in the double basses. This develops into a triad in E flat major symbolising nature in the form of the life-giving waters of the Rhine (a motif recurring in a slightly modified way when the Earth Goddess Erda appears in *Der Ring* 4). The atmosphere darkens when Alberich appears on the scene (Schreier, 196). The initial harmony changes and his robbery of the Rhinegold, accompanied by shrill discord, sets the entire dramatic history into motion. The music differentiates further and further into the various Leitmotifs.
- Tolkien's creation story is found in *The Silmarillion*. The One, Eru, creates the Ainur, the Holy Ones and propounds themes of music to them. They begin to sing and a harmony arises, reminiscent of the Pythagorean idea of the harmony of the spheres. Discord arises when one of the Holy Ones, Melkor, adds themes that are not in accordance with those of the One. Ultimately Ilúvatar calls everything, including Melkor's disharmonies, into being through the word 'Eä', and history begins. This Eä could be interpreted as a musical interval, a so-called perfect fourth: E – A. It is tempting to see Melkor as a personification of the 'devil in music', the term for a tritone or augmented fourth, the most dissonant of chords; Wagner uses one for Alberich's curse of the ring and also for the motif of Fafner in his dragon form. Melkor creates discord, but because of this, Ilúvatar 'augments' the original Music. At the end of Arda all dissonance will at last be resolved.

---

22 Wotan is also called *Licht-Alberich*, and as such the opposite of *Schwarz-Alberich* (Black Alberich), the dwarf. Wagner based this opposition on a theory in Jacob Grimm's *Deutsche Mythologie*. See Shippey (2007, 223-231).

Incidentally, the interval which initiates the motif of the pure Rhinegold is a perfect fourth as well. So is the E-flat – A-flat shift from the creation motif to the first appearance of living beings.[23]

Schreier calls the specific situation in Tolkien's 'Ainulindalë', where Melkor deviates from the initial harmony of the Ainur 'structurally comparable' (195) to the beginning of Wagner's *Ring*, where Alberich disturbs the triads of the Rhinemaidens.

23a. Tolkien's work has often been described in terms of music. Flieger compares the vision behind the history of Middle-earth to a musical score (2005, xiv). Kazimierczak stresses the importance of the sound of language for Tolkien and speaks of his 'linguistic symphony' (56). Ellison refers to the 'operatic qualities' of Tolkien's works (1983, 11); describing a scene from *Götterdämmerung* he feels that 'if Tolkien had been a composer, this is the way in which his operas would have been written' (1998, 40). Schreier calls the musical 'themes' referred to in Tolkien's text reminiscent of Wagnerian Leitmotifs (195-196). In Tolkien's own words, 'such music that was in me was […] transformed into linguistic terms' (*Letters*, 350).

24. A young man loses his family, wandering around by himself for a while, having to cope with many enemies, before he finds his soulmate – and a new, worse enemy.
- Siegmund in *Die Walküre*.
- Both Beren and Túrin in *The Silmarillion*.

25. A fight between a wolf and a dog/hound.
- In *Die Walküre* this is a symbolical duel, as both combatants are human. The symbolism lies in their names: Siegmund, the son of Wolfe (another name for Wälse, who is really Wotan in disguise), fights Hunding, literally 'son of a dog'. After losing an argument with his wife, Wotan has to grant the victory to the dog, but kills Hunding afterwards.
- In the tale of Beren and Lúthien in *The Silmarillion*, the fight is literal. The great hound of Valinor, Huan, defeats and kills a number of werewolves. The last one is Sauron in disguise, who flees when he realises he cannot win.

---

23 For a brief discussion of *The Rhinegold* and 'Ainulindalë', see Naveh, 34f.

Later Huan fights Carcharoth, the chief wolf of Morgoth. He manages to kill him, but at the cost of his own life.

Though the hound wins in both cases, this is a good thing in Tolkien's story but a bad thing in Wagner's. Not a very strong parallel, but remarkable enough to deserve mentioning.

26. A brother and sister in an incestuous relationship.
- In *Die Walküre*, Siegmund (a man of many pseudonyms) and Sieglinde discover they are twins and nevertheless unite in love. Their son is Siegfried.
- In *The Children of Húrin*, Túrin Turambar (a man of at least as many pseudonyms) unwittingly marries his sister Nienor. They are horrified when they discover this; both commit suicide, though not only for that reason. Their unborn child dies with Nienor.

27. A dwarf called Mime (Wagner, *Der Ring* and *Siegfried*) or Mîm (Tolkien, *The Children of Húrin*), who acts, or tries to act, against the hero of the story.

28. Dwarves are greedy and evil (the latter in Tolkien's case mainly found in the *Books of Lost Tales*, after which he changed his mind). Both also connect Dwarves with the forging of precious artefacts like the Ring of the Nibelung, the Tarnhelm, the Arkenstone, Frodo's coat of mithril, and the Nauglamir, the Necklace of the Dwarves in *The Silmarillion*.

Omitted from this list were weak comparisons, for instance the claim that a great river plays a central role (Scott Rohan, 150). However, the role of the River Anduin in *The Lord of the Rings* is not really central, while the River Rhine plays no role at all in the second and third of the four *Ring* operas. There is a link between the two rings and the aforementioned rivers: Alberich robs the gold from which he forges his ring from the river Rhine, while Tolkien's One Ring emerges from the river Anduin after having been lost for centuries. But rings emerging from bodies of water in which they were lost are fairly common in stories. Also, Alberich cursing love and robbing the Rhinegold is of a different dimension than Déagol finding the One Ring.

Winged helmets, worn by Tuor in *The Book of Lost Tales* I, by Gondorians, and by valkyries in traditional Wagner stagings, do not constitute convincing evidence either. Such helmets abound in illustrations of Norse myths and Viking lore, despite the fact that they did not originally belong there and were not put there until the 19th century.

Also omitted are mere additions; that both Siegfried and Aragorn inherit the shards of their father's/ancestor's swords is connected so closely to the reforging of those swords that it does not merit a separate entry.

Stretching was another reason to omit a comparison. Brünnhilde's self-immolation at the end of *Götterdämmerung*, resulting in the destruction of Walhall, is not the same thing as Gollum perishing in the fires of Orodruin by accident or Providence (Higgins). Nor is 'Wotan uses the ring to pay the giants' comparable to 'Sauron betrays the Elves' ('Spengler'). That Fafner and Fasolt both meet a sticky end is the result of Alberich's curse.

Finally, comparisons resting too heavily on personal interpretations instead of mere observations are also left out. When a heavily Freudian analysis (Kasper, 284) claims that 'Frodo violates Gollum' is Tolkien's version of 'Siegfried violates Brünnhilde', referring to the *vagina dentata* myth to explain why Gollum *really* bit off Frodo's finger, this cannot be taken seriously. It may be entertaining to claim that the ring symbolises the female element, and that therefore both stories represent a struggle between sex and abstinence, won by the latter (no wonder that Wotan loses his will to live and the Elves leave Middle-earth). But such insights are not really relevant.

2.2. 'Faint and disparate echoes'

What remains looks impressive enough. Is it, though? Another objection frequently raised against the suggestion that Tolkien borrowed from Wagner is, that both drew from the same Norse sources, such as the *Eddas* and the *Völsunga saga*. Texts like the back cover of the Penguin edition of Jesse Byock's *Völsunga saga* translation seem to support this. The prospective reader is told that '[w]ith its cursed treasure of the Rhine, the sword reforged and the magic ring of power, [the saga] was a major influence for writers including William Morris and J.R.R. Tolkien and for Wagner's *Ring* cycle.'

One example of this 'common sources' approach is Bradley Birzer's lecture. Birzer starts out by quoting the sentence about the two round rings and admits that 'at a superficial level, the stories share several things in common.' Nonetheless, this 'should not lead one to conclude that Tolkien borrowed from Wagner. Rather, Tolkien and Wagner each drew from the same sources.' According to Birzer the similarity between the rings is that they 'cause evil' and the 'moral and physical stretching of [their] original posessor.' The term 'ring of power' only occurs in a direct quote from Tolkien, and not in the vicinity of Wagner's name.

Following the same approach, David Bratman notes that Tolkien 'was antipathetic to Wagner' and ascribes his crossness

> to the assumption by ignorant critics, mistaking common features for influence, that Wagner's work must have inspired *The Lord of the Rings*. A familiarity with the medieval sources that inspired both writers would eradicate that error. (Bratman, 147)

Bratman, who is one of the few to point out (in a footnote) that the often-quoted statement about the two round rings does not refer to Wagner's *Ring* but to 'a mythological farrago in the mind of a critic' (148), goes on to remark that there is one similarity between the two Ring stories after all: invisibility. Tolkien's ring renders invisible, Wagner's comes with a helm of invisibility. Because Bratman acknowledges this, it seems all the more peculiar that he fails to notice that both are Rings of Power with the potential to bestow world domination, and that this potential appears for the first time in the *Ring* cycle, not in the medieval sources.

Another example is provided by David Harvey. He believes that Tolkien's statement about the two round rings does apply to Wagner's operas, but considers it simplistic.

> Tolkien was being dismissive of Wagner's dealings with German myth. There are similarities, but they are broad and general similarities. Both the Rings are symbols of power and carry power within them. Both the Rings carry with them an ability to inspire a lust for power upon those who do not possess them. Possession of the Ring carries a price to be paid. To take the Ring is an exercise in choice.

But he sees differences as well: Wagner's ring is not addictive and not completely evil, while Tolkien's ring is both. Unlike Tolkien, Wagner does not present an essential conflict between good and evil, for 'everyone is flawed'. But Alberich, Mime and certainly Hagen are worse than just flawed, and a conflict between good and evil can enact itself inside one and the same character. Also, Wagner's ring may not be addictive the way Tolkien's is, yet letting go of it is a huge problem for most of the characters who possess it at some point, and the libretto states explicitly that whoever owns it, turns into its slave.

Harvey then points out that common sources explain many correspondences between the two ring stories, but that the 'concept of the Ring as giving the owner mastery of the world was Wagner's own contribution to the myth', as it does not occur anywhere in the sources. Then, near the end of the chapter, he makes a peculiar turn and concludes that it is

> quite clear that Tolkien's work owes nothing to *Der Ring des Nibelungen*, and it is impossible to draw comparisons between the two works. The few similarities that there are operate as faint and disparate echoes of one another, coming from a distant and common source.

This conclusion is incompatible with Harvey's earlier findings. As it was Wagner who first laid the link between a ring and world dominion, it should be obvious that this 'echo' does not come from a common source. Nor is it particularly faint. In fact, the similarities Harvey calls 'broad and general' concern things of crucial importance, yet he shrinks back from the obvious conclusion.

Whatever the case may be, the question of how many similarities on the list given above go back to common sources needs an answer now.

2.3. Common sources
(numbers referring to those in the similarities list)

1. *A dragon guarding a treasure, slain by a hero* appears in the *Eddas* and the *Völsunga saga*. The hero is Sigurd. Wagner used the German version of the name, Siegfried, taken from the *Nibelungenlied*. There, Siegfried has slain the dragon before entering the story; in the *Ring* he does it on stage. Tolkien has no less than five dragons and their slayers: Smaug, shot by Bard the Bowman

in *The Hobbit*; Ancalagon the Black, slain by Eärendil in the War of Wrath at the end of the First Age; Glaurung, killed by Túrin in a way reminiscent of Sigurd's killing of Fáfnir in the *Völsunga saga*; Scatha the Worm, slain by Fram son of Frumgar – and Fáfnir and Sigurd themselves.

3. *Two relatives quarreling about the ring, one of whom kills the other.* The common source for this is the poem *Reginsmál* in the *Poetic Edda*. Here, Fáfnir kills his father Hreidmar over a treasure, which included the ring Andvaranaut. This ring has the property to multiply gold; together with the rest of the treasure, it was robbed from the dwarf Andvari, after which he cursed it. Wagner turns the relatives into giants and Hreidmar becomes a brother, Fasolt. He has another pair of brothers quarrel over it, the dwarves Alberich and Mime, though neither of them kills the other. In Tolkien's story the two relatives fighting over the ring are the cousins Déagol and Sméagol, the latter killing the former.

5. *A broken sword being reforged.* The *Völsunga saga* tells of the reforging of the sword of Sigmund, Sigurd's father, which shattered against Odin's spear. Wagner retains this last part and has Siegfried personally remake the weapon. In *The Lord of the Rings*, the broken sword of Elendil is reforged for his descendant Aragorn. Scott Rohan thinks this similarity should not be attributed to common sources alone, as both Wagner and Tolkien put more stress on the reforging than the sources do (149), but that does not seem a very strong argument.

6. *Many acquire the ring by stealing or robbing it.* See also under 3. In the Norse sources, the gods take Andvaranaut from Andvari; later, Fáfnir robs it from Hreidmar and Sigurd takes it from the lair of Fáfnir the Dragon after having killed him. As shown above, both Wagner and Tolkien also have the ring change hands repeatedly through theft, robbery and murder.

7. *One of the owners of the ring hides in a cave for a long time.* In the Icelandic texts, Fáfnir hides in a cave for an unspecified amount of time; generations have passed before Sigurd comes along to challenge him.

8. *Two characters play a riddle game.* This happens in two different lays of the *Poetic Edda*, *Alvíssmál* (between Thor and a dwarf) and *Vafþrudnismál* (be-

tween the disguised Odin and a giant). The riddle-games between Mime and the Wanderer and between Bilbo and Gollum are both based on these sources.

9. *The ring betrays its bearer.* It already does so in the source texts after Andvari has cursed it, and it causes the death of many.

10. *A hero receives information from a talking bird.* In the Eddaic lay *Fáfnismál*, some birds talk about the treacherous smith who intends to kill Sigurd, who overhears this. Later they tell him about the valkyrie sleeping on the fire-encircled mountain-top. Wagner reduces the birds to one, the *Waldvogel* (Forest Bird). In *The Hobbit* a thrush overhears Bilbo talking about Smaug's weak spot and passes this knowledge on to Bard the Bowman of Esgaroth, who understands the speech of thrushes. This enables him to shoot Smaug.

13b. *A symbolical tree is dying or dead.* Wagner modeled his *Weltesche* directly on the World Ash of Norse mythology, Yggdrasil. A serpent or dragon, Niðhöggr, is said to gnaw at the roots of Yggdrasil. The tree starts to tremble at the onset of *ragnarök*, but nowhere in the sources is it said that it dies or withers, though no doubt it perishes when the world ends. Tolkien's many special trees are more distantly related to it and have other ancestors as well, like the Trees of Paradise, but these do not wither. A debatable case.

15. *A mysterious, bearded figure walks around in a cloak and a wide-brimmed hat.* The god Odin roams the world of ancient Scandinavian myth in this guise. Wagner's Wotan is directly based on him, but Gandalf, too, has Odinic traits. So at first sight this seems to resort under 'common sources'. However, MacLachlan[24] argues there is another parallel between Wotan and Gandalf: both have to find a way to solve the problem of the Ring of Power and both need to find free agents to act for them – a problem non-existent in the Icelandic sources, which do not know about any Ring of Power. It is their involvement with the ring as a vessel of evil power that separates these characters from the Norse god.

In Tolkien's case, it could also be argued that both Gandalf and Saruman represent aspects of Odin. In Norse myth, this ambiguous god has deceitful,

---

24 MacLachlan, 124..

treacherous traits. Such traits are absent in Gandalf, but they surface in his fallen counterpart Saruman. Saruman in his turn bears some resemblance to Wotan as the shady manipulator in *Das Rheingold*.

If the Last Battle, *ragnarök*, is also taken into consideration, even Sauron appears to present himself as an Odinic character. Dimond briefly discusses Noel's identification of Sauron with Odin, but rejects it because the god's adversaries are the monsters, not the heroes of the story (188, n. 5). Equally tenuous seems the parallel between Wotan as the Wanderer who walks around in disguise, and Aragorn, who hides his true identity as heir to the throne of Gondor, roaming through the lands of Middle-earth as Strider (Vill, 65). Aragorn has his days of rulership ahead of him, whereas for Wotan they lie behind him.

18. *Self-immolation on a pyre by one of the characters.* Brünnhilde's pyre is described in the *Völsunga saga* and in two Eddaic lays, *Sigurðarqviða in scamma* (the Short Lay of Sigurd) and *Helreið Brynhildar* (Brynhild's Hell Ride). But before she burns, Brynhild has already committed suicide by casting herself on her sword; she does not immolate herself riding onto the pyre on horseback, like Wagner's heroine. In Book V of *The Lord of the Rings*, Denethor burns himself alive making a reference to 'heathen kings of old', who apparently also burned on a pyre in Middle-earth – the only instance in which Tolkien uses the word 'heathen' in his Ring epic. One wonders, though, whether those kings were still alive when the fire was lit. Yet the moral significance of what happens in either work is almost diametrically opposed, so this 'similarity' had probably best be disregarded.

19. *A warlike young woman ceases being a shieldmaiden.* This is described in the Eddaic lay *Sigdrífumál*: Odin has punished a Valkyrie for granting victory to the man whom he decreed to be slain. Now she will grant victory no more but become a married woman. Wagner applies this to his *Schildmaid* (shield-maiden) Brünnhilde, after changing her from the Icelandic warrior-queen she is in the *Nibelungenlied* into a valkyrie. Tolkien's Éowyn ceases to be a shieldmaiden, too, but unlike Brünnhilde she does this of her own choice when Faramir woos her.

23. *The world is born from music.* The general idea has been present in Western thought since the Ancient Greeks. However, in the case of Tolkien and Wagner the parallels seem to go beyond the general idea, given the presence of 'themes'. (See also the discussion under point 23 of the similarities list.)

25. *A fight between a wolf and a dog/hound.* The Hundings, the tribe of the hound/dog, are a legendary tribe in early Germanic sources, mostly mentioned because of their standing feud with the Wulfings, the tribe of the wolf. In the two Eddaic lays named after him the hero Helgi Hundingsbane slays the Saxon king Hunding (hence his nickname); according to the *Völsunga saga*, Sigmund is Helgi's father, but the author of the saga possibly got his facts mixed up: elsewhere Helgi is a scion of the Ylfing or Wulfing tribe. The sons of Hunding are Sigmund's foes in his last battle, which is the reason why Wagner made Hunding Siegmund's foe in *Die Walküre*.

Wagner and Tolkien also share the werewolf motif found in the *Völsunga saga*; here, Sigmund and Sinfjötli fight in wolf form. In *Die Walküre*, Wagner suggests that Wälse/Wolfe could assume the shape of a wolf, though it remains unclear whether Siegmund could do so as well. Tolkien's *Legend* simply follows the saga.

In *The Silmarillion*, Sauron changes himself into a werewolf to fight Huan, the Hound of Valinor, but is defeated. Beren assumes the shape of a werewolf with the help of Lúthien's enchantments.

26. *A brother and sister in an incestuous relationship.* The *Völsunga saga* has an incestuous relationship between Sigmund and his sister Signý, of which she is aware but he is not. They have a son, Sinfjötli, later murdered by Sigmund's queen. (Sigurd is Sigmund's son by his third and last wife.) Wagner's siblings Siegmund and Sieglinde commit incest knowingly. In *The Silmarillion* and *The Children of Húrin* Túrin and Níniel marry without knowing they are siblings; she becomes pregnant and both kill themselves upon finding out the identity of the other. However, as mentioned before, Tolkien's chief inspiration for this was the Finnish *Kalevala*, not a common source. In this work the hero, Kullervo, seduces his sister Aino. Neither of them knows they are related. Like Níniel

Aino drowns herself when she discovers that Kullervo is her brother, though in Níniel's case her belief that Túrin is dead contributes to her despair.[25]

27. *A dwarf called Mime.* The name Mimir occurs twice in the sources. The first Mimir is a giant guarding the well of wisdom in the *Eddas*. He is beheaded, but his head, carried around by Odin, keeps giving wise counsels. Neither Wagner's nor Tolkien's character have much to do with him.

The other Mimir is the human smith who fosters Sigurd in the *Thidreks saga* and is ultimately slain by him. None of the source texts has a *dwarf* called Mim(e). It was Wagner who combined the German form of the name with the character's profession and the fact that he is a dwarf in at least one of the Norse sources. Tolkien's Mîm is a so-called petty dwarf – and 'petty dwarf' would be an apt description of Wagner's Mime. As will be discussed later, Shippey (2007, 110-111) suggested that Mîm may well be a deliberate allusion to Mime.

28. In the Icelandic sources, Dwarves are great creators of artefacts, but they are not necessarily evil and not always greedy. Wagner's Alberich and Mime are both, though the Nibelungen in general are not described as such in Mime's account in *Das Rheingold* 3. It seems possible that Tolkien was influenced by the images of Alberich and Mime while working at the early stages of his legendarium, and that he changed his views of Dwarves when he became aware of this.

The result from this culling is that the initial list is reduced to about a dozen, depending on how strictly one counts. So even when all elements deriving from common sources are eliminated, a number of similarities remains. Of the remaining parallels, several are ring-related, and these include some of the most important ones.

So in the end, the argument that common sources account for all parallels is untenable. The aforementioned back cover of the *Völsunga saga* is rather misleading and most likely the result of commercial thinking. The combination 'Ring of Power' and Tolkien seems designed to sell; add Wagner, and it may sell even

---

25 One scholar writing about Wagner and Tolkien seems to overlook the story of Túrin and Niniel when he writes: 'The sexuality of the adult world [is] largely absent from the story of Arda. [...] Siblings having sex, as in *The Valkyrie* – is it possible to imagine a motive less attractive to Tolkien?' (Arvidsson 2007, 184)

better. But the ring the cover refers to, Andvaranaut, the 'jewel of Andvari' the dwarf, does not convey power. What it does do is multiply gold, and this only in the *Eddas*; in the *Völsunga saga* it is merely a ring on which the owner puts a curse when he is robbed of it. It was Wagner who made the step from the unlimited multiplication of gold to boundless power, and it was Tolkien who separated this Ring of Power from the accumulation of wealth and gave it a life of its own. For both, boundless power leads to slavery, a reflection on the nature of power not present in any of their common sources.

So, does Tolkien's ring derive from Wagner's after all? Various people have answered this question in various ways. Their answers fall roughly into three categories: No, Yes, and Deliberately so.

Chapter 3

What has it got in its pocketses?

3.1. No

3.1.1. Birzer

Bradley Birzer bases his 'no' to the question whether or not Tolkien got his ring from Wagner partly on the fallacious common sources argument but also addresses some other aspects of the matter. Birzer, like Tolkien a Roman Catholic, calls attention to the personal differences between the composer and the author. He describes Wagner as a socialist who used the pagan myths of the North to give the Germans 'a nationalist identity' and wrote his *Ring* cycle to show that Man could redeem himself and 'attain his own godhood'. Tolkien, on the other hand, was a pious Roman Catholic who viewed 'a sanctified northern, pagan myth as a means to return the modernist, heretical West to Christendom'. He abhorred socialism and communism, to such an extent that he sympathised with General Franco's fascists in the Spanish Civil war, because they defended the Church against the atrocities of the communists, something which Birzer seems to consider perfectly alright or even commendable. Politically, Tolkien leaned towards anarchy or unconstitutional monarchy (*Letters*, 63). He disliked *Götterdämmerung*,[26] understanding 'Wagner's apotheosis in the "Twilight of the Gods" as merely a repeat of man's first sin in the Garden of Eden.' In other words, he had major ideological objections towards Wagner's work.

The information Birzer gives is not always correct or complete. Wagner ceased to be a socialist in his middle age, having come to believe that people are not just the victims of bad circumstances but create their own circumstances (*Eine Mitteilung an meine Freunde*; i.e. A Communication to my Friends).

---

26 A claim that possibly has its source in Curry's *Defending Middle-earth* (48). However, Curry does not substantiate it.

He abhorred the communism of his time as 'a tasteless and pointless doctrine [...] of the mathematically equal division of goods', capable of 'annihilating all the achievements of two thousand years of civilisation, perhaps for a long time',[27] and impossible to bring into practice; people who believed that it could free mankind from dictatorial bondage were either fools, or malevolent. Like Tolkien, Wagner preferred unconstitutional monarchy to any other form of government: 'A state achieves its true ideal in the person of the King. He is the representative of pure human interest' (*Über Staat und Religion*)[28]. Making a monarchy constitutional meant slowly torturing it to death. But he believed this had best be combined with universal suffrage, whereas Tolkien had very little faith in democracy:

> I am *not* a democrat, only because "humility" and equality are spiritual principles corrupted by the attempt to mechanize and formalize them, with the result that we get not universal smallness and humility, but universal greatness and pride, till some Orc gets hold of a ring of power – and we get and are getting slavery. (*Letters*, 246)[29]

Though Birzer points to Tolkien's penchant for anarchy, in the sense of 'abolition of control', he omits Wagner's anarchism. Unlike Tolkien, Wagner was not averse to armed rebellion: he took part in the revolution of 1848 (though without firing any shots himself). The character of Siegfried, conceived during his revolutionary years, is considered a typical anarchist: in Act III of the eponymous opera he shatters Wotan's Spear of Law. Still, both Wagner and Tolkien might have agreed about the abolition of control and perhaps about the abolition of the state as well. In the abovementioned letter Tolkien also claimed he would arrest people who used the word 'state' other than in an inanimate sense, and shoot them if they did not recant, a remarkable statement, even if one considers it was made in a private letter during the dark days of World War II. Wagner wrote about the necessity for history to bring about the downfall of the state, a constraining and dominating power which prescribed

---

27 Said in a talk held at the Dresdner Vaterlandsverein, the Patriotic Society of Dresden: *Wie verhalten sich republikanische Bestrebungen dem Königtume gegenüber?* ('How do republican aspirations relate to kingship?' 1848). German: 'eine abgeschmackt und sinnlose Lehre [...] der mathematisch gleichen Verteilung des Gutes [die] alle Errungenschaften einer zweitausendjährigen Zivilisation auf vielleicht lange Zeit auszurotten [könnte].'
28 '*Über Staat und Religion*' (About State and Religion). German: 'Ein Staat erreicht mit der Person des Königs zugleich sein eigentliches Ideal. Er ist der Vertreter des rein menschlichen Interesses.'
29 At the time Tolkien wrote this (1956), the most glaring example of a failed democracy lay less than a dozen years in the past.

its subjects how to think and act (*Oper und Drama*, I). No doubt he was more serious about anarchism, at least during his revolutionary days, than Tolkien, who was at most an armchair anarchist. But at least in this respect, the two are not diametrically opposed.

Tolkien provided two examples of anarchist societies: the Shire, which has hardly any government at all, as we read in the Prologue to *The Lord of the Rings*, and the rulerless – though not leaderless – community of the Ents, which is not even a society in the usual sense of the word. There are no examples of anarchist communities anywhere in Wagner's operas; the enlightened kingdom in *Lohengrin* and the Nürnberg of the *Meistersinger*, societies free of compunction, maintained by cooperation and mutual support, come closest.

As for Birzer's remark that the *Ring* gave Germans a 'nationalist' – as opposed to 'national'? – identity:[30] even if the work were indeed the chief cause of 20th century German nationalism, it does not follow that it was written with that purpose in mind. In his pamphlet 'Die Kunst und die Revolution' (Art and Revolution), Wagner writes:

> If the Greek art-works embraced the spirit of a fine nation, the art-work of the future must embrace the spirit of free mankind, beyond all the confines of nationality; the national essence in it must be only an ornament, the charm of an individual case amidst a multiplicity, and not a limiting barier.[31]

This dates from the time when Wagner had recently embarked on the first libretto of the *Ring* cycle, *Siegfried's Tod* (Siegfried's Death) later *Götterdämmerung* – he wrote the text backwards, expanding it until it had its present form. In other writings of this period, e.g. 'Das Kunstwerk der Zukunft' (The Artwork of the

---

30 Birzer writes that Wagner wrote his *Ring* 'while Bismarck struggled to achieve German unity', but this only applies to the music. Wagner was not opposed to this unity, though he said rather ugly things of the German people and called Germany 'ein elendes Land' – a miserable country – in a letter to Mathilde Wesendonk of August 3, 1863. In the years before the unification of Germany in 1871 he had a brief period of nationalism for opportunistic reasons: he hoped to receive Bismarck's support for his *Festspiele*. *Die Meistersinger* (1868), the Wagner opera that comes closest to being nationalist, was written during this time. When Bismarck and the Kaiser failed to support him financially, Wagner's nationalism melted away and he became very critical of the *Reich*, even publishing an article against Bismarck in his magazine *Bayreuther Blätter*. For Wagner the German identity was rooted in German art, not in the German state; he used to say he carried Germany within himself.
31 English Translation: Cooke, 264. German: 'Umfaßte das griechische Kunstwerk den Geist einer schönen Nation, so soll das Kunstwerk der Zukunft den Geist der freien Menschheit über alle Schranken der Nationalitäten hinaus umfassen; das nationale Wesen in ihm darf nur ein Schmuck, ein Reiz individueller Mannigfaltigkeit, nicht eine hemmende Schranke in ihm sein.'

Future), similar statements can be found; Wagner was more of an internationalist than many people think, at least in theory.

Birzer is not wrong in thinking that Wagner and Tolkien were doing different things with their ring stories, and for different reasons. But one problem of his argument is that his rejection of any Wagnerian influences on Tolkien is based on Wagner's biography – of which he displays a limited knowledge – rather than on a comparison of the two stories. Another is, that he fails to consider the possibility of negative influence. He uses Tolkien against Wagner apparently without seriously wondering what Wagner's *Ring* is about.

3.1.2. Bratman

Bratman does more or less the same. Seeing that many Tolkien fans also like Wagner he points out that the spirits of their works are actually quite different.

> Wagner's story has a ruthlessness, a scornful joy in destruction, and a resignation to easily avoided tragic fate, that are alien to Tolkien's deep-rooted sense of pity, sorrow, recovery, and hopeful faith in a more positive fate despite all loss. Tolkien weaves an epic tale of wonder and beauty mixed with danger, while Wagner's *Ring* essentially boils down to a kind of soap opera of the gods, featuring the rise and self-inflicted fall of a bombastic heroic demigod, rather as if *The Lord of the Rings* had been all about Boromir. (147)

This assessment of Wagner is somewhat superficial, to put it mildly, and it would not be hard to find equally reductive and funny plot summaries of Tolkien's ring epic – but this would not make them adequate either. The idea that Siegfried is the main character of the *Ring* is a fairly widespread error. This was partly caused by Wagner himself, who had trouble abandoning his original idea of Siegfried as the world's saviour long after his drama cycle had taken a rather different turn, and partly by the general public, which was only too eager to adopt Siegfried as their hero until he ran out of fashion after the Nazi era. The main characters of the *Ring* are Wotan and Brünnhilde.

Bratman also remarks that Wagner's music, unlike Tolkien's prose, does not 'hearken backwards with dignified restraint', but is constantly pushing 'at the limits of the harmonic practice of the day', as if this would somehow disqualify it and hearkening backwards is by definition better and more virtuous (one suspects he does not like the music). His conclusion that no sensitive reader would conflate Wagner's work with Tolkien's seems sensible enough, but conflation is not the point. This is a smoke screen. That people love both Tolkien and Wagner does not mean they cannot see the differences. The question was, whether Wagner influenced Tolkien. As Bratman falls back on the incorrect common sources theory to explain all similarities except the use of invisibility, he is hardly in a position to answer it.

3.1.3. Spear

Another denier is John Spear, who held a talk about Wagner and Tolkien on occasion of the Los Angeles *Ring* performance of 2010. Tolkien was less influenced by Wagner's work than he thought at first: they both use the same sources, but his research showed him that each tends to favour different ones. Also, the popularity of the *Ring* in the Third Reich and Tolkien's anger at Hitler for sullying German myth renders any influence very unlikely. The ring itself is a fairly universal symbol, 'not least of which is eternity'. The major theme of both works could best be summed up by Lord Acton's famous maxim that all power tends to corrupt, but absolute power tends to corrupt absolutely.

If Spear means to say that both must have had Lord Acton's maxim at the back of their minds and that this explains the similarity, he would be mistaken. The maxim dates from 1887, more than a decade after the first performance of the *Ring* in 1876, and Wagner, who died in 1883, never knew it. (Perhaps Lord Acton attended the *Ring*?) As for the argument that the situation in Nazi Germany would preclude any Wagnerian influence: given Tolkien's negative feelings about Hitler, a strong engagement with the issue on his part seems more likely, which in itself is a form of influence.

3.1.4. Müller

The paper 'The Lords of the Rings' by Anja Müller of the University of Bamberg, Germany, also falls into the No-category. Müller begins by saying that she will disregard Tolkien's own statement about the two round rings – which like most people, she applies to Wagner's *Ring* – for the time being. The scope of her paper requires her to focus on the two rings themselves, leaving aside other similarities. Studying their histories and fates, she uncovers a couple of marked differences. Tolkien's ring is irredeemably evil, and hence its destruction is a must. Wagner's can 'recover its innocence by being returned to the Rhinedaughters' disinterested play.' Likewise, the *Ring* cycle builds on the dichotomy of love and power, while 'in Middle-earth the wish for power, represented in the One Ring, is isolated [...] The question, therefore, is not "Power or Love?" but "Power or no power"' (349). The conclusion is that, although both rings are Rings of Power, their characteristic features are different enough to affirm Tolkien's statement that there is no resemblance.

This seems debatable. The two rings are more than just 'rings of power' – both have the potential to grant world dominion and both corrupt (nearly) everyone who possesses or desires them. Moreover, the wish for power is less isolated in *The Lord of the Rings* than Müller seems to think. There is a strong connection between power and slavery in the epic. The One Ring enslaves, while Sauron's ultimate goal is to '*rule* them all [...] and in the darkness *bind* them', as the Ring verse goes (italics mine). The opposite of this enslaving power is freedom: it is the free peoples of Middle-earth that resist the Dark Lord. This opposition between freedom and slavery is also present in Wagner's work. Alberich's design is to subject the entire world to the power of his ring: in *Der Ring* 3 he uses words like capturing, coercing and making others his servants. Only a truly free hero will be able to prevent him from achieving his aim, as Wotan tells Brünnhilde in *Die Walküre* II, 2. There are obvious parallels here, and it remains unclear why such features would not be characteristic.

Müller's assessment of Wagner's ring is debatable, too. It is the Rhinegold that is pure and innocent, not the ring. Even the desire to forge it is evil, as it causes one to forswear love. Some of its evil effects, the enslavement of the Nibelungs, Alberich's bad treatment of his own brother and his evil plans for the world, are evident before Wotan robs it and Alberich curses it. At the end of *Götterdämmerung* III the ring returns to the Rhine and the Rhinemaidens. Does this mean that it recovers its innocence, as Müller believes? As the maidens are seen playing with it at the end of the cycle, it obviously retains its form at that point. But there's something odd about this. In her final monologue, Brünnhilde sings:

> *Das Feuer, das mich verbrennt*
> *rein'ge vom Fluch den Ring!*
> *Ihr in der Flut löset ihn auf,*
> *und lauter bewahrt das lichte Gold,*
> *das euch zum Unheil geraubt.*
> (*Götterdämmerung* III)
>
> ('Let the fire that consumes me
> cleanse from the curse the ring!
> You in the river, dissolve it,
> and keep pure the bright gold,
> that was disastrously stolen from you.')

So the Rhinemaidens are to dissolve the ring in the river after the fire has cleansed it from the curse. The moment Brünnhilde asks the Rhinemaidens to keep the 'bright gold' pure, the Rhinegold motif is heard, suggesting that it is the gold itself she is referring to, not gold as a metaphor for the ring. Later, the motif returns once more when Hagen vainly tries to retrieve the ring. The most likely conclusion is that Müller is mistaken, probably due to the fact that the dissolution of the ring does not take place on stage. All the same, it is implied in both text and music.

In the last paragraph of this first half of her lecture, Müller asks the question: 'Are the similarities the result of mutual influence?' (350) Presumably she knows Tolkien was born after Wagner's death, which makes the choice of the word 'mutual' somewhat odd. If put like this, an affirmative answer is impossible. And indeed Müller's answer is:

> One may compare the stories that are related in Wagner's *Ring* and Tolkien's *Lord of the Rings* to a large pot of stew. New ingredients are constantly added to this stew, they are cooked for a while, until their consistency changes and they adopt different facets of taste. Once in a while a cook comes along, fishes several ingredients out of the stew and serves them.

She goes on to explain that the image of this pot of stew was taken from Tolkien's essay 'On Fairy Stories' where it is called the Cauldron of Story, an image Tolkien took from George Webbe Dasent (*On Fairy-stories* § 25-38). However, Tolkien explicitly points out that the cooks 'do not dip in their ladle blindly'.

3.1.5. Scott Rohan

Michael Scott Rohan answers the question with a qualified 'no'. He attempts to lay the claim that Tolkien plagiarised Wagner to rest, conjuring up a very amusing image of Wagner, 'who'd have made a good Gollum', shouting: 'Thief Tolkien! Ve hates it for effer!' (153). In the end, though, he refutes any allegations of theft made by tireless Tolkien bashers like A.N. Wilson and Philip Pullman, author of the trilogy *His Dark Materials*.

Scott Rohan admits there are similarites between the two ring stories, and he lists no less than twenty that he believes cannot be explained away by pointing to common sources. He also argues that Tolkien knew Wagner's work and in all probability liked his music. Admittedly, there is a resemblance between the two rings, but the ring Bilbo found in the original version of *The Hobbit* was just a traditional fairy tale prop. It was not until Tolkien began to write a sequel to his successful children's book that it acquired an extra dimension and importance. 'Only when the writing was quite well advanced did his Ring become – *chiefly through the demands of the story* (Tolkien, *Return of the Shadow*, 42) – a malevolent entity with a will of its own.' The conclusion would be that

> Tolkien's creative processes had already come a long way down the line on their own, before they reached anything like the Wagner model. By a totally separate route he'd developed the concept of the Ring to a point where that resemblance to Wagner's [...] had actually become almost inevitable' [...] By starting from the same sources, by juggling with concepts, synthesizing them, following Wagner's route without any ininitial intention to imitate – those points of resemblance came to coincide. (155)

Scott Rohan supposes that to Tolkien this would look like doing properly what Wagner had got wrong. Being a fantasy author in his own right, he recognises the way the creative process works. Authors looking back over their own writings years afterwards will recognise things in them that they read and loved or were impressed by, but which they did not know influenced them at the time of writing. In short, the alleged plagiarist becomes the talented writer who transmutes 'what he's read and been shaped by into something entirely his own' (155). In April 2010 the *BBC Music Magazine* contained an article by Scott Rohan in which he stated that Wagner's *Ring* did influence Tolkien's work. So it is chiefly the question whether or not Tolkien was a plagiarist which he answers negatively.

Scott Rohan only briefly summarizes the transformation of Bilbo's fairy-tale prop into the One Ring, but it is worth taking a closer look at what Tolkien himself said about it. In the first phase of writing what would become *The Lord of the Rings*, the invisibility ring Bilbo had come upon under the mountains was merely one among many distributed by 'the Lord of the Ring' to ensnare people. According to the third chapter of this first phase, 'Of Gollum and the Ring' (*Return of the Shadow* III), these rings were all accounted for, except one – Bilbo's. Though it was not yet the Ruling Ring, it was already the 'last and most precious and potent' of the Lord's many rings. The One Ring was waiting to be discovered.

Tolkien began to write the sequel to *The Hobbit* in December 1937 and had reached Rivendell before he stopped to revise his text and answer some questions for himself. Judging by the dates tentatively given by his son Christopher, this must have been some time between February 1938 and October of that year. It is during this time that the concept of the One Ring emerges. Noting that the ring Bilbo had put his hand on in the dark was more powerful than all the others, Tolkien asked himself why the Dark Lord was so eager to have it back. 'In what did its potency consist?' The answer he came up with was:

> Because if he had it he could see where all the others were, and would be master of their masters – control all the dwarf-hoards, and the dragons, and know the secrets of the Elf-kings, and the secret [?plans] of evil men. (*Return of the Shadow*, 225)

This is where the central idea of the Ruling Ring is finally present, as Christopher writes. It is not yet linked to the idea of world domination, but this is only one step further. It is not clear when exactly the idea occurred to Tolkien, as the question and his answer to it were written on different occasions. However, the idea was there when he wrote the second chapter of the third phase, then titled 'Ancient History' (eventually 'The Shadow of the Past'), late in 1938.

A significant period. In March of this year, Germany had annexed Austria, while the westernmost part of Czechoslovakia, the Sudetenland, was occupied by the Germans on the first of October, the day after Chamberlain announced 'peace for our time'. Whether or not Tolkien had faith in Chamberlain's assessment, in a letter to Stanley Unwin of 13 October 1938 he wrote that the *Hobbit* sequel he was working on could turn out to be unsuitable for children, because it was becoming more terrifying, more 'adult': 'The darkness of the present day has had some effect on it. Though it is not an "allegory"' (*Letters*, 41).

Obviously, one of the ways in which the *Hobbit* sequel turned out more terrifying is the dangerous power residing in Bilbo's ring. Though Scott Rohan assumes this was chiefly caused by the demands of the story, it seems likely that external circumstances as mentioned above also played a part in this development. Of course this would support his argument that Tolkien transmuted what he had read and was shaped by into something of his own, and that this does not imply plagiarism. However, when Scott Rohan claims that most of the other similarities on his list can likewise be explained by the way the creative process works, his argument becomes less convincing, and especially his use of the word 'coincide'.

Can it be coincidence that Tolkien originally called the supreme agent of evil the 'Lord of the Ring' while Wagner referred to it as the 'Lord of the Ring', *des Ringes Herr*? The singular form actually survives in the definitive version: at one point Pippin calls Frodo 'Lord of the Ring' (*The Fellowship of the Ring*, II, 1). In view of this, Gandalf's subsequent 'Hush!' takes on a somewhat ambiguous meaning...

Can it be coincidence that the One Ring enslaves the bearer, while the possessor of the *Ring des Nibelungen* is described as 'des Ringes Knecht', a phrase that best translates as 'the slave of the ring'? And what about the fact that in order for the world to be saved, both rings have to return to their place of origin and do so in the end? That both rings perish in a cathartic cataclysm involving a great fire? It is here, that the no-arguments founder. Had Tolkien internalised these elements of Wagner's *Ring* to such a degree that they popped up involuntarily when he was wondering about the true nature of Bilbo's ring? Or is something more going on after all?

3.1.6. Ridpath

The most creative and ambiguous denial comes from Michael Ridpath, who addresses the question in a crime novel, *Where the Shadows Lie*. The controversy pops up at an Internet forum. One poster suggests that Wagner's *Ring* cycle influenced Tolkien. Another promptly brings up the *Völsunga saga* as their common source, whereupon a trollish third poster calls Tolkien a liar and a plagiarist.

Without further mentioning Wagner, Ridpath settles things by introducing a jealously guarded family saga in which the dwarf Andvari's ring – the original one from the *Völsunga saga* – is found in the river Rhine by a mecieval Icelander. It turns out to be a thing of evil, giving the bearer great power while slowly taking possession of him. To be destroyed it must be cast into the fires of Mount Hekla. A member of the family that owns the saga happens to have studied under Tolkien in Leeds. He kept in touch with his professor and allowed him to read the story – in 1938, when Tolkien, attempting to write his sequel to *The Hobbit*, was suffering from writer's block. In other words, Tolkien was inspired by a family saga about an evil ring of power. A ring, moreover, found in the river Rhine – precisely where it had ended up at the conclusion of Wagner's *Götterdämmerung*...[32]

3.2. Yes

3.2.1. Hillard

Another novel in which Tolkien plays a role, *Mirkwood*, also briefly mentions Wagner. In a discussion, one character brings up Tolkien's habit to borrow 'names, nouns and other stuff'. When the female protagonist asks 'what's wrong with borrowing, when he used it to create such great stuff?' he replies: 'Precisely, my dear. Tolkien felt no unease in this. To him, every name and

---

32 Ridpath makes clever use of the fact that the 14th century Icelandic *Mödruvallabók* refers to a certain *Gaukur's saga*, which has never been found. However, his claim that Tolkien had written only one chapter of the *Hobbit* sequel by March 9, 1938, doesn't fly: Tolkien had written four chapters, one of which contained most of the elements the thriller suggests were inspired by *Gaukur's saga*. See *Return of the Shadow*, 11-109.

every tale was a place to begin a new story. Which reminds me. Hell, I'm just a professional middleman, but I'd say Wagner's opera, *The Ring* – about the one ring that could rule the world [...] – all sounds pretty familiar. Except Wagner wrote it in 1869' (Hillard, 130-131). Despite the incoherent phrasing, the suggestion is obvious.[33]

3.2.2. Shippey

The answer Shippey gives to the question in his paper 'The Problem of the Rings' is an Elvish 'yes and no' more than anything, with a dash of 'Deliberately' added to the mix. Shippey limits himself to one aspect of the comparison: the way the composer and the author handled their Icelandic source material. While studying the sources he wanted to use in his *Ring*, Wagner encountered one of the great conundrums, or, in German, *Königsprobleme* of 19th-century comparative philology: how do all the different versions of the story of Sigurd the Dragonslayer relate to each other? More specifically, what happened with the ring Sigurd gave to, or took from, or swapped with Brynhild? The sources are in conflict. The philological amateur Wagner, Shippey argues, did not succeed in creating a solution acceptable to the professional philologist Tolkien, who must have rejected his treatment of the sources.

In the *Ring* cycle, for example, the dwarvish smith Mime is an 'utterly degraded' character, unlike his counterpart Regin in the *Eddas* and the *Völsunga saga*. Siegfried kills him without compunction. Shippey suggests that the story of the petty-dwarf Mîm and Túrin Turambar in *The Children of Húrin* was intentionally written against this episode in the opera. Not only did Wagner turn Siegfried's foster father into a dwarf, he also degraded the entire dwarvish race by making the character both ridiculous and despicable (though Mime is also knowledgeable, and a victim of his more sinister brother, Alberich). Against this, Shippey argues, Tolkien sets another dwarf, giving him a name almost identical with that of Wagner's dwarf. Just as Mime betrays Siegfried, Mîm betrays

---

33 In 2011 the Tolkien Estate initiated a lawsuit against Hillard, mainly for using a cover too suggestive of Tolkien's own works, though the way Tolkien was depicted in the book was also considered problematic. No mention was made of the plagiarism suggestion. The matter was settled the same year, and at the time of writing (Oct. 2011) a movie based on Hillard's book is said to be in the making, featuring Tolkien as a character.

Túrin, but as a member of a dispossessed, persecuted race he has a reason for this behaviour. Túrin spares him, and his compassion puts Siegfried's lack of mercy in an unfavourable light.

A couple of years earlier, Christine Chism had made the same case for Bilbo Baggins as Siegfried's antithesis: 'In *The Hobbit*, Tolkien rewrites the moment of Siegfried's murder of Mime' (Chism, 77). Mime is after Siegfried's life, Gollum is after Bilbo's, and Bilbo's first impulse is to kill his loathsome foe. But then, understanding what a miserable existence Gollum leads, he is struck with compassion and spares him. It is his pity that ultimately saves Frodo and maybe Middle-earth. Without Gollum, the Ring would never have been destroyed: Frodo succumbs to its power at the last moment and is only saved because Gollum bites his finger off and falls into the fires of Mount Doom.

Chism has a point here: Gollum does resemble Mime, who has an obvious Gollum-moment in *Siegfried* I, 3 when he fantasizes about attaining the ring, singing: 'Mime the bold, Mime is King, Prince of the Elves, Ruler of the Universe!'[34] Compare this with Gollum's 'Perhaps we grow very strong… Lord Sméagol? Gollum the Great? *The* Gollum!' (*The Two Towers* II, 2). Gollum's dialogue with himself, his split personality, in a way recalls Mime's double-tongued speech after Siegfried has slain Fafner: the dwarf believes he is talking sweet, but in reality he is telling the young hero that he plans to give him a sleeping draught and cut his head off once he has fallen asleep.

That Bilbo spares Gollum would make him, and later Frodo, much more of a merciful anti-Siegfried than Túrin with his own delusions of mastery could ever be. Moreover, Mîm never threatens Túrin personally and only turns against him *after* he has been spared, because one of his sons was killed by one of Túrin's men – which was the reason behind Túrin's generosity to begin with. What the episode actually shows is how vindictive a dwarf can be.

There is little room for pity in Wagner's *Siegfried*; if any of his operas is about pity, it would be the work of his old age, *Parsifal*. Its hero is supplementary to the two-dimensional Siegfried and grows wise through compassion, much like Frodo, who decides not to kill the villainous Saruman at the end of the

---

34 German: 'Mime, der Kühne, Mime ist König, Fürst der Alben, Walter des Alls.'

Ring epic.³⁵ Or, if one insists on finding compassion in the *Ring* cycle, it could be found in Brünnhilde. At first she is a '*kalte, fühllose Maid*' (cold, unfeeling maiden), bred to carry dead heroes to Walhall without an ounce of pity. But in *Die Walküre* II she is overcome with compassion for Siegmund and Sieglinde and their unborn child, to such a degree that she defies her father, Wotan.

Yet Shippey seems right insofar as it remains remarkable that Tolkien introduces a *dwarf* called Mîm, even though the idea to make the smith who fosters Siegfried a dwarf was not Wagner's own (his addition to the source material was making Mime the brother of the original ring owner). In the prose introduction to the *Reginsmál* and in the saga *Norna Gests tháttr* Regin is said to be a dwarf in stature (*dvergr of vöxt*); he is possibly identical with the Regin mentioned in the catalogue of Dwarves in the *Völuspá*.³⁶ Be that as it may, if Tolkien did indeed write the afore-mentioned episode of the Túrin story against *Siegfried*, he obscured it by changing the characters' circumstances as thoroughly as their motives. And he was not merely writing against Wagner, but also against his own source, the Eddaic lay *Fáfnismál*. In this lay Sigurd, acting on the advice of a flock of birds, likewise slays the foster-father who intends to murder him. In the *Legend*, the birds warn Sigurd against Regin; the dragonslayer turns around, sees Regin creeping towards him with hatred in his eyes, and kills him. The hatred and Regin's sneaky approach are Tolkien's own addition: in the original lay Sigurd immediately acts on the advice of the birds and decapitates the smith without any other justification. In a way, Bilbo sparing Gollum could be seen as Tolkien correcting the harshness of the Icelandic sources that he had already mitigated in his *Legend*.

Wagner, too, tries to mitigate the harshness of the scene. The Waldvogel, his one remaining bird, does not advise the hero to kill Mime but only tells him to listen carefully to his words. Having tasted the dragonblood, Siegfried can

---

35 Correspondences between Parsifal and Frodo have not escaped notice either, see Ryan 1966 (though he seems to mix up the title of Wagner's opera with the character of the original Celtic story) and this German website: http://home.arcor.de/hobbitkunde/hobbitkunde/hobbitkunde/hobbit_text.html (retr. date 08-11-2011)
36 In *Wagner's Ring in 1848* Haymes writes that *Das Lied vom Hürnen Seyfried*, one of Wagner's German sources 'tells of a youth raised by dwarf smiths in the forest' (8), but this is wrong on several counts: there is only one smith (with a servant), he is human and he does not raise Siegfried but takes him on as an apprentice. The dwarfs enter the story at a later point: they are the owners of the hoard. This shows how tricky it is to keep track of what Wagner took from which source and what was his own invention.

hear Mime's murderous thoughts, instead of his innocent-seeming words. So can the audience; Wagner could not have spelled out the danger more clearly. Ridding himself of his foster-father once his murderous intentions become clear is Siegfried's own decision. Maybe he could have chased him away, though in that case Mime would undoubtedly have continued plotting against him. In any case Wagner (who admitted in his letter to Röckel of 1854 that Siegfried was not flawless), did not make up the smith's murder plans, nor his death at the hand of the hero. He merely used them, and so did Tolkien in his *Legend*.

If anything can be held against Wagner in the case of Siegfried and Mime, it is that the latter is wholly despicable and unlike Gollum wholly irredeemable. He is also a much flatter character than Regin, who is torn between his love for Sigurd (mentioned in the introduction to the lay), his duty to revenge his brother and his lust for gold. The reason is that in order for Siegfried to shine despite his act of violence, his opponent cannot have sympathetic traits. Hence Wagner's vilification of Mime. Unfortunately for him, unlike Regin in the source texts and in the *Legend*, Mime is made too silly to be perceived as a serious danger to the hero, so when Siegfried casually finishes him off this seems overkill. This tends to backfire, to the detriment of Siegfried as a character. What makes it worse, is that Mime looks suspiciously like the caricature of a Jew. Though nothing in Wagner's text suggests that he is one, many have identified him as such based on other evidence.[37] Possibly Tolkien was aware of this identification. In that case it could be that he was thinking of Mime when he compared his own Dwarves, who are much more dignified than the *Ring* dwarfs and also a little less gold-hungry, to Jews in his BBC radio interview of 1964, and in one of his letters (*Letters*, 175).

Ultimately, if the Mîm episode in *The Children of Húrin* is meant as a critical gloss to Wagner's *Siegfried*, it has probably more to do with giving a dwarf back some dignity than with the compassion of a hero whose fury and lack

---

37 The readers will have to take my word for this. Entire books have been written about this subject (the best one being *The Darker Side of Genius* by Jacob Katz, Waltham MA: Brandeis University Press, 1986), but I will not go further into it. Its importance for the argument in this particular book is too marginal.

of restraint causes the death of several people who might have stood between him and his fate.

Shippey could probably have made a stronger case by pointing out that Tolkien's use of the incest motive from the *Völsunga saga* was diametrically opposed to Wagner's use of it in *Die Walküre*. Whereas Wagner condoned and even applauded the incest by having both siblings commit it knowingly and willingly, Tolkien made it so abhorrent to them that they feel bound to kill themselves when they find out what they have done. Wagner broke a taboo for reasons he considered valid, like Signý does in the saga. To her, vengeance is more important than anything, including the lives of her children, while Wagner proclaims that true love overrides all social conventions. In his analysis of the Oedipus myth (*Oper und Drama* II, III) he maintains that people abhorred what Oedipus and his mother had done because it went against convention, against our familiar relations with our mother and the ideas based on them, not because incest between a mother and a son is morally wrong per se. It is also possible he had the concept of the 'twin souls' from Plato's *Symposium* in mind. According to a story told there, humans originally had four arms, four legs, and a single head with two faces, but Zeus feared their power and split them in half, condemning them to spend their lives searching for their other half to be complete again.

Tolkien reinforces the incest taboo. He uses this episode from the *Völsunga saga* in the *Legend*, adding the hint, not present in the original, that Sigmund might and perhaps ought to have guessed that the nightly visitor who shared his bed was his sister. This also underlines the sinfulness of the act. This way Tolkien indirectly rejects the idea that vengeance overrides the incest taboo. He was not always undividedly happy with the pagan ethics of the North.

Noting that many elements in Wagner's *Ring* cycle 'find at least an echo in Tolkien', Shippey acknowledges that Wagner's conception of the ring may 'have given Tolkien a hint, and a most important hint.' But Tolkien rejected Wagner's treatment of the sources, and two world wars 'and all that went with them' divided him from the German composer. 'Of this divide Tolkien at least was fiercely conscious and deeply resentful' – as evidenced by his denouncement of Hitler. If Tolkien took anything from Wagner, this was perhaps no more than the idea that something could be done with the idea of the Ring of Power, something more, and more laden with significance than anything in an ancient source, but at the same time and very definitely not what Wagner had done with it. (113)

Shippey somewhat overstates his case when he contrasts Wagner's view of power unfavourably with Tolkien's, claiming that the former 'understands and sympathises with the desire for power, if it could be acquired without paying the price for it.' It is not clear why he thinks so, but maybe he bases himself on the fact that Wagner does not distance himself from some of his more power-hungry characters. In a diary entry of March 28, 1878, Wagner's wife Cosima noted 'that he had once sympathised completely with Alberich'[38] at the moment Wotan robs him of his ring; the dwarf's pain is clearly audible in the music. Whatever his crime, the gods treat him very shabbily. But understanding someone's suffering is not the same as condoning their every act. Alberich ends up as powerless as he was at the beginning, precisely as Wagner wanted him to be. In one of the discarded endings of *Götterdämmerung*, Alberich is actually said to become 'free' again once his ring has been returned to the Rhine. Later, Wagner struck this line identifying the villain as his own victim, but it only stresses his awareness of the enslaving properties of power, rather than suggesting any belief in its desirability.

Wagner also identified with Wotan, sympathising with his moral plight, and it is true that Wotan, as power-hungry as any in the first opera of the cycle, is not the villain of the story. It is obvious, though, that Wagner does not endorse his behaviour. Wotan's initial wrongdoings condemn him, and the main reason that he engenders sympathy – and not just Wagner's – is that he learns to love and to reject power in the course of the drama. Rather than sympathising with the lust for power, Wagner shows that even the desire for it corrupts, and that power can only be acquired at the cost of love. All but one of the characters who possess the Ring or want to obtain it, pay the ultimate price – death – even if they are not power-hungry but just powerful, like Siegfried.

---

38 German: 'daß er einst völlige Symphatie mit Alberich gehabt.'

Apparently, Shippey overlooks the fact that the great dichotomy in the *Ring* is Love versus Power – Love as the natural state of mankind and Power as its corruption with the help of the Law – and that the composer of the *Ring* is unmistakably and unequivocally on the side of love. When he lists the powerful Tolkien characters who refuse to take the Ruling Ring for themselves and finds no corresponding refusals in Wagner's work, Shippey is technically correct, though one powerful character, Wotan, renounces the ring at some point and another, Siegfried, gives it to Brünnhilde as a love token. Brünnhilde learns to give it up, too, though one could argue that she is not particularly powerful at that moment. In any case, even if no powerful character would give up the ring at all, this still would not prove that Wagner sympathised with the lust for power. If anything it suggests that his view was more cynical than Tolkien's – that he had fewer illusions about powerful people, and did not really believe in the 'forces of good, in might for right' (Ross). That more characters withstand (Gandalf, Bilbo with some help, Aragorn, Elrond, Galadriel, Faramir, Sam) than succumb to the lure of the One Ring (Isildur, Déagol, Sméagol-Gollum, Boromir, Denethor, and ultimately Frodo) in *The Lord of the Rings* could even be said to undermine its thoroughly evil image, uplifting though it is. However, this has little bearing on Shippey's main point: Tolkien may have noticed the potential of Wagner's ring, but if he took anything from Wagner it was not to copy him – on the contrary.

Despite this 'yes and no', Shippey's latest utterance on the matter seems meant to put the spirit of Wagner back into the bottle again. In his introduction to the 2011 essay collection *Tolkien and the Study of His Sources*, he writes about the Professor's annoyance with people who claim

> that he must have "got it out of" some earlier work. Wagner is a frequent culprit here, put forward by those aware that there are Rings in both men's works, aware of little else about either, and anxious to demonstrate a fancied cultural superiority. (9)

Possibly this return to a more defensive attitude has something to do with the publication of the *Legend*: its 'Wagnerian' subject matter only invited further comparisons. There is some truth in the statement above, though it is a pity that it tars the more knowledgeable people with the same brush as the cultural snobs.

3.2.3. Haymes

A prime example of the Yes category is 'The Two Rings' by Edward Haymes, a professor of German Literature, who among other things wrote about the connections of Wagner with the *Nibelungenlied*. In a balanced comparison of the two ring stories, Haymes investigates the backgrounds of the two creators, the context in which their works arose and the posibility that both merely drew from the same ancient sources. His conclusion is that common sources are an insufficient explanation for the resemblance between the two rings.

> Tolkien must have absorbed Wagner's notion of the ring even though he probably knew the Icelandic sources Wagner had used better than the composer himself [...] There are too many aspects of Wagner's specific adaptation of the ring motif that show up in Tolkien for this to be an accident.

Haymes shows there are many differences as well. Tolkien's work is epic, while Wagner's is dramatic. Tolkien did not associate power with money and does not explicitly present love in all its manifestations as the antithesis to power, while sex is avoided altogether. For Tolkien, virtue lies in self-denial, in Wagner it lies in the affirmation of the self. Yet despite all these differences, the similarities are decisive for Haymes and 'Tolkien stands convicted of being a closet Wagnerian.' He concludes by comparing Tolkien's refusal to acknowledge that 'he had learned much from Wagner's mythopoesis and his art as a whole' to Wagner's very shabby treatment of almost everyone he was in some way indebted to. However, he stresses that Tolkien was 'not as petty a man as Wagner,' which is something of an understatement. Haymes could have added Wagner's posthumous connections with the Third Reich to his discussion, but in any case he investigated the subject conscientiously before reaching his conclusion.

3.2.4. Bayreuth and sundry

Many simply take it for granted that Tolkien's work is based on, influenced by, or indebted to Wagner's *Ring*, as Shippey suggested (though it is a mistake to believe that people who claim so are no more aware of Wagner's work than they are of Tolkien's; many of them are well-informed Wagnerians). 'The opera cycle is of tremendous importance for Tolkien's work', owing 'a debt to Wagner and his liberal reworking of Nordic and Teutonic mythology'.

An enthusiastic newspaper article about two different performances of the *Ring* in Britain in the year 2005 bears the title 'The return of the original Ring Lord'.[39] It appears to be 'beyond all reasonable doubt that Tolkien was heavily influenced by Wagner's *Ring*, and *The Lord of the Rings* (together with *The Hobbit* and perhaps also *The Silmarillion*) ought to be seen as a variant within the ring tradition of the Nibelung Cycle' (Arvidsson 2007, 148). A reviewer of the Dutch translation of the *Legend* bluntly dismisses any suggestion that Tolkien was independent of Wagner, seeing influences both in the two alliterative poems and in *The Lord of the Rings*. He concludes his review by recommending the *Ring* over the *Legend* (Van Vredendaal, 31, 36). The introductory essay to the essay collection *Wagner & Cinema* bears the title 'Why Wagner and Cinema? Tolkien Was Wrong', and at the end of it the statement about the two round rings is quoted and rejected without any other argument than a counter-quote by video artist Bill Viola that '[i]t's hard to avoid Wagner's latent presence'[40] (Joe, 19).

Unsurprisingly, in Bayreuth the joke is on Tolkien. There, a theatre company stages abridged, parodising versions of one or more Wagner operas every summer as an alternative to the *Festspiele* in the same town. In 2007, the company chose the *Ring* cycle, called their play *Her den Ring* (the German title of *The Lord of the rings* is *Der Herr der Ringe*), produced a poster that blatantly mimicked the posters of Jackson's film version, and at some crucial moments incorporated Tolkien-elements in the text. After Alberich has stolen the Rhinegold to forge the ring that will grant him world domination, the following exchange takes place between him and the Rhinemaidens:

Alberich:	Too late. Whinge, if you must. Your own fault. You three have driven me crazy, you felt so secure, and you betrayed the secret to me.
Flosshilde:	What will you turn into now?
Wellgunde:	Gollum?
Woglinde:	Sméagol?
Alberich:	Sauron!

---

39 Quotes from Pantle; Emerick; Duchen.
40 The author more or less leaves the impression that Tolkien was referring to *The Lord of the Rings* films as well as the book; she took the Tolkien quote from Ross's column in the *New York Times*, which does not always keep the book and the films apart.

The suggestion is obvious and the audience roars with laughter. An extensive comparison of Wagner's *Ring* with the film version of Tolkien's epic yielding 26 pages of sometimes far-fetched similarities, wonders if Sauron is not actually a megalomaniac version of Alberich (Vill, 9).

Faced with the question whether 'Tolkien stole Wagner's creation', Simon Rees, the dramaturgist of the Welsh National Opera, replies:

> It seems very strange that Tolkien could take a subject that was so directly parallel and swear that it didn't come out of Wagner's *Ring*. The more I look at the two pieces, the clearer it is to me that Wagner produced a piece of extraordinarily united and unified work that you can tap from every angle and it remains as sound as a bell. And that *The Lord of the Rings* is the conception of a very much lesser imagination, though still a very interesting and powerful piece of writing. (Leech)

The English conservative philosopher Roger Scruton remains circumspect regarding the question of influence, merely claiming that 'Wagner made Tolkien possible'. But then he leaves no doubt as to the fact that in his opinion, the latter falls far short of the standards set by the former:

> Unlike Wagner [...] Tolkien did not have the ability to remake the religious experience through art. His novel has smatterings of the great conflict between good and evil, and an abundance of mysteries. But it does not re-create the experience of the sacred that Wagner has always in mind in the tetralogy.

3.2.5. Ross, Kasper, and sex

In the opinion of the American music critic Ross there is no point denying Wagner's influence on Tolkien, 'not when characters deliver lines like "ride to ruin and the world's ending"[41] – Brünnhilde condensed in seven words.' As in the *Ring*, the old order disappears, but power is transferred in a peaceful, not an apocalypticic way (Sauron would disagree). 'For Tolkien, myth is a window on an ideal world, both brighter and blacker than our own. For Wagner, it is a magnifying mirror for the average, desperate modern soul.' But Tolkien misses one very important thing:

---

41 Éomer, believing his sister to have fallen in the Battle of the Pelennor Fields (*The Return of the King* II, 6).

When Tolkien stole Wagner's ring, he discarded its most significant property—that it can be forged only by one who has forsworn love. (Presumably, Sauron gave up carnal pleasures when he became an all-seeing eye at the top of a tower, but it's hard to say for certain. Maybe he gets a kick out of the all-seeing bit.)

Ross is not the only one to point out that Tolkien ignores the sexuality so prominently present in Wagner's work. The German theologian Hartmut Kasper suggests that Tolkien has merely encoded the sex for the protection of child-readers and that it is 'easy to decipher' for adults – see the reference to the vagina dentata myth mentioned in 2.1 (286). But a reviewer of a book about the erotic impulse in Wagner writes: '[T]here's something adolescent about Tolkien's entirely sexless world, whereas Wagner was pushing the boundaries of what was possible, both in matters of sex and in his musical idiom.'[42] Haymes recalls a Wagnerian musicologist reading *The Lord of the Rings* who complained: 'There is no sex and everyone is always stopping for tea.'

3.2.6. The racism card, Schwartz & Arvidsson

Many statements illustrate the problem, mentioned by Birzer, that Wagner is used against Tolkien. Tom Nairn calls Tolkien shallow, compared to Wagner's emotional depth, and believes that the former's attempt 'to recreate the pagan epic Beowulf' fell flat because 'Tolkien lacked the poetical soul to do so'. In the eyes of A.N. Wilson, long-standing Tolkien relativist, *The Lord of the Rings* is weak, 'Wagner for kiddies, Wagner without a brooding sense of spiritual catastrophe'.[43] The author of a book discussing Joyce's *Finnegan's Wake* voices a similar opinion: 'Wagner is Tolkien for grown-ups' (Hodgart, 131). As he adds that the *Wake* is 'Wagner for rather learned and linguistically sophisticated grown-ups', the suspicion arises that he is a little out of his depth here. Anyway, criticising the author by means of the composer seems to have become an aim in itself, and we have moved from questions about similarities, borrowing and inspiration into bashing territory.

---

42 Bradley Winterton in the *Taipei Times* of August 14, 2011.
43 Wilson is not entirely dismissive of Tolkien. He praises 'the sheer power' of Tolkien's narrative and his invention of the mythology and language of the Elves, finding *The Silmarillion* 'deeper' and more impresssive than *The Lord of the Rings*. But Wilson also concluded that Tolkien 'was not really a writer'. Of course, this became the headline of the article.

It gets worse when Wagner the anti-Semitic Hitler favourite is conjured up to haunt the conservative Tolkien. One method is insinuation. Ivo van Hove, who staged a demythologised version of the *Ring* cycle in Flanders, is a borderline case: 'Wagner did not only influence the mythological subject-matter and the form of the narrative, but also the political, ideological and even nationalistic overtones of [*The Lord of the Rings*], which was written during the Second World War.' Though Van Hove never makes this explicit, the wording makes the combination Wagner-Tolkien sound faintly unsavoury. Van Hove obviously does not know that Tolkien was far from happy with the rising tide of British nationalism during the War (see especially his letter to his son Christopher from 23-25 September 1944, *Letters* 92-94).

A person calling himself 'phil' who read Ross's article in the *New Yorker*, muses in his weblog about the similarities between the two rings and devotes some thoughts to Wagner, the Nazis and Tolkien. Wagner, 'like Tolkien, seems to set up (maybe unintentionally) an equation between evil and the dark-skinned races.' This was what tainted Wagner's *Ring*, because the Nazis turned it into their national myth. They could do this because the work was 'so powerful and like all great art, so malleable'. His conclusion: if you love Tolkien's work,

> the Ring Cycle story — and its place in history, at the hands of the Nazis — provides some interesting food for thought. Since, in some ways, Tolkien's Ring story is almost like an updated version of the Wagner Cycle, you have to wonder if a German-authored version of *The Lord of the Rings* would not have undergone the same treatment. (philosophistry.com)

Does 'phil' have a point – would the ring epic, published in 1930 by one J.R.R. Tollkühn, have been safe from being hijacked by the Nazis? And what role does racism play in this context?

Wagner described two of the villains in his ring as *Schwarz-Alben* ('Black Elves'), basing himself on the *Prose Edda* and Jacob Grimm's interpretation of it. However, he never ascribed them a black skin, nor did he ever suggest that the two roles be performed by dark-skinned singers. Both have been interpreted as Jews, which does not come entirely out of the left field, though nothing in the text or the stage directions indicates that they are. Of course not: they are Dwarves, not human beings. Whatever Wagner may have believed he was doing when he created them, he knew better than to assign mythical beings a racial designation belonging to humans.

Tolkien's story does have dark-skinned evildoers. Most of these are orcs. Leaving aside his later attempts to make them either totally corrupted humans or talking machines (*Morgoth's Ring*, 409-442), Orcs are not human. The human Haradrim, who fight on Sauron's side in the Battle of the Pelennor Fields, are also dark-skinned, but they are not described as irredeemably evil, rather as fierce, proud and cruel. At some point, looking at one of their fallen warriors, Sam wonders if he was really evil of heart and if he would not have preferred to stay peacefully at home (*The Two Towers* IV). Like the Easterlings, the Haradrim are said to be victims of Sauron's lies and after the Fall of Barad-dûr Aragorn makes peace with them, while orcs are hunted down and killed.

Superficially seen, the use of apparently non-western peoples as Sauron's allies may seem unfortunate. But there is no ideological basis for racism in the epic: the Haradrim and Sauron's other human allies are not corruptible because they are racially inferior to other humans, but because they are men. Anyone reading Tolkien's letter of 18 April 1944 to his son Christopher, who was training as a pilot in South-Africa then, knows his position: 'The treatment of colour nearly always horrifies anyone going out from Britain, & not only in South Africa' (*Letters*, 73). In the 'Akallabêth', the story of the Fall of Númenor, some of the worst atrocities such as human sacrifice, also instigated by Sauron, are attributed to the white Men of the West, the Númenoreans, and condemned – Tolkien held a rather dim view of mankind in general.

However, as the Nazis did misappropriate the *Ring* even though it was not written to propagate fair-haired and fair-skinned Germanic superiority,[44] it is hard to say whether a hypothetical pre-war German counterpart of Tolkien would have been safe from the cultural annexation policy of the Nazis. It could

---

44 Siegmund is actually described as *braun* (brown), and the words German(ic) or race are never used anywhere in the text. The sinister Hagen is the 'inferior' result of mixed breeding, and as this is instigated by the chief villain, Alberich, it could be constituted as a condemnation of interraciality, though a very understated one in that case. Also, it is Hagen himself who draws attention to it. If one insists on looking for claims of German superiority in Wagner, both *Tannhäuser* and *Die Meistersinger* would be more promising candidates. As for the term race (*Rasse* in German): Wagner always opts for the more neutral *Geschlecht* (kindred) when he refers to the various groups of beings in *Der Ring*, such as dwarfs, gods, giants, etc.

be that they would have loved the heroism of the Germanic looking Rohirrim, whose language Tolkien translated with that of his equally Germanic Anglo-Saxon ancestors. It is easy to misunderstand his work. For years, *The Lord of the Rings* was banned in the Soviet Union because the darkness from the East was interpreted as a reference to the totalitarian Soviet Union (Grushetskiy), despite the fact that this kind of interpretation always angered Tolkien.

In an article about Tolkien's life, writings and world view, the Danish historian Jesper M. Rosenløv notes that critics use the similarities between *The Lord of the Rings* on the one hand and *The Ring of the Nibelung* and the Nazi-cult of all things Norse and Germanic on the other hand to discredit Tolkien and attribute racist and fascist motives to him. He points to Tolkien's descripton of evil creatures as scimitar-bearing, dark-skinned or slant-eyed figures from Southern and Eastern regions as one of the reasons (114). In the end, though, Rosenløv refutes the accusation that Tolkien was a fascist, pointing out that such critics confuse conservatism with fascism and that his letters show where he truly stands. Which in itself is true enough (though Nazism should not be confused with fascism either and by refuting the former one does not automatically refute the latter). In any case, all this makes clear that Tolkien's story is vulnerable to superficial reading.

The Austrian Guido Schwarz also sees racist tendencies in Tolkien's *The Lord of the Rings*, above all in the depiction of the Easterlings, in the First Age mostly found among the people supporting Morgoth and in the Third Age among the followers of the evil overlord Sauron. This reminds him of the ideology of the Nazis, who considered people from the East racially inferior to themselves. Tolkien contrasts these bad guys with the fair-haired characters on the side of good, like the Rohirrim and the Elven-lady Galadriel, for Schwarz the epitome of a-sexual purity. He conveniently forgets that Tolkien's ideal of beauty is Lúthien Tinúviel, more fair than mortal tongue can tell – and her hair is raven black.

Having mentioned Galadriel, Schwarz conjures up the spectre of Wagner by claiming that Tolkien 'introduced a Lohengrin-scene' to his epic: when the Fellowship is about to leave Lórien, Galadriel appears in a swan-ship (93). A tenuous connection: in the opera *Lohengrin* the hero arrives, not in a swan-ship, but in a boat drawn by a swan, and when King Ludwig of Bavaria played Lohengrin in a swan-shaped boat he did so mostly because in real life swans refuse to draw boats and one has to be inventive. Swanships are not just a recurring motif in *The Lord of the Rings* and *The Silmarillion*, they also occur regularly in prehistoric art from the Mediterranean to Scandinavia. One does not need to drag in Lohengrin's boat to explain their presence in Tolkien's ring epic.

It looks as though Schwarz uses Wagner to compromise Tolkien by association in his attempt to warn readers against 'fascistoid' tendencies, both in Tolkien's work and in themselves as fans. That the opera *Lohengrin* contains a remark about 'hordes from the east' to match Tolkien's Easterlings would support such an interpretation. Wagner's characters are referring to historical events, the Magyar invasions of the German lands during the Carolingian period, and possibly at the same time alluding to the situation of the kingdom of Saxony, where Wagner lived at the time. Hitler, of course, applied it to the Soviet Union. As for Tolkien, in his view the Easterlings and the Haradrim, though servants of the enemy, needed to be liberated from tyranny just as much as the inhabitants of Middle-earth who fought against Sauron (*Letters*, 240-241). In addition, it is only to be expected that your enemies come from the East if you situate your good guys in an area bordering on, or close to, a western sea. As he wrote:

> In any case if you want to write a tale of this sort you must consult your roots, and a man of the North-west of the Old World will set his heart and the action of his tale in an imaginary world of that air and that situation: with the Shoreless Sea of his innumerable ancestors to the West, and the endless lands (out of which enemies mostly come) to the East. (*Letters*, 212)

Later Tolkien wrote to a correspondent that the goodness of the West and the badness of the East do not refer to modern times but spring from the demands of the narrative (Scull & Hammond, 640). This reads like a deliberate attempt to steer the adressee away from interpreting the tale as an allegory of World War II. If it was, Tolkien was being naïve: a decade after the war the majority of his public would almost inevitably think of the recent past when reading about enemies in the East, and though not an allegory, the story was applicable. Meanwhile, narrative necessity only works as an argument if one takes for granted that it is natural for 'a man of the North-west of the Old World' to situate the enemy territory in the East. That Tolkien held such notions confirms his own suggestion that his work had best be considered as a fantastic or alternative history of this world as seen by an inhabitant of the British Isles, instead of pure fantasy.

The Battle of the Pelennor Fields can serve to illustrate this. Shippey has argued that this clash of armies more or less follows the account given by the Gothic historian Jordanes of the Battle of the Catalaunian Plains, near present-day Châlons, France (1982, 12). In this crucial battle, which took place in AD 451, the combined forces of West-Romans, Visigoths and their allies defeated the hosts of Attila the Hun and his Ostrogoth allies, preserving Western civilisation from the 'Easterlings'. If this battle was indeed used as a template for the Pelennor Fields, the picture Tolkien paints here – possibly influenced by Jordanes' negative description of the Huns[45] – looks more black-and-white than the historical event underlying it. The Gondorians and their allies are good, their enemies are evil or serve an evil, demonic overlord. From an historical point of view the Hunnish chieftain, Attila, is an ambiguous figure: some sources depict him as a tyrant and 'the scourge of God', while in others he is a benevolent ruler. The name Attila is probably Gothic in origin, the diminutive of *atta*, 'father'. 'Little father' does not sound too bad – though it may have been a charm to play down the terror incited by the person so named.

Tolkien was well aware of the different views regarding Attila: in the *Legend*, his son quotes a passage from his lecture notes about the Völsungs in which he wrote: 'Attila (when legend or history is not on his side), is represented as grasping and greedy' (341). Faced with the choice between presenting Attila as the evil Scourge of God or as the Little Father, he followed Icelandic literature, which is furthest removed from actual history, as well as being the product of the most northwestern country of Europe. *The Legend of Sigurd and Gudrún* follows the Eddaic lay *Atlakviða* in making Attila the bad guy (both the late lay *Atlamál* and the *Völsunga saga* have lost sight of the Hunnish conqueror; in the former he is just a local chieftain, in the saga actually Brynhild's brother). In the *Nibelungenlied* Attila (Etzel) is a benevolent ruler and the unwitting

---

45 'Species pavenda nigredine [...] quaedam deformis offa, non facies; habensque magis puncta quam lumina.' (A fearsome, swarthy race [having] a kind of malformed lump for a face; and having points rather than eyes.)

victim of an internal Burgundian feud, whereas in the second *Legend* poem Atli (aka Attila) is as violent and greedy as in the *Atlakviða*. And if the Battle of the Pelennor Fields is modelled on that of the Catalaunian Plains, Tolkien clearly opted for the version in which the forces from the East are unequivocally evil in this case as well. In doing so, he has some historians on his side, but not all historiography. In Hungary and Turkey Attila is a hero, and the German Emperor Wilhelm II used him as an example of a great military leader.

In the historical accounts the Goths often follow Attila because of the loot his victories promised them, whereas in the *Legend* they are only too happy to turn against him. This was Tolkien's own addition, not something he found in his Icelandic sources. As the Goths were Germanic, what he actuallty does here is put all the Germanic peoples on one side against the non-Germanic, Asian Huns, betraying a latent racism in this early work. Maybe he annexated the Goths for the side of the 'good guys' because the idea that speakers of one of his favourite languages were fighting for a Hunnish tyrant was appalling enough for him to manipulate his sources. That does not make him a fascist, but it does betray racial bias against certain types of Asians. This is confirmed by one of his letters, where he calls Orcs 'degraded and repulsive versions of the (to Europeans) least lovely Mongol-types' (*Letters*, 274). At the same time, it shows that he was aware of the bias.

In any case, if Schwarz sees fascistoid tendencies at work in Tolkien's story because the enemies in it come from the East, he overlooks the fact that from an English point of view the Germans were the 'enemies from the East' a mere ten years before the publication of *The Lord of the Rings* – the British actually called them Huns. Schwarz seems to apply the situation in post-war Germany (and Austria) to the work of an English author, and though he claims to do so in order to warn Tolkien readers against fascist tendencies in themselves, he ought, perhaps, to have realised that the author's position differed from that of his German and Austrian readership.

Still, Schwarz is not the only one to raise this objection; The Swede Stefan Arvidsson also mentions Tolkien's anti-Easterling attitude in relation to Wagner, and his judgement is not to Tolkien's advantage either. For Wagner the enemies are above and among us, but for Tolkien, he writes, they are found 'with the others. The enemy [...] is linked with Slavic and Eastern malevolence and a filthy machine-cult, and he fights, not surprisingly, under red and black standards' (163). In other words, Tolkien is being anti-communist here, and from their point of view the Soviets were right to ban *The Lord of the Rings*.

Margaret Sinex argues that Tolkien's descriptions of these non-westerners, particularly the Haradrim, borrow the colour codes of medieval texts describing Saracens. When his work echoes those texts, ranging the Saracen-like people among the enemies, he is not expressing any personal views about non-white, non-western peoples but using a topos from the literature he knew best. Tolkien applied the standard colour scheme for Saracens from several medieval texts to the Haradrim: red, black and yellow (Sinex, 183ff). That Arvidsson overlooked the references to yellow may account for his identification of the Southrons with more recent opponents of the West (though the sickle in the Soviet flag was yellow, too). On the other hand, Hooker also sees a link between the red banners of the Southrons and the Red Flag of Communism, pointing at Tolkien's very negative opinions of this ideology (182). In the end, both medieval and more recent colour schemes probably contributed to Tolkien's choice of colour here.

Noting that Tolkien shared Wagner's passion for Northern culture, Arvidsson quotes from the famous lecture on *Beowulf*, claiming that Tolkien saw Norse mythology 'as a tool to intervene in his own time':

> It is the strength of the northern mythological imagination that [...] put the monsters in the centre, gave them victory but no honour, and found a potent but terrible solution in naked will and courage [...] So potent it is, that while the older southern imagination has faded forever into literary ornament, the northern has power, as it were, to revive its spirit even in our times. It can work, even as it did work with the *goðlauss* viking, without gods: martial heroism as its own end. (*MC*, 25)[46]

Tolkien, Arvidsson adds, made this statement in 1936, and 'one is quite happy it wasn't said in German' (Arvidsson 150).

---

46 'Without gods' is Tolkien's own translation of Old Norse *goðlauss*; this does not mean godless in the sense of impious and wicked, but in the sense of independent of the gods.

However, he omits the conclusion of the passage above: 'But we may remember that the poet of *Beowulf* saw clearly: the wages of heroism is death.'[47] If Arvidsson had read the passage more carefully; if he had realised that the author of *Beowulf* was a Christian and that Tolkien wrote *The Homecoming of Beorthnoth, Beorthelms Son* to *denounce* martial heroism as its own end, he might have recalled Faramir's words 'I do not love the bright sword for its sharpness, nor the arrow for its swiftness, nor the warrior for his glory' (*The Two Towers* III, 5). Then it might also have dawned on him that the passage was cautioning – a timely warning in 1936! – against precisely the thing he claims the author to be advocating.

Despite their serious allegations, both Schwarz and Arvidsson claim to like *The Lord of the Rings*. At the very least their remarks show an attempt to take a critical distance which is too often absent when Tolkien fans and even scholars write about their beloved author, and which would be refreshing but for the bantering tone and tongue-in-cheek attitude (worse in Schwarz than in Arvidsson).

Edward Rothstein, a music critic who writes quite sympathetically about *The Lord of the Rings* and Tolkien's struggle against the evils of modernity, sounds more grimly serious when he warns that

> [t]he tastes that made Wagner so attractive to the Germanic lands during World War II are partly Tolkien's. His accounts of the virtuous battle against Sauron are accompanied by a quasi-fascistic love for the Nordic as opposed to the Southern [...], a preoccupation with differing races and creatures bred in service to a cause.

This somewhat misleading description – why does Rothstein omit to say that only the Enemy breeds creatures in service to his cause? – makes one wonder if it is at all possible to love 'the Nordic' (a word, by the way, that Tolkien disliked because the ending was French in origin) in a non-fascistic manner. Or at least, whether such a thing is possible for those people who keep associating it with the Nazi period, instead of realising that the Nazis distorted its image. Tolkien had a point when he wrote about his 'burning private grudge against this ruddy little ignoramus Adolf Hitler [...] Ruining, perverting, misapplying, and making

---

47 In an English abstract of this book available online Arvidsson also cuts off the quote before the final sentence and concludes that Tolkien saw Norse mythology as a tool to intervene in his own time, only leaving out that it was good he didn't say it in German.

for ever accursed, that noble, northern spirit, a supreme contribution to Europe, which I have ever loved, and tried to present in its true light' (*Letters*, 55f).[48]

Fred Inglis started out by decrying Tolkien as a fascist (Inglis 1981, 197). Called on his misuse of the term he modified his judgment after revisiting Tolkien's work, but remained quite negative:

> Tolkien is no Fascist, but his great myth may be said, as Wagner's was, to prefigure the genuine ideals and nobilities of which Fascism is the dark negation. (Inglis 1983, 40)[49]

3.2.7. Hate-speak

From here we enter the territory of those who use Wagner against Tolkien because apparently, they hate both. To prevent this survey from becoming too depressing, two examples will have to suffice. Giving his opinion about Jackson's films, the American political analyst James P. Pinkerton shows no love whatsoever for Northern mythology and throws the baby out with the bath water:

> [...] to enter into the Ringworld and its realm of elves and orcs, is to be reintroduced to what "Rings" creator J.R.R. Tolkien called "that noble northern spirit" – that is, Nordic lore. Yup, we're blasting back to the past, to paganism, to the blood-and-fire bombast of Richard Wagner operas [...]. The historically minded will remember that the Nazis loved all this mythology. The whole of the Third Reich was awash in runes, lightning bolts and valkyries riding. Yet Hitler discredited these sagas when he went off to his own Götterdammerung in 1945. But now the Norsemen, minus the swastikas, are making a cultural comeback. [...] all Americans might recall that the basic irrationalism exalted in "Rings" once led other peoples into the abyss.

---

48 Two Dutch authors can serve as an example here. In an interview published two weeks after his death, Harry Mulisch speaks of the barbarian, dark side of German culture, of which the 'mudstream of the occult' brought about by Richard Wagner in the 19th century was a manifestation, and which became dominant during the Nazi era. In his texts Wagner had harked back to 'this strange, a-cultural Edda and Siegfried-rubbish, the Nibelungen and all that.' Mulisch was a cultured man, but the North and its ancient literature were obviously outside his range of interest and knowledge. Another Dutch author, Hella Haasse, broke off her study of Scandinavian language and literature because of the Nazi abuse of Norse myth. (*Het Vierde Leven*). As she was a guest at the Hobbit dinner with J.R.R. Tolkien in Rotterdam in 1958, one wonders if they had occasion to talk about this.
49 Described in Yates 1995. This article contains a number of excellent refutations to various kinds of Tolkien bashing up to 1992.

Writing these lines, Pinkerton must have forgotten the adagium that abuse does not preclude proper use. Whenever Hitler is allowed to discredit anything simply because he used it for his own evil ends, he is granted a posthumous victory. Unfortunately, people often reason in this way, and it appears that Tolkien's words about Hitler's effect on the Northern spirit was spot on. Pinkerton, who apparently does not know much about the book version of *The Lord of the Rings*, Tolkien's religious background and the differences between paganism and Nazism, wrote his article almost six decades after the defeat of the Nazis.

The last example represents all those who voice this kind of opinion online. It is taken from a comment to a satirical description of Jackson's *Lord of the Rings* films:

> I'll never understand the 60s love affair with Tolkien. He wasn't an environmentalist (unfortunately), he was an anti-urban fascist. He stood for all the crap we hippies despise: Victorian virtue, national obligation, and Wagnerian racism. All this poison finds its way into Lord of the Rings.[50]

Such vitriol makes it abundantly clear why many Tolkienites, fans and scholars alike, are so eager to rescue the English Professor from the German Meister, whose bad image after the Second World War is somewhat less undeserved than that of the noble Northern spirit due to his anti-Semitism. Yet Wagner also loved that spirit. Despite everything it may be worth asking whether he is really such bad company. And if Tolkien's *Ring* cannot hold its own in the vicinity of Wagner's, no degree of separation will save it in the end. But its undiminished popularity more than half a century after its publication shows that there is nothing to fear on that count: it can hold its own very well.

---

50 http://lorenrosson.blogspot.com/2006/06/tolkien-fascist.html (retr. date 24-06-2010). A somewhat funny variant of this kind of writing was an article in the Norwegian newspaper *Dagen* of January 6, 2004, 'Ringenes Herrer og Antikrists Ånd' (*The Lords of the Rings* and the Spirit of the Antichrist), in which the author, a Lutheran priest, on discovering that Wagner, Hitler and Tolkien used the same medieval sources and that Tolkien was a Roman Catholic idolator, concludes that *The Lord of the Rings* cannot be other than anti-semitic. If this is not immediately clear to the reader, it is because Tolkien went about it much more subtly than Hitler did.

3.3. Deliberately

3.3.1. Hall

In this category we find those who believe that Tolkien's story was written with the intention of challenging Wagner's work. Ross is something of a question mark here: though he does not explicitly say so, he seems to suggest intent on Tolkien's part when he writes that it is possible to see the ring epic 'as a kind of rescue operation' to save Norse myth from its corruption by the Nazis, 'perhaps even saving Wagner from himself.'

In 1978, Robert Hall argued that Tolkien intended his work to be Anti-Nibelungen. Wagner called his cycle *ein Bühnenfestspiel für einen Vorabend und drei Tage* ('a stage festival play for a preliminary evening and three days'), which according to Hall corresponds with the one-part *Hobbit* and the three volumes of *The Lord of the Rings*, a comparison also made by John Spear. In addition to this, both stories have what is essentially the same theme, 'how to thwart the designs of a totally evil being [...], who seeks to achieve universal domination through a Ring which he has forged' (Hall, 352).

There, the resemblance ceases for Hall: while Tolkien was an optimist who believed in the ultimate victory of good and the restoration of the true monarchy, Wagner was a pessimist who saw the destruction of all existing structures and the return to a natural state of anarchy as the only solution. Tolkien's work, therefore, is a comedy while Wagner's is a tragedy. Despite Wagner's population of dwarves, gods, giants, and water sprites, his *Ring* is about the individual actions of thoroughly human characters and their consequences, whereas in Tolkien's story a variety of different races and peoples acts as a collective working towards a common goal.

In all its brevity, Hall's summary of the two ring stories cleverly highlights their basic similarity, and he has a good point when he contrasts Wagner's individualism with Tolkien's collectivism (though he is mistaken about the later Wagner's political beliefs and overlooks Tolkien's anarchism). However, that *The Lord of the Rings* was originally conceived as one book and published in three parts for purely practical reasons, undermines the main premise of his theory. The comedy-versus-tragedy argument is debatable. The ending of Tolkien's story is too elegiac for a comedy, while the ending of the *Ring* is ambiguous (more about this in Part II).

3.3.2. O'Donoghue

Referring to Tolkien's (alleged) disavowal of Wagner's work as a model for his own, O'Donoghue admits there are several similarities (184-186). However, she considers *The Lord of the Rings* a 'purposeful countering of Wagner. The thrust of Tolkien's narrative undermines and deliberately reverses what happens in Wagner.' The un-Wagnerian Frodo offers a 'comic inversion of heroism' and his epic struggle to destroy the ring by throwing it into the Crack of Doom, where it was first forged, is 'the ultimate anti-Wagnerian' twist (184-185). As both rings are dissolved in the end, one in water and the other in fire (or molten lava), it remains unclear what exactly is so anti-Wagnerian about the destruction of Tolkien's One Ring, but no further explanation is given. That Frodo constitutes an antithesis to Siegfried's 'brutal heroism' is undebatable, but it loses much of its significance in view of the fact that Siegfried ceased to be the main character of the *Ring* long before Wagner finished the work, and that he is not presented as an example to be emulated despite Nazi claims to the contrary.

O'Donoghue's claim that Tolkien profoundly resented the 'racist appropriation [...] of Norse material which Wagner's work had come to represent' does carry some truth, but her statement that he was 'opposing the supremacist agenda of right-wing ideologists' suggests a conflation of 'right-wing' and racist (and perhaps also fascist) that probably never existed in Tolkien's mind. Furthermore, her belief that it is the Elves – 'the most gifted and civilized of the peoples in the *Lord of the Rings*' – that Tolkien identifies as Jews, instead of the Dwarves (the Elves are even said to speak a Semitic language!) does not exactly inspire confidence in the grasp she has of her subject. She admits that Tolkien 'unconsciously reproduced some of the prejudices of the twentieth century', but does not identify these prejudices – perhaps because doing so would undermine her analysis of his ideological position?

3.3.3. Spengler

'Spengler',[51] writing for the *Asia Times Online* shortly after the release of the second *Lord of the Rings* film, also suggested that Tolkien was deliberately countering Wagner. In a colum turning out to be an ode to traditional American values written for his Asian readership, he suggests that Tolkien wrote his epic 'as an "anti-*Ring*" to repair the damage Wagner had inflicted upon Western culture.' *Der Ring* had propagated the heroic *Uebermensch*-cult that ultimately led to the New World Order of Nazi Germany, and in a follow-up to this column 'Spengler' proposes that Tolkien's work purposefully 'sought to undermine and supplant Richard Wagner's operatic *Ring* cycle, which had offered so much inspiration for Nazism.'[52]

Like others, 'Spengler' lists the many points of resemblance between the two rings, but focuses especially on their common base, 'the crisis of the immortals'. Both the twilight of the Gods and the departure of the Elves symbolise the decline and loss of power of the European aristocracy, which had determined the high culture of the West for many centuries. Avoiding the 'neo-pagan despair' that Wagner's *Ring* displays in the face of this crisis and rejecting its literally godless conclusion, the Catholic Tolkien took Wagner's materials and recast them – like Siegfried recast the shards of his father's sword into a new form, offering hobbitical 'modesty, forbearance and renunciation' as an alternative solution. Today's hobbits are the 'reluctant heroes of the new American Empire [… who] want nothing more than to till their fields and mind their homes.' (One wonders what the spiritual father of the hobbits would have thought of their recruitment into the service of a foreign superpower, especially in light of his anti-American letter to his son Christopher of 9 December 1943, *Letters*, 65).

---

51 'Spengler' is the pseudonym of David P. Goldman, an American writer and economist. It refers to the German philosopher Oswald Spengler, whose main work, *Der Untergang des Abendlandes* (The Decline of the West), München, 1923, is a theory about the cyclical rise and fall of civilisations. Oswald Spengler considered the scope of Wagner's works a sign of cultural degeneration (O. Spengler, 375ff). This almost begs the question what he would have thought of Tolkien's legendarium.
52 Like Shippey, 'Spengler' argues that Túrin is the anti-Siegfried, but he also calls him the anti-Beowulf. The latter is rather a howler. 'Spengler' seems unaware of the fact that the Anglo-Saxon epic *Beowulf* was a life-long favourite of Tolkien's, written by a Christian poet for a Christian audience. Compared to this, suggesting that Wagner was a neo-pagan is a minor mistake.

According to 'Spengler', Tolkien was succesful: *The Lord of the Rings* has superseded the *Ring* and is more popular nowadays than Wagner's work. That Hitler's embrace had probably reduced Wagner's popularity fairly effectively before Tolkien's work could do anything of the kind is something he fails to consider. It could be that *The Lord of the Rings* filled the seat vacated by Wagner's *Ring*, resonating with the post-war audience in a familiar way, but without the baggage weighing down the older *Ring* story, and catering to different needs. That it was far more popular than the other ring story in the decades following its publication is very likely. A statement C.S. Lewis is reported to have made in the last interview before his death would support this: Lewis complained, maybe jokingly, that he had wanted to write a new prose version of Wagner's *Ring* cycle, but that he feared that the word 'ring' might lead people to think of Tolkien's work (mentioned by Birzer).

Still, despite the large dint in his reputation after World War II and despite the rise of *The Lord of the Rings*, Wagner was never completely superseded. The first LP recording of *Das Rheingold*, for instance, reached the Top Ten in the United States in the late fifties alongside artists like Elvis Presley and Pat Boone, and stayed there for weeks. That Tolkien's epic will make the world forget Wagner's *Ring* seems wishful thinking sprung from the anti-Wagner bias permeating 'Spengler's' columns. It ignores the fact that the appeal of Wagner's work lies foremost in the music, not in the story. Tolkien's epic may be more popular and more widely known today, yet the 'rapturous response' to the films in which Spengler puts so much stock has ebbed away by now (though it will no doubt resurge once the *Hobbit* films are released – and ebb away again after a while).

It is true that the One Ring has been used as a lure to draw attention to Wagner's opera cycle,[53] maybe in the hope of attracting a younger audience: the average Wagnerian is much older than the average Tolkien fan. Perhaps future stagings will contain allusions to *The Lord of the Rings*. In fact, Wotan actually cuts off Alberich's finger to get at the ring in the Weimar cycle of 2008-2011,

---

[53] For example http://www.starkinsider.com/2011/06/in-photos-san-francisco-operas-ring-cycle.html (retr. date 07-11-2011). Frank Nimsgern's musical *Der Ring* is promoted by stressing Tolkien as much as Wagner, though it is mainly based on *Der Ring des Nibelungen*: http://www.openpr.de/news/184392/Frank-Nimsgern-Der-Ring-das-Musical.html (retr. date 11-03-2011)

though the original stage-directions say nothing about this; if this is not a nod at Tolkien, it is a remarkable coincidence. Meanwhile, the popularity of Wagner's *Ring* is on the rise again. The season 2009/2010, for instance, saw more than 20 productions of the complete cycle the world over, not counting those of separate *Ring* installments and other Wagner works.[54] In New York, a *Rheingold* performance was projected on a big screen in Times Square; in Cologne the same *Rheingold* was turned into a pantomime with sound effects and an allusion to Tolkien in the form of Gollum. In Bayreuth an abridged *Ring* for children is in the making, to the horror of many a Wagnerian, while a 'Tiny Ring' – excerpts of Wagner's work combined with a kid's play – was staged in Amsterdam in 2011. The Luxemburg Opera House recently offered an abridged *Ring* for adults.

Though Tolkien has more fans, the number of Wagner Societies matches that of Tolkien Societies, even when all the separate *Wagnervereine* in Germany are counted as one. Secondary literature on Wagner's *Ring* has no problem keeping up with that on Tolkien. The greater the distance to the Nazi era, the more the resistance to the *Ring* seems to decrease. If Tolkien did write his Ring story with the intent to push Wagner's into the background he did not succeed nearly as well as Spengler would have liked.[55]

While greed remains a root of evil and money remains a highway to power, Wagner's tetralogy will not be superseded by a Ring story, which hardly addresses this particular aspect of the corrupting effects of power, but focuses on a different one. Given the dangerous and often unwholesome power of money, bankers and brokers more than a hundred and fifty years after its first conception, *Der Ring des Nibelungen*, is as relevant as ever, perhaps more so.

3.3.4. 'Thief Tolkien'

This does not invalidate the idea itself, though. One does not have to hold a popularity contest between two geniuses and their work to accept the possibility

---

54 See: http://www.wagner-nsw.org.au/ravens.html (retr. date 11-03-2011)
55 An interesting case is the crossword puzzle in the *St. Louis Post-Dispatch* of November 13, 2009. The clue for 1 across was: 'Composer of famous Ring cycle'. The clue suggested Wagner, the answer was Tolkien. Whose work was considered more famous here?

that Tolkien meant his story at least partly as a correction to Wagner's, whose view of evil he did not share.

Recalling Scott Rohan's argument that Tolkien 'transmuted what he had read and been shaped by' into his own thing one might ask: did he at some point realise that Bilbo's ring had come to share some qualities with the Ring of the Nibelung? We will never be sure whether he did or not, but it seems unlikely that the resemblance did not at some point jump out at him on rereading. And Tolkien often reread and rewrote his own texts.

It is possible to engage deeply with a statement, a worldview or a vision of reality one does not agree with, precisely because one disagrees with it; often it is such disagreement that triggers action. What if this is what happened to Tolkien with regard to Wagner's *Ring*? He knew it well, he studied the libretti while he was working on *The Hobbit* (which he did from 1930, possibly 1928, onward) and he could read the source texts in the original languages. It seems likely that the Ring of the Nibelung had been simmering in the cauldron of his mind for quite a while before he embarked on the *Hobbit* sequel. Then, while he was working on it, all of a sudden the fairy-tale ring that Bilbo put his hand on under the mountains turned out to have acquired a couple of characteristics reminiscent of that same Ring of the Nibelung.

What if Tolkien seized on this discovery as an opportunity to put things right that he thought Wagner had got wrong? He had suddenly found himself with a Ring of Power, a ring lost in the dark by someone whom he thought had no inkling of its true nature. And he was going to return it to its place of origin. If this made him seem a thief, so be it; he knew himself to be better equipped to handle this ring than its previous bearer had been. Scott Rohan was on the right track when he conjured up his image of Wagnergollum and Tolkienbilbo.

As insiders know, Tolkien wrote two different versions of the Bilbo-Gollum encounter in *The Hobbit*. The scene in the 1937 edition was fundamentally changed and expanded for the revised edition of 1951. In the first version, Gollum is a creep who plans to eat Bilbo if he wins the riddle game they hold in the dark, but he is willing to give Bilbo a present if he loses. The present is the ring that Bilbo has found in the tunnels. When he loses the riddle game and discovers he cannot give Bilbo the present because it is gone, Gollum plays fair. Though he would still like to have the hobbit for supper, he shows Bilbo the way out of the underground tunnels. Meanwhile, Bilbo has realised that the ring he has found must be Gollum's intended present. But as he considers it his possession now and reasons that Gollum promised it to him anyway, he keeps his mouth shut and lets Gollum show him out.

As mentioned above, this fairly innocent ring changed into a dangerous and evil thing while Tolkien was working on the early phase of the sequel, not long before the outbreak of World War II. The story as told in the 1937 version of *The Hobbit* was no longer compatible with the much more sinister nature the ring had acquired in the sequel. Initially, Tolkien did not do anything about this. When Rayner Unwin, who read the first part of *The Lord of the Rings* in 1947, said that he considered this a weakness, Tolkien initially thought any radical alterations were 'of course impossible, and unnecessary' (Scull & Hammond, 319). The Foreword to the sequel, or perhaps its opening chapter, would suffice to clear things up.

Shortly afterwards, however, he changed his mind and rewrote the passage. In the revised *Hobbit* of 1951 Gollum is a much more unpleasant character. Instead of promising Bilbo a present, he claims that he will show him the way out if the hobbit wins the riddle game, yet he plans to kill and eat him anyway. But his precious ring, which he needs in order to make himself invisible and sneak up on the hobbit, is missing. Bilbo in his turn uses the ring, which he now realises must be Gollum's missing Precious, to escape from the tunnels, with Gollum's shrieks of 'Thief Baggins! We hates it forever!' ringing in his ears. When he finally tells the Dwarves about it, he lies to them: they still get to hear the original story of how he came by it, though now this version of events has become incorrect. This was Tolkien's way to have both stories without being inconsistent. It even adds a dimension: In Chapter II of *The Fellowship of the Ring* Gandalf tells Frodo that Bilbo's lie about the ring put him onto the right track regarding its true nature. Gollum's treacherous intent and Bilbo's lack of truthfulness are telling illustrations of the evil nature of the ring.

In itself this would suffice to explain why Tolkien changed the text of *The Hobbit* after all, though it was not imperative to do so and he does not seem to have considered it of vital importance, given his initial willingness to adapt the sequel to the version of 1937. However, what if he had yet another motive for rewriting the passage in the end: the realisation that the Ring of Power Bilbo had stumbled on in the dark bore more than a passing resemblance to Wagner's Ring of the Nibelung? Did Tolkien decide to acknowledge this resemblance somehow in the text itself? In hindsight, the second version may seem inevitable, but strictly speaking not all elements in the revision were necessary.

If Gollum is the slave of the ring, he can no longer promise it to Bilbo as an award for winning the riddle game, and that he intends to eat the hobbit regardless of the outcome fits the change in his personality. But does he need to find out what has happened? Does he have to curse Bilbo for a thief? Should we envisage Tolkien writing down Gollum's cry of 'Thief Baggins' with a gleam in his eye? He may have foreseen that some critics familiar with the *Ring* might call him a thief, but he knew he could deny this in good conscience. He could swear that just like Bilbo he had *found* the ring, not stolen it, and anyway the one who cried 'thief' had originally been a robber himself, if such a term is applicable to someone bending ancient sources to suit a vision of his own. Perhaps Sméagol killing Déagol is Wagner doing his worst with the ancient Icelandic sources? Moreover, in writing it this way, Tolkien could even allude to the passage in *Das Rheingold* in which Alberich is said to have ordered the Tarnhelm, the invisibility helm, to prevent a *thief* from creeping upon him and stealing the Ring while he is asleep. That Bilbo 'steals' the ring from Gollum, who robbed it from Déagol, is reminiscent of Loge's advice to Wotan how to acquire the ring in *Das Rheingold* 2: 'Was ein Dieb stahl, das stiehlst du dem Dieb.' (What a thief stole, you steal from the thief.)

To add more fuel to this theory: Tolkien said of himself that he was 'a hobbit in all but size' (*Letters*, 179), so it is not difficult to see Bilbo as his alter ego in this passage. Wagner was a small fellow with a rather big head – a suitable Gollum model. Bilbo and Gollum were distantly related, like the English and the Germans, and one of Tolkien's ancestors came from Germany. Finally, the English tend to consider German a somewhat throaty language, and 'gollum' is described as a throaty sound.

All jokes aside, given the many (mostly philological) inside jokes Tolkien made in his books,[56] he was very well capable of playing such a trick. Not that it mattered too much to him: he could probably have lived with the idea that the joke would never reach the general public – in fact he did live with it for a couple of years, until he discovered in 1950 that Allen & Unwin had used his revised text after all. But if the revision does indeed allude to Wagner's *Ring*, Tolkien's use of phrases like 'the Lord of the Ring'[57] and elements such as the need to return the ring to its place of origin and the twilight of the immortals, may indeed be intentional.

---

56 See especially Shippey (1982).
57 In a letter to A. Furth of 31 August 1938 Tolkien actually refers to his *Hobbit* sequel as 'The Lord of the Ring', singular! (Scull & Hammond, 220)

Chapter 4

Other Approaches

4.1. The evils of power

4.1.1. Werner

Some people focus mainly on the rings of power, for instance David Werner of La Verne University, California, in 'My precious illusion – Rings of Power in Wagner and Tolkien', a presentation on occasion of the Los Angeles Ring festival in May/June 2010.[58] His approach is quite original in that it does not merely compare the two rings but draws the Eden myth into the comparison. Just like the two rings, the forbidden apple gives power ('you shall be like God') that corrupts. Neither the apple nor the two rings live up to the eater's/ bearer's expectations; they are linked with a curse of death and ageing and soon lead to fratricide. To get rid of the curse, one must give up the illusion of power. The journey back to life involves closing the circle: gaining access to the Garden of Eden again (Christianity) is comparable to returning the rings to their respective places of origin. This is a personal quest. The goal of life should be 'getting the gold back where it belongs,' as Werner said, using the Wagnerian symbol of the Rhinegold which is stolen in order to forge the corrupting ring.

His presentation did not address the question of influence, though in an email to the author of this book Werner wrote that of course Wagner's *Ring* influenced Tolkien's and suggested that if Tolkien denied this – which as we saw is probably not the case – he must have done so because he considered the question 'dopey'.

---

[58] Available as a video through: http://laverne.edu/academics/institutional-review-board/faculty-research-and%20-scholarship/faculty-research-lectures.php (i-tunes needed).

4.1.2. Luke, and Ross again

Werner's stress is on the personal aspect of mythology, which he sees as a reflection of what is going on inside a person's life. Helen Luke, too, focuses on the personal aspect. In her Christian-Jungian analysis *The Ring* she finds some differences as well as similarities between both stories, but she is not interested in the question whether Tolkien borrowed his ring from Wagner. In fact, she considers them to be one and the same symbol, emerging 'from the unconscious into this world' and she consistently uses the word 'ring' in the singular. Her essay is mostly concerned with the *Ring*, and *The Lord of the Rings* is only brought up occasionally to serve as a contrast. In Luke's view, 'the circle of wholeness and the ring [singular!] of Alberich and Sauron are [...] the positive and negative poles of the Self'. To her, the ring is not intrinsically evil – it is made evil through the way people use it, which means that she either overlooks or disregards the fact that both rings are explicitly made either by an evil character (Sauron) or with evil intentions (Alberich), and need to be destroyed.

The most interesting part of the analysis for non-Jungians is when Luke focuses on the very different power symbolism in the two stories, and explains this difference by looking at the historical periods in which they originated. The 19th century saw the rise of power through capital, hence Alberich's attempt to achieve world domination by exploiting the human greed for riches. All other values threaten to fall victim to the passion for gold.

In the 20th century, on the other hand, power is foremost 'sought and wielded for its own sake, often heavily disguised under the mask of selfless devotion', and Luke considers this a danger to mankind compared to which the greed of gold is harmless. She argues that

> the fanatic of Communist or Nazi persuasion will suffer poverty and hardship [...] and will sacrifice personal desire and feeling, believing sincerely that he does all this for the good of humanity – and so the ring is delivered up to the Sauron in the unconscious whose rule means the ultimate destruction of love, of the free spirit of man, and of humanity itself. (29)

The Jungian character of Luke's observations may not appeal to everyone, especially not to readers who also (or mainly) situate Sauron in the universe at large as a personal agent of evil, the Middle-earth equivalent of a fallen angel.

Yet it is worth considering the possibility that the difference between the two rings reflects two different ways in which the quest for power has manifested itself in the course of history. When power uses ideology, one gets the Ruling Ring; when power uses money, one gets the Ring of the Nibelung. Tolkien's ring, then, is the mirror of totalitarians, Wagner's of capitalists. This could, for instance, explain the renewed popularity of Wagner's *Ring* in the face of the early 21st century's neo-capitalist excesses – though the renewed popularity of classical music may have something to do with it as well.

Vill also contrasts Wagner's criticism of capitalism and authoritarianism with Tolkien's criticism of totalitarianism and its destructive violence, the latter especially in Jackson's film version (69-70). Ross, however, explicitly ties up the notion of a Ring of Power with the rise of technologies of mass destruction, which first appeared on the horizon in the 19th century.

> Pre-modern storytellers had no frame of reference for such things. Power, for them, was not a baton that could be passed from one person to another; those with power were born with power, and those without, without. By Wagner's time, it was clear that a marginal individual would soon be able to unleash terror with the flick of a wrist.

He illustrates this with a prediction by Oscar Wilde that future wars will be fought by a chemist with a bottle on each side. A striking illustration, even though Wilde was born in 1854, at at time when Wagner had already written the text of his *Ring* and some of the music.

4.1.3. What power?

Ultimately Luke's view seems too simplistic: in both cases, absolute power is the ultimate goal. Alberich robs the gold because of the boundless power it will give him over others, not because it can make him rich. Once he has forged the ring, he enslaves his own people. His ultimate goal is not buying everyone, but making everyone give up love, like he himself has done: '*Wie ich der Liebe abgesagt, alles was lebt, soll ihr entsagen!*' ('As I have forsworn love, all living things will have to renounce it!') as he announces in the third scene of *Das Rheingold*. In other words, he is the ultimate egoist, not just a hyper-capitalist. And Third Age Sauron, whose original virtue used to be 'that he loved order and co-ordination and disliked all confusion and wasteful friction' (*Morgoth's Ring*, 396), has long since given up any pretense that he is working towards an abstract ideal. Quoting an Orwell biographer who remarks that 'the love of power is stronger and more perverting than any material or economic motive,'[59] the musicologist and Wagner expert Cooke applies these words to Wagner, but they apply at least as much to Tolkien – who was working on *The Lord of the Rings* when Orwell's *Animal Farm* was published, and finishing it when *1984* came out.

But what is this power? In the *Ring*, power and love are opposed like darkness and light. Only by forswearing love can power be achieved, and this leads to the violation of Nature. When Alberich, having forsworn love, robs the Rhinegold in order to forge the ring and enslave others, the light is extinguished. Wotan on the other hand shrinks back at the last moment from sacrificing love to power and world dominion. But he, too, has violated Nature before the beginning of *Das Rheingold* by cutting a branch from the World Ash to use as his spear of Law, causing the tree to wither. The law may seem a necessity, it is nevertheless an instrument of domination and, in Wagner's view, a violation of what is natural. The Walhall-*Leitmotiv*, closely associated with Wotan, too, grows out of the original Ring motif, to which the Rhinemaidens sing that 'he who forges the ring from the gold can claim the world as his own.'

However, just as Wotan is flawed, so is the law, and the spear motif does not descend without a reason. Wotan uses his spear to subdue Alberich and steal his ring. In *Die Walküre* Fricka brandishes the law in order to demand punishment for the adulterous and incestuous love of Siegmund and Sieglinde; this passage combines the spear motif with that of the ring, which symbolises the lust for power. The law itself has become an instrument of destruction, and therefore it has to go. Wotan's reluctant and as yet partial change of attitude is accompanied by an equally reluctant transformation of the spear motif at the end of the opera: the motif attempts to ascend but never quite succeeds; it only does so in the Act III of *Siegfried*, when Wotan has ceased to fear his own end (Berne, 157, 165). In the next scene the sword Nothung, with its ascending motif, shatters Wotan's spear: Siegfried's anarchy, which Wagner

---

59 George Woodcock, *The Crystal Spirit*, London 1967 (q. Cooke, 271).

at one stage equated with true freedom, destroys the corrupt law. In the end, though, not even this act of freedom is able to overcome the lust for power. At the end of *Götterdämmerung* it is love, manifested through sacrifice that takes the place of the law. Wagner is, in fact, working with the traditional Christian matrix here, though the content he puts into it is not traditionally Christian at all.

Tolkien's case is somewhat more complicated. Although Helen Luke sees the love-power dichotomy at work here as well, others seem almost at a loss when they try to define the precise nature and workings of power in *The Lord of the Rings* and elsewhere. For Richard Jenkins, the Ring of the Nibelung represents moral choice and its consequences, but Frodo 'appears to have no intrinsic lust for power [...] and the supposedly corrupting effect of the ring upon him seems to be external to his nature, forcibly and arbitrarily imposed from without.' He fails to see why Shippey's idea that the One Ring is addictive would make this morally interesting, but then he seems to think that being addicted absolves a person from responsibility, something with which not everyone agrees. Jenkins also overlooks the fact that Shippey combines the nefarious effects of the ring on the bearer's mind with its independent will towards evil – it is actively trying to get back to its maker (Shippey 1982, 107-111). But he has a point when he wants to know why the Ring corrupts Frodo in the end.

For Müller, the power in Tolkien's ring story is a 'disinterested force of its own'; evil arises when one tries to achieve power for power's sake. But this, too, does not explain why Frodo eventually succumbs to the lure of the Ring, though he has never desired power for power's sake. Arvidsson notes that for Wagner, power is diametrically opposed to love, but that in Tolkien's Ring epic, power is 'a wholly abstract quality [...]: omnipresent but without any clear objective [...] Power becomes immaterial.' And depolitised, which he considers deplorable.

Attempting to find the true motive behind Sauron's lust for power, Arvidsson fumbles in the dark, suggesting that this is no more than 'a kind of metaphysical desire to destroy'.[60] He overlooks something here: when Frodo asks Gandalf why the Dark Power would want to enslave the hobbits, Gandalf's reply is that

---

60 Arvidsson had already suggested this in a previous study (2005, 119).

'miserable slaves would please him far more than hobbits happy and free' (*The Fellowship of the Ring* I, 2). Why seek pleasure in slaves, if destruction is what you are after? It is Morgoth, the antagonist of *The Silmarillion*, who wants to destroy, to reduce the world to *nil*, as Tolkien himself explains in an essay published in Volume 10 of *The History of Middle-earth*. What Sauron seeks is domination:

> He did not object to the existence of the world, so long as he could do what he liked with it, and, more specifically, it was the *creatures of earth*, in their *minds* and *wills*, that he desired to dominate. (*Morgoth's Ring* 394-398)

Elsewhere he writes that if Sauron had been victorious

> he would have demanded divine honour from all rational creatures and absolute temporal power over the whole world. (*Letters*, 243-244)

In short, as for Wagner, power is domination for Tolkien, too: not just domination of other people, but of their minds and wills. In itself, this is in keeping with Luke's analysis. Capitalism only needs to bully people or buy them, ideologies need to brainwash or break them. But as mentioned before, Third Age Sauron has shed any ideological pretense. He comes dangerously close to embodying pure totalitarianism and thereby to being an allegory.

In a way, though, Arvidsson is not far off the mark when he concludes that the true villain of *The Lord of the Rings* is 'the biblical snake'. This explains why not even the most innocent of the book's characters, the hobbits, are wholly immune to the lure of the Ring: who is safe from the insidious whisperings of Satan? Even Sam is tempted: 'He saw Samwise the Strong, Hero of the Age, striding with a flaming sword across the darkened land, and armies flocking to his call as he marched to the overthrow of Barad-dûr' (*The Return of the King* VI, 1). The reader does not get to look into Frodo's mind when he claims the ring for himself at the end of his quest, but the picture is not all that difficult to fill in.

4.1.4. Views of evil

The question, then, would be: why is power so dangerous, of all things – both for the wielder and for those subjected to it? Because it is absence of love? Because it enslaves us, through oppression or by promising to give us what we want?

In *The Battle for Middle-earth*, Fleming Rutledge remarks in a footnote: 'I would not compare Tolkien with the staggering genius of Wagner, except in one sense: I think Tolkien goes even deeper into the nature of Power as an active force and its hold on each being' (96, n. 5). Rutledge does not go any further into this, but maybe we can. In Wagner's *Ring*, power is compensation for lack of love. Alberich does not steal the gold until the Rhinemaidens he tries to woo have rejected him. Wotan does not seek power, mutilating the World Ash, until his youthful love for Fricka has cooled. Fasolt covets the ring because he has had to give up the goddess of love, Hagen because he is the offspring of a loveless union, loved by no one. In contrast, Siegfried gives the ring away because he loves. Power is a surrogate for the one thing that is not for sale.

In Tolkien's story, though, nothing won by power is able to satisfy in the end. Power is not even a surrogate for love; instead of giving us anything but love, it robs us of ourselves, it sucks us up – Christine Chism strikingly compares the One Ring to a black hole – and we end up like empty cloaks under empty crowns, invisible and practically non-existent. People crave power when they chase illusions, the way people take drugs for the illusion they create. No wonder power is addictive in *The Lord of the Rings*. But it is total power itself that proves to be the illusion. Gollum's disappointment at what he found under the Misty Mountains is symbolical of the disappointment to which the lust for power will lead.

Does this make Tolkien's analysis of power deeper? It could be that Wagner's view of it looks less deep because it seems so simple. Love, and the lust for power will have no hold on you – because you do not need it. Yet 'Frodo undertook his quest out of love – to save the world he knew from disaster at his own expense, if he could' (*Letters*, 327) – and nevertheless he was unable to resist the temptation of the Ring of Power in the end. As a Roman Catholic, Tolkien probably rejected any ideas about the capacity of fallible human beings to solve the problem of power through love, convinced that human love can only take us so far, as the power we are up against is stronger than we are.

In the end, though, Wagner, too, came to doubt the power of earthly love, though he never entirely gave up on it. After the failed revolution of 1848 and the forced exile which landed him into great personal trouble, his optimism about what love could achieve waned. Before long, it turned into a kind of Schopenhauerian pessimism even before he read Schopenhauer; when he did, he recognised much of his own thinking in the philosopher's work. Simply put, Schopenhauer believed that goodness and redemption could only be achieved by renunciation of the world and abnegation of the will. Wagner briefly changed the textual ending of his *Ring* to reflect these ideas. Ultimately, though, the music gets the 'last word', and the theme heard at the conclusion of the cycle is one associated with love, but it sounds peacefully resigned rather than triumphant (more about the ending of the *Ring* in 4.6).

Evil, for Wagner, is existentialist. It lies in the act: *zum Reif zu **zwingen** das Gold* (***forcing*** the gold into the Ring). The opposite of this coercion is freedom: it takes a free hero to return the gold to where it belongs. In the end this free hero turns out to be not Siegfried, who fails, but Brünnhilde, freed by love to do what is right, though at the cost of her own life. The main surface difference with Tolkien's solution is that she manages to do it on her own.

Tolkien's view of evil is essentialist: the evil of the Ring is the evil of its maker – and its maker is a satanic creature, too powerful for a mere mortal to overcome. His capacity for evil is concentrated in the Ring, which has a mind of its own and tries to get back to him by using its temporary possessors to achieve this goal. Good intentions alone are not enough to destroy it. Frodo can take it to the brink of destruction, but is unable to throw it into the fires of Mount Doom: he too, fails. In this respect at least he does resemble Siegfried. It is Gollum who destroys it by biting off Frodo's ring finger and tumbling into the volcano with the ring, something made possible by Frodo's mercy towards Gollum at an earlier stage. Ultimately, though, Frodo is saved by grace, an act of God. The life it costs is Gollum's, but in one of his letters Tolkien states that if he had not been attacked by Gollum, Frodo would probably have come to see that he had to 'cast himself with the Ring into the abyss' to achieve its destruction (*Letters*, 330). An act that would have brought him very close to Brünnhilde.[61]

In one respect, Wagner's presentation of evil is quite problematic. For those who love it, most of the time his music is too compelling to convey a proper sense of the true nature of evil, even when it is intentionally disharmonious or shrill. Alberich and Hagen are undoubtedly evil, but the music accompanying their words and actions lends them a certain dark grandeur. It best approaches the squalor of evil expressing the utter depravity of Mime in the first two acts of *Siegfried*. However, the suspicion – not entirely unfounded – that Mime is intended as the caricature of a Jew makes this only more problematic.

In *The Silmarillion*, Tolkien barely skirted the pitfall of depicting evil as grand – even bringing music into the equation – when he had Fëanor declare: 'The deeds that we shall do shall be the matter of song until the last days of Arda' (*Silmarillion* 88). A similar sentiment is found in Homer's *Iliad*, where Helen predicts that she and Paris 'shall be themes of song for men of the future' (VII, 430-432). The older Tolkien avoided such sentiments. When King Théoden of Rohan decides to battle Saruman's army at Isengard, he seems to echo Fëanor when he says to Aragorn: 'Maybe we shall cleave a road, or make such an end as will be worth a song.' But he immediately adds: 'if any be left to sing of us hereafter' (*The Two Towers* I, 7). Théoden's decision is not rooted in defiance or even in the desire to be remembered, but in a sense of duty in the face of death and final defeat. Likewise, when Sam considers defending Frodo's body after the attack by Shelob, he wonders 'if any song will ever mention it: How Samwise fell in the High Pass and made a wall of bodies round his master.' However, he soon realises there is too much at stake. If he gives up the quest to make a last stand, no one will sing of it, 'for the Ring'll be found, and there'll be no more songs' (*The Two Towers* II, 10).

Nothing in the entire *Ring* cycle taxes a Wagner-loving audience the way Frodo and Sam's desolate and joyless journey through Mordor taxes even the most devoted of Tolkien readers. The chapter about the scouring of the Shire is a

---

61 In his weblog entry "Wagner and Tolkien Thread: Strange Ring Fellows" (3 January 2011, retrieved 3 October 2011), Andy Higgins compares Gollum to Brünnhilde, as both are consumed by fire while holding the ring. Yet the fundamental difference between Gollum's involuntary and Brünnhilde's voluntary destruction is too big for the comparison to be wholly convincing.

thoroughly unromantic and realistic anticlimax to an epic quest story. Ultimately the evil characters in *The Lord of the Rings* lack grandeur. As Rosebury puts it: 'It is one of the triumphs of Tolkien's literary judgement [...] that fully accomplished evil is represented by states of personality (or unpersonality) which no sane reader could envy' (Rosebury, 47).

4.1.5. Fear of the end

Yet there is more. In Wagner's *Ring*, the lust for power and the concomitant lack of love spring from fear of the end. '*Alles was ist, endet*,' (All that is, ends) sings Erda, the Earth Goddess, in *Das Rheingold* 4. Wotan's power as a god and ruler is finite; his desire to keep Alberich's ring for himself springs from his refusal to accept this finiteness. That he heeds the warning of the goddess and flees the curse of the ring by relinquishing it is his first halting step towards insight. In a way, the entire *Ring* is the story of how Wotan learns to relinquish power and accept his own end. As Wagner wrote to his friend, August Röckel, in a famous letter of 25 January 1854: 'Without the necessity of death, life is not possible. [...] We must learn to die, to die in the most complete sense of the word: fear of the end is the source of all lovelesness. [...] Wodan rises to the tragic height of willing – his own downfall.' Later in this same letter he adds that, in fact, we are Wodan (quoted in Wapnewski 1982, 186).[62] That Wotan has not yet learned this in *Das Rheingold* leads to his robbery of the ring and Alberich's curse.

Fear of the end, fear of one's own mortality, is an important theme for Tolkien as well. 'All this stuff', Tolkien writes about his Middle-earth stories, 'is mainly concerned with Fall, Mortality, and the Machine.' He applies this above all to human creativity, not to political power, but the idea is the same:

---

62 German: Ohne Notwendigkeit des Todes keine Möglichkeit zum Leben [...] Wir müssen sterben lernen, und zwar sterben in vollständigsten Sinn des Worts, die Furcht vor dem Ende ist die Quelle aller Lieblosigkeit [...] Wodan schwingt sich bis zu der tragischen Höhe, seinen Untergang – zu wollen.' *Wodan* is the form of the god's name in the first concept of the *Ring* cycle.
Wagner's rejection of the desire for immortality was influenced by his lecture of the philosopher Feuerbach. In his *Gedanken über Tod und Unsterblichkeit* (Thoughts about Death and Immortality), published anonymously in 1830, Feuerbach postulated that Christian belief in immortality resulted from mankind's growing egoism in theory and practice. The only true immortality lay in great deeds and inspired works of art.

Clinging to the things made as 'its own', the sub-creator wishes to be the Lord and God of his private creation. He will rebel against the laws of the Creator – especially against mortality. Both of these (alone or together) will lead to the desire for Power, for making the will more quickly effective, – and so to the Machine (or Magic). (*Letters*, 145)

In other words, to the One Ring. One of its properties is that, like the nine rings Sauron made for Mortal Men – who *did* seek political power – it prolongs mortal existence without adding more life to it. The rings stretch life until it has thinned out into nothingness. Such a property is not attributed to the Ring of the Nibelung, but the treasure of gold that Alberich has produced by using his ring, and of which it forms a part, grants eternal youth, according to *Das Rheingold* 4. This is the main reason why Fafner, who unlike his brother is not infatuated with Freia, is willing to exchange the goddess with her life-giving apples for the treasure. In other words, both the composer and the author link the prolongation of existence to a mechanism carrying the power to achieve this, though in Tolkien this is more pronounced than in Wagner. And both consider resistance to finiteness and mortality the deepest cause of human corruption.[63]

4.2. A poisoned imagination?

4.2.1. Chism and the poisoned sources

'The sub-creator wishes to be the Lord and God of his private creation', Tolkien wrote in his much-quoted letter to Milton Waldman (*Letters*, 145). This leads to the desire for power and from there to the mechanism of the magic ring. According to Chism one of the things the One Ring represents is Tolkien's view of the dangers inherent in mythmaking and world-building. While working on his ring epic, he had a prime example of world-creation gone wrong close at hand: Nazi Germany. The national-socialist cannibalization of medieval narratives into pseudo-historical racialist mythologies, and the inspiration Hitler found in Wagner's particular brand of cannibalism, most importantly the

---

63 MacLachlan explores the parallels between Tolkien's approach of death and mortality and Wagner's in depth. Referring to a television interview of 1968 in which Tolkien stated that *The Lord of the Rings*, like all literature, is about death, he endeavours to show how the ring epic defines the life of purpose that makes the confrontation with death a meaningful ending, and in what way Wagner's *Ring* can shed new light on this. See MacLachlan, 67f..

'mythology for Germany' (Chism, 75) of the *Ring*, must have made it obvious to Tolkien that mythmaking was anything but innocent.

Müller also sees a link with National Socialism. She argues that the essay 'On Fairy Stories' contains a negative comment to Wagner's mythmaking:

> The remark that Fantasy can also be abused if man creates a sub-creation to his own praise, can easily be read as a lash at the religion of art that had emerged from Wagner's artistic myth and the ideological abuse of which was plainly before Tolkien's eyes in 1939, as a corrupted and degenerated "fantasy". (Müller, 354)

Chism, however, goes much further. Early on in her paper, she rejects Tolkien's dismissal of the suggestion that *The Lord of the Rings* was influenced by the Second World War, mostly because he protested too much. Tolkien may have claimed that his One Ring represented what he calls, with a Nietzschean turn of phrase, the 'will to mere power' (*Letters*, 160),[64] for Chism it is also a dark exploration of the powers of aesthetic production itself. To illustrate this she contrasts Tolkien's earlier writings about artistic creation, such as the optimistic *Mythopoeia*, written in 1931, with the essay on fairy stories, where Tolkien shows a first awareness of the potential misuse of fantasy, and with the late, pitch dark poem *The Sea Bell* (1962, a pessimistic rewriting of the poem *Looney* of 1934). Here, a bold quest for a world full of wonders and strange new peoples and tongues leads a traveller to an empty, unresponsive territory over which he vainly claims lordship. It ends with a disillusioned homecoming and a total loss of communication. Now *The Sea Bell* is explicitly linked with *The Lord of the Rings*. In its fictional source, the Red Book of Westmarch, it is subtitled 'Frodos Dreme'. Though the poem was probably not written by Frodo himself, as Tolkien tells us, it suggests feelings of loneliness and emptiness on Frodo's part after losing the One Ring (*The Adventures of Tom Bombadil*, 9). Chism wonders why this ultimate symbol of evil is allowed to overshadow a lifelong desire for fantasy. Her answer involves Wagner's *Ring*.

---

64 *Der Wille zur Macht* (The Will to Power) is the title of a compilation of texts written by the German philosopher Friedrich Nietzsche. Was Tolkien thinking of Nietzsche while he wrote his phrase 'the will to mere power'? As the work was among the favourite texts of Nazi ideologists and Tolkien wrote the letter in which the phrase occurs in 1952, it could be that he did and implicitly rejected Nietzsche's ideas along with Sauron's evil ring. (He could not know at the time that the book was a distortion of these ideas by Nietzsche's fascist sister Elisabeth: the extent of her manipulations did not become known until 1959.)

Like Shippey, Hall and 'Spengler', Chism suggests that Tolkien intentionally wrote against Wagner's misuse of his sources, but she connects this more explicitly to the misuse of Germanic myth during the Second World War. Wagner's work, and in particular his *Ring*, which extols the ruthless heroism of Siegfried – in this respect Chism also falls victim to the misconception about the character's status mentioned earlier – was an important element in paving the way for the distortion of Germanic myth into an aggressive, nationalistic and genocidal ideology. Tolkien observed this with dismay. Therefore, he made 'his difference from Wagner a defining moment of his mythos' (Chism, 76). He must have asked himself, whether a work of art could 'remain innocent in itself though cursed in its uses,' and his answer was negative. The National Socialist misuse of myth, inspired by Wagner's work, led Tolkien to doubt the innocence of mythmaking itself, Chism argues, assuming Tolkien shared the misconception regarding the character of Siegfried.

The arbitrary and slippery symbols of mythology can be counteracted with allegory, fixated and entwined with history. Tolkien's tool to counteract the corruption of mythology into an evil, destructive ideology was the One Ring, an 'empty allegory of the will to power' (Chism, 80). Whatever the cost, it must be renounced – and Tolkien, with much pain, does indeed renounce it in his story. We see the cost in Frodo, left worn and empty after the destruction of the ring, and in Middle-earth itself, bereft of myth after the departure of the Elves, and fading into history.

Ultimately *The Lord of the Rings*

> is a fantasy that wills its own disenchantment into history, a mythology that [...] assents to its own mortality and agrees to fade. Unlike Wagner it refuses apocalypse, laboriously caves out history's costs, pressures and fragile delights, drags its remaining fingers through the blood and brings itself in the end to write: *This shall be*. (Chism, 87)

This painful renunciaton of fantasy, such a far cry from the enthusiasm with which Tolkien had embraced it in the early thirties, would explain why he abandoned the attempt to write a sequel to *The Lord of the Rings* at an early stage (*Peoples of Middle-earth*, 409-421). It would explain why he was unable to revise *The Silmarillion* in any systematic way despite his fervent attempts to do so during the years following the publication of his major opus. It would explain the melancholy of *Smith of Wootton Major* (1967), in which Smith, Tolkien's alter ego, gives up his imaginative star. And finally, it would explain why he wrote a month before his death that he had 'lost confidence' in his ability to finish *The Silmarillion* (see *Letters*, 431). His

> war-driven, self questioning investigation of the uses of mythology had brought him to a point with no energy to move forward and yet had worn away at the enabling presuppositions for going back. (Chism, 88)

The argument that Tolkien grew disillusioned with the power of the imagination and renounced it in the form of the Ruling Ring looks fairly convincing at first sight. As we saw above, it is true that Tolkien links the misuse of creative power to a magical mechanism like the One Ring. Also, if Chism is right, this would explain why power is such an immaterial thing in *The Lord of the Rings*, as Arvidsson noted. However, the argument raises doubts, not in the last place because of Tolkien's well-known disavowal of allegory, which he contrasted with history, 'real or feigned' (*The Lord of the Rings*, Foreword). To see Chism bring together what Tolkien separates is intriguing, but not wholly compelling.

Perhaps disenchantment could explain why Tolkien failed to finish *The Silmarillion*, but by the time he wrote the above-mentioned letter he was 81 years old and knew that he was running out of time. Before that, he had kept trying to finish the work for almost two decades, which would suggest that he was not aware of having 'renounced' fantasy – or he would not even have tried. Yet Chism's wording implies awareness: Tolkien 'comes to a conclusion,' he 'counteracts' and 'decides against' something. Ultimately, the main reason for his failure to turn the work closest to his heart into a coherent whole compatible with his published Middle-earth books, was probably mostly due to the problems he had with the flat-earth cosmology of the earlier versions. As he conceived of his subcreated world of Arda as our own world in an early stage of (pre)history – we are now supposed to be 'at the end of the Sixth Age, or in the Seventh' (*Letters*, 283) – or as an alternative history of the past (Interview), he concluded that it had to be round. Making it so would involve 'devastating surgery', as Christopher Tolkien puts it (*Morgoth's Ring*, 383), which might lead to its destruction, and ultimately he was not prepared to go through with the operation.

Smith of Wootton Major does not constitute compelling evidence for Chism's theory either. Smith gives up his star of imagination, an obvious case of disenchantment. However, instead of throwing it away or destroying it he passes it on to a new generation, which would be a rather dubious thing to do if imagination itself had been poisoned.

Further, if Tolkien believed mythmaking to be a gift from the Creator and a human birthright, as *Mythopoeia* proposes, why allow mere mortals like the Nazis to spoil this gift? Why consider a return to history the only viable antidote to the poisonous 'mythology' of Nazi Germany, as Chism suggests? Nazi ideologists also attempted to pervert the Christian message, but this did not turn Tolkien into a non-believer. 'Abusus non tollit usum. Fantasy remains a human right,' we read in 'On Fairy Stories' (§ 80) and though Tolkien wrote the essay before World War II, it was not published until 1947 – without retractions or added warnings about the dangers of mythmaking illustrated by its misuse during the recent war.

Verlyn Flieger has a different take on the essay's meaning as considered against the backdrop of the Second World War. It contains heavy criticism against the treatment of myths as mere sources of knowledge about our ancestors and their beliefs, precisely because this approach had acted as a stimulus for cultural nationalism. The essay affirms 'myth's intrinsic value as story, not as source of extrinsic information' (Flieger 2003, 34).

Meanwhile, though it is true that the *Sea-Bell*, *Leaf by Niggle* and *Smith of Wootton Major* all in their own way question the unlimited freedom of human imagination, the main problem does not lie with the imagination itself, but with its uses by fallible human artists. Turning away from the sources of the imagination because the Nazis poisoned them is, in fact, blaming the victim.

Another problematical part of the argument is Chism's use of Wagner's 'master-*Ring*'. Its creation is compared to 'forging a vicious nation-state that instrumentalizes a Wagnerian fantasy' and even to Sauron's artistry, which 'destroys what it engages' (Chism, 81). Together with the chief Nazi ideologist, Alfred Rosenberg, Wagner is identified as a national socialist 'inheritor of

Romanticism', somewhat peculiar given the fact that his works are considered to be the culmination of the German Romantic movement. One begins to wonder if the author is aware of the fact that Wagner died before either Hitler or Rosenberg was born. Yet there seems to be a contradiction here. The *Ring* was apparently innocent before the Nazis contaminated it, or else it would be nonsense to ask whether a work of art could *remain* (italics mine) innocent if it was cursed in its uses.

On the whole, it seems better to assume that Tolkien did not renounce fantasy because of a previous mythmaker's real or perceived aberrations, and was less certain about the direct connection between Wagner's mythical music drama and the horrors of the Second World War than Chism seems to be. It is certainly possible that he thought Wagner had not used his mythmaking powers well in every respect and did indeed set out to counteract the ruthlessness of Siegfried with the pity of Bilbo. Chism does not mention this, but the passage in which Bilbo decides not to kill Gollum was written after the Second World War. Also, Tolkien may have been of the opinion that Wagner had misrepresented the 'noble Northern spirit' he mentions in his diatribe against Hitler, and that this had somehow contributed to making it 'forever accused'. But could it have escaped him altogether that on the whole, the *Ring* cycle runs counter to Nazi ideology? As Bryan Magee puts it:

> The implications of *The Ring* are the precise opposite of fascism: that the pursuit of power is incompatible with a life of true feeling, and threfore the attainment of it destroys the capacity for love; that because power is inwardly destructive of the people who wield it, it is in the very deepest sense anti-life; that necessary order should rest not on force but on consent and the honouring of agreements; and therefore that the dishonouring of agreements, because it ensures that things can be settled only by force, and therefore will be settled by force, is the most disruptive of crimes. (B. Magee, 44)

That the *Führer* was fond of a work that condemns the lust for power and domination and practically dictated his own downfall, is one of the ironies of history. (Nazism was a death cult, but that Hitler prepared his own *Götterdämmerung* and that of millions of others from the very beginning, has to remain conjecture). It is no coincidence that the Allies used parts of *Götterdämmerung* for their propaganda broadcasts into Germany, assisted by a dissident granddaughter of Wagner, Friedelind, who had rejected her family's embrace of Nazism and fled

Germany in 1939. Not that it proves much, but Friedelind Wagner compared Hitler to Alberich and did not believe her grandfather would have agreed with the National Socialist regime (Carr, 220).

In any case, the essential message of the *Ring* cycle, the one that remained once the various notions chasing each other in Wagner's head during its composition period had run their course, was that the only thing worth cherishing in the end is love. Brünnhilde says as much in one of the rejected endings of *Götterdämmerung*; in the definitive version it is implied by the music, when the orchestra plays the theme of redemption by love three times during the finale of the cycle. It is hardly fair to reduce the *Ring* to Siegfried's failings, and it is hard to believe that Tolkien would have agreed to attend even a single part of the *Ring* if he believed this was all Wagner's work amounted to. In any case, whatever Tolkien may have thought of the *Ring* cycle and the role it played in Hitler's Germany, that his own Ring epic renounces an imagination whose sources were poisoned by Nazi misuse and that it takes back his earlier writings on the justification of mythmaking, remains debatable.

4.2.2. From myth to history

It is true that myth, or 'story and song', to use the last words of *The Silmarillion* (304) makes way for history at the end of *The Lord of the Rings*; the last of the High Elves leave Middle-earth and the Age of Men begins. But a shift from mythology to history was Tolkien's intention from an early stage onward, when he set out to write a mythology for England, or rather, a 'body of more or less connected legend' which he could dedicate 'to England; to my country'[65] (*Letters*, 144). This was years before Hitler entered the stage and the Nazis did their worst with the mythology Tolkien loved best.

However, while the notion of myth becoming history was an early one, the way this plays out in *The Lord of the Rings* differs markedly from what Tolkien had in mind several decades earlier. In its initial design, his legendarium took the form of a frame narrative about the mariner Eriol, or Ottor Waefre. He was the fictional father of Hengist and Horsa, the 5th century brothers who led

---

65 Anders Stenström has shown the much quoted phrase 'a mythology for England' to be Carpenter's combination of several of Tolkien's statements concerning his original project.

the Anglo-Saxon migration to the Isle of Britain. In his boat, he set out from Heligoland, the present-day German Isle of Helgoland near the 'Angle', the area of origin of the Angles. Searching for Atlantis he ended up in Tol Eressëa, where he was to learn the ancient history of Middle-earth, which he would then take back to England – in this earliest version of the legendarium (*The Book of the Lost Tales 1*) originally a part of Tol Eressëa, broken off by the gods and transported to the geographical position of present-day Britain. On Tol Eressëa, Eriol was to marry an Elvish woman; their son Heorrenda would bring an Elvish strain into the English population. As the language of the Anglo-Saxons was probably meant to derive from that of the Dark Elves (*Lost Road*, 179), Tolkien would have created a threefold connection between the Elves and the Anglo-Saxons, a cultural, a racial and a linguistic one.

In the second version the island, now called 'Luthany' (later Leithien) after a work by the Catholic mystic poet Francis Thompson, is in its present place from the outset, but it was meant to pass from a mythical into a historical stage. The Elves, who dwelt in the British Isles before the coming of Men, would vanish. Their city Kortirion, would eventually become Warwick. Meanwhile, Eriol himself had become Ælfwine, an Anglo-Saxon born around 849, descended of Ing, King of Luthany.[66] Still later he acquired the name his Half-Elven son had in the first version, Heorrenda, also Tolkien's putative name for the *Beowulf* poet. Eventually this history of Middle-earth would come down to J.R.R. Tolkien.

In 1936, things took a different turn again: after a bargain struck with C.S. Lewis Tolkien began the story 'The Lost Road', set in his own time, which was to involve time-traveling to the past by two of Ælfwine's 20th-century descendants. It was at this stage that the Downfall of Númenor, Tolkien's private version of the Atlantis story, entered the tale. None of these concepts were carried through to the end, but the use of the 'Lost Road' frame marks a first shift away from mythology and towards history.

---

66 Not to be confused with the Ing who was the forerunner of the Elf In(g)wë. For the relationship of Ing with the historial Inguaeones, mentioned by the Romans, see *The Book of Lost Tales 1*, 304-305. Ing, or Yngvi, possibly was the original name of the god Freyr.

Still later, at the end of 1945, roughly a year after the sequel to *The Hobbit* had come to a standstill, Tolkien embarked on yet another story, 'taking up in an entirely different frame and setting what little had any value in the inchoate Lost Road,' as he wrote to Stanley Unwin (*Letters*, 118). This story is known as 'The Notion Club Papers' (*Sauron Defeated*, 145-327). It is a last attempt to retain the frame previously represented by the 'Lost Road'. The protagonists, one of whom is still Ælfwine's descendant, live in the early 1980s, three dozen years after Tolkien embarked on this story and almost a decade after his death. These men find their way back to Númenor by way of dreams. Some time prior to 1942 Tolkien had written a second version of the fall of Númenor, 'The Drowning of Anadûnë' (*Sauron Defeated*, 332-440) which he probably planned to incorporate into this new frame narrative. Flieger speculates on what might have happened if Tolkien had completed the book:

> The traditional method of starting a mythology at the beginning with Creation would have been replaced with the far less conventional narrative entry from what for Tolkien would have been the middle, (i.e., modern, reader-contemporary period). The imagined End (which he never got to) would still be far off in a future quite clearly still ahead of our own world. In addition, the shift would have augmented the rather tenuous and changeful thread of historical and territorial continuity – whether as Tol Eressëa or actual Britain – with the para-psychological thread of continuity through memory. (Flieger 2004, 60)

So, why didn't he complete it?

The most obvious answer is that he needed to get on with the *Hobbit* sequel, eagerly awaited by his publisher and his readers. But approximately six years later, in the letter to Waldman, Tolkien called his idea of creating a mythology, or legendarium, dedicated to his own country 'absurd' and the purpose 'overwheening' (*Letters*, 144f) and said that his crest had long since fallen. Another good reason for abandoning it, one would say. Yet in his commentary to 'The Fall of Númenor' in *The Lost Road*, Christopher Tolkien writes that Ælfwine, who was to form the link between the legendarium and English history, still played a role in his father's writings after the completion of *The Lord of the Rings* (*The Lost Road*, 21). The Anglo-Saxon mariner did not make it to the 1977 *Silmarillion*, but in his foreword to *The Book of Lost Tales 1* Tolkien's son expresses his regret at having published *The Silmarillion* without any kind of framework, a 'suggestion of what it is and how (within the imagined world) it came to be' (*The Book of Lost Tales 1*, 5).

However, this could hardly have involved Ælfwine. In the Prologue of his Ring epic, Tolkien had introduced the 'Red Book of Westmarch', written by Bilbo and Frodo Baggins and finished by Sam Gamgee. This tome incorporated Bilbo's 'translations from the Elvish' – the tales of the Elder Days, the matter of *The Silmarillion*. Tolkien, as the mediator between the material of Middle-earth and the present-day public, 'translated' this book into English. Thus, the Anglo-Saxon mariner winding up on Tol Eressëa and returning with Elvish myths had become redundant, and we must assume that Christopher Tolkien never found any texts in which Ælfwine was given a new role (Noad, 67-68).[67]

Why did Tolkien change his mind? As Michael Drout sees it, he wanted to separate his invented legendarium from his historical scholarship: immediately after the last chapter of *The Lord of the Rings* in 1948, Tolkien wrote Appendix F, denying explicitly that the Rohirrim actually spoke Old English, though at first sight they do. His explanation is that he had merely used Old English because its relationship with modern English mirrored that of the language of Rohan with the original language of the hobbits, which he had 'translated' into modern English. Yet in *Peoples of Middle-earth*, Christopher Tolkien notes that this contradicts the foreword 'Concerning Hobbits': here, the hobbits are said to speak a language very similar to Modern English (10-17). Also, the Old English names of the Rohirrim were present since the first stage of composition of the Ring epic. The conclusion, according to Drout, is that we must 'be sceptical about appendix F and not be completely convinced by the author's protestations that his work on Middle-earth did not have some created connection to English history.'[68] As he puts it, '[t]he connections, deeply buried [...] remain for those who can find them' (Drout, 242).

---

[67] Noad believes a construction in which a meeting of Ælfwine and Bilbo led to the former's expedition to Tol Eressëa would have been possible, but this disregards the fact that Bilbo already knew the Elvish material via Elrond and other denizens of Rivendell. There was nothing new to find out for Ælfwine in the West.
[68] Honegger reconciles the views of Tolkien and those critics who maintain that the Rohirrim are Anglo-Saxons by arguing they are a Germanic archetype, 'the embodiment of the common Germanic ideal of the northern heroic spirit and as such not to be identified with any known (Germanic) peoples' (Honegger 2011, 128).

They are not that deeply buried, though: quite a few reviewers saw connections with England, and with North-Western Europe in general, when *The Lord of the Rings* first came out. And does the wish to separate creative storytelling from scholarship sufficiently explain why the author cut all explicit ties with the historical past of England from his epic? After the success of *The Hobbit* in 1937 he had tried to get the material from the Elder Days published while the narrative frame still connected them to England.

Fimi mentions two other possible reasons why the connection of the legendarium with England was more or less severed. Tolkien's English nationalism had waned; the opposition between the Celtic and Anglo-Saxon traditions of Britain had lost its significance for him. His mythology for England had become a mythology, first for all of Britain, and from there for North-West Europe (Fimi):

> Those days, the Third Age of Middle-earth, are now long past, and the shape of all the lands has been changed; but the regions in which Hobbits then lived were doubtless the same as those in which they still linger: the North-West of the Old World, east of the Sea. (*The Lord of the Rings*, Prologue 1, 'Concerning Hobbits')

In the second place, 'courtesy of World War II he also had an acute awareness of the dangers of insisting on [...] national purity; he knew how origin and cultural myths could be misused and appropriated' (Fimi 2009, 130).[69] Thomas Honegger notes that in the first versions of his legendarium, Tolkien 'comes close to the medieval concept of nation as being defined in terms of its territory, its people, and its language' (Honegger, 2007, 11f). But when people and territory are replaced by blood and soil, the 'Blut und Boden' mysticism of the Nazis comes too close for comfort. That Tolkien never came to realise this, seems unlikely. Bachman & Honegger argue that he was aware of it and that this may have led to his writer's block of 1941/1942. Like Chism, but in a more nuanced way, they also discuss the relation between Tolkien's Ring epic and the ideology of Rosenberg.

---

69 Fimi argues that Tolkien originally modelled the material culture of Númenor and Gondor on that of the Vikings: the winged Gondorian helmets resembled the helmets which the 19th century mistakenly attributed to Germanic gods and Valkyries, possibly due to the costumery of Wagner operas.
However, after World War II Tolkien claimed that the model of the Gondorian crown was that of the ancient Egyptian South Kingdom, to which he had merely added wings; he rejected the idea that it was Norse. Fimi calls this suspicious (2009, 172).

It was the combination of myth and nation rather than imagination that had become tainted after the war; mythology and territory had become very uneasy bedfellows. Through no fault of Tolkien's, the Anglo-Saxon connection had become problematic, and even the idea of transmission via 'racial memory' introduced in the 'Notion Club Papers' no longer looked innocent. Explicit ties had to be cut. It is by no means impossible that the fate of Wagner's *Ring*, deserved or undeserved – if Tolkien had an opinion about this, it is not available to the general public – contributed to his change of tack. If this theory holds water, Chism was on to something, but her conclusion was simply too radical.

Whatever was the case, in *The Lord of the Rings* the link between the legendarium and England was made implicit and reduced to elements like the Shire and its hobbits, the culture and language of Rohan (despite Appendix F), and the name Eärendel, taken from the Anglo-Saxon poem *Críst* and slightly modified. In Honegger's view the substitution of Ælfwine with hobbits makes the epic 'more English than ever' (Honegger 2007, 126). Yet it was with considerable regret that Tolkien retouched the connections between his legendarium and the legends and history of his country, or he would not have continued to play with the idea of retaining Ælfwine. He balked at the thought that Shire names were to be translated into foreign languages (*Letters*, 249-251), and after the publication of *The Lord of the Rings* he wrote to an admiring reader that he must have succeeded in restoring 'to the English an epic tradition and present them with a mythology of their own' (*Letters*, 231). Perhaps he hoped against hope that a time would come again in which Ælfwine could make his return?

On the other hand it is telling that in his last story, *Smith of Wootton Major*, England itself is not mentioned, though the names of the characters and places are all English. While it is possible to guess how they relate to the tales of Arda, the snatches of myth Smith sees and experiences in Faery have a generic character. The realm of Faery, as Tolkien knew well enough, is accessible through many woods.

Concluding, the shift to history in Tolkien's work was intended from the beginning, but after 1945, its character changed. The product of the sources was relabelled, so to speak, and what was meant to turn into the history of England turned into generic – human – history instead at the end of *The Lord of the Rings*. Thereby, it also became better suited to acquire a huge popularity far beyond its original target audience: identification with hobbits is by no means limited to English readers, as Tolkien himself noticed during his visit to Rotterdam in 1958 (*Letters*, 265). In the end, by failing to create a mythology for England, Tolkien created much more than that.

Finally, and most likely unintentionally, this shift also brought it closer to Wagner's approach. Wagner made a shift from history to mythology, to which his curious essay 'Die Wibelungen' of 1850 bears witness (see Wilberg's study). He exchanged a projected hero from German history, the Emperor Friedrich Barbarossa, for Siegfried and the other mythical protagonists of the *Ring*, who had, and have, a far more universal appeal despite their German names.

Chapter 5

Conclusion

Ever since the publication of Tolkien's epic quest story *The Lord of the Rings*, people have been comparing this work to Wagner's four part opera cycle *Der Ring des Nibelungen*. The chief reason for this was the presence in both works of a dangerous ring that promises world power, a much-coveted object that must be eliminated at its place of origin in order for the world to be saved from the evil designs of the ringmaker. As Wagner's work preceded Tolkien's by roughly 80 years it was inevitable that the question of influence, the question whether it was among Tolkien's sources, should arise. That Tolkien knew Wagner's *Ring* is certain. What he thought about it is a matter of debate. There is reason to assume he was not averse to the music, to put it cautiously. The text poses a bigger problem.

The comparison between the two famous Ring stories is complicated by several factors. The first of these is the controversiality of both Wagner as a person and a number of his operas, among them the *Ring* cycle. Wagner was an anti-Semite and an opportunist who shamelessly used others to promote himself and his work. He was also among the favourite composers of Adolf Hitler, and an important character from the *Ring*, Siegfried, became an icon of Nazi Germany. Though Wagner died before Hitler was born, his anti-Semitism, his use of Germanic mythology and his worship of German art have led to the idea that his works themselves are ideologically suspect and carry the seeds of misuse. Though he was a musical and dramatic genius, being compared to Wagner is not necessarily a compliment. That the book said to have been influenced by the *Ring* cycle was written during and after the Nazi era further muddies the waters, as does the fact that Tolkien has been accused of fascism and racism for story-internal reasons that have little or nothing to do with Wagner.

The second complication is Tolkien's alleged denial of any resemblance between his ring and Wagner's: 'Both rings were round and there the resemblance ceases.' A closer look at the context of this statement shows that it does not seem to pertain directly to the *Ring*. Yet the presence of the word with its strong Wagnerian associations in this same context leaves room for doubt. On the other hand it is only too easy to turn Tolkien's rejection of the comparison against him, suggesting that this is precisely what he would say if he knew his work was derivative.

Thirdly, Wagner and Tolkien had some sources in common, notably three important works of medieval Icelandic literature: the *Poetic Edda*, the *Prose Edda* and the *Völsunga saga*. Obviously, common elements deriving from such sources must be eliminated first for any comparison to make sense. However, this still leaves us with a professional philologist who knew the material inside out on the one hand, and on the other a philological amateur better versed in music as a medium of expression.

As it turns out these complicating factors tend to have a negative effect on many a discussion of the Wagner-Tolkien relationship. Often ignorance, preconceived ideas and some kind of hidden agenda prevail. The association of Wagner with the Nazi period is used against Tolkien. Wagner is accused of being a Third Reich ideologist. The context of the statement about the two round rings is overlooked. Tolkien is dismissed as derivative and his epic as a lesser work. The common sources are invoked to explain away all similarities by people who never even bothered to study them.

The approximately thirty elements which Wagner's *Ring* and Tolkien's main works (*The Lord of the Rings*, *The Hobbit* and *The Silmarillion*) appear to have in common can be reduced by about two thirds when held up against the backcloth of Norse myth and legend – give or take a few other sources of common inspiration. The remaining elements cannot be eliminated in this way and are mostly ring-related. Given Tolkien's certain knowledge of Wagner's *Ring*, the conclusion that it influenced him seems inevitable and maintaining the opposite becomes futile. It can even be argued that both the revised edition of *The Hobbit* and *The Lord of the Rings* contain some tongue-in-cheek allusions to Wagner's work. That Tolkien had different beliefs and purposes does not necessarily undermine this, as influence does not automatically imply imitation. Anyone familiar with both the ring epic and Wagner's opera cycle knows that *The Lord of the Rings* tells an original story, whereas the *Ring* retells an existing story in an original manner. It is equally clear that they represent different approaches and propose different solutions to the problem of power. In itself, there is no need to protect Tolkien against the evil power of the *Ring*, whether real or imagined.

Merely listing similarities and thereby establishing Tolkien as a possible closet-Wagnerian is both reductive and risky. It ignores their fundamental differences, exposing Tolkien to accusations of epigonism and plagiarism, often but not exclusively by people who are not really familiar with his work. (Interestingly, this category seems to include both Wagner-hating Tolkien bashers and Wagnerians.) Assuming that the influence was at least partly negative could be a viable way out of this.

Realising at some point that the compelling symbol Wagner had created with Alberich's ring had insinuated itself into his imagination, Tolkien may have made conscious use of this by setting straight what he thought Wagner had bent. This included fundamental aspects like the underlying world view of the *Ring* cycle, its analysis of the evils of power and the suggested remedy, and also Wagner's use of their common sources, of which Tolkien, as a professional philologist, had a better knowledge. The contrast between Bilbo's merciful treatment of Gollum in *The Hobbit* and Siegfried's more callous treatment of Mime, a comparable character, could serve as an example to corroborate this hypothesis. However, if Túrin Turambar's treatment of the dwarf Mîm (*Unfinished Tales* and *Children of Húrin*) was intended as a similar attempt to correct Wagner, it turned out less convincing.

It is possible to investigate the relation between the two rings without addressing the question of influence. The stories can be seen as latter-day representations of the Eden myth. They can be interpreted in a Jungian way. Their different power symbolism can be analyzed in terms of 19th-century capitalism respectively 20th-century totalitarianism, or in terms of an existentialist versus an essentialist view of the power of evil. For Wagner the dichotomy of power and love is immanent. For Tolkien, who believed evil power to be of supernatural origin, the struggle against it is transcendent. Their shared conviction that it is fear of death which fuels the desire for power does not point to influence:

Wagner saw this as the cause of lovelessness, whereas in Tolkien's view it instigates rebellion against God, sprung from the wish to rule one's own creation, including the laws of mortality.

This inherent danger of mythmaking leads back to the idea that Tolkien may have been deliberately writing *The Lord of the Rings* against Wagner. If the disastrous misuse of mythology in Nazi Germany, especially of Wagner's *Ring* myth, more or less scared Tolkien into questioning the innocence of mythmaking itself, *The Lord of the Rings* could be interpreted as a work that lets myth fade into history. However, a closer look at the actual history of his mythmaking rather suggests that it was the combination of myth and nation rather than myth and imagination that caused a change of track in his writing: after World War II the explicit links of his secondary world with England disappeared. In this, his approach incidentally resembled Wagner's, whose plans for an opera about an historical Holy Roman Emperor made way for his mythical *Ring* cycle.

Part Two

Myths, Fairy Tales and Endings

> 'Myth is the beginning and the end of history.'
> Richard Wagner, *Oper und Drama*

> 'Fairy tale does not deny the existence of sorrow and failure: the possibility of these is necessary to the joy of deliverance.'
> J.R.R. Tolkien, 'On Fairy Stories'

Chapter 6

Romanticism and Mythmaking

6.1. Introduction

Both Wagner and Tolkien held a view of myth at variance with the predominant use of the word in everyday language. When people call something a myth, they usually mean it is not true. Wagner and Tolkien would strongly have disagreed, however different their approach – Wagner focusing on the ritual aspect of myth, Tolkien stressing the language aspect. Their common ground is a positive view of myth rooted in 19th century romanticism.

Comparing the two John Ellison argues that essentially both belong to the Romantic Movement. Or rather, that they can be said to represent its final flowering in their respective countries (Ellison, 14). In the case of Wagner, Nietzsche and the poet Von Hofmannsthal made this assessment in the late 19th century, Thomas Mann a few decades later. As Tolkien was born around the time when the Romantic Age was coming to a close, it is more surprising to see him assessed in this way. Bidlo makes a case for Tolkien as a Neo-romantic.

According to Ellison the similarity between Tolkien and Wagner lies in their (sub-)creation of secondary worlds that takes over the imagination. In either case it goes beyond a tale of a Ring of Power: it resides in their elemental opposition of good and evil, involving a fall; in their concern about the defilement of nature, a direct result of corruption through the lust for power; in their regrets about loss of innocence and oneness with nature; and in their preoccupation with death and mortality. All these are essentially themes brought to the fore in the Romantic Age. Moreover, both Wagner and Tolkien

> provoked violent and sometimes contradictory emotions and reactions which often seem curiously similar. (...) There is passionate adherence, outright rejection, and, most interestingly, an ambivalence which sways between the two extremes. All of these attitudes seem to arise in response to the intensely personal nature of the appeal both artists make to the individual imagination. (19)

Tolkien's position is more exposed than Wagner's because he is a romantic 'in the midst of a later and more cynical age' (20). But one day, when people will be able to view him and his works in a historical perspective, this will pass, as it has passed with Wagner – Ellison glosses over the fact that Wagner remains a controversial figure even now.

Like Chism, Ellison compares Frodo with Siegfried, though in a much more positive way. Siegfried is 'not an obvious "lookalike" for Frodo', but they are approximately of an age and their distinctive attribute is their innocence. Like Frodo and hobbits in general, Siegfried is close to nature. He reacts instinctively ('hasty', as Treebeard would put it) and sometimes violently, just as Frodo reacts harshly when he exclaims what a pity it was that Bilbo didn't stab Gollum, 'the vile creature' (*The Fellowship of the Ring* I, II). Gandalf's ensuing lecture about pity has a Wagnerian resonance, Ellison notes, referring to *Parsifal* with its Schopenhauerian influences. His conclusion is that 'Tolkien (...), unconsciously echoing elements in the late Romantic history of ideas, seems in consequence a very typical product of late romanticism' (16).

One element of 19th century Romanticism Ellison does not mention in his 1988 essay is nationalism. However, he discusses its cultural variant in an article comparing *The Lord of the Rings* to Wagner's *Meistersinger of Nürnberg*. Without wanting to suggest that this work influenced Tolkien he notices 'striking parallels between Tolkien's "myth" of the Shire and Wagner's of Nuremberg':[1] both depict an idealised pre-industrial society rooted in national history. There is no real government, identity is expressed by traditions, family ties are strong, and rules exist but should not be taken too seriously. Despite this picture of wholeness – '*heile Welt*' in German – the creators of these merry idylls built in a warning against parochialism and complacency: the unexpected evil the hobbits find upon their return to the Shire, vis-à-vis the '*Wahn*' (delusion) monologue of the protagonist, Hans Sachs, and his warning in word and music about 'evil times' at the end of the opera. The similarity between the two works, Ellison concludes, 'resides to some extent in cultural nationalism,

---

[1] There is at least one huge difference: *Die Meistersinger* philosophises about art and its importance for society. Nothing of the kind happens in the Shire, where the songs that are the subject of heated discussion in the opera are simply sung, in a much more natural way than anything the young *Meistersinger* hero, Walter von Stolzing, comes up with.

or regionalism' (Ellison 1998). He does not further elaborate to which extent this is the case, but the article definitely adds nationalism to the mixture of romantic ingredients in the works of both artists.

6.2. National myths

In the 19th century the longing for a national mythology was felt in many European countries and regions - and many acted on it. In Denmark N.F.S. Grundtvig's *Nordens Mythologi* (1808 and 1832) helped shaping Danish national consciousness;[2] so did his son Sven's compilation of Danish ballads, a generation later. In Norway Asbjørnsen and Moe compiled a collection of folktales, *Norske Folkeeventyr* (1841-44), which did not only further the emancipation of the Norwegian language from Danish, but also formed an important contribution to the study of comparative mythology in Europe. In Finland Elias Lönnrot combined Finnish mythical lays and folklore into the *Kalevala* (1888). This soon gained the status of a national mythology and inspired the movement that led to Finland's independence from Russia in 1917. Though its authenticity was questioned later, it has retained its status until today and is celebrated each year on February 28, the national Kalevala Day.

The search for national myth also led to forgeries. The poetry cycle by the mythical bard Ossian (1765), which the Scottish poet MacPherson claimed to have translated from the Gaelic, was largely unauthentical. The Celtic bard was compared to Homer and his poems acquired a huge popularity in large parts of Europe, counting Napoleon and Goethe among their fans. Their authenticity soon came under attack, though. As it turned out, MacPherson had indeed used ancient Gaelic ballads but altered them to suit the tastes of his time. In addition he had added a great many fabrications of his own. The name Ossian itself was adapted from Irish mythology, where Oisin is the son of Finn mac Cool – Fingal in the Scottish text.

Another elaborate forgery inspired by the national mythology hype of the 19th century was the Frisian *Oera Linda Bok*, 'discovered' in 1860 and published in 1872 but unmasked as a forgery soon after. Written in fake Old Frisian in a

---

2 Agøy 1995 discusses the similarities between Grundtvig and Tolkien: both found fruitful ways to reconcile their Christian faith with their love of pagan myth.

runic-looking script allegedly based on the sun wheel, it purported to contain the mythology and history of Frisia from 2194 BC until 803 AD, introducing funny etymologies in the process (such as Neptune deriving from 'Neef Teunis', Nephew Tony). Recent research suggests that it was an elaborate hoax intended to fool, among others, Frisian nationalists who resisted the dominant Dutch culture (Jensma). Most of the suspects were Frisians themselves.

6.2.1. Tolkien in England

In England the longing for a national mythology was also felt. Because they needed to maintain their own particularity and cultural heritage as minorities within the larger entity of the United Kingdom, Scotland, Wales and Northern Ireland all had strong national identities. England, as the dominant force, much less so. During the heyday of European nationalism the country was felt to have too little national identity, and to boost this identity the Victorians invented 'Anglo-Saxonism'. The period preceding the Norman Conquest was depicted as a Golden Age pervaded with the true English spirit of freedom and democracy. For a while, this Anglo-Saxonism fulfilled the role of a national myth.

However, Anglo-Saxon mythological material from this time was scant, due partly to the early christianisation of the British Isles, partly to the above-mentioned Norman Conquest (the latter deeply deplored by Tolkien). The simultaneous revival of the Viking age with its Norse mythology and Icelandic sagas opened the gates to a parallel, related culture which met the demand for non-classical, non-biblical myths and stories. It soon became hugely popular (see Wawn). In the preface to his translation of the *Völsunga saga* (1888), William Morris wrote: 'This is the Great Story of the North, which should be to all our race what the Tale of Troy was for the Greeks'.

Tolkien undoubtedly read this sentence: when he won the Skeat Prize for English in 1914 one of the books he bought for the money was precisely this translation. It did not quite work out the way Morris – and probably also Tolkien – had hoped, despite the 'northernness' of England and the relationship of English with the North-Germanic languages (Shippey 2007, 192-194). The saga is Norse in origin and in written form ultimately belongs to the Icelanders, who are rather particular about their 'ownership' (Björnsson 16).

The 'matter of Arthur', popular though it was, and is, could not offer a real substitute either. It is Celtic in origin and reached England mostly by way of France. For those reasons it was not the most suitable candidate for a specifically English mythology. In Tolkien's words, it was 'imperfectly naturalised' (*Letters*, 144). Not to mention that his favourites, the Anglo-Saxons, were Arthur's enemies. Tolkien even goes as far as claiming the 'true tradition' of fairies for the 'Engle', the English, while 'the Iras and the Wēalas [the Irish and the Welsh] tell garbled things' about them (*The Book of Lost Tales* 2, 290).

In 1910, when the Romantic Age was past but nationalism remained as strong as ever, E.M. Forster's *Howards End* appeared. In this novel, the character Margaret Schlegel (an Englishwoman of German heritage), wonders:

> Why has not England a great mythology? Our folklore has never advanced beyond daintiness, and the greater melodies about our countryside have all issued through the pipes of Greece. Deep and true as the native imagination can be, it seems to have failed here. (...) England still waits for the supreme moment of her literature – for the great poet who shall voice her.[3]

Whether Tolkien read this is not attested, but if he did, it is quite likely that he considered it a challenge. Around the same period when Forster wrote his book, Tolkien and three of his closest friends, Geoffrey Bache Smith, Rob Gilson and Christopher Wiseman, had founded the so-called TCBS club while still at school. At first this had been no more than a convivial society, but somewhere along the line these gifted young men came to cherish the conviction they had something important to offer on the moral and spiritual plane. In the words of Bache Smith they believed that they 'had been granted some spark of fire that was destined to kindle a new light in the world.' Especially Tolkien was considered capable of carrying the torch. At the last meeting of the TCBS in December 1914, called 'The Council of London', the four friends agreed that he should pursue his poetic calling.

The TCBS did not survive the First World War, in which all four took part. Gilson fell in battle and Bache Smith succumbed to an injury. In *Tolkien and the Great War*, John Garth maintains that it was both survivor's guilt and the

---

3 E.M. Forster, *Howards End*, New York, 1910, q. Flieger, 2004, p. 43. Perhaps not quite incidentally, Wagner is mentioned in this novel. He is cast in the role of bad guy, though Forster himself loved Wagner's operas and adapted the *Leitmotiv*-technique for his novels.

sense of destiny fostered by the TCBS and enhanced by the death of several of its members, which formed the catalyst for the creation of Tolkien's legendarium (Garth 308ff.).

Remarking that the relationship of war and mythology merits attention, Verlyn Flieger points out that Tolkien's poem 'The Voyage of Éarendel the Evening Star', inspired by an Anglo-Saxon poem and anticipating the cosmology of his secondary world of Arda, was written only a month after England entered the First World War in August 1914. She believes that 'the imminence of war, with its implied destruction of existing culture, fuelled, if it did not create, Tolkien's desire to give his country a mythology' (Flieger 2004, n. 2). The war was probably a catalyst rather than a stimulus, bringing his latent nationalistic feelings to the surface. During a debate at a students' society in the autumn of 1914, after the outbreak of the war, Tolkien spoke against the motion, 'This house deprecates an ideal of nationalism' (Scull & Hammond, *Chronology*, p. 56). Given the circumstances, this seems no more than natural, and it would also explain 'the aggressive nationalism of *The Book of Lost Tales*' (Fimi, 130).

Two years earlier, in 1912, Tolkien had discovered the Kalevala. 'I would that we had more of it left – something of the same sort that belonged to the English' (Carpenter, 67), he wrote. It got his imagination going. Between 1914 and 1924 he wrote his own, partly versified 'Story of Kullervo' about this hero of the Kalevala, and also the drafts of two essays on the same subject. Towards the end of World War I, a year after Finland had gained its Kalevala-inspired independence from Russia, he embarked on a Kalevala-inspired tale of his own, 'The Lay of the Children of Húrin'. This is the first version of the tale of Túrin and his sister Nienor, published in *The History of Middle-earth* 3. It was obviously influenced by the Kullervo episode, and Flieger suggests that it was the example of the compiler of the Kalevala, Lönnrot, as much as the stories themselves, that inspired Tolkien.

> [Lönnrot] had reconstructed for Finland a world of magic and mystery, a heroic age of story that may never have existed in precisely the form he gave it, but which nevertheless fired the Finns Finland with a sense of its own independent worth. It seems clear that Tolkien envisioned himself doing exactly that, constructing a world of magic and mystery, creating a heroic age that,

although it might never have existed, would give England a storial sense of its own mythic, and therefore national, identity. (Flieger 2005, 29)

Whether or not Tolkien was heeding E.M. Forster's call in *Howards End*, following Lönnrot's example and trying to replace the lost myths of the Anglo-Saxons, and whatever role the First World War played, he did make a serious attempt to give England such a mythic identity, as his letter to Waldman attests. As convincingly shown by Fimi (2009, 63-7), his claim that the Arda legendarium was first and foremost philology-inspired, and that he devised his Elvish languages before he created a world in which they could be spoken, was mostly a retrospective construction.

The huge popularity of *The Lord of the Rings* and its Englishness notwithstanding the attempt to create an English mythology foundered, measured against Tolkien's original intentions. Fimi ascribes his 'inability to "re-construct" a "mythology for England" [...] to his non-involvement with folklore' (Fimi 2009, 55). He did not have a high opinion of folklore: in his essay 'On Fairy Stories' he characterised folktales as 'lower mythology' ('On Fairy Stories', § 42). But given the scarcity of original English folktales (Shippey 2007, 188) he did not have much to work with in that respect anyway. In addition, his mythology was highly personal from the outset: the tale of Beren and Lúthien with its strongly autobiographical elements was one of the cores. Nor did it help that his tales left the impression of being Celtic rather than English, due to the influence of Welsh on a considerable portion of Tolkien's nomenclature. The reader who was asked to write a report on the *Silmarillion* material for Allen & Unwin in 1937 objected against the 'eye-splitting Celtic names', though Tolkien himself disagreed that they were Celtic (*Letters*, 25).

One wonders how many of Tolkien's fellow-countrymen were waiting for a new mythology designed for England, even though he was not so much attempting to reconstruct the lost mythology of England as trying to create 'a body of more or less connected legend' that he could dedicate to his country. In any case, today precisely such a body exists: *The History of Middle-earth*. And though it never became an official 'mythology for England', Tolkien's work and world have found a place in the hearts of millions in- and outside of his own country.

6.2.2. Wagner in Germany

Whereas the longing for an English mythology, or one that could serve as such, seems to have been limited to individuals like Morris, Forster and Tolkien, in Germany it became a part of the Romantic movement. Just like England, Germany lacked a mythology of its own. It had a national epic, the *Nibelungenlied*. But for all its ancient roots and its traces of older material, this work belongs essentially to the courtly, Christian Middle Ages. Despite the popularity of its hero, Siegfried, and the Siegfried-mania of the 19th and the 20th century up to the end of World War II, it could not fulfil the role of a national mythology in the sense of a sacred narrative with a cosmogony, gods and heroes, reflecting the values and beliefs of a nation.

In Germany, the desire for such a mythology first arose in the late 18th century, the period that saw both the rise of Protestant Bible criticism and a newly awakened interest in national history and the pagan past. This took place in a country that was no unified nation, but a hodgepodge of larger and smaller states. During the Napoleonic wars the Holy Roman Empire, all but in name extinct, had formally been dissolved and the French invasion of Germany only created additional feelings of frustration. When the French army departed, political unity was nowhere in sight; it would not be achieved until the 1870s. Any German unity could only be cultural, and a national mythology was considered one of the means to accomplish this.

The new sacred narrative had to encompass Christian morality and ethics but should not be rooted in the essentially 'foreign' bible stories or in outdated Catholic 'superstitions'. Greek mythology, being both foreign and unchristian, was even more unfit. From the 1770s, onwards – a century before William Morris had the same idea for his country – a number of intellectuals suggested that a revival of the Norse pantheon could provide the basis for a new German religious imagery. However, the early Romantics rejected such an idea. The national gods of Germany should not be figures like Hermann – aka Arminius, the leader who defeated the Romans in the Teutoburg Forest – and Wotan, but art and science, said the philosopher Friedrich von Schlegel, the most vocal advocate of the new German mythology. It is hardly coincidence that Margaret

Schlegel, the Forster character who muses about England's lack of a real mythology is of German descent and has the same surname as the philosopher.

The lodestars of the new Schlegelian mythology of the future had to be figures like Kepler, Luther and Goethe and, quite remarkably, Mohammed (Williamson, 55).[4] Whereas Friedrich looked to historical figures of great stature his brother, August Wilhelm, looked to a specific period in history. To him the Middle Ages were a great source of inspiration for the new sacred narrative; he claimed that the spirit of chivalry originated in the combination of Germanic strength and bravery and Oriental spirituality (Williamson, 77). Wagner's opera *Lohengrin*, begun in 1845, is a first sign of the influence this reading had on him. The shining Grail knight, Lohengrin, fits Friedrich Schlegel's picture perfectly, whereas it is the pagan woman Ortrud, the agent of evil, who invokes the old Germanic deities Wotan and Freia to help her deceive and dissemble (*segne mir Trug und Heuchelei*).

However, Wagner was not only influenced by the Schlegel brothers, but also by their opponent Jacob Grimm, a pioneer of Germanic philology. To Grimm, myth resided in the soul of the nation, proceeding from the unconsciousness of the people, not so much from the achievements of individuals. Nor could any cosmology be based on scientific insights. Also, all mythologies were closely connected to the language, the customs and the specific history of the peoples among which they originated. It was impossible for an individual to invent a mythology, as the early Romantic theoreticians suggested – one guesses Grimm might not have applauded Tolkien's attempt to create a mythology for England. He also disapproved of adapting old myths for a wider audience, as they could only be truly enjoyed in their historical form. One suspects he might not have liked Wagner's Ring too much either, though without him it would not have come into existence. But Jacob Grimm died in 1863, before any of its parts were performed.

---

4 Schlegel made his call for a new mythology in the *Gespräche über Poesie* (Dialogue on Poetry, 1800), which soon acquired the status of a manifesto. Mohammed and Luther made his list because they had founded a new religion, respectively a new church, and one of the things Schlegel aspired to was the creation of a new 'Bible', which he described not as a single book but as 'an infinite idea that would unify all of art, philosophy, and experience' (Williamson, 55).

In his *Deutsche Mythologie* (1835),[5] a monumental, exhaustive and fairly unreadable study of Germanic mythology, Grimm tried to reconstruct the religion of the ancient Germans with the help of mythical tales, local customs and folklore. This included the fairy stories he had collected together with his brother Wilhelm (published in 1812). Though Grimm was rather anti-Catholic and paid much attention to the struggle of the Germanic tribes against the rising tide of Christianity, his reconstructed ancient Germanic religion 'looked remarkably like an enlightened or liberal form of Protestantism' (Williamson, 105): Wotan more or less became a monotheistic deity. After Grimm, the poet Heine, whose works also influenced Wagner, went a step further and argued for a pantheist faith as the logical continuation of this merger of Germanic myth and liberal Protestantism. In his poem *Deutschland* (1840), Heine invoked Siegfried to call for the unification of Germany and after the unsuccessful revolution of 1848 he used Siegfried's death to lament its failure.

Ultimately, the ideas about Germanic mythology propagated by the Grimm brothers won out over those of the Schlegel brothers and their likes. It helped that Grimm's *German Mythology* was not just anchored in half forgotten old stories but also in everyday customs, popular sayings and old wives' tales, all elements of popular culture in danger of being wiped out by industrialisation and modernisation. 'Thus, the construction of a national mythology involved less an outright process of "invention", than viewing the existing landscape with new, "mythopoeic" eyes.' (Williamson, 120). Much of Grimm's material was only preserved in non-German sources which he conveniently annexed for his purposes; even *Beowulf* was incorporated. Yet the result resembles a 'mythology for Germany' more than almost anything else. The exception is Wagner's Ring.

Wagner read the *Deutsche Mythologie* in 1843, and though he considered its structure too convoluted, he was impressed to such a degree that he spent years to acquire, or borrow, and read anything on German mythology and the earliest history of the Germanic peoples he could lay his hands on. Grimm's work became his mythological Bible and for many years he carried it along

---

5 This laid the basis for the work of later philologists like Tolkien, who knew and used it, though he did not always agree with Grimm.

wherever he went. It became the seed for his Siegfried project, which would take about half a dozen years to germinate and more than thirty to develop into the complete *Ring* cycle. He used many other sources as well, but it was this work that set him on the trail that eventually would lead to his magnum opus. He also made good use of Grimm's perhaps greatest achievement, the *Deutsches Wörterbuch* (German Dictionary, begun 1854), the philological counterpart of the *Mythologie*.

Writing the Ring, however, Wagner was not focused on presenting a mythology for Germany along traditional lines. Inspired by Friedrich Schlegel and other early Romantics, he wanted something new, a myth that could change the future. And if Tolkien did indeed take his cue from the remark made by Margaret Schlegel in *Howards End*, it could perhaps be maintained that both he and Wagner are each in their own way indebted to Schlegel's ideas.

Wagner had started out as a Christian nationalist focusing on the German(ic) past, to which *Lohengrin* and some of his early prose writings bear witness. The 1848 Wibelungen essay[6] marks a shift of interest from history to mythology and lays the foundation for his ideas about myth, as Wilberg has shown. Before he chose Siegfried as the subject for his next work Wagner had considered an opera about the Emperor Frederick Barbarossa. The results of his research about this figure can be found in this essay, where he had him claim *Weltherrschaft*, ('world dominion') as the leader of *das älteste Volk* ('the oldest people'). Given the popular belief that Barbarossa would once return to lead his people and given the course German history took in the 20th century, this has a fairly sinister ring. However, the idea was not Wagner's own – in the Middle Ages the Holy Roman Emperors, who were predominantly German, had laid claim to world dominion, or rather worldly dominion alongside the spiritual dominion of the Pope, but with equally universal claims. Moreover, towards the end of the essay Wagner rejected the need for an emperor in a revolutionary passage preserved in the first impression, but struck after the revolution had failed (Wilberg, 92).

---

6 Wibelungen is Wagner's version of Waiblingen, the German name from which the word Ghibelline is derived. He believed Wibelungen to be a misrepresentation of Nibelungen.

As 19th-century nationalism was not a conservative and reactionary but rather a revolutionary and socialist movement,[7] it is not surprising to see Wagner embrace a socialist internationalism at the same time. He played an active part in the Dresden uprising of 1848-49. When it failed he fled into exile, narrowly escaping the long prison sentence to which his friend Röckel was condemned. After doing some hard thinking and concluding that artistry and politics did not go together, at least not for an artist of his kind, he turned his back to the latter. It was at this point that he came to view myth, 'this originally nameless poem of the people'[8] ('Zukunftsmusik') as a timeless expression of the purely human, not corrupted by religion, history and convention. Ultimately, nationalism was to be superseded.

During this period Wagner began *Der Ring des Nibelungen*, a work conceived as a socio-political manifest disguised in ancient Germanic bearskins, but gradually turning into a paradigm for the mythical artwork of the future. Around the same time, he also wrote the draft for an opera about Jesus – declaring him non-Jewish in the process! – and a sketch for another opera about the Greek hero Achilles. In 1856, while still working on *Siegfried*, he drew up a prose outline and some musical sketches for a Buddhist opera, *Die Sieger* (The Victors) under the influence of his lecture of Schopenhauer. Unlike the *Ring*, none of these projects took off, but the subject matter of two of his later operas, *Tristan und Isolde* (written 1856-59) and *Parsifal* (written 1877-1882), is not German(ic) either, although the storylines were largely based on the medieval versions of the German poets Gottfried von Straßburg and Wolfram von Eschenbach, not on their French originals. These operas are German works: cultural elements from abroad turned German in Wagner's hands. But they also serve to show that Wagner was a cultural cosmopolitan as much as he was a cultural nationalist (Lachenicht). To put it in the words of the playwright Hauptmann, he was 'as Greek as he was German and as Asian as he was European' (*Über Wagner*, 210).

---

7 It is important not to look at 19th-century nationalism through a 21th-century, post-war lens.
8 German: *dieses ursprünglich namenlos entstandene Gedicht des Volkes*. 'Zukunftsmusik' was first published in a French translation under the title 'La musique de l'avenir' (1860) to acquaint the French with Wagner's ideas; the German version was published in 1861 in Leipzig. It was Wagner himself who put the title in inverted commas. He had used the term – invented by his critic Ludwig Bischoff – before in 'The Artwork of the Future', but did not approve of its use by either his friends or his enemies.

By the time he wrote his last work, *Parsifal*, Wagner's idea of myth had changed once again into the concept of a dream-inducing art that would lead to insight into the true nature of the world. His artwork of the future was to be a total experience encompassing all the arts, a religious act, harking back to Ancient Greek theatre or his ideas about it. For that reason he called *Parsifal*, a *Bühnenweihfestspiel* ('Festival Play for the Consecration of the Stage'). This was not an attempt to replace religion with art, something Wagner considered impossible. To him, art and religion were simply two sides of the same coin, both expressions of the mythical experience of being ('Die Kunst und die Religion'). All the same, such mystical ideas could easily be interpreted as propagating a religion of art in which the artist – read: Wagner – was the High Priest. They figured prominently in the Wagner cult that arose during the composer's lifetime and culminated during the years between the two World Wars. As mentioned above, Tolkien may have meant the 'On Fairy Stories' passage warning against the abuse of Fantasy (§ 80) 'as a lash at the religion of art that had emerged from Wagner's artistic myth' (Müller, 354). It is perhaps debatable whether Wagner set out to create works like the *Ring* or *Parsifal* to his own praise, but he did nothing to discourage the personality cult – on the contrary.

Whatever he wanted to achieve with his works during the various stages of his life, though, it was never his aim to revive ancient German mythology. This would only have supported the socio-political status quo by giving it a hallowed past, while Wagner actually rejected the status quo. Nor did his attempt to create a new myth for his time result in an unequivocally nationalist work. Some of his contemporaries saw this quite clearly: after the premiere of the *Ring* in Bayreuth in 1876 the critic Speidel commented: 'We would very much like to know what is national about Wagner's text book *The Ring of the Nibelung*?'[9] (Gregor-Dellin 1991, 725f).

At the same time, though, he was thoroughly German. 'The idea that a people could be held together by their attachment to myth was one that led him to choose Germanic legend as a subject in the first place' (Haymes 2010, 17).

---

9 *Wiener Fremdenblatt*, 15 October 1876. German: 'Wir möchten aber wohl wissen, was an Wagners Textbuch "Der Ring des Nibelungen" national ist?'

Moreover, he believed in the superiority of German art and culture, to which he applied the qualification 'heilig' (holy or sacred) in *Die Meistersinger*. This could be part of the reason why the *Ring* came to resemble a mythology for Germany anyway. Unfortunately this is also part of the reason why it was so vulnerable to misuse by the Nazis and why so many modern Germans have an uneasy relationship with Wagner and his works.

So, ironically, while Wagner accomplished something he did not set out to do (with some disastrous results), Tolkien did not accomplish something he did set out to do. Wagner, on the other hand, was not as successful as he would have liked in his endeavour to create 'the artwork of the future', also because he put the burden of achieving this on a single artist, a universal genius.[10] Tolkien showed more realism and a better sense of proportion when he wanted to leave 'scope for other minds and hands, wielding paint and music and drama.' (*Letters*, p. 145).

6.3. Modern myth

Mary Cicora, contrasting myth and history in her study of Wagner's Ring, claims that myth implies 'consciousness, immortality and timelessness', while history implies 'self-consciousness, mortality and temporality'. As a modern myth is mythological in a self-conscious way, 'for that reason, it is paradoxically *not* mythological.' In her discussion of the *Ring* cycle, Cicora maintains that the romantic irony contained in the self-reflection of the characters, especially that of Wotan – who is both a god and a human being with a modern self-awareness – undermines the work's mythological nature (7, 12). This would confirm Dahlhaus's assessment that Wagner restored myth in order to destroy it (Dahlhaus 1996, 111). Ross wonders if this was not what irritated Tolkien most: 'that Wagner wrote a sixteen-hour mythic opera and then, at the end, blew up the foundations of myth.'

If it was, Tolkien apparently did not try to restore those foundations with *The Lord of the Rings*. If any of the characters of his Ring epic can be said to

---

10 The composer Peter Cornelius wrote an opera, *Der Barbier von Bagdad* (1858) which is basically a parody of Wagner as a man boasting of his competence in dozens of different professions.

show the above-mentioned self-reflection it is the hobbits, from whose perspective most of the story is told.[11] Sam and Frodo, for instance, are aware of the fact that they are part of an ongoing (hi)story (TT, IV, IX), and it is this post-modern self-awareness that arguably disqualifies *The Lord of the Rings* as myth. The same goes for the repeated intra-textual references to the book the hobbits are writing about their adventures. Vladimir Brljak shows how Tolkien's metafictional devices undermine the authenticity of the myths and stories told in his works, even claiming that reading them as 'myths' means 'under-reading' them (22).

Could a case be made for the mythical status of *The Silmarillion*, or at least for the tales of the First Age that make up most of its contents? At first sight these tales do not seem to contain much self-reflection. Some of them read like true myths, such as the story of Aulë and the making of the Dwarves, or the Kinslaying at Alqualondë. In another instance, though, and a crucial one at that, a character shows himself keenly aware of playing a role in (hi)story: Fëanor, who announces after the Doom of Mandos that 'the deeds that we shall do shall be the matter of song until the last days of Arda' (*The Silmarillion*, Ch. 9). What follows proves him right – but that is precisely the reason why the narrative needs him to say it in the first place. The song knows too well it is being sung. In places even the Music of the Ainur, the Ainulindalë, could be argued to display the kind of narrative self-consciousness that, according to Cicora, would unmask Tolkien's mythology as a modern and un-mythological work. If he had succeeded in aligning the cosmology of his sub-created world with that of the primary world, as he tried to do in the 1950s (*Morgoth's Ring*, 383-390), this would probably have undermined their character of true myth still more.[12]

---

11 Dimitra Fimi speaks of an 'omniscient narrator', but this seems a misjudgement. The narrator of *The Hobbit* is omniscient and intrusive, as in the first part of *The Lord of the Rings*. By the time the hobbits reach Bree, though, the narrative mode changes into Third Person Limited (though there are a few authorial intrusions later on). The viewpoint character is usually Frodo, sometimes another hobbit, occasionally Aragorn or Gimli. Often, the narrative mode even approaches Third Person Objective: the narrator only records what he observes.

12 However, for a discussion whether there really exists a fundamental difference between true and artificial myth ('*Kunst-Mythos*'), see Wilberg, 322-352. It could be interesting to apply these insights into Wagner's work to that of Tolkien and discover if Wagner was really the 'last great mythopoet of the Occident' (Wilberg, 344, quoting Wipf's 'Der Aufstieg Wotans im germanischen Götterpantheon', *Tribschener* Blätter 82, 1978).

Arvidsson explicitly asks whether or not the Ring stories of Wagner and Tolkien can be called myths. As he defines myth as 'an authorised religious tale with everything this implies of supernatural sanctioning', *The Lord of the Rings* can hardly be called one, he says, for it does not have the 'paradigmatic truth' that Wagner's *Ring* achieved. There are several reasons for this: 1) it lacks the kind of authorising context which in Wagner's case has the form of opera houses all over the world, with Bayreuth as a central 'temple'; 2) whereas Wagnerism became a cultural and political movement that influenced and determined the lives of its adherents,[13] Tolkien-fans do not base their lives on Tolkien's writings and ideas; 3) his Ring story contains too much humour to be a proper myth; 4) it mostly avoids addressing adult aspects of human life like sex, work and politics; 5) it fails to conform to the basic formula of myth: 'original perfection > threat > hope of perfection in case people act correctly' (Arvidsson 2007, 180-2).

The argument that Tolkien would not qualify according to the first criterion does not hold water, given the numerous Tolkien moots, festivals, symposia and conferences that take place on a regular basis in various parts of the world, often over a period of several days and in some cases at the same location every year. The Oxonmoot is the Tolkien equivalent of Bayreuth, be it cheaper and without a waiting list of about ten years. These gatherings give the attendants a stronger sense of being an 'initiate' than does attending Wagner operas, as they are less anonymous. Apparently Arvidsson does not know much about the international Tolkien community. This also casts some doubts on the validity of 2). If there is such a thing as Tolkienism as a way of life, it remains more marginal than Wagnerism was around 1900, and few people convert to Tolkien's particular brand of Catholic anarcho-conservatism. Yet Arvidsson seems to underestimate the extent to which Tolkien's epic has been integrated into the collective consciousness of our times, albeit partly thanks to Jackson's film version.

The third argument against *The Lord of the Rings* being mythical, while the *Ring* is, seems a little stronger. Tolkien's humour in *The Lord of the Rings* works

---

13 Even now, some consider it an incentive to renew the world, or to build a new world on the ruins of the old one, which is believed to be in its death throes. See for instance Peter Berne's book *Apokalypse*.

(though *The Silmarillion* would undoubtedly qualify as mythical according to this criterion) the humour in Wagner's operas less so. But as it is situational and musical – the part of Mime in *Siegfried*, for instance, has a strong *buffo* (comical) element – rather than verbal and largely depends on the performance, it is not quite fair to judge it by the texts alone, as Arvidsson seems to do. If well-executed, some of Loge's scenes in *Das Rheingold* and of Mime's scenes in *Siegfried* can be funny enough. But generally speaking, in the *Ring* instances of comic relief are few and far between. Whether Arvidsson is justified in claiming that 'paradigmatic truth' and humour are incompatible remains a matter of debate, but this falls outside the scope of the current discussion.

The fourth reason is largely true as well, certainly regarding sex and work.

Reason five is the most interesting one. Brünnhilde's sacrifice and the destruction of Walhall together with the old gods at the end of *Götterdämmerung* open the possibility for a better future, if only the theatre audience is prepared to take action afterwards. Therefore, the *Ring* is a myth and more specifically, a revolutionary myth, says Arvidsson. The audience cannot sit back and sigh in relief, because the happy future and the new world order are not provided or promised by the story. They have to be established by the public. 'A new world must be built without the authorities. Here and now.' (Arvidsson, 131-2). Tolkien, on the other hand, 'does not link the hope for perfection to the actions of human beings. No hope is put in Man.' So, his text is not mythical and Arvidsson rejects the claim by 'most of today's [Tolkien] scholars' that it is. (184)

This is somewhat problematic. Firstly, it looks a little as though Arvidsson puts up a straw man: first he mentions the books and articles that discuss Tolkien's work in terms of myth, and then he applies his own definition of myth to one of them, *The Lord of the Rings*, to conclude that it does not qualify. But contrary to his opinion few Tolkien scholars nowadays consider *The Lord of the Rings* a myth. It could be argued that it has mythical traits, and the term 'myth' did indeed figure in several early studies prior to the publication of *The Silmarillion*. Generally, though, Tolkien scholars and readers alike view the work as an epic or a novel. It is Tolkien's corpus of stories, poems and other texts about the Elder Days – roughly the time before the Third Age – that is usually discussed in terms of myth and mythology. Both *The Lord of the Rings* and *The Hobbit* are rooted in this mythology and contain mythical elements, but without being myths themselves in the strict sense of the word.

Arvidsson also complains that the people who apply the term myth to Tolkien's work rarely explain what they mean by it. However, there is a reason for this: these people simply use Tolkien's own terminology for what he was trying to create, plus the formula coined for it by his biographer, 'a mythology for England' (Carpenter, 89). Instances in which Tolkien refers to his own writings in terms of 'myth' and 'mythology' abound (Book 10 of the History of Middle-earth, *Morgoth's Ring*, would be a rich source – see Noad, 31-38), but in the letter to Waldman he writes about 'a body of more or less connected legend' (*Letters*, 144) and in a letter of September 1963 about his 'legends' (*Letters*, 333). Commenting on his older tales, he tends to put the word mythology between quotation marks, as if to denote its artificiality, or because by then he had abandoned the idea of creating a mythology (Brljak, 17).

What did he mean by 'myth'? He was undoubtedly aware of the claim to authority contained in the narrower definitions of the term, like the one Arvidsson gives. But it is very unlikely that Tolkien, the orthodox Catholic, ever intended to create an authoritative religious tale to rival that of his own Church. So if he thought of a mythology as a body of stories about creation, the cosmos, the sacred and the nature of the world, it was probably either to copy the form without the function or to disguise the religious tales of his own faith in an idiosyncratic symbolism of what he considered to be a typically English cut.

There is yet another explanation for his use of the terms 'myth' and 'mythology': that he was not doing so as a mythopoet, a sub-creator, but as a scholar studying the text corpus of an ancient, vanished civilisation – a position not unlike that of a compiler and translator of an epic about hobbits found in a weighty tome called *The Red Book of Westmarch*. And while his mythology may not be a call to action here and now, as a source of inspiration for a world-wide audience it takes no back seat to the greatest mythopoeic work of the 19th century, *Der Ring des Nibelungen*.

Chapter 7

Nature and its Defilement

Nature plays an important role for both Wagner and Tolkien. For Wagner, myth originated in the encounter of man and nature. Tolkien's concern for nature permeates all his works, but especially *The Lord of the Rings*. Being in close connection with nature is a positive thing in the *Ring* cycle as well as in the Arda legendarium. Yet it goes further: both Wagner and Tolkien gave nature, benevolent as well as malevolent, an active role.

Wagner often uses personification: there are the Rhinemaidens, who are water sprites and there is Erda, the wise earth-goddess. The Forest Bird is a creature of the air, Loge is fire incarnated, a 'wandering flame' (*Die Walküre* III, 3), representing the intellect. The giants, living on the 'earth's back' (*Siegfried* I, 2), stand for nature's raw strength. All four classical elements are present, represented by sentient creatures, and all play a pivotal role in the story. None of them are entirely personal, the Forest Bird least of all, while Loge reverts to impersonal fire after *Das Rheingold*. In addition, there is non-personified nature: the World-Ash, the river Rhine, the storm at the beginning of *Die Walküre*, the forest with its animals, especially prominent in Siegfried, and perhaps even the pure gold counts. All of these nature elements, sentient and non-sentient alike, have their own musical motifs.

Personified aspects of nature are found in Tolkien's *Silmarillion*: most of the Valar fall into this category. In *The Lord of the Rings* we have Tom Bombadil – possibly a personification of nature itself – and the river-daughter Goldberry, the highly original Ents and the Eagles.[14] There is an abundance of non-sentient nature: forests, mountains, rivers, etc.. But Tolkien also introduces a category of semi-sentient beings, aware and active, but not communicative, and not particularly benevolent: Old Man Willow, the Watcher in the Water, the Huorns, Shelob, and maybe the mountain Caradhras ought to be included

---

14 Though the thinking fox in *The Fellowship of the Ring* I, III is an anomaly.

here as well. When wind, falling stones and snow defeat the Fellowship on its flanks, there is a strong suggestion that it is the ill will or the malice of the mountain itself that causes this (*The Fellowship of the Ring* II, III). In the film Saruman is behind this, as though the mountain could not have acted of its own accord. This misses the point Tolkien is making repeatedly: that nature actively intervenes in the story (the movie also misses the point with the Ents, whose intervention depends on Pippin's ruse). Nature is not merely a victim in *The Lord of the Rings*.

Yet a victim it is: in both Ring stories the corruption through power goes hand in hand with the defilement of nature (Ellison 1988, 17). In 1976 Sir Reginald Goodall wrote: 'We've destroyed in the last fifty years more than in the aeons before… Nature is so finely balanced that we disturb the purity of the world. We can't help it. That is the original sin, and that is what the whole *Ring* is about.' (q. Ellison) He was writing about Wagner's tetralogy, but the statement might well be applied to Tolkien's story. In either case it is something of a generalisation, but the theme is unmistakeably prominent in both works. It is a relatively modern theme: before the 'dark satanic mills' came into being and the Luddites began their protest against them, it was hardly an issue.

Wagner was among those to whom it was a growing concern. While the main theme of the *Ring* cycle is Love versus Power, it could arguably be subtitled as Nature versus Law: he blamed much of what was wrong in the modern world on the laws made by those in power to protect their own interests. This often resulted in infractions against nature. Wotan fashioned his Spear of Law from a branch cut from the *Weltesche*, the World Ash, a violation causing the tree to wither. Not surprisingly the Leitmotif representing this spear shows a downward movement, as opposed to that of Siegfried's sword, represented by an upward movement. Wagner's *Weltesche* is essentially Yggdrasil, the World Ash of Norse mythology. In the *Poetic Edda* (*Völuspá* and *Grimnismál*) various serpents gnaw at its roots and branches and it has more to suffer than men are aware of. At the onset of *ragnarök* the tree begins to tremble, but though its ultimate fate remains unclear, nowhere in the sources is it actually seen to wither. This is Wagner's own addition to the sources. (So is the idea that Siegfried is the representative of Nature: his actions are not based on any conventions, but on what Nature dictates him to do.)

Violence against trees plays an important role in Tolkien's work as well: the Age of the Trees ends because the giant spider Ungoliant destroys the luminous trees of Valinor with Morgoth's help. In the Second Age Sauron orders the White Tree of Númenor to be chopped into pieces and burned in the fires of the great temple he built for the worship of Melkor. At the end of the Third Age Saruman ravages the forests around Isengard to feed the fires of his engines at Orthanc. His Orcs also cut down trees purely for mischief, leaving them to rot where they fell. Returning to the Shire after the fall of Sauron, the hobbits discover that Saruman has gone ahead of them and caused the Party Tree to be cut down. Tolkien's trees, however, are always in some way restored, either because a sapling survives, or because a new tree is planted, as in the Shire. As Tolkien wrote a year before his death: 'In all my works, I take the part of trees against all their enemies' (*Letters*, 419).

Environmental and ecological issues in *The Lord of the Rings* have been discussed at length by Curry, while Davis argues that there is a constant conflict between civilisation and nature in Middle-earth, with the Ents and the Entwives as prime exponents (61ff). The Ents stand for wild, untamed nature; their chief desire is to communicate with trees and plants. The Entwives on the other hand have tamed nature and bent it to their will, cultivating trees and plants to do their bidding and bear fruit. In the course of time the Ents have grown estranged from their wives, until they entirely lost sight of them, and at the time of *The Lord of the Rings* the Entwives seem to have vanished from the face of the earth. Though seemingly on the side of nature, Tolkien makes it clear that this situation is unhappy. The Entwives represent the caretaking side of civilisation and the Ents need them as their complements, their other halves. In this, he is more balanced than Wagner was: at the end of the *Ring* cycle, civilisation as it exists then is wiped out in its entirety by fire and water.

If anyone represents the destructive side of civilisation it is the fallen wizard Saruman, even more so than Sauron. The Dark Lord may be Alberich's counterpart as the forger of an oppressing Ring of Power; it is Saruman who more obviously parallels Alberich as the modern industrial who would sacrifice the world around him to meet his selfish ends. The Nibelungs used to be a carefree people until Alberich enslaved them, sending them down into dark caverns filled by black clouds and sulphurous vapours, to sweat and toil for him.

He rules them by fear; wherever he appears, screams and laments are heard. Nibelheim is an obvious reference to the devastations of industrial capitalism. So is Isengard; its description, like that of the Shire after the hobbits' return, is coloured by Tolkien's 'personal experience of the invasion of the countryside by the products of industrial capitalism' (Ellison 1988, 17):

> But no green thing grew there in the latter days of Saruman. (...) Shafts were driven deep into the ground; their upper ends were covered by low mounds and domes of stone, so that in the moonlight the Ring of Isengard looked like a graveyard of unquiet dead. For the ground trembled. The shafts ran down by many slopes and spiral stairs to caverns far under. (...) Iron wheels revolved there endlessly, and hammers thudded. At night plumes of vapour steamed from the vents, lit from beneath with red light, or blue, or venomous green. (*The Two Towers*, III, VIII)

In Jackson's film we see the Orcs at work in the pits of Orthanc, supervised by the wizard; envisaging Alberich in such an environment takes no great effort of mind. The fortress of Barad-dûr in Mordor is described as a similar place, only on a much grander scale, but as it is not shown its horrors remain much vaguer.

Tolkien introduces one element lacking in Wagner's work: infringement of the nature of sentient beings. Morgoth changes Elves into Orcs; Saruman crossbreeds Orcs and human beings to produce half-Orcs. This is an idea that could only have arisen in the age that saw the development of genetic experiment. The Nibelungen become industrial slaves after Alberich has brought them under his sway with the help of the ring,[15] but their fundamental nature does not change.

---

15 When Wagner saw the London docklands in 1877, he seems to have remarked that this was Alberich's dream come true (Spencer/Millington, 368).

Part Two: Myths, Fairy Tales and Endings

Chapter 8

A World too Much? Fantasy versus (Stage) Drama

8.1. Myth and drama

When it comes to genre, Wagner and Tolkien seem diametrically opposed. Not because one was a composer while the other was a writer, but because Wagner's works are dramatic, whereas Tolkien preferred fantasy to drama, considering it the 'most nearly pure form' of art ('On Fairy Stories' 2008, § 67). Now obviously, opera is not the same thing as drama, but Wagner saw himself as a dramatist rather than an opera composer. His ideal was to unify all forms of art – narrative, poetry, music, dance, painting, architecture, the *Gesamtkunstwerk* ('total work of art') – in the theatre.

However, the wellspring of drama was myth. And myth, writes Wagner, is born from the poetic imagination: the working of the brain is able to shape phenomena, separated from their natural reality, into comprehensive new images… and this working of the brain is what we call '*fantasy*' (*Oper und Drama*, II, II).[16] When Tolkien wrote:

> The mind that thought of light, heavy, grey, yellow, still, swift, also conceived of magic that would make heavy things light and able to fly, turn grey lead into yellow gold, and the still rock into a swift water. If it could do the one, it could do the other; it inevitably did both. (…) In such "fantasy," as it is called, new form is made ('On Fairy Stories', § 27),

he did not express a fundamentally different and opposite thought.

---

16 German: '… vermag aber die Tätigkeit des Gehirnes die (…) von ihrer Naturwirklichkeit losgelösten Erscheinungen zu den umfassendsten neuen Bildern zu gestalten… und diese Tätigkeit des Gehirnes nennen wir Phantasie.' German 'Phantasie' generally means imagination, but here a translation with '*fantasy*' seemed called for.

8.1.1. Dramatic narrative

Even before he developed his views on myth and drama in his treatises of the late 1840s and beyond, in Wagner's view drama and fairy tale were never in opposition. As mentioned in II.1, the first opera he wrote, *Die Feen* (1833), was about fairies and partly situated in Faery, the magic realm. During his entire life he continued to use fairy tale motifs and supernatural elements in his works. The Flying Dutchman has to sail the seas forever unless a mortal girl promises him everlasting fidelity. In *Lohengrin* an evil sorceress has changed the innocent Elsa's brother Gottfried into a swan, but the hero changes him back at the end. Magic potions play a role in *Tristan und Isolde* and *Götterdämmerung*. *Siegfried* contains elements from The Boy Who Went Out to Learn Fear and Sleeping Beauty (Brünnhilde on her rock, an element already present in the source texts), and when Mime cries 'nun ward ich so alt wie Höhl' und Wald, und hab' nicht sowas gesehn!' ('Now I've grown as old as cave and wood and haven't seen anything like it!') he is using a stock phrase from many fairy tales. The entire third *Ring* opera lacks tragic conflict and resembles a fairy story more than anything. *Das Rheingold* has too much unresolved conflict to qualify as a fairy tale proper, but it contains several fairy tale elements; one book even describes it in modern terms as 'a fantasy prelude - a dungeons and dragons story of gods, giants, dwarfs and magic gold' (White/Scott, 92). The last instalment of the *Ring* cycle develops from myth into heroic tragedy, but apart from the aforementioned magic potions it also contains a fairy tale allusion: Waltraute's question in *Götterdämmerung* I, 3, 'Schwester, schläfst oder wachst du?' (Sister, are you asleep or awake?) recalls a similar question in Grimm's fairy tale 'One-eye, Two-eyes and Three-eyes' (Von Wolzogen, 46).

The *Ring* does not qualify as Aristotelian drama proper. Wagner went against the rules by showing things on the stage which in classical drama are reported by a messenger or through teichoscopy (Dahlhaus 1990, 37), for instance Alberich becoming invisible and changing shape in *Das Rheingold*, the Fire magic at the end of *Die Walküre*, the slaying of Fafner in *Siegfried* and the ending of the cycle, with Brünnhilde's pyre, the conflagration of Walhall and the flooding of the Rhine. Thomas Mann went as far as considering Wagner a creator of epic theatre instead of a dramatist (q. Wilberg, 276).

Even so, he considered himself first and foremost a dramatist. As mentioned before, unlike the majority of opera composers he wrote both the libretti and the music, underpinning his creative practice with theoretical treatises like *Oper und Drama*, 'Das Kunstwerk der Zukunft' and 'Zukunftsmusik'. As his ideas about what he was doing and aimed to achieve tended to change in the course of time, these texts sometimes contradict each other. But one thing did not change: he considered Drama the most fundamental form of art, encompassing all others and proceeding in its totality from Ancient Greek drama, which had been prefigured by myth. The greatest representative of this had been Aeschylus, whose trilogy *Oresteia* was the model for his *Ring*. Wagner held this work in great reverence, preferring it to the literature of his own time and to the works of the other ancient Greek dramatists because of its epical qualities and its greater nearness to myth (Wilberg, 278-9). He also admired the 17th century Spanish playwright Pedro Calderón de la Barca, whose 'total theatre' combined spoken text, poetry, song and dance and definitely influenced Wagner's concept of the total work of art. But he began his career as a dramatist by attempting to emulate another great example. As a teenager he wrote a tragedy, *Leubald*, which contained elements from at least half a dozen Shakespeare plays. His second opera, *Das Liebesverbot* ('The Ban on Love') written in 1836, is loosely based on *Measure for Measure*. The reason that he rejected the term 'music drama' after first having invented it, is that he considered his works dramas pure and simple, in fact, the only dramas worthy of the name since Shakespeare's times (Dahlhaus 1990, 10).

8.1.2. Faërian drama

As several scholars have shown, Tolkien's works contain many Shakespearean echoes and allusions (Shippey 1982, et. al.). However, his letters suggest he held a somewhat dim view of the Bard, who he claims to have 'disliked cordially' (*Letters*, 213). In a footnote to this letter he wrote about his 'bitter disappointment and disgust from schooldays with the shabby use made in Shakespeare [*Macbeth*] of the coming of "Great Birnam wood to high Dunsinane hill".' Therefore he 'wanted to devise a setting in which the trees might really march to war', which resulted in the march of the Ents to Isengard (*The Two Towers* I, IX). Though he may have exaggerated his dislike of the playwright, his disappointment in *Macbeth* reverberates in his essay on fairy stories, where he writes that 'very little about trees can be gotten into a play' ('On Fairy Stories', 2008. § 73).

Because of the dominance of Shakespeare and his plays, literary criticism in England 'tends to be far too dramatic', Tolkien maintains. Unfortunately, people who prefer Drama to Literature are bound to misunderstand 'pure storytelling', constraining it 'to the limitations of stage plays'. But Drama is 'fundamentally different from narrative art' and 'naturally hostile to fantasy'; 'Fantasy (...) hardly ever succeeds in Drama' (§ 70-73). Fantasy, in Tolkien's view, is the art that forms the operative link between the imagination and the final result, 'Sub-creation'. By this he means a secondary world, unlike our primary world and free from 'the domination of observed fact', which commands 'Secondary Belief' because it possesses 'the inner consistency of reality'. This is difficult to achieve; it requires labour and thought and demands 'a special skill, a kind of Elvish craft'. If successful, it is 'a rare achievement of Art: indeed narrative art, story-making in its primary and most potent mode' (§ 66-69). *The Lord of the Rings*, which he considered 'a practical demonstration' of the views expressed in the essay (*Letters,* 310), can make a very good claim to being such a rare achievement of narrative art.

Tolkien applauds Drama when it is of Faërian origin and presents a Secondary World through Enchantment, an elvish craft to which the fantasy of mortal men can only aspire. So, leaving aside the question whether he truly believed that this could be experienced by mortals or thought he had experienced it himself, it is not the dramatic per se he objects against. He was also very well capable of creating dramatic tragedy, as *The Children of Húrin* proves; no character in any of Tolkien's works bears more resemblance to a protagonist from classical Greek tragedy than Túrin Turambar does. Greenman argues that the 'Quenta Silmarillion' is an Aristotelian tragedy, even though it is not written in verse. At the same time both the story of the *silmarils* and that of Túrin are fantasy tales, with Elves, Dwarves, 'gods' (the Valar), magical artefacts and monsters. If one replaces Elves by water nixes and/or valkyries, they are not so unlike Wagner's *Ring* - yet that is Drama. To be sure, it is music drama and therefore more than a play, but it remains subject to the limitations of the stage. It is, in fact, the stage presentation, the material aspect of drama that bears the brunt of Tolkien's attack on fantasy drama. What was his problem with staging Fantasy?

In the first place he objected against counterfeiting 'fantastic forms'. Once, he reports, he saw a children's pantomime of Puss-in-Boots in which the metamorphosis of the ogre into a mouse was shown on the stage. 'Had this been mechanically successful,' he wrote,

> it would either have terrified the spectators or else have been just a turn of high-class conjuring. As it was, though done with some ingenuity of lighting, disbelief had not so much to be suspended as hung, drawn and quartered. (§ 70)

What Tolkien is in fact suggesting here is that whatever means are used to create magical effects in the theatre, and however successful they are, he will not willingly suspend disbelief. The process as well as the result is fake, and he wants the real thing.

To remain consistent he also ought to have objected against fantasy films, animated or otherwise, as any 'magic' a film is able to achieve is likewise mechanical and counterfeited. In a note to 'On Fairy Stories' he mentions the 'cinematograph' among the visual arts but does not express any opinion about it, which makes us none the wiser. But despite the fact that he considered *The Lord of the Rings* unfit for dramatisation and did not think much of the radio play the BBC made of the work in 1955/56 (Scull & Hammond, *Chronology*, 479-80), he was not averse to the idea of a film adaptation when an American company approached him a year later with a proposal. This was to be a mix of live action and animation. He actually liked the concept art, which seems to have resembled the drawings of Arthur Rackham. When he received the script by Morton Grady Zimmerman he picked it apart (*Letters*, 270-77) and the whole project foundered, but apparently the visuals were not the stumbling block. In 1969 he sold the film rights to United Artists. Conversations he had with Arne Zettersten around 1970, however, suggest that he always remained sceptical about a film adaptation (314).

Returning to the fairy tale essay, the Puss-in-Boots example is highly interesting. Why make mince meat of a pantomime for children,[17] who need very little material and mechanical aid to fuel their superior imaginations? Perhaps it was so badly done that not even the youthful audience fell for it, which would have made it eminently suitable for Tolkien's purpose. But Puss-in-Boots also happens to be one of the fairy tales Wagner used in his *Ring* cycle. In *Das Rheingold* Alberich transforms himself by means of the Tarnhelm, first into a *Riesenwurm*, a huge serpent that looms threateningly over Loge, then into a toad. This enables Loge to catch him, like the pussy catches the ogre-turned-mouse, though fortunately for Alberich and the rest of the cycle he does not get eaten. This remains conjecture, but could it be that Tolkien was not merely thinking of the pantomime when he used this particular example, but also of Wagner's work, which he may have attended at some unspecified date in the 1930s before he wrote his essay?

Shippey argues that Tolkien may have found fault with Wagner's anachronistic incorporation of another fairy tale, Grimm's 'The Boy Who Set Out to Find Fear', into the legend of Siegfried,[18] and he thought that Wagner 'had botched the very kernel of the whole Norse/German heroic tradition' by turning Siegfried into a brute and a lout (2007, 109; see also Part III). If this is the case, Tolkien must have been very unhappy with the anachronistic incorporation of a post-medieval French fairy tale into an ancient legend of Germanic origin: Puss-in-Boots (*Le Chat Botté*) was written in the late 17th century by the Frenchman Charles Perrault.

---

17 I am assuming here that Tolkien saw the pantomime as an adult, accompanying one or more of his own children, given his sophisticated analysis and the fact that he did not mention that he saw the pantomime as a child. But it is also possible that he reconstructed his own childhood feelings about the performance in more sophisticated terms.

18 However, the prototype of this and similar fairy tale characters possibly *was* Siegfried. Tolkien himself incorporated an element from the fairy tale 'Rapunzel' (also from the Grimm collection) plus an allusion to the 'impossible quest' fairy tale type in his story of Beren and Lúthien. Ironically, like many of Grimm's fairy tales, 'Rapunzel' was also French in origin, dating from the 17th century. It moved to Germany with the Huguenots.

8.1.3. Visual representation

Tolkien's other objection against Drama as a vehicle for fantasy is that, in itself, Drama is already trying to create a 'bogus' or 'substitute magic' by presenting imaginary people in a make-belief reality. To add 'a further fantasy or magic is to demand (...) an inner or tertiary world. It is a world too much.' He has never seen such a thing done successfully, and though he concedes it is theoretically possible, it is not the 'proper mode of Drama, in which walking and talking people have been found to be natural instruments of Art and illusion.' (§ 72).

Of course, someone writing in the 1930s can hardly be blamed for being ignorant of later developments in drama; when Tolkien wrote his essay Bertold Brecht's anti-illusionary 'alienation effect', meant to encourage a more critical attitude among the audience towards the spectacle on stage, was not widely known yet. But even in the late thirties his position was far from self-evident. The term magic, applied to a theatre performance, suggests an attitude uncommon among educated 20th century people. He, of all people, must have been aware of the difference between make-belief and magic, so what is the term 'bogus magic' doing here with reference to Drama per se?

The argument about the 'tertiary world' is also somewhat peculiar: the stage world and anything in it, whether 'realistic' or 'fantastic', *is* the secondary world. A tertiary world may (but does not necessarily) arise in the case of a 'play inside a play', but to make a case against it. Tolkien really ought to have said more than just that it is a world too much. However, this is not what he was trying to do. In his crusade on behalf of Fantasy, he argued against fantasy drama by turning Drama proper into something it is not.

He began his discussion of Drama and Fantasy by contending that Fantasy is an art best left to words. 'In painting (...) the visible presentation of the fantastic image is technically too easy: the hand tends to outrun the mind, even to overthrow it. Silliness or morbidity are frequent results.' (§ 70). In Note E to the essay he works this out, discovering in surrealism 'a morbidity or unease very rarely found in literary fantasy'. In the same note, he expresses the opinion that illustrations 'do little good to fairy-stories'. The only visual representations of his work he is known to have appreciated besides his own are the illustrations of Pauline Baynes, Cor Blok and 'Ingahild Grathmer'.[19] None of these are close to photographic realism, those by Blok least so.[20] The same goes for his own illustrations. Despite his limited technical skills his non-Middle-earth drawings show a degree of realism often absent in the illustrations he made for his own work,[21] while several of the more realistic Middle-earth pictures, like 'Old Man Willow' (Tolkien 1995, no. 147), would not be recognisable as fantasy illustrations if it wasn't for the captions. Barring a few exceptions, his illustrations to his own work leave at least something to the imagination. As Tolkien writes, still in Note E:

> The radical distinction between all art (including drama) that offers a visible presentation and true literature, is that it imposes one visible form. Literature works from mind to mind and is thus more progenitive. (§ 113)

The term 'imposing' is reminiscent of his words regarding applicability and allegory in the Foreword to the second edition of *The Lord of the Rings*, a work he strongly insisted was not allegorical. Though people often confuse them, according to him the difference between the two is that 'the one resides in the freedom of the reader and the other in the purposed domination of the author.' Freedom is a key term in this context: in addition to the reasons given in the main body of the essay, Drama also proves unfit as a vehicle for Fantasy because it curbs the freedom of the imagination; Fantasy thrives on a free imagination and cannot exist without it.

At first sight this argument seems more powerful than those about the lameness of special effects and the tertiary world that is one too many. An often heard objection against illustrations of Tolkien's works – and this includes Jackson's film version of *The Lord of the Rings* – is that they override previous images already present in the mind. Frodo gets to look suspiciously like Elijah

---

19 Tolkien chose Pauline Baynes to illustrate *Farmer Giles of Ham* (Scull & Hammond, *Chronology*, 340); he approved of Blok's work and bought two of his paintings (*Chronology*, 581, 587, 590); because he liked the designs of Ingahild Grathmer (pseudonym of Princess, later Queen Margrethe of Denmark) they were chosen to illustrate the 1977 Folio Society edition of *The Lord of the Rings*.
20 Ruth Lacon coined the phrase 'visual applicability' to characterise this type of illustration. See: http://networkedblogs.com/l57V5 (retr. date 25-6-2011).
21 Compare, for instance, the drawings in Hammond & Scull 1995: 17 (Foxglove Year) and 27 (Tumble Hill near Lyme Regis) to 88 (Mirkwood) and to Plate 37 (entitled 'Fangorn Forest', though it originally illustrated the passage from *The Silmarillion* where 'Beleg finds Gwindor in Taur-nu-Fuin') in *Pictures*.

Wood, while Gandalf becomes indistinguishable from Ian McKellen. (Tolkien himself got his inspiration for Gandalf from a postcard based on the painting *Der Berggeist* by Joseph Madlener, dating from the 1920s,[22] but this is not a portrait and therefore less likely to dominate the imagination. It is interesting, though, that one of his main fantasy characters was partly inspired by a visual work of art.)

But does it also work that way on a theatre stage? Pictures and movies are (relatively) permanent, a theatre performance is not. More importantly, it is always an interpretation, and never the drama itself. It suggests a way of looking at things without imposing it on anyone, and it is always possible to reject a theatre performance without rejecting the drama itself. Or to appreciate an excellent staging and first class performances without having a high opinion of the piece in question.

Commenting on the essay, Flieger considers Tolkien's discussion of Fantasy and Drama debatable, 'not only for his evaluation of drama as the vehicle for fantasy, but also for his criticism of "special effects".' ('On Fairy Stories' 2008, § 137). However, in her capacity as the editor of the essay, she does not enter the debate. In the second half of her paper 'The Lords of the Rings' (see n. 62), the first half of which was discussed in III.1, Müller does. Basing herself on the views Tolkien expostulates in 'On Fairy Stories' she calls him a 'logocentric': for someone like him the word was the supreme vehicle of the imagination (356). The relationship between a word and the thing it denotes, signifier and signified, is immediate. In visual representations this immediacy does not exist, and this renders Tolkien's analysis of the incompatibility of Drama and Fantasy problematic. One might add that his bold statements concerning word-art as the prime vehicle for Fantasy will probably hold little appeal to non-logocentric artists. Wagner, whose chief medium was music, felt that words were unable to convey the essential. This may have been the reason that he came to prefer mythical subjects to historical ones: for him myth is terse, it is performance rather than speech, like ritual, with which it was originally connected (Dahlhaus, 47).

---

22 According to Carpenter's biography, Tolkien wrote 'origin of Gandalf' on the envelope of the postcard. (66-7), which was printed in 1935.

8.2. Fantasy drama

Though she does not mention the Puss-in-Boots episode, Müller thinks that Tolkien's condemnation of dramatic fantasy was also directed at Wagner's *Ring* cycle. His reaction is so vehement, she suggests, because the cycle can indeed be regarded as a Fantasy drama. For Tolkien, myth is sub-creation through fantasy and she argues that this is what Wagner does: his *Ring* 'acquires the character of a sub-creation precisely as (...) the product of a creator who works something new out of mythological material' (Müller, 351). There are differences, too: Tolkien had a much more humble view of the artist as a sub-creator under God than Wagner, who created a pseudo-religion around his own art, something Tolkien must strongly have objected against (but see 1.2.2. for Wagner's own view). And whereas for the philologist the power of language was rooted in the relationship between words and things, the composer found it in sound, because he did not 'separate sound language and word language'. Still, in Wagner's operas,

> the narrative element, so cherished by Tolkien, has a central function (...), interrupting the action again and again in order to establish coherence (...). In these moments the focus of attention is directed away form the narrating figure to the narration itself. These narrative interruptions may well be compared to those which Tolkien employs. (355)[23]

The suggestion that some of Wagner's operas are fantasy dramas receives support from a Dutch newspaper columnist musing about the thread running back from Liliana Bodoc (an Argentine fantasy author) via Tolkien to Wagner. His fifteen-year old daughter, an avid reader of Bodoc's novels, had previously devoured *The Lord of the Rings*. Then, as a member of the choir performing in *Parsifal* for the Brussels Opera, she discovered Wagner. Though she expressed a dislike for modern stagings and was disappointed to hear they had even conquered Bayreuth, she was wildly enthusiastic about the opera itself. Her father was flabbergasted, until it occurred to him that she was no stranger to Wagner's world thanks to the fantasy novels that are the main fare of the kids nowadays

---

23 One Wagner biographer calls the *Ring* 'a musical epic more than anything' (Gregor-Dellin 1990, 56). Dahlhaus speaks of a 'scenic epic' (1990, 39). In 'Zukunftsmusik', however, Wagner claims that the only suitable opera text is one in which the poet no longer describes, but presents his object in a way which convinces the senses – 'and this is Drama alone'. Apparently he forgot the long narrative stretches of his Ring.

called 'young adults' by the book industry. At first he wondered how degrading it would be if Wagner were to become the early hero of a shady literary genre hardly taken seriously. But then he realised it had always been that way, as the composer based his texts on popular myths and sagas. His conclusion: for today's kids Wagner could again become the storyteller he was from the outset, and this could once more make Wagner's fantasy as self-evident as it was meant to be (Groot, *Trouw*).

One probably needs to be both a true Wagnerian and an inveterate optimist to have this much faith in the magical powers a Wagner opera can exert over today's fantasy-loving young adults. The majority of them may never go back beyond Tolkien. Meanwhile, one of the more remarkable things mentioned in the column is that the staging had no influence on the girl's appreciation of the opera, which must have fit her idea of the fantastic.

According to Müller, Wagner also considered the use of stage machinery detrimental to fantasy. He criticised the opera practice of his own time, which insisted that things had to be presented with the utmost material realism to bring about a fantastic effect without any co-operation of the imagination (*Oper und Drama*, I, IV). Against this he set the performance conditions of Shakespearian drama, with their appeal on the imagination to complete what is presented in a rudimentary way on the stage. They will result in far better performances than any attempts at detailed material realism. Müller concludes that Tolkien's rejection of fantasy in drama is based on precisely such attempts at achieving fantastic effects through purely material realism, in other words, on the same hyper-realistic performance practice Wagner rejected. Tolkien quite simply succumbed 'to the illusions brought forth by realism in stage performance'(357).

Müller admits that Wagner did give quite a few stage directions, but she suggests that just like set pieces these must be seen as leaving room for the imagination. Their 'exact realisation on stage is eventually impossible, and most likely has never been intended to be fully put into practice.' (355) A prime example of such impossibility would be the use of invisibility on the stage. In *Das Rheingold* 3, Alberich dons the Tarnhelm and, having become invisible, he torments his brother, Mime, who cannot fight back against the unseen attacker. According to Wagner's directions, the singer is to leave the stage after putting on the helm and sing on through a speaking-tube, a solution Bratman calls 'inevitably crude' (147). In modern stagings, more advanced special effects can be used to make the singer sound as though he is still present. Sometimes, though, Alberich simply stays on the stage and the audience has to imagine him away. Many people do not mind, like Tolkien apparently did not mind depicting an invisible Bilbo. His drawing of the hobbit visiting Smaug inside the Lonely Mountain (Tolkien 1995, no. 133) shows the invisible visitor as a black silhouette surrounded by a white cloud. In his comment he explains that '(as my children, at any rate, understand) he is really in a separate picture or "plane" being invisible to the dragon' (*Letters*, 35). Apparently his children had enough imagination to ignore the fact that, as special effects go, this one was inevitably crude.

May we assume that his 'Apology for Fantasy' is overstating the point when it rejects fantasy drama as categorically as it does? Tolkien was not just making an analysis, he was on a mission to propagate fantasy and sub-creation in a drama-loving culture, and he probably thought this justified some exaggeration. He was simply being territorial about his preferred form of art, wanting to claim it for the kingdom of Language. But the imagination is not only triggered by words (and for some people not even primarily). When it is capable of seeing an invisible hobbit in a different plane, it should also be able to see an ogre turn into a mouse in a different plane.

On the other hand, Wagner may have intended his stage directions more literally than Müller thinks. Regarding special effects he had 'both a childlike delight in the ingenuities of stage deception and an absolute belief, one wholly representative of his time, that what had been imagined should be represented literally' (Carnegie, 85). He was a musical genius and a great dramatist, but when it came to visualising his own works he was no visionary and his attempts at achieving realism often resulted in the opposite. Unlike the Swiss scenic designer Adolphe Appia (who among other things introduced controlled lighting in the 1920s) and his own grandson Wieland (who followed Appia's lead in the 1950s), he did not look beyond the obvious. For the premiere of the *Ring* at the Bayreuth *Festpielhaus* in 1876, for example, he had ordered a realistic-looking papier-mâché dragon from England. Even after it turned out that the neck had been shipped to Beirut by mistake, he kept insisting that the dragon be used during the performance. Instead of terrifying the audience, the neckless monster hung its head as though begging to be put out of its misery and when Siegfried killed it, the public burst out laughing. Wagner's assistant stage manager in 1876, Richard Fricke, recorded some of the discussions about this first production of the *Ring* in his diary. Among other things he warned the Master, so enamoured with stage machinery, that too much realism could easily backfire. Reading a grand scene was one thing, because then 'the imagination is fully engaged; but as soon as [it] is presented visually, when all our other senses are on the alert, the image created in our imagination risks becoming ludicrously shrunken' (Carnegie, 89). One feels that Tolkien might have applauded Fricke.

Sometimes, Wagner was on the verge of despair when faced with the difficulties of translating his grand visions adequately into the realities of the stage. As Cosima recorded in her diary on 23 September 1878, he remarked in exasperation that after having invented the invisible orchestra, it was time for him to invent the invisible stage. People have interpreted this as an invitation for posterity to abandon the traditional stagings; in the 1950s Wieland Wagner used this remark to defend his minimalist approach, which would allow the audience to experience the drama without being distracted by machinery and set designs. Though this turned out to work well for many opera-goers (protests by traditionalists notwithstanding), Wagner's diatribe was probably not meant to be taken too seriously, as he added that he also would have to invent the inaudible orchestra.

8.3. Music, words and the invisible stage

This, of course, begs the question what difference the music makes for the 'fantasy' dramas that constitute Wagner's *Ring* cycle. How much about trees can be got into an opera? Would Tolkien have approved of fantasy opera, as opposed to fantasy drama? As he counted drama among the visual arts, he was apparently not thinking of opera when he wrote 'On Fairy Stories'. One of his favourite composers, Weber, is best known for operas like *Der Freischütz*, which contains some supernatural elements, and *Oberon*, a straightforward fairy tale opera. Perhaps he merely liked the music and never attended either of those works in the theatre. On the other hand, in these cases disbelief does not run too huge a risk of being hung, as they do not demand too much by the way of special effects. Wagner's *Ring* does – of all his works, it offers by far the most formidable staging challenge.

If we take Tolkien's question about the trees literally, we find that Wagner put two of them in his *Ring*: the World Ash and the tree in the middle of Hunding's house, from which Siegmund draws the sword put there by Wotan. The latter, also an ash, is visible on the stage (assuming we are not dealing with one of those performances in which it is not). It received a wound when Wotan thrust the sword into it, and as such it can be considered a representative of the wounded, dying World Ash representing Nature marred. The World Ash is usually not shown on the stage. But Wagner put it to music: it has its own motif, played by the orchestra every time someone mentions it and occasionally when it is not mentioned. One half of it is related to the Treaty motif, also known as the Spear motif – the spear is a branch broken from the ash – and the *Götterdämmerung*-motif, while the other half is related to the Nature motif and the motif of the goddess Erda. It is part of a complex structure of musical relations, and if it does not stimulate the conscious imagination, it certainly evokes imaginative associations. Wagner composed his World Ash of musical motifs, textual references and a visible stage tree. Apparently, at least something about trees can be got into a Wagner opera.

But trees as such do not make a fairy tale, or fantasy. Of course, Wagner's Leitmotifs add elements to the story that neither words nor visuals can convey. When Sieglinde sings of the stranger thrusting a sword into the tree, she does not know it was Wotan, but the Walhall-motif played by the orchestra identifies him as such. The same Walhall motif is related to the Ring motif – a comment on the power of the law. Alberich's curse is an inversion of the Ring motif – the downside of power being doom and death, etc. But is music able to modulate drama into fantasy? As the Ride of the Valkyries proves, it can suggest galloping horses, but is it, for instance, capable of creating a believable dragon? How does a dragon sound?

Anyone unfamiliar with the *Ring* cycle who wants to know what Wagner's take on this was should try the version conducted by Sir Georg Solti from 1958-65.

Fafner, the dragon, manifests himself in *Siegfried* II,2 and by the mere sound of him he is awesome: wonderfully dark and hollow and accompanied by terrific tubas. It seems unnecessary to see him – almost better. Many lovers of Wagner's *Ring* cycle, though, do not merely listen to the music; they also buy tickets and attend performances, wanting to see the drama unfold as well as hear it, longing for a total experience of the total work of art. But there is no need for every minor detail to be presented on the stage. The audience has imagination as well as eyes and ears. And of course, the music tells the tale in its own way.

It is the music, rather than the text, which here takes over the function of the spoken word in drama (Dahlhaus 1996, 23). It transmits the essence of the drama; the staging cannot compete with it, only support it – or undermine it if it is very bad, though the music is good enough to prevail most of the time, as it did during the 1876 premiere despite the dragon. Sometimes Wagner showed himself aware of the imaginative power of his music regardless of visual representation. In his essay 'Beethoven' (1870) he wrote that the music expresses 'the inner essence of the gesture' [of what happens on the stage] 'with such direct comprehensibility that, once the music absorbs us completely, it actually renders our eyes unable to watch the gesture intensively, so that in the end we understand it without even seeing it.'[24] No invisible stage, perhaps, but an unseen stage, or at least a vaguely seen one.

For the *Festspiele* of 1965 Wieland Wagner represented the dragon by two giant fiery eyes moving across the backcloth – moving beyond a neckless paper dragon inviting ridicule, and leaving it to the music and the imagination to do the rest. Sometimes less is more. When Tolkien represented Sauron by a single, great, fiery eye, instead of trying to capture him with too detailed verbal descriptions (besides the eye he only mentions a black hand), he showed himself eminently aware of this. Tolkien knew how to use words, but he also knew when to limit his use of them.

---

24 German: '[spricht] das innerste Wesen der Gebärde mit solch unmittelbarer Verständlichkeit aus, daß sie, sobald wir ganz von der Musik erfüllt sind, sogar unser Gesicht für die intensive Wahrnehmung der Gebärde depotenziert, so daß wir sie endlich verstehen, ohne sie selbst zu sehen.' (Q. Dahlhaus 1990, 114/5).

In addition to this he was not entirely consistent in his blanket rejection of all visual forms of fantasy: apparently it does not apply to his own illustrations of his work. Of course, he knew what his mental images looked like, but why encroach upon the magic of language by depicting an invisible Bilbo on a 'different plane'? Or by trying to sketch Sauron for the dust jacket of *The Return of the King* – a water colour drawing showing an orange eye in a grey head with a kind of spiked crown, with underneath it a black arm stretched out over a vague mountain range. Its unfinished state suggests the artist did not think much of it himself, but why even try when you have written such a perfectly suggestive fiery eye?

By rejecting the stage machinery of his time because it did not leave enough to the imagination and replacing it by his own kind of material realism, Wagner was also less than consistent. The suggestion that he underestimated the imaginative power of his own music is preposterous – but then, why insist on a papier-mâché dragon? His biographer Gregor-Dellin is not the only one to suggest that his staging ideals are cinematic, that they presuppose film techniques and represent a 'super-cinema-fantasy' (Gregor-Dellin 1982, 105), as though he had visualised the work as a film *avant-la-lettre.*

As for *The Lord of the Rings*, that Tolkien sold the film rights despite his misgivings may have something to do with his hopes, maybe unconsciously that it would somehow be possible to approximate his inner visions through the medium of film. Zettersten contradicts his belief – shared by his son Christopher[25] – that it was unfit for visual dramatisation by asserting that it has proved eminently suitable for the white screen. Any flaws found in the films are to be ascribed to the script, to the changes Jackson and his fellow-scriptwriters made to the original story. Their success is largely due to the strength of Tolkien's own visual imagination and his ability to translate the images he saw before his mind's eye into language (Zettersten, 311-319). This is a somewhat peculiar assessment, as Tolkien's descriptions, especially of people and their attire, tend to be generic and suggestive rather than descriptive and personal. Concerning Legolas's appearance, for instance, we never get to read much more than that he is 'a strange

---

25 Who claimed that *The Lord of the Rings* was 'unsuitable to transformation into visual dramatic form' (*People in the News*).

Elf clad in green and brown' and has 'a fair Elven face'. Boromir is said to be 'a tall man with a fair and noble face, dark-haired and grey-eyed' (*The Fellowship of the Ring* II, II), which is not saying much at all, given the many Tolkien characters who have dark hair, grey eyes and fair and noble faces. Anyone who has ever seen more than one drawing of Treebeard by more than one artist knows how much Tolkien's description of the Ent left to the imagination of his readers. Locations like Rivendell, Lórien or Minas Tirith are described in ways that inspire different mental images in different individuals. Zettersten's assessment is a little unjust as well: if Jackson and his crew deserve credit for anything, it is for their ability to visualise Tolkien's world in ways that appeal to countless fans from culturally very diverse backgrounds.

Still, even cinematic renderings of fantasy texts will inevitably fall short of Tolkien's Faërian Drama: 'If you are present at a Faërian drama you yourself are, or think that you are, bodily inside its Secondary World' ('On Fairy Stories', § 74). Whether the virtual reality of a sophisticated computer game is a closer approximation to this than cinematic drama, as Péter Kristóf Makai argues, seems debatable. While it incorporates the player in the secondary world of the game, the adventures experienced there do not necessarily make a good story or good drama. And the cyberworld does not (yet?) offer the complete range of sensory perceptions that help create primary belief in human participants in Faërian drama (one assumes), so the immersion is not total. As it remains technology-based, it is not qualitatively different from the 'high-class conjuring' mentioned in 'On Fairy Stories' (§ 70). Makai probably correctly supposes Tolkien would have disapproved of his idea that the secondary world of virtual reality has much in common with Faërian drama as he envisaged it (49). Compared to film, its interactivity perhaps takes it a little bit closer to the world of Faëry – but no more than that. Remarkably enough, Makai's article implicitly links Tolkien and Wagner on two occasions: the first time when he identifies Tolkien's Faërian Drama as 'the ultimate *Gesamtkunstwerk*' (41), the second time when he proposes computer simulations as another step on the road to a 'twenty-first century version of the *Gesamtkunstwerk*' (51).

Summarising, Wagner may have attached too much importance to realistic props in a pre-cinematic world, while Tolkien may have feared that no props would ever be real enough to create a good fantasy drama on the stage – though he remained open to the possibility of a fantasy film. In the end, though, it is for the public to decide whether Secondary Belief has been achieved or not. Fantasy and Drama remain only diametrically opposed for those who insist on getting literal magic where only figurative magic or technology exist. Their preferred means of enchantment differed, but both Wagner and Tolkien were fantasists and mythmakers – and the *Gesamtkunstwerk* the former tried to achieve may not be too far removed from the latter's profoundly desired Faërian Drama.

Chapter 9

Tragedy, Elegy, Eucatastrophe

9.1. Tragedy versus comedy

At first sight another fundamental difference between Wagner and Tolkien, related to the drama-versus-fantasy aspect, lies in the endings of both ring stories. In accordance with its status as a fantasy or fairy tale, *The Lord of the Rings* has a happy ending: the ring has been destroyed, the chief agent of evil vanquished, the world saved and freedom guaranteed. Law and order have been restored and the king has returned to rule wisely and benevolently. Wagner's *Ring*, on the other hand, ends in tragedy and destruction: many of the characters are dead, many hopes have been dashed, the gods have perished and Walhall has gone up in smoke.

Hall summarises these outcomes by calling Tolkien's work a comedy and Wagner's a tragedy. In Weinreich's view, Middle-earth has little to do with the dark fantasies around the Nibelungs, though its creator was admittedly indebted to the world of Norse and Germanic saga. The tale of the Nibelungs is purely tragic; whatever the heroes try to achieve, they are doomed to fail. Something of the same occurs in *The Silmarillion* as well – examples are Fëanor and Túrin – but even here the ultimate message is one of healing: the world will be renewed with the Second Music of the Ainur. Tolkien's message is a joyous one, Weinreich concludes, pointing to the author's Christian world view and his concept of *eucatastrophe* from 'On Fairy Stories', the sudden joyous turn that 'denies universal final defeat and in so far is evangelium' (§ 99). This is incompatible with the *ragnarök*-inspired Nibelungen saga (*Polyoinos*, Plagiate?). Scott Rohan concurs: 'Wagner's story is not eucatastrophic, but classically tragic.'

9.2. Revolution versus restoration

This position is problematic. Although Tolkien was an orthodox Roman Catholic, his world view was closer to the Germanic outlook on life than Weinreich's term 'incompatible' (*unvereinbar*) suggests. In that respect, the following quote from the Beowulf lecture is illuminating:

> The monsters had been the foes of the gods, the captains of men, and within Time the monsters would win. In the heroic siege and last defeat men and gods alike had been imagined in the same host. Now the heroic figures, the men of old, *hæleð under heofenum* [healed under heaven], remained and still fought on until defeat. For the monsters do not depart, whether the gods go or come. A Christian was (and is) still like his forefathers a mortal hemmed in a hostile world. (*The Monsters and the Critics and Other Essays*, 22)

In the next paragraph he writes that the author of Beowulf is 'rehandling in a new perspective an ancient theme: that man, each man and all men, and all their works shall die. A theme no Christian need despise' (*The Monsters and the Critics and Other Essays*, 23). The main difference was that for Tolkien the final victory of Heaven was a given. His message 'is a double one. It speaks of doom and inevitable battle, and it speaks of eternal peace' (Burns, 178).

Tolkien's legendarium does indeed contain several references to the healing of Arda at the end of time. But Tolkien was not an optimist. In a BBC interview of 1968, he remarked that his ring epic does not have a happy end. This may seem strange, as it is unmistakably eucatastrophic. Yet it does not end with a joyful fanfare but rather with an elegiac sigh: the immediate threat to Middle-earth has been removed and Frodo has helped save his world, but it is lost to him. Arvidsson remarks that from a political point of view Tolkien's Ring epic ends on a positive note. But if the author had wanted to create a happy ending, he could have stopped after the destruction of the Ring, the coronation of the King and the hobbits' joyful homecoming. That was not what he did. The High Elves with their beauty and wisdom leave Middle-earth and 'the world begins to sink into the greyness of history'. Frodo is damaged beyond repair and must leave together with them, for 'you cannot go home, if you have saved the world' (Arvidsson 2007, 166-7). If the poem 'The Sea Bell' from the Tom Bombadil cycle is really a dream of Frodo, as the subtitle suggests, the picture becomes even darker for the protagonist of the story (see also Chism).

Furthermore, any defeat of the Shadow is temporary, as Gandalf remarks at an early stage of the story (*The Fellowship of the Ring*, I, II). At some point, Tolkien even embarked on a Fourth Age tale entitled 'The New Shadow' (*The Peoples of Middle-earth*, 409-22), which he abandoned once he realised it could never become more than a thriller (*Letters*, 344). All the same, the title is telling. Arvidsson goes as far as saying that, due to Man's lust for power and his urge towards revolt against the order of creation, the coming Age of Men lies under a shadow from the start. In Wagner's work, though, the downfall of the gods bodes well for the future of mankind (2007, 159).

In fact, the *Ring* does not have any ending at all within the framework of the story in Arvidsson's view. The corrupt world of the gods collapses, and with it the myth itself. The ending is projected into the world of the theatre audience, which is encouraged to create the happy ending themselves, to build a new world without the authorities (2007, 132). Wagner's *Ring* is a self-destructive, revolutionary myth. In *The Lord of the Rings*, Arvidsson only sees a restoration of sacred kingship according to medieval standards, quoting Tolkien's words that 'the tale ends in what is (...) like the re-establishment of an effective Holy Roman Empire with its seat in Rome' (*Letters*, 376).[26] In other words, we are dealing with revolution versus restoration, not happy ending versus tragedy. However, this disregards the fact that the absence of a definite ending can just as well mean that the cycle will restart. Wagner himself remarked that the music of his *Ring* could always begin all over again, as his wife Cosima noted in her diary on 23 July 1872.[27]

9.3. The end of myth

As for Tolkien's work, if one looks at his legendarium as a whole, which Arvidsson does not do because he is focused on *The Lord of the Rings*, it is clear that whatever is restored at the end of the story, it is not myth. Myth does not survive the ending of the Ring epic any more than it survives the end of the Ring cycle – on the contrary, the epic documents its loss.

---

26 This brings Wagner's 'Wibelungen' essay to mind. Here, his ideal hero was Frederick Barbarossa, ruler of the Holy Roman Empire, seeker of the Holy Grail and for a while his ultimate priest-king. This historical hero was replaced first by the mythical Siegfried, whose shortcomings proved too serious, and later with the equally mythical Parsifal, who does eventually become a priest-king.

27 German: 'es gibt keinen Schluß für die Musik' (...) 'sie kann immer von vorne wieder anfangen'.

In the Arda legendarium the demythologising process takes place in stages. At the beginning the gods, later renamed the Valar (Powers), demiurges of the Neo-Platonic kind, roam across the whole of Arda. After the earliest times they withdraw to the Blessed Realm. After their last intervention in Middle-earth at the end of the First Age, this withdrawal process is completed. In the closing years of the Second Age the Blessed Realm itself is removed from the circles of the world. After the end of the Third, the last divine emissaries of the Powers and the last Elves who met them in the flesh depart from Middle-earth, leaving the world to humankind. Myth has definitively withdrawn from Middle-earth.

Ellison explicitly links these endings to a preoccupation with death and the acceptance of death. At the end of *The Lord of the Rings* and Appendix A, which closes with the passing away of a disillusioned Arwen, this theme undermines the feelings of triumph following Sauron's downfall. 'The epilogue of *The Lord of the Rings* is open-ended, even tragic', characterised by the longing for an irrevocably vanished past and at the same time by the acceptance of inevitable change (Ellison, 1988, 18).

Though Ellison calls the tale of Arwen an epilogue, the book's published version has no official epilogue, just a series of appendices, of which 'The Tale of Aragorn and Arwen' is the first. They were published at the end of the third volume of *The Lord of the Rings*. But Tolkien did write, or embark upon, several versions of yet another epilogue in which Sam reads a letter from King Elessar to his children and answers some of their questions. However, the publisher disliked the idea and convinced Tolkien this epilogue had better be left out. In 1992 all versions of it appeared in *Sauron Defeated*. Together with the appendices, they attest to Tolkien's reluctance to end his magnum opus.

People have occasionally made fun of the many endings of Jackson's film version of the epic, which contains at least half a dozen of them, but almost all are present in the book, along with at least one ending absent from the film, the chapter 'The Scouring of the Shire'. Just like the demythologisation process of Middle-earth, the ending of the epic also takes place in stages, as though the author was addicted to his creation, or to the creating process itself, and was following some self-prescribed detox programme. When Tolkien had the

Vala Ulmo tell King Turgon in the 'Quenta Silmarillion': '[L]ove not too well the work of thy hands and the devices of thy heart' (*The Silmarillion*, 125), he knew exactly what he was talking about. It was difficult for him to let go and he was a notorious non-finisher, as the many fragmentary texts published after his death make clear; one volume actually carries the title *Unfinished Tales*.

Arvidsson calls the appendices a clumsy, futile attempt to answer the childish question 'What happened next?' (167). This ignores the fact that four of the six do not deal with this question at all, while the other two and especially the 'Tale of Aragorn and Arwen' serve as final closure, not as a pitiful attempt to prolong the party after the spirit has gone out of it. The countless fans who cannot get enough information about Tolkien's Arda will profoundly disagree with his assessment, pointing out that, instead of merely telling a story, Tolkien built an entire world. The appendices provide the kind of back-story that adds both body and depth to this world. Also, they confirm that 'there is no true end to any fairy-tale' ('On Fairy Stories', § 99; see also note H).

9.4. The end of the world?

A century before Tolkien spent some years tying up the loose ends of his major opus, Wagner started his long wrestling match with the ending of his. In the course of twenty-six years, from 1848 to 1874, he wrote and composed four endings for the *Ring*, or six, if the revisions of the first ending are counted. The original ending was that of *Siegfried's Tod* (with an English apostrophe), the initial version of what was to become *Götterdämmerung*. This was the first of Wagner's *Ring* libretti, and it was finished by December 1848.

In this version, Siegfried and Brünnhilde ascend from their funeral pyre to Walhall to purify Wotan of his crimes. Brünnhilde has the last word, telling the gods that they have been absolved from their guilt because Siegfried has taken it upon himself. The Nibelungs are no longer slaves – even Alberich shall be free. The first revision adds a suggestion by Brünnhilde to add Siegfried to the pantheon of gods,[28] but later Wagner made her admonish the gods to lay down their powers and leave the world to mankind. The conflagration consuming Walhall and everyone in it is absent from both these versions. There was a second revision in 1850, but this is fragmentary and Brünnhilde's closing speech was not preserved.

After this Wagner decided it was necessary to dramatise the back-story and expand his opera about Siegfried's death backwards into a cycle of four. By this time he had reached the conclusion that Walhall had to go up in flames, and in 1852 he changed the ending accordingly. It also became heavily influenced by his lecture of Feuerbach, who argued that love has primacy over all other human endeavours. Now Brünnhilde dismisses gold, divine splendour, house and court, pomp and circumstance, the deceptive union of treaties and the dissembling custom of law in her closing speech, leaving only blessed love; Wagner stressed its redemptive powers even more strongly than Feuerbach had done.

Then he read Schopenhauer's Buddhism-influenced philosophy. The philosopher stressed the illusory nature of existence, and the need for the negation of the will and the annihilation of being. Again, Brünnhilde's last speech changed. Enlightened and redeemed from rebirth, she announces that she will close the gates of eternal becoming behind her. Her final lines now are: 'The blessed end of all things eternal, do you know how I attained it? Grieving love's profoundest suffering opened my eyes for me: I saw the world end.'[29]

This ending, dating from 1856, remained unchanged for eighteen years, among other things because Wagner abandoned the composition of the *Ring* to write two other works, *Tristan und Isolde* and *Die Meistersinger von Nürnberg*. One is inclined to think he also had trouble letting go and that both are the products of procrastinating. Eventually he returned to his *Ring* with his patron, King Ludwig II of Bavaria, breathing down his neck. In 1874, when he finished the

---

28 In the 1937 revision of the 'Quenta Noldorinwa' in *The Shaping of Middle-earth (HoMe 4,* 205*)* Túrin Turambar is counted among the sons of the gods/Valar after the Dagor Dagorath, the Last Battle. He and his sister Nienor were to be glorified much like Siegfried and Brünhilde at the end of *Siegfried's Tod*. Tolkien later abandoned the idea, but unless Tolkien knew the original ending of Wagner's work, this is an interesting case of parallel thinking.
29 German: Alles Ewgen selges Ende/ wißt ihr, wie ich's gewann?/ Trauernder Liebe tiefstes Leiden/ schloß die Augen mir auf:/ enden sah ich die Welt. –

Part Two: Myths, Fairy Tales and Endings   159

composition of *Götterdämmerung*, he struck the Schopenhauerian text, adding a note that it was superfluous, because the music sufficiently expressed the meaning of the words.

A great deal has been written about the ending of the Ring cycle. According to one view, the replacement of the Feuerbachian ode to love with the Schopenhauerian rejection of the illusory world and the negation of the will means that pessimism won out in the end. One of the representatives of this view, Darcy, points out that as early as 1854 Wagner wrote to Liszt that the world was fundamentally evil: it belonged to Alberich and should be done away with (52). While this may have been the disappointed, penniless exile unloading, Wagner never returned to his pre-revolutionary optimism. This interpretation does not necessarily mean that the end is unequivocally pitch black and tragic. If renouncing the will and rejecting the world as an evil illusion in true Schopenhauerian fashion is the only way to cope with existence, it should be considered positive that Brünnhilde succeeds in doing so. Even if one refuses to consider an ending influenced by Schopenhauer's particular brand of Buddhism a good thing, the fact remains that Alberich has not prevailed. The curse on the ring is lifted and his plan to make everything alive renounce love, stated in *Das Rheingold* 3, has been foiled. His attempts to recover the ring have foundered. So have Hagen's; his final words to the Rhinemaidens, '*Zurück vom Ring!*' (Away from the Ring!), are easily interpreted as an additional, general warning against the pursuit of power.

The music, however, does not point towards a purely Schopenhauerian ending. The motif[30] known as 'Redemption through love' (Wagner himself called it, more ambiguously, the 'glorification of Brünnhilde'), repeated thrice at the conclusion of the cycle, is introduced in a context that does not exactly suggest an abnegation of the will. Brünnhilde has just told Sieglinde that she needs to live, as she is carrying Siegmund's child, Siegfried, who will find joy in victory. Sieglinde, who now wants to live for her child instead of following her lover into death, bursts out in a panegyric starting with the words '*O hehrstes*

---

30 It has been questioned whether this is truly a *Leitmotiv*, as it occurs only twice in the entire cycle. However, this has no bearing on the present argument.

Wunder' (Sublimest wonder), sung to precisely the motif which plays such a prominent role at the end of the *Ring*. Wagner composed it in 1855,[31] the year after he read Schopenhauer and a few months before he wrote the prose sketch for the Schopenhauerian ending. In 1872, he inserted the motif in the finale of *Götterdämmerung*, the moment when Brünnhilde's blissfully greets Siegfried, with whom she is to be reunited. This, too, hardly suggests a departure for a Nirvana devoid of passion and love. Yet around this time Wagner also versified the Schopenhauerian ending, though he eventually decided against putting it to music. All this serves to show that his 'response to Schopenhauer's philosophy was not to let it dominate the Ring exclusively' (Lee, 202).

To Wapnewski all the changes and reinterpretations leave the impression that the work refused to end and tried to prevent itself from doing so through the introduction of ever new twists and turns (191). 'Maybe it is not the least of Wagner's achievements that he evaded an unambiguous solution, that he accepted the open ending even though he may not have wanted it. A finale that is not definitive' (194). Lee considers the entire cycle a work in progress. For Ellison, too, Wagner's Ring has an open ending, just like Tolkien's epic. The survivors at the end of Wagner's Ring are 'mortal men doomed to die'. The hoped-for new order has been put into doubt and no one can foresee how the future will turn out (Ellison, 1988, 18).

Some are more positive about the way the cycle concludes. Dahlhaus points out that none of Wagner's fateful stories end without a glimmer of hope. Regarding the ending of the *Ring* he speaks of a dialectic in which salvation – Siegfried as the redeemer of the gods and saviour of the world – turns to ruin with Hagen's betrayal and to salvation again thanks to Brünnhilde's sacrifice (1990, 102). Müller describes it in more Tolkienian terms:

> The fall of Walhalla simultaneously means '*Erlösung für Gott und Welt*' (redemption for god and world), and the final scene hints at a new era. The idea of redemption, central to all of Wagner's musical dramas, constitutes a thoroughly eucatastrophical element, which may not always be present on stage but is always hinted at in the music. (353)

---

31 First noticed by Deathridge.

Kitcher & Schacht suggest that the ending holds out 'the prospect of something like victory even in failure and defeat' (62). They explicitly reject the view that the final version and the Schopenhauer-based one express the same thing. The orchestral conclusion does not negate the will but transforms it 'into a new form of love' (195). Visually, the last scene of the work may be one of destruction, but the orchestral ending of *Götterdämmerung* renews everything that has gone before, infusing 'the themes of nature, gods and heroes[32] with a different and greater light' (200). The final paragraph of their book is worth quoting in full:

> And though the world ends, the earth remains, still capable of renewal, still charged with this promise that we have come to know. We also know that everything that comes to be in it must end, including all order and the very best of lives and loves. But in their mere presence, however ephemeral, they have the power to illumine the world in a manner that vindicates all. (201)

Is this a eucatastrophe, a sudden joyous turn that denies universal defeat? Perhaps this would be overstating the matter, and the first version was undoubtedly more eucatastrophic than the final one. In fact, the term eucatastrophe does not seem entirely suitable: Tolkien coined it first and foremost for the story of the Gospel, which he considered historically true and the wellspring of all 'fairy tale' eucatastrophes, like the one in *The Lord of the Rings* ('On Fairy Stories', § 104-5). To apply it to Wagner's *Ring*, the ending of which was not inspired by an orthodox view of the Gospel, is stretching the term almost to breaking point.

Still, the *Ring* cycle is not a pitch-dark tragedy, as little as Tolkien's epic is a comedy with a happy ending. Both Wagner and Tolkien had trouble finishing their major works, not in the last place because tinkering with them must have become habit-forming. Ultimately, Ellison's assessment that both works have an open ending is probably closest to the truth.

---

32 That is, the Nature, Walhall and Siegfried Leitmotifs, heard at the end of the *Ring* cycle together with the motif of Redemption by Love.

Chapter 10

Conclusion

Wagner and Tolkien have more in common than a Ring of Power and the story they created around it. Moving beyond questions of influence and deliberate borrowing, it is possible to discern four more parallels and mirror situations. The first of the mirror situations concerns their involvement with national myth. In the 19th century, the age of romanticism and rising nationalism, Wagner followed the generation of German poets, philosophers, and philologists who began the search for a new national mythology suited to unite a culture lacking political cohesion. Building on their achievements he used recently unearthed material of Germanic and more specifically Norse origin to raise a monumental myth of his own carrying socio-political overtones and claims to universality: his *Ring* cycle. Such claims were not unjustified: he did succeed in creating a myth, not just for his time but for posterity as well. However, because of his choice of subject matter this work also became the national German myth for which his predecessors had searched and longed. In the next century, this led to misuse, but the *Ring* proved strong enough to survive this.

Almost three quarters of a century later Tolkien, deploring the lack of a native English mythology and possibly taking his lead from the compiler of the Finnish Kalevala, tried to fill this gap, fuelled by a sense of mission after the death of two of his closest friends in the First World War. More than thirty years later, he had to concede that this attempt to create a body of legend for his country, England (and by extension North West Europe) had more or less foundered. Yet in the mean time, out of it had come a story, *The Lord of the Rings*, that conquered far more than his corner of the world. It soon became a myth for his own century and beyond. In view of this, the question whether it is a myth in the religious sense of the word or rather an artificial myth aware of its own artificiality is of minor importance. The same applies to Wagner's *Ring*.

An obvious parallel is a shared interest in nature and especially their disapproval of its destruction by the corrupting powers of evil. In both the opera cycle and the epic, trees are the exponents of violated nature, and both works bring out the dark sides of unchecked industrial capitalism in their depictions of Nibelheim, respectively Isengard. Tolkien, writing in an age of genetic experiment, adds the infringement of the nature of sentient beings.

Another mirror situation seems to be present in a preference for opposite, in Tolkien's view even opposing, genres: drama versus fairy tale/fantasy. Tolkien built part of his essay on fairy stories on this opposition, considering mythmaking the province of fantasists, or sub-creators, as he called them. He thought that fantasy was best left to words. Claiming that fantastic forms on the stage will always be counterfeit and unable to achieve suspension of disbelief, he rejected human fantasy drama, contrasting it with 'Faërian Drama', in which the spectator is bodily present inside the secondary world. As a typical logocentric he may have succumbed to the illusions of material realism in stage practice. But even if he did not, no visualisation of his work (apart from his own art) would probably ever have met his demands, not even a film or the virtual reality of a present-day computer game.

Wagner considered himself first and foremost a dramatist, but for him drama did not exclude fairy tales and the fantastic. Both had their origin in myth as a product of the innate human capacity to create new images (the latter a perception he shared with Tolkien). He called his operatic works dramas, but several of them and especially the *Ring* transcend the boundaries of Aristotelian drama, containing both lengthy stretches of narrative and fantastic elements meant to be shown, not told. For that reason people have called them epic theatre or musical epics and stressed their cinematic character. Yet a case can be made for their quality as fantasy dramas, especially if the evocative power of his music is taken into consideration – and despite Wagner's own shortcomings when it came to visualising his work on the stage.

His exasperated wish for an invisible stage could be called symptomatic: achieving a perfect performance of *Der Ring des Nibelungen* remains one of the greatest challenges in the world of opera. Wagner's *Gesamtkunstwerk* and Tolkien's Faërian drama may not be very far apart after all.

The respective endings of the *Ring* and *The Lord of the Rings* also appear to be fundamentally opposed. Simply put, the former ends in tragedy, the latter in joy. A closer look, however, shows that this is too simplistic. The ending of the ring epic is pervaded by loss and its author denied it was happy. The world may have been saved, but not for everyone, and the fall of Barad-dûr marks the fading of myth into history. On the other hand, though most of the characters are dead at the end of the Ring cycle and the world of the gods has perished, the chief mechanism of evil is gone and the music holds out a glimmer of hope for mankind. If the endings are in opposition, it is rather because Tolkien restores ancient authority while Wagner sets it afire.

Both had trouble concluding their major work. In Wagner's case this was caused by his shifting world views due to his lecture of various philosophers and his hesitance to leave any of these the final say, in Tolkien's by a reluctance to let the final curtain fall on myth, leaving only a world where mysteries will be replaced by thrillers. Their mournfully joyous and hopefully tragic conclusions had best be categorised as open endings: here, mirror situation and parallel coincide.

Part Three

The Amateur and
the Professional

'We, the readers of ancient texts, need such a vivid imagination to fill the gaps in the old, worn-out manuscripts that it almost becomes an art in itself.'

Arnaldur Indriðason
The King's Book (*Konungsbók*), chapter VII

Chapter 11

Sources and Resources

11.1. Pure and adulterated northernness

As mentioned in Part I, Carpenter reports in his biography how Christopher Wiseman recalled a young Tolkien making jibes at Wagner because he held the composer's interpretation of the ancient Norse myths in contempt. But what sense would it make from an artistic or literary point of view to denounce creative artists for not being true to the spirit of their source texts – unless being true to them was their stated intention?

In Wagner's case, it was not. Whenever he read such old texts – or any texts, for that matter – it was not in order to discover what they might be saying, but to see what he could make them say. He was well aware of his own subjectivity as a reader. In 1857 he wrote to Marie zu Sayn Wittgenstein, the stepdaughter of Franz List, that he seldom read what was in front of him but rather what he projected into it (Von Westernhagen 1966, 11). His objective was inspiration rather than academic soundness. He did not in the first place embrace Norse myth for its Northern qualities or out of a fondness for all things Germanic, but because it was myth, which he believed held universal truths. As he wrote in *Oper und Drama* (II, III): 'The incomparable thing about myth is that it is true at all times.'[1]

If Wagner got things wrong according to Tolkien's standards, of course it does not follow that his work, in this case the *Ring* cycle, is flawed per se. As a creative

---

[1] German: Das Unvergleichliche des Mythos ist, dass er jederzeit wahr (...) ist.' Wagner was discussing the Greek Antigone myth when he wrote this, but there is no reason to believe it does not apply to other myths as well. Spencer (61) berates those who generalise the statement, but he seems to overlook that Achilles, Philoctetes and later Ulysses are mentioned in the same paragraph, which then moves from the specific to the general.
Incidentally, this suggests that Wagner did not intend his *Ring* to be an allegory any more than Tolkien intended *The Lord of the Rings* to be one - despite claims to the contrary by people 'confusing allegory with applicability', as Tolkien put it in the Foreword of his epic.

artist, he was under no obligation to stick closely to his sources. Christopher Tolkien seems to be saying something similar in his introduction to *The Legend of Sigurd and Gudrún* when he writes that

> Wagner's treatment of the Old Norse forms of the legend was less an "interpretation" of the ancient literature than a new and transformative impulse. (...) Thus the libretti of *Der Ring des Nibelungen*, though raised indeed on old foundations, must be seen less as a continuation or development of the long-enduring heroic legend than as a new and independent work of art. (*Legend*, 10)

Shippey interprets this as a polite rephrasing of Tolkien's 'gruff dismissal' of any Wagnerian influences as found in *Letters*: 'Both Rings were round and there the resemblance ceases' (2010, 301). Tolkien was referring to *The Lord of the Rings* and his son to the *Legend*, but the common factor is the rejection of the idea that it was all borrowed from Wagner, thus Shippey. Tolkien thought that most modern rewritings or interpretations of old material, and notably Wagner's, 'led to failures of tone and spirit'. What upset him was that

> Wagner was working, at second hand, from material which he knew at first-hand, primarily the heroic poems of the Elder Edda and the later Middle High German Nibelungenlied. (Shippey 1982, 220)

Returning to the subject years later, Shippey suggested that Wagner seemed 'an enthusiastic amateur', fascinated by the same works as Tolkien, but unable to read the Old Norse ones in the original and follow any scholarly debates about them. It was because the amateur Wagner could and did not show these texts due respect, that Tolkien denied all connections between Wagner's *Ring* and his, despite the fact that he attended performances of it and probably got something out of it as well.

If he did indeed remain at odds with Wagner for philology-related reasons, this would confirm the fundamentally philological nature of his inspiration. It would say as much about him as it does about Wagner, whose 'wrong' treatment of the source texts has probably more to do with what he wanted to achieve than with lack of skill in the field of philology. Tolkien, the professional, was probably as territorial about their 'common ground' as Shippey says he was.

But this may not have been all. Jeff Sypeck, commenting on the publication of *The Legend of Sigurd and Gudrún*, wonders if it was Wagner's radicalism that

Tolkien objected to, or his 'Saruman-like' devastation of the 'archaic forests' of Northern myth. It would be interesting to know why exactly Tolkien wrote the lays in *The Legend of Sigurd and Gudrún*. The more obvious reasons were that he wanted 1) to unify the Edda poems dealing with the tale of the Völsungs (*Legend*, 6), smoothing out or solving contradictions and placing them in the larger framework of Norse mythology; and 2) to show that it was possible to use ancient Norse metres, notably the demanding *fornyrðislag*, in modern English by reviving them for posterity. However, neither of these reasons explain why he wrote these lays when he did, 'in the earlier 1930s' (*Legend*, 5), the estimated period of origin.

One possible explanation has to do with the anti-German feelings resulting from the First World War. Many people in Britain resisted German influences in every area where they perceived them to be present, and one of these areas was close to Tolkien's heart. Five years after the 1918 armistice, he complained that philology was seen as a purely German invention and that some were treating it as though one of the reasons for fighting the war was putting an end to it (Garth, 289). Perhaps the poems were first conceived at that time; perhaps the idea was that the British public had to be made aware of the large non-German areas of philology. Though their inspiration is philological, there is very little German about the *Legend* poems; one might say they are as Norse as anything not written in the Norse Middle Ages can be.

Another explanation could have something to do with his perusal of the *Ring* libretti – assuming he did not only read *Die Walküre* together with the Lewis brothers in March 1934, but the other texts as well. Though 1934 seems on the late side to qualify as 'earlier 1930s', it is not entirely impossible. Perhaps Tolkien had been studying the libretti for some time by then and decided to write something much closer to the originals. If the plan to retell the story of the Nibelungs preceded his lecture of Wagner's texts, he would even have killed two birds with one stone by studying them: preparing himself for the (aborted) attendance of the *Ring* in Covent Garden, and making himself thoroughly acquainted with the workings of the enemy.

That he was familiar with Wagner's version of the story as an adolescent was, in fact, symptomatic. Wagner's recasting of the *Legend* was seductive enough to become the dominant version soon after it appeared, overshadowing the sources within a couple of decades after their rediscovery by the general public. In a letter of 20 November 1851 to Liszt, Wagner claimed that his version combined all the elements of the Siegfried tale spread throughout the Germanic world: 'In the autumn of 1848 I sketched for the first time the *complete myth of the Nibelungen*, such as it henceforth belongs to me as my poetic property.' (italics added)

Due to the composer's huge popularity during the last decades of the 19th century and the first years of the 20th up to the first World War, most people only knew the story through his tetralogy. This situation did not change after the First World War, though this rendered the composer's work less popular outside his own country, nor even after the Second World War, despite the setback due to Nazi misuse:

> It was Wagner's version that conquered the stage and today it is probably the only one that may still appeal to an educated audience outside Iceland and Scandinavia (...) because of his masterly way of combining Icelandic myth with staging and music. (Lönnrot 41)

In the opinion of the Danish philosopher Sørensen, who put the mythical lays of the Edda in a modern, charming new jacket,[2] the comparison between the *Ring* and its sources shows how accurately Wagner condensed Norse myth and saga (Sørensen, 69f). 'Wagner's achievement is to synthesize his sources so seamlessly and cogently that his version seems to be the original one' (O'Donoghue, 137). Cooke wrote that 'it might even be argued that the *Ring* is as valid and coherent a dramatic synthesis of the complex mythology of Northern Europe as we are ever likely to get' (86). A.S. Byatt knowingly introduces Wagnerian elements in her retelling of *ragnarök*, the end of the Gods. In the source texts Odin does not break off a branch of the World Ash to fashion a spear, wounding the tree in the process, nor does he engrave this spear with runes of law and contract. It was Wagner who added these elements; all the same Byatt incorporated them in her rendering of the myth (39 & footnote, 52, 112). In other words, it was not originally there, but it should have been.

---

2 Villy Sørensen, *Ragnarok. En gudefortælling*. Viborg: Centrum, 1982. English version: *The Downfall of the Gods - Ragnarok*. Lincoln: University of Nebraska Press, 1989.

It does not seem too wild a guess that Tolkien would have balked, had he been alive to read all this, especially Cooke's statement. Brilliant musicologist though he may have been, Cooke was perhaps less qualified to say if and to what extent Wagner's version offers a valid synthesis of Northern mythology. The word synthesis is, in fact, not entirely correct, as the composer added important elements of his own. Whatever is the case, though, Wagner did not wreak havoc in the Mirkwood of Northern myth: this 'dark archaic forest' is still there for anyone to visit.

All the same, it could be argued that it deserves more visitors than it gets since World War II, whether or not Wagner shares the blame for this with the Nazis. If nothing else, that the *Ring* obscured the original texts must have been a source of indignation for Tolkien. That many considered it the genuine article can only have been infuriating, like the fact that some who knew the source texts, actually considered it an improvement. A friend of Wagner's, Heinrich von Stein, wrote for instance:

> It is quite simply as though the Ring were an original text which was no longer available to the Edda poets and partial comprehension of which can therefore be traced only here and there in their poems: so much does everything in the drama seem to be restored to its original unity and to be newly created and brought to life.[3] (E. Magee, 125)

Apparently the *Ring* cycle radiated such authenticity that many who made its acquaintance felt they had touched upon true Northern myth. Take the young C.S. Lewis, for instance. In the autobiographical *Surprised by Joy* (1955), he wrote how 'pure northernness engulfed' him upon reading the words *Siegfried* and *Twilight of the Gods* and seeing Rackham's illustrations for Wagner's *Ring* (1910 & 1911) at the age of thirteen. If he ever told Tolkien about this after the two became friends in 1926, one can easily imagine the latter disabusing Lewis of the notion that Wagner's tetralogy represented the true spirit of the North. After which he invited him to join the *Kólbitar* (Coalbiters), an informal group of Oxford scholars who used to gather around a merry hearth fire to discuss Icelandic myth and language. The rest is history.

---

3 German, transl. Elizabeth Magee: 'Es ist [...] einfach und geradezu, als ob der Ring eine den Eddadichtern nicht mehr zugänglich gewesene Urschrift sei, deren teilweises Verständnis man demnach in ihren Liedern nur hie und da verspürte: so sehr scheint im Drama alles zu seiner Ureinheit zurückgeführt und neu geschaffen und belebt.'

It probably did not go like that. However, it does not seem too far-fetched to believe that Tolkien was eager to counter such ideas, in his eyes misplaced, by writing something much closer to the medieval sources. Not necessarily because Wagner's *Ring* was a bad piece of work, but because the public took it for something it was not.

The Icelandic scholar Ólason remarks that, compared to the one in the *Poetic Edda*, Wagner's version of *Ragnarök* was a radical innovation. It would probably have shocked the ancient Icelanders: in the Eddaic lays, the world of the gods and the world of men remain separate. The Edda speaks to us with a number of different voices; its polyphony arises from different kinds of stories belonging to different worlds. In Wagner's *Ring*, several of these stories are welded into a single tale and the polyphony is lost. If Ólason's assessment is correct, 'The New Lay of the Völsungs' would have shocked the ancient Icelanders just as much: this poem, too, is a fusion of mythical and heroic lays.

On the other hand, 'the use 19th century poets, such as Wagner, made of these old stories is not altogether different in nature from how they were used in 13th-century Icelandic works' (Ólason, 46). Both the *Völsunga saga* and the *Thidreks saga*, for instance, are late compilations, based on old, heroic lays, in the case of the *Thidreks saga* lost lays of German origin. Their anonymous authors at times combined story elements in entirely novel ways. As such they can be considered the predecessors of Wagner – and of Tolkien. Incidentally, that Wagner handled the old stories more or less like the author of the *Völsunga saga* did, would not have been a recommendation in the eyes of Tolkien, who had a few bones to pick with this 13th century Icelander (*Legend*, 220-232).

Cooke takes the scholars to task who accuse Wagner of having misrepresented his sources:

> One can sympathise with scholars who have spent their lives studying ancient mythology or medieval poetry, trying to thread their way meticulously through confusions and contradictions in search of the true original meaning, and who then find that Wagner has taken only such elements as served his purpose, and fused them, altered them, even added to them, just as he liked. [...] But they fail to realise that his purpose was entirely different from theirs: he was not trying to dramatize old myths or poems for their own sake, but to interpret through his art such of their meaning as seemed to him still to have relevance for his own time. (83)

Whether or not Tolkien was one of those scholars, might we assume that he believed the only appropriate reaction to a work whose content or influence was not to his liking to be another work of art, another story, like the *Legend*? After all, telling a story was his natural way to get a point across.

Even so, this does not quite answer the question: Why the early thirties? Arvidsson's review of the *Legend* in the Swedish newspaper *Dagens Nyheter* offers a tempting answer. Arvidsson, who also notices that the lays were written 'at a time when Tolkien and his friend C.S. Lewis seem to have had their most intensive Wagner period', sees a connection between the genesis of the lays and the rise of Nazism with its annexation of a misrepresented Norse mythology into a cult of German superiority.

As the *Ring* cycle became an ingredient in this cult due to Hitler's Wagnerolatry, the problem sketched above, that *this* was what true Northern myth was like, would have become acute with Hitler's rise to power. Tolkien may have felt that action was called for. This would not imply that he foresaw the extent of the damage that Hitler – with Wagner as his unwitting executioner – would do to Norse myth, only that he must have had at least an inkling of what was going on in Germany during the 'earlier thirties'. Unfortunately, no Tolkien letters from this period have been published and biographical accounts do not offer relevant information either. Though the scenario remains a distinct possibility, whether Arvidsson is right has to remain conjecture.[4]

Whatever is the case, Tolkien may have overestimated the possibility of changing the picture by means of poetry and story. It was not Wagner's superior storytelling that made his *Ring* the prevailing version of Northern or Germanic mythology for many years to come; the plot has flaws. It was his intensely powerful music and the way in which story, text and music combined into a seamless unity. When Shippey's review of the *Legend* appeared under the headline 'Tolkien out-Wagners Wagner' this, too, failed to take the impact of Wagner's music into account. But it is essential to do so. As John Culshaw wrote:

---

4 Chism also mentions the *Legend* poems in the context of Tolkien's war and postwar repudiations of Wagner's Ring. As they had not yet appeared when she wrote her article, she refrains from speculating about his motives to write them apart from pointing out how intensely dedicated he was to 'these medieval sagas' (76).

> What Wagner did in The Ring was to connect two basic human instincts or responses – the response to music, which is indefinable, and the response to the retelling of a myth, which is something all of us share in common (54).

In the *Ring*, myth and music enhance each other and both are necessary to appreciate the work in full, but the music plays the leading role. It tempts those who love it into believing in the myth more than the myth itself does. The poems of *The Legend of Sigurd and Gudrún* have a music of their own, but this is not of the kind that slays its ten thousands, their formal mastery notwithstanding. Whether they will become a viable alternative to the story of Wagner's *Ring* outside the – admittedly wide – circle of Tolkien devotees, remains to be seen. However, as a means to convey the power of ancient Icelandic storytelling (other than the *Poetic Edda* itself) they are unrivalled. If Tolkien's professionalism out-Wagners Wagner, it is probably here.

But how much of an amateur was Wagner precisely? Which sources did he use, and how did he use them, compared to Tolkien?

11.2. Sigurd versus Siegfried

One source that Wagner and Tolkien possibly had in common is not medieval, though it was set in the Middle Ages and belonged to the 19th-century Romantic revival of that period. This is the novel *Der Zauberring* (The Magic Ring) by the German baron Friedrich de la Motte Fouqué. It was published in 1813, the year of Wagner's birth, and featured valiant knights, fair damsels, sorcerers and of course the magic ring from the title. It was hugely popular in its time and in 1825 Robert Pearse Gillies translated it into English. Amy Sturgis, who restored the translation and wrote a scholarly introduction, argues that as it directly inspired William Morris and George MacDonald, it made *The Lord of the Rings* possible. She calls *The Magic Ring* a missing link in the story of Tolkien's One Ring, which began with the tale of Siegfried from the Eddas and the *Nibelungenlied* and developed through time to Wagner's tetralogy and *The Lord of the Rings*. Her conclusion is that the novel 'is a key part of this narrative chain' (Magic Words).

It is possible that Tolkien knew *The Magic Ring*. On March 10, 1920, he read a paper on 'The Fall of Gondolin' to the Exeter College Essay Club, and according to the minutes this was 'exceedingly illuminating', marking him 'as a staunch follower of tradition, a treatment indeed in the manner of such typical romantics as William Morris, George MacDonald, de la Motte Fouquet[5] etc...' (Scull & Hammond, 110-111)[6]. This suggests some familiarity with Fouqué's work among the club members, Tolkien included. Fouqué's ring grants the owner a certain power over the spirit realm, and this recalls the way the One Ring gives Sauron power over the Ringwraiths. But whether this makes the novel a 'key part' in the chain leading from the medieval sources to Tolkien's ring epic remains a matter of debate.

Wagner must have known *Der Zauberring*; another of Fouqué's novels, *Undine*, was among his favourite books. His uncle, Adolf Wagner, a scholar and translator and the major intellectual influence of his adolescent years, was the author's personal friend. During his school years in Leipzig in the 1820s, young Richard may have come across this and other works by Fouqué in his uncle's personal library, and he was an avid reader. It is difficult, though, to pinpoint a direct influence.

A more traceable influence was Fouqué's dramatic trilogy *Der Held des Nordens* ('The hero of the North'), of which *Sigurd der Schlangentödter* ('Sigurd the Serpent Slayer', 1808) was the first part. This is the first post-medieval retelling in German of the tale of Sigurd as found in the *Völsunga saga* and the *Poetic Edda*, which Fouqué may have read in the original – in 1808 no German translations existed yet. This dramatic trilogy also features the first re-use of Germanic alliterative verse in a post-medieval work of literature, though Fouqué applies it in a limited number of passages. Using evidence from both this drama and *Der Ring des Nibelungen*, Elizabeth Magee has argued that it must have influenced the *Ring*, though Wagner does not list it among his sources and mentions the *Serpent Slayer* about as often as Tolkien mentions Wagner's *Ring*. It is possible that it was not a direct prompt.

---

5 A misspelling by the minutes secretary.
6 Pointed out to me by Jessica Yates, who also provided me with a copy of the minutes.

Nor was the *Nibelungenlied*, despite popular belief. In 1844, Theodor Vischer, an art philosopher, published a detailed concept for an opera based on this work. The poet and early feminist Louise Otto Peters tried to interest composers in this project by publishing parts of a Nibelungen libretto by her hand in the August - December 1845 issue of the *Neue Zeitschrift für Musik*. Robert Schumann, the magazine's founder and editor in chief, took the project into consideration but due to health problems never got round to writing anything. Others, among them the Danish composer Niels Gade, wrote (fragments of) a Nibelungen opera, but these works, if they were finished at all, are forgotten today. Wagner... declined. It was not until he discovered the ancient Icelandic texts that he was sold on the idea. As he wrote in 1851 in 'A Communication to my Friends':

> Although the splendid type of *Siegfried* had long attracted me, it first enthralled my every thought when I had come to see it in its purest human shape, set free from every later wrappage. Now for the first time, also, did I recognise the possibility of making him the hero of a drama; a possibility that had not occurred to me while I only knew him from the medieval *Nibelungenlied*. ('Eine Mittheilung an meine Freunde', *Gesammelte Schriften und Dichtungen. Band IV,* 312)[7]

So to him the Norse Sigurd conveyed a sense of authenticity that the German Siegfried lacked. Also, Wagner apparently considered the German tradition too superficial for operatic purposes; as an old man, Gade remembered him remarking during a conversation they had in 1846: 'I must study these Old Norse Eddaic poems of yours; they are far more profound than our medieval poems' (Björnsson, 99). Moreover, one might venture to guess that the presence of gods and other non-human creatures in the Icelandic poems and sagas opened possibilities which the German epic failed to offer him. It was above all myth he was looking for, and the *Nibelungenlied* is not mythical. And finally it could perhaps be said that Wagner had a fine enough nose to catch a whiff of the true Northern spirit when he came across it – even though he failed to acknowledge it as such and claimed it to be *urdeutsch* (*ur* meaning 'original',

---

7 German: 'Hatte mich nun schon längst die herrliche Gestalt des Sigfried angezogen, so entzückte sie mich doch vollends erst, als es mir gelungen war, sie von aller späteren Umkleidung befreit, in ihrer reinsten menschlichen Erscheinung vor mir zu sehen. Erst jetzt erkannte ich die Möglichkeit, ihn zum Helden eines Dramas zu machen, was mir nie eingefallen war, solange ich ihn nur aus dem mittelalterlichen Nibelungenlied kannte.' Transl. William Ashton Ellis. Wagner never even read Otto's texts; he always wrote his libretti himself.

but also 'very'). This does not mean that he only drew from Norse tradition – though this material takes up more than 80 percent of the work – merely that it was his chief impulse for writing *Der Ring des Nibelungen*.

Ironically, Wagner was wrong to take the Sigurd tradition of the Icelandic poems and sagas for a 'non-wrapped' version, older than the Middle High German epic and closer to the ancient Germanic origins. As Tolkien put it in his introduction to the *Elder Edda*: 'Let none who listen to the poets of the Elder Edda go away imagining that he has listened to voices of the Primitive Germanic forest' (*Legend*, 18).[8] Both traditions of the Siegfried story probably grew out of a couple of tales, now lost, which were based on a set of events that took place during the Dark Ages on the banks of the river Rhine. At some point this story was uprooted, to use Tolkien's term, and brought to Scandinavia, where it acquired specifically Northern characteristics and developed into a number of contradictory versions which all differ from their Southern counterpart.

This work, the *Nibelungenlied*, was in all likelihood written not long after the year 1200 by an anonymous author in the duchy of Austria. It is a heroic verse epic in a feudal, courtly and Christian setting. No traces have been found of a pre-existing oral tradition, but scholars assume there must have been one. Such traces do exist for the Northern tradition. The Icelandic texts were written between approximately 1220 (the *Prose Edda*, authored by Snorri Sturluson) and the late 13th century (the anonymous *Völsunga saga*). The authors of these texts were Christians, but the setting is neither Christian nor courtly. In one respect Wagner may have been right: they preserve more of the pagan character of the original tales than the *Nibelungenlied* does, though the debate to what degree they are Christian and what it was their authors wanted to achieve still goes on today.

As the philologists of Wagner's days often were not aware of these things yet, he is not to be blamed for being mistaken. He was well-read; it would not be exaggerated to say he knew as much as was possible to know – for a non-philologist, that is – about the Old Norse originals. But what had he read?

---

8 This 'Introduction' was written during the 1920s; since then, the term *Elder Edda* was abandoned by scholars. It is misleading, as its lays were written down after the 'Younger Edda'. Nowadays it usually goes by the name of *Poetic Edda*, while the Younger one is called the *Prose Edda* or *Snorra Edda*.

When someone asked him this question after the publication of the *Ring* libretti, Wagner responded by drawing up a list of ten texts whose study had made him familiar with his subject. This list contains both primary and secondary sources (*Dokumente,* 19). Most of the secondary ones are of no direct concern to the purpose of this book, though Jacob Grimm's *Deutsche Mythologie* deserves to be mentioned here. The same goes for the Middle-High German source texts.

Of the ten entries on Wagner's list, only four were translations of Norse originals, but they cover a great deal of material. They were, in this order: *Edda, Völsunga saga, Wilkina and Niflungasaga* and *Heimskringla. Wilkina and Niflunga saga* are other names for what is better known as the *Thidreks saga.* By *Edda,* Wagner meant both Eddas. Of the *Prose Edda* he had two translations in his personal library in Dresden, where he lived during the time he studied the *Ring* material and where he wrote part of the text. One of them lacked the sections dealing with the Nibelungs (!), though it contained seven mythological poems from the *Poetic Edda.* Wagner also owned a translation of the *Völuspá* by Ludwig Ettmüller (or Eddamüller, as his friends called him), a philologist Wagner met during his exile in Zürich after he had to flee from Dresden. There he acquired Ettmüller's complete Edda translation (1837), which he had previously borrowed (E. Magee, 44). In Zürich he also read Simrock's translation, the first complete and metrical rendering of the *Poetic Edda* into German and still the most well-known, shortly after it appeared in 1851.

Ettmüller's '*Vaulu-spá*' (1830) was a bilingual edition, with an introduction, notes, appendices and a glossary. It was preserved along with the major part of Wagner's personal library, and the sections containing the original text and the glossary are both well thumbed, indicating that he made serious attempts to understand the Old Norse. Maybe it leaped 'across the barrier of the difficult language, and gripped [him] in the very act of deciphering line by line' (*Legend,* 18) – it is too tempting not to quote Tolkien here.

Wagner also owned the heroic lays of the *Poetic Edda* in the prose translation of the Grimm Brothers, though this edition lacks some of the lays he used for his *Ring.* He did have a complete original-language edition of the *Poetic Edda,* Von der Hagen's *Lieder der älteren oder Sämundischen Edda* (Songs of the Elder or Sæmund's Edda, 1812). This seems to indicate that he knew at least a modicum of Norse. How much he knew is difficult to say. Spencer thinks he was unable to read the originals (59), while Elizabeth Magee suggests Wagner merely 'sampled the poems in Von der Hagen's Old Norse edition for the flavour of their original language' (30). Von Westernhagen, on the other hand, thinks that he could read them (1966, 36).

That he knew no Old Norse at all seems too conservative a view of Wagner's linguistic abilities. He knew his languages: he was fluent in French, familiar with Latin, Greek, English and Italian, and he also read Middle High German.[9] The library at Wahnfried, his residence in Bayreuth, contained Ettmüller's *Altnordisches Lesebuch* of 1861, with original Icelandic texts, and Wimmer's *Altnordische Grammatik* of 1871. He probably went on studying the language even after having completed the text of the *Ring*, quoting and reciting the Edda to his friends long after the libretti were finished, as Cosima's diaries attest. His philological awareness enabled him to make the connection between *Deutsch* (German, derived from a word meaning 'people' or 'folk') and *deuten* – ('to interpret for the people'), though he mistakenly believed the latter was the primary word, instead of the former. He was familiar with Grimm's Law, which describes the shift of Indo-European voiced and voiceless stops into Proto-Germanic voiceless stops and fricatives (for instance Latin *decem* -> English ten; Latin *tertius* -> English third, etc., etc.). And one of his alleged mistakes was not really a mistake. When he found out that *ragnarök* meant 'end' or 'judgement', not 'twilight' of the Gods, which is *ragnarökr*, he even considered changing the title of his fourth *Ring* opera (C. Wagner, 122) but in the end he decided against it.

Regardless of how well Wagner was able to understand the original texts, one thing should be clear: his lecture of them thoroughly changed his way of writing. Nothing in his previous opera libretti foreshadows the linguistic opulence of the *Ring* texts, which abound with puns, neologisms and etymological derivations, not to mention the alliterations. This could well be the result of his study of

---

9 He knew, for instance, that Middle High German *cappa* (a loan from Latin) meant 'cloak' and had not yet acquired the meaning of 'cap', as it had in his time. For that reason he changed the *Tarnkappe* from the Nibelungelied into a *Tarnhelm*: a helm was much easier to handle on the stage (see Cooke, 204). Also in the Norse sources, Sigurd found a helmet among the dragon's treasures, the *ægishjalmr*.

the Edda 'and the cultural and linguistic substratum that he uncovered there, both in the poems themselves and in the secondary sources' (Hauer, 55).

All but one of Wagner's Icelandic sources mentioned on the 1856 list were also used by Tolkien for *The Legend of Sigurd and Gudrún*, while elements from them also found their way into his Middle-earth writings. The sole exception is the *Heimskringla*, a collection of tales about the kings of Norway from legendary times up till 1177; the part Wagner used for his *Ring* is the *Hákonarmál*, in which Valkyries play a role. Christopher Tolkien summarizes this work in his commentary to Part V of 'The New Lay of the Völsungs' (*Legend*, 215), but only to illustrate the role of Valkyries in Norse tradition, not because his father used it.

For our present purpose there is no need to go into much detail concerning Tolkien's precise source texts. Suffice it to say that he read them in the original, lectured about them at Oxford University and must have owned original language editions of each of his sources as well as translations. He also possessed a vast amount of philological knowledge that Wagner lacked, not merely because he was a professional, but also because in Tolkien's day the study of philology had developed considerably since Jakob Grimm and his colleagues and rivals – Wagner's authorities – had begun to cultivate the field.

Now how did the amateur Wagner treat his source material, compared to Tolkien the professional? Do the two have things in common?

Chapter 12

Language

12.1. Words, grammar and syntax

12.1.1. Tolkien's archaisms

A philologist is literally a lover of words, but to say that Tolkien loved words would be an understatement: he was passionate about them, both as a scholar and as a writer of fiction.[10] Phonaestetical considerations played a large role in this passion, especially with regard to his invented languages. So did historical linguistics, the study of the older stages of languages and their literature, his own included. No wonder that as an author, Tolkien was famous or, as not a few would say, notorious, for his archaic language. The oldest version of 'The Fall of Gondolin' (1916/17), the first tale set in what would become his world of Arda, is rife with old-fashioned words, obsolete grammatical forms and archaic syntax.

Take, for instance, these words of the young Eärendil during the flight from the city: 'Mother Idril, thou art weary, and warriors in mail ride not among the Gondothlim, save it be old Salgant!' (*The Book of Lost Tales II*, 190). In 'The Music of the Ainur', dating from the same period, Rúmil of Tirion says things like: '... the Eldar dwell till the Great End unless they be slain or waste in grief [...], nor doth eld subdue their strength, except it may be in ten thousand centuries; and dying they are reborn in their children, so that their number minishes not, nor grows' (*The Book of Lost Tales I*, 59). In 'The Coming of the Elves' Manwë says things like: 'Tell us how ye came; how ye found the world; what seemeth it to you who are its first offspring, or with what desires doth it fill you' (*The Book of Lost Tales I*, 116). This was the kind of language Tolkien loved: in 1966, he told Dick Plotz of the Tolkien Society of America in an

---

10 The interplay between the scholar and the author is explored in depth in Gilliver, etc.

interview that he considered the quasi-biblical language he had used in the earlier stages of his legendarium his best, but that his publishers did not agree (Scull & Hammond, 679). Later he modernised his grammar somewhat, but retained much of the old-fashioned vocabulary.

The *Legend*, written about fifteen years after the first texts of the legendarium, is also rather archaic in style. Here, Tolkien deploys words like *wanhope*, *rede*, *sheer* (in the sense of clear), *dreed*, *boot* (in the sense of remedy), *conner* and *dight*, and verb forms like *dost*, *spake*, *clove* and *bounden*. His tendency to prefer originally Germanic words to (mainly Romance) loan words is already visible in these early poems, despite his attachment, quite pronounced in the *Legend*, to the word *glory* (from Latin *gloria*).

An example of archaic syntax is 'of gold he dreamed him'. For the most archaic words and phrases, Christopher Tolkien provided a gloss. This is the more remarkable as his father wrote in his 'Prefatory remarks on prose translation of "Beowulf"' (1940) that

> words should not be used merely because they are "old" or obsolete. The words chosen, however remote they may be from colloquial speech or ephemeral suggestions, must be words which remain in literary use [...] among educated people. [...] They must need no gloss. (*The Monsters and the Critics and Other Essays*, 55)[11]

Would a literary audience in the 1930s have needed the glosses that were thought necessary eighty years later, one wonders?

The language of the children's book *The Hobbit* is hardly archaising but *The Lord of the Rings* shows a partial return to his earlier style. Some of the archaic syntax and many of the obsolete forms are missing, but the text still contains phrases like 'And on a time evil things came forth, and they took Minas Ithil and abode in it, and they made it into a place of dread,' or 'I was not sent to beg any boon' (*The Fellowship of the Ring*, II, II). Words like *ere*, *nigh*, *wrought*, *wroth*, *save* (in the sense of except), *but* (in the sense of only), *heed*, *deem*, *fey* and *sire* (in the sense of father), and many other old-fashioned words still figure frequently, as do phrases like 'they knew it not' or 'what say you?'. The language

---

[11] Tolkien goes on to denounce William Morris's use of the word 'leeds', from Old English 'leode', for 'people'.

Isildur uses in the ancient scroll Gandalf found in Minas Tirith is even more archaic, but as this scroll dates from more than three millennia before the events of *The Lord of the Rings*, the difference is relatively small – much smaller than, say, the difference between Classical Latin and present-day Italian.[12] Middle-earth is a conservative world.

A phenomenon occurring frequently in Tolkien's texts is inverted word order: 'In a ravine she lived', we read of Ungoliant in *The Silmarillion*, and 'Fair shall the end be!' cries Fëanor before he swears his oath. 'Great was the triumph of Morgoth' and 'Unhappy was the lot of Húrin'; the examples are too numerous to count. In the *Legend*, inverted word order is even more frequent. 'Long lay the shadow'; 'Their words he heard'; 'High stands a hall on Hindarfell', 'Steep stands the path'; 'A maid have I seen'; 'Green run the roads to Gjúki's land' are all examples taken from three successive stanzas on a single page (116). But then, this is poetry in which not only the metre determines the word order, but also the dramatic tension the poet wants to create and the stress he wants to put on certain words. The prosody demands inversion.

In his ring epic, Tolkien uses inversion much more sparingly, and almost exclusively in the dialogues, though Isildur's scroll also contains a few examples. 'Only to the North these tidings came', and 'This I will have as weregild', Elrond (quoting Isildur) says in the 'Council of Elrond' chapter in *The Fellowship of the Ring*. In the chapter 'Minas Tirith' in *The Return of the King*, Denethor's first words are: 'Dark indeed is the hour.'

Typically Tolkienian is the modernisation of an Old English term like *dweomerlace* (Layamon) or *demo/erlayke* (several medieval poems) into 'dwimmerlaik', used by Éowyn against the Nazgûl King. No 'gloss' is given in the text, suggesting that an equivalent in the Common Speech did not exist. However, by discussing the Old English occurrences of its components, Shippey arrives at a possible interpretation: dwimmerlaik is a combination of 'creature of sorcery' and 'sport of nightmare'. This is not a meaning at which the average reader will arrive without help, but Tolkien hands out 'crutches' in the form of re-

---

12 The original language of the scroll was either Sindarin or Quenya; possibly Gandalf provided an archaising translation into the Common Speech to give an impression of age. Or else it was the translator of the Red Book of Westmarch into English, Tolkien, who did so. We can only speculate here.

lated words, such as Dwimordene, the Rohirric name of Lothlórien, (wrongly) associated with deceit, and Dwimorberg, the mountain into which Aragorn ventures to call the ghosts of the Oathbreakers to his aid (Shippey 2007, 169ff). The reader, having seen the Nazgûl King before, knows that Éowyn is dealing with someone turned into a ghost by the deceits of the Enemy, and the right associations will establish themselves. Or so Tolkien hoped.

12.1.2. Attack and defence

Being intimately familiar with the older stages of the English language and able to write poetry in Old English, Tolkien knew exactly what he was doing when he used each of these words, forms and phrases. They help to create historical depth as much as references to past events do; Tolkien believed that people could 'feel history in words' (Shippey 1982, 87). However, the amount of criticism directed at his archaising style over the years shows that it does not work like that for every reader. As one critic put it when the last instalment of *The Lord of the Rings* appeared: 'Far too often Mr Tolkien strides away into a kind of Brewers Biblical, enwreathed with inversions, encrusted with archaisms' (Carpenter, 225).[13] In 1977, after the publication of *The Silmarillion*, a reviewer spoke of 'excessive archaisms, quasi-Biblical echoes, and assorted inverted eftsooneries' (Adams). More recently, a similar criticism was aimed at *The Children of Húrin*: 'The inverted word order, the strange names, even the cadence of the sentences, all seem pompous and overblown' (Kilian).

It seems best to let Tolkien come to his own defence here. When Hugh Brogan wrote him a letter criticising the archaic style of parts of *The Two Towers*, he reacted by pointing out that people often confuse 'bogus medieval stuff' with real archaic English. Many of the things he had said could not be said 'in our slack and often frivolous idiom'. He illustrated this using a sample from the chapter 'The King of the Golden Hall', the one Brogan was most critical of, calling it terrible. When King Théoden says: 'Nay, Gandalf! [...] You do not know your own skill in healing. It shall not be so. I myself will go to war, to fall in the front of the battle, if it must be. Thus shall I sleep better,' this is merely

---

13 Other critics include Edmund Wilson, Philip Toynbee, and Harold Bloom, who called Tolkien's style worse than that of the *Book of Mormon* (Bloom, Introduction).

moderated or watered archaism, as he points out. In really archaic mode the King's first sentence would have run: 'Nay, thou (n')wost not thine own skill in healing.'

The modern version would have been something like: 'Not at all, my dear G. You don't know your own skill as a doctor. Things aren't going to be like that. I shall go to the war in person, even if I have to be one of the first casualties' – 'And then what?' Tolkien asks.

> Theoden would certainly think, and probably say "thus shall I sleep better"! But people who think like that just don't talk a modern idiom. You can have 'I shall lie easer in my grave', or 'I should sleep sounder in my grave like that rather than if I stayed at home' - if you like. But there would be an insincerity of thought, a disunion of word and meaning. For a King who spoke in a modern style would not really think in such terms at all, and any reference to sleeping quietly in the grave would be a deliberate archaism of expression on his part (however worded) far more bogus than the actual "archaic" English that I have used. Like some non-Christian making a reference to some Christian belief which did not in fact move him at all. (*Letters*, 225)

Nobody could have explained it better, though if people prefer a defence by someone other than the Professor himself they could try Ursula LeGuin's article on the speech of Elfland. LeGuin even foresees the argument that could be brought up against Tolkien's reasoning: that the language of the past was perfectly contemporary and prosaic for its speakers: 'Did the real Achilles speak in hexameters? Would the real Beowulf please stand up and alliterate?' Her own reply: 'We are not discussing history, but heroic fantasy. We are discussing a modern descendant of the epic' (LeGuin, 206).

Brian Rosebury rightly berates critics who complain about Tolkien's archaic style, showing that it is absent from large chunks of *The Lord of the Rings* and giving examples of the opposite: Barliman Butterbur does not wear an apron, he has it on, and the hobbits do not dismount, but get off their ponies. The diction and syntax of the book are 'predominantly non-archaic' (Rosebury, 41f and 147). Rosebury is probably right, but this may be precisely the reason that the archaic parts draw so much attention. Then the posthumous publication of Tolkien's earlier works, written in a much more old-fashioned style, clinched the matter: in Tolkien's writing style, archaisms abound.

A critic like Brian Attebery shows some awareness of what style Tolkien emulated in his more elevated texts but nevertheless does not quite seem to get it. In his review of *The Children of Húrin* he writes:

> Tolkien's style – indeed, his entire approach – was derived from English narrative poems such as Beowulf and Gawain and the Green Knight, from the Norse sagas and, especially in the case of this latest book, from Wagner. [...] This is Tolkien in Wagnerian mode. Indeed, it may be possible to say that this is *echt* Tolkien.

While it is true that the *Völsunga saga* inspired *The Children of Húrin*, Tolkien did not need Wagner in order to write in the style of the sagas, as he knew them more intimately than the composer did. It would have been impossible anyway, as Wagner's *Ring* is not written in saga style at all, but in a verse form derived from the *Poetic Edda*.

12.1.3. Wagner's archaisms

That Wagner wrote a four-part drama entirely in alliterative verse, unprecedented in mid-19th-century Germany as well as elsewhere, earned him an amount of criticism, not to mention ridicule, that easily outweighs anything heaped on Tolkien. The same goes for his archaic language. In his essay *Am Mythenstein* (1861) Wagner's Swiss contemporary, the author Gottfried Keller, dismissed Wagner's pretention that he was creating the Artwork of the Future. He called the language of the *Ring* 'archaistisches Getändel' (archaistic dilly-dallying), not even suited for the spirit of the present, let alone for that of the future.

Another critic who wrote unfavourably about the archaisms in the *Ring* was none other than Arthur Schopenhauer. Wagner greatly admired the philosopher, whom he considered a kindred spirit, and in 1854 sent him the libretti of his *Ring*, with a dedication. Schopenhauer, a great stylist, was not amused by what he found and scribbled his scathing comments in the margin. Though he had other quarrels with Wagner's style, the artificially archaic vocabulary bore the brunt of his displeasure.[14] The word *freislich*, for instance, in 'freislichen Felsen' (fearsome rock – *Die Walküre*, III, 3) was among those that drew the attention

---

14 Schopenhauer's ultimate verdict, 'He has no ears. A deaf musician!' never reached Wagner in this form; it was reinterpreted in the sense that Schopenhauer had said 'I admire Wagner as a poet, but he is no musician.'

of the philosopher's red pencil, and he was not the only one to denounce it. This purely Middle High German word fell out of use during the 16th century; 19th-century translators of the *Nibelungenlied* (where it is spelled *vreislich*) and other medieval texts tended to avoid it (Schuler, 54f). Wagner did not need the word for alliterative purposes here, as he could easily have used *furchtbar*, one of its modern equivalents. Obviously, he loved it. The vocabulary of his *Ring* tetralogy shows that he was as fond of archaisms as Tolkien was and that he, too, preferred Germanic words to loan words – which poses fewer problems in German than it does in English. But he did not try to restrict himself to words that an educated audience would understand without help.

A list - by no means exhaustive - includes *Friedel* (lover), *Wal* (the bodies of slain warriors), *Mage* (kinsman/-woman), *Minne* (love), *Mut* (mind, heart, or mood ; Wagner rarely uses the word in the modern sense of courage), *feig* (in the MHG sense of 'fey', not cowardly) *Misswende* (turn for the worse), *wabern* (to make a swaying movement, hence, to flicker), *tapfer* (in the old sense of strong), *empfah(e)n* (to receive, mod. G. 'empfangen'), *mordlich* (murderous), *queck* (alive), *kiesen* (to choose) and *Harst* (fray).[15] In some instances Wagner removed affixes belonging to later stages of German linguistic development, using *schlingen* instead of *verschlingen* (to devour), or *gehren* instead of *begehren* (to desire). Wagner probably found the latter in Ettmüller's Edda translation.[16] *Unkündig* (unknowing) became *unkund* (the umlaut on the former was caused by the /i/), a return to MHG *unkunt*, meaning both unknowing and unknown. In a few cases. Wagner actually managed to reintroduce previously archaic words into the German language, such as *Hort* (hoard), *Recke* (warrior), *Harm* (grief, or vexation) and *Lohe* (blaze) (Panagl, 84-86).

The word *wabern* probably came from *Die Deutsche Heldensage* (The German Heroic Legend, 1829) by Jacob Grimm. Interestingly, its Old English cognate, *waefre*, occurs in the name of Ottor Waefre in *The Book of Lost Tales I*. Here,

---

15 According to one anecdote, singers sometimes demanded that the text be translated into German before they were prepared to study their parts.
16 In one of the examples given above, Tolkien seems to do the same when he writes *minish* instead of *diminish*, but this is a different case. *Minish* is derived from ME *minushen*, a loan from Old French *menuisier*, from Latin *minuere*, while *diminish* is a 15th-century merger of this verb with another ME loan from Old French, *diminue(n)*, meaning approximately the same. Tolkien simply chose the verb that suited him best.

Ottor is the seafaring father of Hengest and Horsa. In modern English this verb became 'to waver', and 'wavering fire' is how Tolkien translates the Old Norse *vafrlogi*, the wall of flames surrounding the sleeping Valkyrie on the mountain, in the *Legend*. In German the word *Waberlohe* was especially coined to translate *vafrlogi*: Ettmüller, Wagner and Simrock all use it (Schuler, 57). Wagner was usually quite aware of what he was doing. His use of the verb *sprengen* in the sentence '*sonst spreng ich dich fort*' (or I'll make you run), for instance, is in accordance with the fact that *sprengen* is the causative of *springen* (to leap, run), like *legen* (to lay) is the causative of *liegen* (to lie).

Wagner further used the Germanic suffix -ing to denote descent: Wölfing, Neidinge, Irming,[17] just like Tolkien did when he coined 'tribal' names like Beornings, Bardings and Eorlingas (O.E. plural of Eorling). Wagner also used the suffix -ung: the *Ring* has Wälsung, where the *Legend* has its Norse cognate, *Völsung*. This possibly betrays the non-philologist. Wälsung is used as a patronym: Siegmund is the son of Wälse (Wotan). But the German cognate would be Wälsing; Wagner adapted this to increase the resemblance with Völsung. In a footnote to his study *Finn and Hengest* Tolkien maintains that the occurrence of Völsung as the main name of an individual shows that the suffix *-ung* was 'originally not genuinely patronymic' (41, n. 18).[18] He may be right, though according to some there was such a deity as Völsi in Norse mythology (symbolised by a horse phallus), who possibly represented the fertility aspect of Odin – which could explain why the Völsungs are said to be descended from him (*Saga of the Völsungs*, 9).

The text of Wagner's *Ring* also contains obsolete grammatical forms, though he does not use them as often as Tolkien does. Examples: *brann* (burned) for *brannte*, *frug* for *fragte* (asked), *pflag* for *pflegte* (used to), *Mannen* for *Männer* (men). Archaic syntax, on the other hand, occurs often: the text contains numerous old genitive and dative constructions where modern German has a preposition: '*des Ringes* waltet, wer ihn gewinnt' (whoever wins the Ring, has

---

17 Wittig the Irming from *Die Walküre*, III,1 was taken from the late medieval German Dietrich epics, where Witege was a vassal of king Ermanarich, Norse Iormunrek – to whom Tolkien refers in the second lay of his *Legend* (281). The Old English cognate of this name is Widia - and a Widia is the grandson of Wade of the Helsings from the poem 'Widsith', mentioned by Tolkien in *The Lays of Beleriand*. Plenty of connections here…

18 The O.E. cognate of Völsung is Wælsing (= Sigemund), and *Beowulf* gives his father's name as Wæls.

power over it), 'wehre *dem Kuß* [...] nicht' (do not resist the kiss), or 'willst du *mir* fliehn?' (would you flee from me?), and many more.

Wagner was also fond of inversions, like *'Der Welt Erbe gewänne zu Eigen, wer aus dem Rheingold schüfe der Ring, der masslose Macht ihm verlieh.'* (Literally: The world's heritage would win for his own who would create from the Rhinegold the ring that boundless power would give him.) In *Die Walküre* I, 1 Siegmund tells Sieglinde about his misadventures by telling her: *'Vermählen wollte der Magen Sippe dem Mann ohne Minne die Maid'*. (Literally: To wed wanted the kinsmen's tribe to the man without love the maid – note that the sentence begins with the verb which in normal German syntax would come at the end!) Later in this act, when Sieglinde asks her guest if his name is really *Wehwalt* (Woe-warden), he replies: *'Nicht heiss ich so, seit du mich liebst.'* (Not is that my name, since you love me). She asks on: *'Und Friedmund darfst du froh dich nicht nennen?'* (And 'Peace-guard' may you not happily call yourself?) In such cases stress, the build-up of dramatic tension and the structure of the music, already present in Wagner's head when he wrote the text, determine the wording. Generally, it can be said that Wagner's archaisms are not there for their own sake, but to serve the fullness and conciseness of the linguistic expression; *Klangmalerei* (sound-painting) serving as a kind of verbal instrumentation (Westernhagen 1973, 22). This could be considered a parallel to the prosody-determined inversions in Tolkien's texts.

12.1.4. Wordplay

Both Tolkien and Wagner loved to play with words. In Tolkien's works, the wordplay often has a philological character. Old English *máðm*, for instance, 'precious object' or 'treasure', found its way into the Shire as 'mathom': a thing for which the hobbits had no direct use, but which they did not want to throw away. The Old English word for murder, *morðor*, became the name of Sauron's evil realm (in Tolkien's Elvish language Sindarin Mordor means 'dark land', but that does not cancel the allusion). The name of the fattest Dwarf in *The Hobbit* is Bombur, and *bömburr* literally means Fatbelly in Old Norse – a very apt name. But Old Norse *bumba*[19] means 'drum', and a drum is the instrument Bombur plays in the Dwarven orchestra!

From the name of the drowned continent of Atlantis Tolkien coined the Quenya verb form *atalantë*, meaning 'downfallen': in his secondary world the island-continent Atalantë (or Númenor) underwent the same fate as Atlantis did in the primary world. In 'The Notion Club Papers' he introduced a character named J.J. Rashbold, a translation of German *tollkühn*, the name that became Tolkien after the bearer emigrated to England in the 18th century. Other puns are more complicated, like the one on the name of the Brandywine river, which is the English translation of a pun on an Elvish name in the original language of the hobbits!

Not all his puns were philological: in the Tom Bombadil chapter in *The Lord of the Rings* Goldberry speaks of the 'ring' in Frodo's voice, and two characters in the children's book *Mr. Bliss* are named 'Day and Knight'. The 'Crack of Doom' in which Frodo has to cast the One Ring has changed from a moment in time – the announcement of the Last Judgement – into a place name. When Frodo gives his name in Bree as 'Underhill', this is a reference to his dwelling place under the Hill in the Shire. And not everything that looks like a pun is one: Tolkien points out that the similarity of Elder – as in Elder Kindred, the Elven folk – to Eldar is accidental (Guide, 212).

Wagner also loved to play with words. Brünnhilde's announcement in *Die Walküre* II for instance, 'zur Wal kor ich ihn mir' (I chose him to be among the slain) plays on the meaning of Valkyrie, Old Norse *Valkyrja*, 'choser of the slain'. He was especially fond of name games. Some of these, like Wotan – *wüten* (to rage: Wotan *wütet*, rages, against the Wälsungs),[20] were etymologically sound, others, like Gutrune – *Gute Runen* (good runes), were based on popular etymology: the real meaning of the name is 'secret lore of the gods'; the *–gud* in the Norse name Gudrún has nothing to do with the Germanic word for 'good'. It

---

19 Probably a loan from Latin *bombus* (from Greek βόμβος) an onomatopoeia meaning 'booming sound' – hence 'bomb'.
20 He may have changed the name of the god to bring out the etymology more clearly. Initially, he had called him Wodan, the North-German form of the name; the South-German name was Wuotan, with the High German soundshift d > t. Wagner settled for Wotan, a pan-German compromise between the two. This version of the name stuck.

is possible that Wagner knew this but could not care less, but it is not a pun Tolkien, being well aware of the real meaning of the name, would have made.

Another example of wordplay is found toward the end of *Das Rheingold*, when the Rhinemaidens are heard lamenting the loss of the gold. On hearing them, Wotan asks: '*Welch Klagen klingt zu mir her?*' (What complaint do I hear?) To which Loge replies: '*Des Rheines Töchter beklagen des Goldes Raub*' (The Rhinedaughters lament the robbery of the gold), calling the crime by its proper name. At that moment, *Klagen* takes on its second meaning of indictment, complaint in the legal sense: while asking his question, Wotan knows quite well he is guilty of trespassing against his own laws by not returning the Ring to the river Rhine.

To remain with Wotan, his spear, which guarantees the continuous existence of the world, is called the *Haft der Welt*. This is a poetic metaphor of the kind called *kenning*, which occurs in Old Norse and Old English poetry, a circumlocution using a figurative compound instead of a simple noun (more about this below). The German word *Haft* has more than one meaning, and the phrase *Haft der Welt* can mean 'custodian of the world' but also 'bondage of the world'. Wotan's spear enforces the law: it guards the world like a prison guard. If Wagner did study the *Prose Edda* in the original, his use of the word *Haft* is probably an allusion to its Old Norse cognate, *haft* or *hapt*. This means 'bond', for instance to tether horses or restrain prisoners, but it is also used in a *kenning* for 'god'. The *Prose Edda* (*Skáldskaparmál*, 'Poetic Diction') mentions the term *hafta-guð* as a kenning for Odin: the god is the tie that binds the world together. In *Die Walküre* II, 1 Fricka reproaches Wotan for loosening '*des Himmels Haft*' (heaven's hold) if he allows Siegmund and Sieglinde to get away with their incest and adultery. In Norse myth it is a positive thing that the world remains bound together: once it falls apart this means *ragnarök*, the doom of the Gods. In the *Ring*, the breaking of Wotan's *Haft der Welt* precedes the necessary end of the old world.

Götterdämmerung I, 3 contains a very significant pun: Striding through the flames to claim Brünnhilde as a bride for Günther, Siegfried tells her that 'ein Freier kam', meaning both 'a suitor came' – he has transformed into Günther using the Tarnhelm – and 'a free man came'. The latter is highly ironical.

Siegfried is supposed to be a free hero, but Hagen has ensnared him by giving him a draught of forgetfulness: instead of being free, the hero has become someone else's tool. 'Freien' (to woo, related to English 'friend') and 'frei' (free) are etymologically related, but the pun works well enough without it.

Calling Wagner a 'born philologist' (*Richard Wagner Handbuch*, 189), is perhaps exaggerated, but for an amateur, he had a great deal of linguistic sensitivity. Panagl gives another good example of what he could achieve when well-informed. In the mystical texts of Middle Age Germany, the verb *entzücken*, (to snatch away), an intensifier of *entziehen* (to take away from), acquired the figurative meaning 'to enrapture'. At the end of *Götterdämmerung* II, 5 Brünnhilde realises why Siegfried has turned away from her: '*Gutrune heißt der Zauber, der den Gatten mir entzückt*'. This is impossible to translate, as the original meaning coincides with the modern one of becoming enraptured, and both meanings apply simultaneously. In translation the sentence might run: 'Gutrune is the name of the sorcery that spirited (or magicked) my husband away', but this hardly does justice to the original.

12.1.5. Philological jests

If Tolkien read the entire *Ring* text, but even if his foray into it together with the Lewis brothers was limited to *Die Walküre*, he may have noticed how Wagner handled language. If he attended to the entire tetralogy, but even if he attended only to *Siegfried*,

> he must have taken some interest in Wagner's unique and unusual approach to German grammar and syntax, one aimed at getting to the emotional centre of each word and tying it so intimately to the music that one became indivisible from the other. (Martin, 130)

This must remain conjecture, but the kind of linguistic play described above was right up his street. His works contain numerous examples of what Tolkien himself called 'low philological jests' (see Shippey 1982/1992). For instance:

1) The name of the dragon Smaug in *The Hobbit* is the past tense 3rd person singular, either of a primitive Germanic verb **smugan* (to squeeze through a hole), as mentioned in *Letters* (31) or of the Norse verb *smjúga* (to creep). Its Old English cognate is found in a spell against *sméogan wyrme*, the 'penetrat-

ing worm', but the verb *sméagan* also means 'to inquire into' and in adjectival form 'subtle, crafty'. And Smaug certainly is a subtle serpent with a penetrating mind! In addition, 'Sméagol', Gollum's original name, is derived from the same verb – he was an inquisitive character before the *Ring* overcame his mind.

2) The Old English phrase 'orþanc enta geweorc' (the skilful work of giants), from a poetic fragment about ancient Roman remains in Britain, inspired Tolkien to create a race on the border of extinction, the *Ents*. At the same time, Orthanc ('cunning mind' in the language of Rohan) is an indestructible piece of stonework serving as the abode of a clever wizard who becomes the enemy of the Ents but is defeated by them in the end. Three words, turned into a subplot that stretched over several chapters.

'The constant interaction of a poet with ancient idiom sharpens the philological vision and creates virtuosity in the handling of linguistic forms' (Panagl, 88). Panagl is speaking of Wagner here, but it applies to Tolkien with a vengeance. And Tolkien did not make mistakes, like Wagner did when he took the old word *Schwäher* to be identical with *Schwager*, brother-in-law, whereas it actually means father-in-law.

An area in which Tolkien's ring epic is certainly superior to Wagner's is the stylistic variation in direct speech (which is all Wagner's text consists of). In the tetralogy, almost everyone uses more or less the same language, from Fafner to the Forest Bird; difference is expressed by type of voice, by the music the characters sing and by the *Leitmotive*. Perhaps Wotan sounds a tad more pompous than the others, or Loge a tad more glib, or Alberich more harsh, but on the whole, the stylistic range of the *text* is not very wide. If, for instance, Mime is ridiculous or pathetic, it is the music accompanying him and his presentation that make it so, not so much his verbal style. The most characteristic speaker is Siegfried, recognisable by his straightforwardness and bluntness.

In Tolkien's dialogues, the reader encounters a great variety of styles. Hobbit speech is mostly colloquial, Elvish speech elevated and archaic. Tom Bombadil speaks rhythmically, as though he is talking in verse, Saruman sounds like a glib politician, and Fangorn is slow and long-winded. The language of the orcs is coarse, Gandalf and Aragorn adapt to the person they are speaking to (Shippey

2000, 72-4). The differentiation goes even further: Frodo, the 'gentlehobbit', and the working-class hero Sam use different registers, while Gollum's speech is just pathological. In a way Tolkien combined and fused the elevated style of the 'matter of Beleriand' and the down-to-earth (though not pedestrian) style of *The Hobbit* to write what is generally considered his masterpiece. That he preferred the former is ironic, that he did not use it throughout his ring epic shows that his writer's instinct was sound enough.

12.1.6. Kennings

Kennings, the poetic metaphors that use circumlocution to denote a noun in Old Norse and Anglo-Saxon poetry, have already briefly been touched on in the passage about the *Haft der Welt*, a kenning for Wotan's spear. In a kenning, a word is often identified with a thing it is not, and background knowledge may be necessary to grasp the meaning. When the sky is called 'Ymir's skull', this is a reference to the creation account of Norse mythology in the *Völuspá*, in which the skull of the slain giant Ymir is used to fashion the sky (with his brains as clouds). The definition of a kenning Snorri gives in *Skáldskaparmál* is broad, including simple, epithet-like kennings like 'wave steed' for ship, as well as more elaborate ones, like 'feeder of war-gull', in which 'war-gull' is a kenning for raven and the whole phrase boils down to 'warrior'.

Neither Tolkien nor Wagner use elaborate kennings, but they both use the kind that presupposes background knowledge. Tolkien uses them more sparingly than Wagner does, and mostly in the *Legend*. In the 'The New Lay of the Völsungs' Sigurd is 'Grani's burden'; his sword is 'serpent's bane' or 'Grimnir's gift'. Rerir is 'the raven's lord', because of the many corpses he leaves for the ravens to feast on. The 'trees of lightning twisted branching' offer a beautiful image but fall just short of being a kenning, as they contain the word to which the expression is referring – lightning.[21] In 'The New Lay of Gudrún' Fáfnir's gold is 'the serpent's treasure', the halls of Atli are 'forest-girdled' (surrounded by a wooden palisade, or by warriors, as the word tree often means warrior in Icelandic poetry – in which case this would be an example of a more elaborate

---

21 If he had used 'radiance' or 'brilliance' it would have been a kenning.

kenning. On the other hand it is also possible to take forest-girdled more literally). 'Oak branches' are gallows; 'snaketongued' arrows are presumably poisoned.

The Hobbit also has a few kennings: the names Bilbo gives himself when he is facing Smaug, such as 'web-cutter', 'stinging fly', 'Ring-winner', 'Luck-wearer' and 'Barrel-rider'. All these are kennings like 'Ymir's skull': one needs to know the story behind them to grasp them, which the reader does, whereas Smaug does not. The same goes for 'Ringbearer' as a kenning for Frodo in *The Lord of the Rings*, though this is of the kind that is hardly more than an epithet.

Wagner uses kennings, too, though he often adds some kind of flowery adjective. '*Der Wassertiefe wonniger Stern*' (the blissful star of the watery depths) and '*der gleißende Tand der Tiefe*' (the depth's glittering finery), for instance, both refer to the Rhinegold. Apart from the added adjectives this is in keeping with the poetry of the ancient Icelandic skalds, in which there is a connection between gold and water. Gold is described with kennings like the 'gleam of the water' or the 'fire of the sea', or even more specifically as 'the red metal of the Rhine'. (O'Donoghue, 134).

Other Wagnerian kennings are '*des Vertrages Pfand*' (the contract's security) for the goddess Freia, who will become the property of the giants if Wotan fails to pay their wages. Alberich is the '*Nacht-Hüter*' (guardian of the night), and '*der Erde Nabelnest*' (the earth's navel nest) is Nibelheim, the subterranean dwelling of the dwarfs. Siegfried becomes '*des Wurmes Würger*' (the serpent's strangler) and '*der Hort der Welt*' (the world's hoard). Wotan is the '*Herr der Raben*' (lord of ravens, reminiscent of the Norse kenning *hrafn-áss*, god of ravens). He also is '*des Felsens Hüter*', the guardian of the Rock on which the valkyrie sleeps, and a '*Schwurwissender Eideshort*' (an oath-knowing hoard of vows), which looks more elaborate than it is. Tolkien does not use kennings for Odin. But then, Wagner's Wotan is the protagonist of the *Ring*, whereas *Legend*-Odin is a supporting character. In any case, this shows that Wagner studied the language and style of his sources thoroughly enough to pick up on this highly characteristic trait.

12.2. Alliterations

12.2.1. Stave rhyme rediscovered

Around the time Wagner was born, the rediscovery of Germanic alliterative poetry outside Scandinavia – found in Old Norse, Old- and Middle-English, Old Saxon and Old High-German texts – lay half a century in the past, and a number of translations had seen the light. The first ones were prose interpretations or retellings rather than poetical renderings trying to do justice to the originals. In 1763, for instance, Thomas Percy published five Old Norse poems, literally translated into English prose from Latin versions produced by 17th century scholars from Scandinavia. English and German prose translations of Eddaic lays appeared in the *Analytical Reviewer* of November and December 1788, respectively Gräters anthology *Nordische Blumen* (Nordic Flowers, 1789). The originals with their stave rhyme and irregular metres were considered primitive and crude; in the first verse translation of the *Völuspá* to appear in German (1784) the translator, the Austrian Jesuit Denis, replaced the alliterating half-lines with regular iambic verses to suit 18th century tastes. So did A.S. Cottle in his partial translation of the *Poetic Edda* into English (1797).

The first post-medieval alliterative texts Germanic style did not appear until the 19th century. De la Motte Fouqué never translated any Eddaic lays, but his aforementioned work *Der Held des Nordens* (1808) is the only German language drama preceding the *Ring* which is based on Norse rather than Middle High-German sources. Though most of it is written in Shakespearian blank verse, parts of it have stave rhyme, be it somewhat randomly. Wagner was the first to use this rhyme in any systematic way in the modern era.

12.2.2. Some technicalities

The most commonly used verse form in Germanic alliterative verse was the long-line: a line, divided into two half-lines, the on-verse and the off-verse. Each of these has two lifts, always stressed syllables, and an unspecified number of unstressed syllables or dips. The third lift - the first of the off-verse – is the so-called head-stave, Old Norse *hofudstafr*, the term Snorri coined when laying down the rules for this kind of poetry in the *Skáldskaparmál*, the third part of his *Prose Edda*.

This head-stave defines the alliteration. It must alliterate with one or both lifts of the on-verse. The second lift of the off-verse must not alliterate with the head-stave. All vowels and diphthongs also alliterate with one another; sk (in English sh), sp and st only alliterate with themselves. Ideally, the alliterating syllables have different vowels. Other technicalities involve metrical patterns, syllable length and the distribution of stressed and unstressed syllables, but in a discussion of Wagner's *Ring* these are of little relevance.

In most Old Germanic texts, like *Beowulf*, the long-lines follow each other, but Eddaic poetry is always broken up in stanzas. There are several different Eddaic metres. Of these, the most important are *fornyrðislag*, which basically consists of four long-lines, and *ljóðahattr*, four-line stanzas of which the even numbered ones are long-lines and the uneven lines have three lifts, of which at least two alliterate. *Málahattr* is a variation of *fornyrðislág*.

The poetry of the Edda differs from that of other old Germanic poetry in yet another aspect. Old Norse had fewer unstressed syllables than the other Germanic languages, which lends Eddaic verse a remarkable terseness and 'an almost demonic energy', as Tolkien put it (*Legend*, 17). Below a quote from 'The New Lay of the Völsungs' to show what a *fornyrðislag* stanza looks like; the speaker is the dwarf Andvari, robbed of the ring that allows him to multiply gold:

> 'My **r**ing I will curse
> with **r**uth and woe!
> **B**ane it **b**ringeth
> to **b**rethren two;
> **s**even princes **s**lays
> **s**words it kindles -
> end **u**ntimely
> of **Ó**din's hope.'[22]

Below is a *ljóðahattr* stanza (of which the first *Legend* poem contains three and the second none). It is from Chapter V, 'Regin'; the speaker is one of the birds

---

[22] In the typography of *Legend*, the half-lines are separated, but the more usual way of presentation is the long-line: 'My ring I will curse with ruth and woe!' etc.

whose language Sigurd understands after the fat from Fáfnir's roasting heart has touched his tongue.

> Who a **f**oe lets **f**ree
> is **f**ool indeed,
> when he was **b**ane of **b**rother!
> I **a**lone would be **l**ord
> of **l**inkéd gold,
> if my **w**ielded sword had **w**on it.
> (*Legend*, 69)

It would take decades for the scholars to analyse all the technicalities and for the translators of the *Poetic Edda* – usually the same people – to master them. Yet even Simrock's German translation of 1851 does not adhere strictly to all the rules given by Snorri and neither does Benjamin Thorpe's first complete translation into English, published in 1866.

12.2.3. Wagner's verse

When Wagner first began to write the text of *Siegfried's Tod* in 1848 he had not yet discovered stave rhyme as the guiding principle. Once he had, and realised what he could achieve with it, he made many adaptations to the text, inserting alliterations where previously there had been none. '*Deinem Rat nur zoll ich lob*', for example, became '*Deinem **R**at nur **r**ed' ich **L**ob*' (both roughly mean: I praise your counsel alone); '*Eine Nacht am Ufer harrst du mein*' (One night you wait for me at the river bank) became '*Eine **N**acht am Ufer harrst du im **N**achen*' (One night at the river bank you wait in the barge). Many more examples could be given. However, despite all these changes, Wagner's verses do not always conform to the basic principles of Germanic alliterative poetry.

In his study of Wagner's alliterative verses, Hermann Wiessner argues that most of the irregularities in the *Ring* can be traced back to Ettmüller's translation of the heroic lays of the Edda, and the explanation of the Old Norse metres he gives in his introduction.[23] Ettmüller's knowledge was conform the insights of his time and based on the Danish scholar Rask's work on the Icelandic

---

23 See also Schuler 29, 30. He made the discovery before Wiessner, who apparently did not know his work. Schuler only mentions it in passing, though.

language.²⁴ However, Ettmüller makes an important omission. He does not mention that in a long-line, the third lift must alliterate with either or both the first and the second one. He does not even use the term *Hauptstab* (*hofudstafr*, head stave). As a translator, he probably noticed that Eddaic poets occasionally deviate from this. However, those cases form a small minority in the *Poetic Edda*, and there was no good reason to omit it. Rask does mention the head stave and its role in Norse poetry.

In his own translation, Ettmüller occasionally drops the ball at times. Like his fellow Edda translator Simrock, he alliterates *s* with *sch* – not allowed, *sch* being the German equivalent of Norse *sk* – but on the other hand he adheres to the rule that *st* and *sp* can only alliterate with themselves, though they both begin with the same *sch*-sound in German. As stave rhyme is based on sound and not on spelling, there was no need to do so in a translation into German. His division of lifts and dips over the lines is not always convincing. Nevertheless, his verses are usually correct.

Wiessner, who quantified the results of his research, concludes that Wagner succeeded quite well in adapting his text to the rules of Germanic alliteration techniques. The Icelandic ethnologist Björnsson also takes a brief look at the composer's use of Eddaic stave rhyme. Quoting one wrong and one correct passage from the *Ring* libretto he concludes that Wagner would not have scored a high grade if he had been an Icelandic high-school student, but that he would not have failed the test of alliterative skill (Björnsson, 108). His compatriot Þorstein Gylfason, who translated the *Ring* into Icelandic, is somewhat more critical. Like Björnsson, Gylfason accuses Wagner of over-alliterating and of repeatedly using secondary alliteration (ab/ab), his most common offence. However, he admits there are examples of this in the Edda, too, which 'may well have given Wagner the idea'.²⁵ He concludes that

> even if I have pointed out some flaws in Wagner's execution of his task these do not, in my opinion, diminish the status of the Ring as a tour de force of versification in the Icelandic manner. (Gylfason, 83)

---

24 Ettmüller used Mohnike's German translation of the work; apparently he did not read Danish, which is a bit surprising in someone able to translate Old Norse. Among historical linguists, Rask is credited with having first conceived of the idea underlying Grimm's Law.
25 Tolkien also uses secondary alliteration in the *Legend*, but not very often.

Yet Wagner's deviations from the rules are quite significant. Firstly, while Eddaic verse is written in stanzas, the *Ring* text is not, a few exceptions such as Siegmund's Spring Song and Siegfried's Forging Song notwithstanding. Lines with four lifts alternate with shorter lines containing three or two lifts, alone, in pairs or in groups. The only discernible structure is that which the rhythm of the music adds to the text. We are dealing with free, rhythmic verse here, not with anything conforming to a regular metre.

That the *Ring* is not strophic throughout is understandable. Wiessner's argument that the strophic form does not allow for dialogue (75) is debatable: the Eddaic lays and the *Legend* prove otherwise. However, the need for variety in the music precluded the use of uniform stanzas. Nor did strophic verse go well together with Wagner's new way of composing, of which his *Ring* cycle is the first example. It was he who invented the *unendliche Melodie*, the neverending or continuous melody, replacing the dualist operatic structure prevailing in his days, in which recitatives alternate with arias and everything is numbered. Also, Wagner did not attempt to revive Eddaic verse, but non-strophic Germanic verse in general, despite the fact that he took much of his material from the *Poetic Edda*.

Another thing is that many of the long-lines in the *Ring* fail to conform to the rule regarding the head-stave. A calculation based on Wiessner's quantification shows that almost one third of them deviate from it. Pointing out that not all Eddaic long-lines conform to the pattern, like Wiessner does, is misleading: the deviations in the lays of the Edda do not nearly amount to Wagner's 33.4 percent. In addition to that, five percent of the *Ring* lines deviate in ways that cannot be blamed on Ettmüller's omission concerning the head-stave.

One peculiarity shows that Wagner did understand the phonetic basis of stave rhyme: some of his verses do not alliterate according to German standard pronunciation, but according to his specific dialect, Upper Saxon. This dialect does not differentiate between the voiceless stops p, t and k and their voiced equivalents b, d and g.[26] In his Upper Saxon dialect '*Es **b**rummt und **b**raust und **p**rasselt hierher*' (It buzzes and fizzes and rustles this way), was a correct

---

26 In *Die Meistersinger von Nürnberg*, for instance, Isol**d**e rhymes on woll**t**e.

long-line (Wiessner, 51 f.). So Wagner did not merely imitate Ettmüller, who was Swiss.

Recapitulating, and leaving aside the many additional rules, the three basic patterns of the Germanic long-line, including the Eddaic *fornyrðislag* metre - are: a a / a x; a x / a x; and x a / a x (only correct under certain circumstances). In addition, there is the line with three lifts, found among others in the Ljódahattr metre. Wagner uses this type of line quite often. At least two of these three lifts must alliterate; the patterns are a a a, a a x, a x a, or x a a. It is easy to find examples of all of these in the *Ring*. Only a few are given here, all from *Das Rheingold*: as Wagner wrote the libretti backwards, logic would dictate that the last text he wrote would show the greatest technical proficiency.[27]

Correct lines:

a a / a x:

Schwarzes, **sch**wieliges / **Sch**wefelgezwerg! (Swarthy, scaly sulphurous dwarf!)

a x / a x:

Der **W**elt Erbe / ge**w**änne zu Eigen[28] (The world's heritage would win for his own)

x a / a x:

Lasst mich in **R**uh! / Den **R**eif geb' ich nicht! (Leave me in peace! I'll not give up the Ring!)

Incorrect lines:

a a / x a (Not infrequent in Simrock's Edda translation either):

Falsch und **f**eig ist / was dort oben sich **f**reut (False and fey is what feasts above)

x a / x a:

Um dich du **K**lares / wir nun **k**lagen (For you, bright thing / we now lament)

---

27 This is confirmed by Wiessners quantification. This notwithstanding the fact that Wagner rewrote parts of the other libretti, notably *Götterdämmerung*.
28 This is also an example of secondary alliteration: a b / a b, **W**elt – ge**w**änne ; **E**rbe – **Ei**gen. This pattern is among the most frequent in Wagner's text.

a a / a a (Over-alliteration):

> Wie **b**ang und **b**leich / ver**b**lüht ihr so **b**ald! (How soon you wither, anxious and pale!)

Correct lines with three lifts:

a a a:

> **A**lles was **i**st, **e**ndet (All that is, ends.)

a a x:

> **H**üte dich, **h**errischer Gott! (Take heed, haughty God!)

a x a:

> **F**lieh des Ringes **F**luch! (Flee the curse of the Ring!)

An incorrect one, without any alliterations at all:

x x x

> Den Ring muss ich haben!' (I must have this ring!)[29]

Sometimes one alliteration runs on for a number of lines, more or less entering into serial relationships with others:

Bin ich nun **f**rei? Wirklich **f**rei?	(Am I free now? Truly free?
So **g**rüß euch denn	Then thus I give you
meiner **F**reiheit erster **G**ruß!	my freedom's first greeting!
Wie durch **F**luch er mir geriet	Since by curse it came to me,
ver**f**lucht sei dieser **R**ing!	accursed be this Ring!)

Also, Wagner often links a sequence of verses by alliteration. The Germanic poets also did this on occasion, so they may have inspired him, but in such verses the consonant of the last lift of a long line determines the head-stave of the next line, while Wagner uses this feature in a rather random way.

---

29 Said by Wotan; much later, Hagen repeats this almost verbatim, only changing the verb: 'Den Ring soll ich haben!' (I shall have that ring!), another line without alliteration.

Doch, **w**ie du **w**uchsest	(But just as you grew
kannst du auch **w**inzig	can you also make yourself
und **k**lein dich **sch**affen?	tiny and small?
Das **k**lügste **sch**ien mir das,	That would seem the cleverest way,
Gefahren **sch**lau zu ent**f**liehn:	to flee slyly from dangers;
das aber **d**ünkt mich zu **sch**wer!	but methinks that would be too hard!)

When Schuler investigated the metrical and alliterative patterns in the *Ring* he came up with several dozens of different structures, stretching over up to seven lines of usually unequal length, with no discernible strophic pattern. Wiessner could not discern any such pattern either, but he found examples for most of Wagner's lines in Ettmüller's Edda translation. Ettmüller's lines, however, were lifted out of the regular stanzas in which they had their proper place. Wagner's equivalents rarely form part of a stanza, and precisely that makes them different from the Eddaic lines. They are not wrong per se; Gylfason notes that Wagner 'usually seems to prefer what we Icelanders call *sérstuðlun*, independent alliteration' (Gylfason, 80).

All this raises the question, whether he actually worked according to a fixed set of rules. While it is true that he reiterates some weaknesses found in Ettmüller's text and introduction, it seems unfair to blame the Swiss translator for Wagner's 'errors', as not all of them can be traced to him. It seems unlikely that Wagner never noticed how far he was straying – unless he had no inkling of the intricacies of Germanic alliterative verse even after studying it, which is hard to believe. If he ignored the strophic form of the *Poetic Edda* because it was unsuitable for his music dramas, he could just as easily decide that Snorri's rules were too strict for his purpose.

Was he trying to create a new kind of alliterative verse for the *Ring*? Wiessner rejects this idea (63), but Haymes, noticing that Wagner's theoretical writings about *Stabreim* lack any references to existing ancient Germanic works of alliterative poetry (22), draws a different conclusion:

> Almost more important than alliteration was the new verse form Wagner created. Although it may have been inspired by Germanic verse forms, at least those from Iceland described by Ettmüller, it was – in 1848 at least – unique to Wagner. If one reads his description of the new verse required for true drama, there is almost as much emphasis on the rhythmic organisation and its approximation of true speech than on the alliteration itself. (Haymes 2010, 23)

This description is found in *Oper und Drama*, where Wagner calls *Stabreim* the oldest attribute of poetic speech, which fits together 'kindred speech-roots' that 'sound alike to the physical ear', to 'combine similar objects into a collective image' (II, VI).[30] Elsewhere he speaks, entirely in the spirit of Jakob Grimm, of 'the stave rhyme in which the people itself once made poetry, when it was still poet and mythmaker', claiming it was the idea of a 'new rhythmic revival of the melody through its justification by verse, by speech itself', that pointed the way to stave rhyme ('Eine Mitteilung an meine Freunde').[31] From a linguistic point of view it seems strange to claim that stave rhyme fits together 'kindred speech-roots', but it was not etymological kinship Wagner had in mind. It is the common initial consonant that constitutes the 'kinship' of root words (*Oper und Drama*, II, VI). If anything, this confirms that he was first and foremost a musician, even when he wrote about language.

Also, he was not the kind of man to toe the line. His admiration for Shakespeare was partly based on his belief that the Bard was no stickler for rules, but wrote freely according to his own insights, the way Wagner himself did. In the course of his career he shows less and less interest in the established poetic and musical conventions of any particular period and place. In this respect he resembles some of his own heroes, particularly Walter von Stolzing in *Die Meistersinger von Nürnberg*. Walter flouts the rules of the guild of Master Singers, or rather, he finds himself unable to adhere to them, because his inspiration brooks no restraint. But he still gets the girl. Behind this lay the conviction that a genius – and Wagner knew only too well that he was one – is exempt from following the rules, and more generally, that rules are stifling and curb the freedom of artistic expression.

When Breig remarks that the metrical principles of Wagner's alliterations are not in every respect identical with those of Old Norse poetry (*Wagner Handbuch*,

---

30 In German the entire quote runs as follows: 'Im Stabreime werden die verwandten Sprachwurzeln in der Weise zueinander gefügt, daß sie, wie sie sich dem sinnlichen Gehöre als ähnlich
lautend darstellen, auch ähnliche Gegenstände zu einem Gesamtbilde von ihnen verbinden.' In 'Zukunftsmusik' he says something similar, adding that the first human speech must strongly have resembled singing.
31 German: '[den] Stabgereimten Vers, in welchem einst das Volk selbst dichtete, als es eben noch Dichter und Mythenschöpfer war'; 'eine neu zu gewinnende rhythmische Belebung der Melodie durch ihre rechtfertigung aus dem Verse, aus der Sprache selbst'. NB: it should be noted both *Oper und Drama* and *Eine Mitteilung* postdate the *Ring* texts; Wagner was theorising about what he had been doing.

418), this is something of an understatement. As Breig himself points out, rhythm is more important than alliteration in Wagnerian *Ring* verse, though the composer treated them equally in *Oper und Drama*; that the textual lifts coincide with musical accentuation is the main formal characteristic of the *Ring* (419). To which could be added that musical phrases with an accent on the fourth and last lift of a long-line more or less invited Wagner to make this lift the head stave, instead of the third. A few examples: '... wer aus dem **R**heingold / schüfe den **R**ing' (who would forge the Ring from the Rhinegold) in *Das Rheingold* 1; and 'Rette mich, **K**ühne / rette mein **K**ind' (Save me, brave woman, save my child) in *Die Walküre* III, 2.

However, using Waltraute's account in *Götterdämmerung* I, 3 as an example, Dahlhaus argues that putting so much stress on the musical accentuation is an exaggeration. According to him Wagner used stave rhyme to both counteract and justify the irregular rhythm of the verses; its musical importance is limited. The alliterations served to justify the dissolution of the classical musical period, the prosaification of his tone language. This would explain the irregularity of the lifts (Dahlhaus 1996, 152) – and thereby, one might add, the fact that the *Ring* texts fail to conform to the rules of Germanic alliterative verse. Again, the music is the determining factor. According to Wagner himself, the music preceded the poetry; in 1844 he wrote that to him the 'musical scent' of an opera was present before anything else:

> I have all the notes, all the characteristic motifs in my head, meaning that when the verses are ready and the scenes have been arranged, the opera is, in fact, already finished, and the detailed musical treatment is more a matter of calm and pensive revision. (*Briefe 2*, 358)[32]

All this goes a long way to explain Wagner's rather free use of the rules of Germanic stave rhyme in general and of Eddaic verse in particular. As he wrote, *Stabreim* bent itself 'in natural and lively rhythm to the actual accents of our

---

32 German: 'Ich habe alle Töne, alle charakteristischen Motive im Kopfe, so dass, wenn dann die Verse fertig und die Szenen geordnet sind, für mich die eigentliche Oper ebenfalls schon fertig ist, und die detaillierte musikalische Behandlung mehr eine ruhige und besonnene Nacharbeit ist.'

speech' ('Eine Mittheilung an meine Freunde'),[33] and someone who believes that it is the rhyme that bends to natural speech will probably not see the point of subjecting his language to the strictures of formal poetry. In this, Wagner showed himself to be a typical child of his romantic times, apparently believing stave rhyme to be a kind of primal speech, instead of an art form likely to develop in a certain type of language. But to quote Tolkien's words again: 'Let none who listen to the poets of the Elder Edda go away imagining that he has listened to voices of the Primitive Germanic forest.'

The suggestion that alliteration is a natural mode or speech would have surprised the numerous critics of Wagner's *Ring* cycle. The *Wörterbuch der Unhöflichkeit* (Dictionary of Impoliteness), a compilation of vituperative criticisms of the composer and his tetralogy, contains denunciations like a 'dog trot of alliterations', 'casserole clattering', 'stammering poetry' or a 'grumpy lump sticking in the singer's throat'.[34] The alliterations also gave rise to several parodies, one of them starting with the traditional German tongue twister *Wir Wiener Wäscherinnen waschen weiße Wäsche* (We Viennese laundry maids wash white laundry – or underwear), sung by a Rhinemaiden.[35] After a while it relapses into rhyme, though: perhaps the author discovered that writing in alliterations is a really daunting task and found himself unable to maintain it throughout more than a couple of scenes.

Time has not healed the aversion of many people against Wagner's stave rhyme: 'It often leads to strained, and even more often to unnecessarily long-winded and repetitive turns of phrase, to forced images and comparisons,' quotes Rosendorfer in his booklet *Bayreuth for Beginners*, adding that 'the weakness for stave rhyme Wagner believed the German soul to possess was apparently

---

33 German: 'der, nach dem wirklichen Sprachaccente zur natürlichsten und lebendigsten Rhythmik sich fügende, [...] stabgereimte Vers' (Wagner's emphasis, 'Eine Mittheilung an meine Freunde', *Gesammelte Schriften und Dichtungen. Band IV*, 329). Wagner was of the opinion that rhyme was un-German and once remarked to his wife that he'd rather not see German poetry in print (C. Wagner, entry for November 18, 1870). Despite this, Siegfried's caricature of Mime in Act 1 of *Siegfried* has several rhyming lines (in Norse poetry, the combination of end rhyme and stave rhyme is called *runhenda*). In *Tristan und Isolde*, Wagner combined alliteration and end rhyme, and *Parsifal* has end rhyme throughout again.
34 Hundetrab von Stabreimen (36), Kasserolengerassel (40), Stotterpoesie (80), Knorrigen Klumpen [...] der dem Sänger im Halse steckenbleibt (40).
35 In 2009, this parody was successfully performed in the city of Lübeck.

non-existent'(97).³⁶ The Dutch publicist Van Amerongen complained about 'those accursed *alliterations* that cover the libretti like mould'(39).

12.2.4. Tolkien's development

During his life, Tolkien wrote a great deal of alliterative poetry, not only in modern English, but also in Old English and in Gothic. His alliterations have not been subjected to the kind of parody or impolite criticism aimed at Wagner's Ring verses, but then, he did not start out by throwing a consistently alliterative work at a general audience completely unused to it, let alone an extremely long one like *Der Ring des Nibelungen*.

The first published text of his hand containing original alliterative verse or 'head rhyme', as he called it, was *The Homecoming of Beorhtnoth, Beorthelms's son*, a fictional dialogue based on historical events, at first only published in a scholarly magazine. The second one was *The Lord of the Rings*. Here the alliterative poetry constituted only a small part of the text, and it was the final stage of a development that had started many years before, during and shortly after the First World War.

The first samples of Tolkien's alliterative poetry are found in the earlier stages of his legendarium, and all of them concern tales from the First Age. They were published in Vol. 3 of *The History of Middle-earth*, *The Lays of Beleriand*. Among them are 'The Flight of the Noldoli from Valinor', which contained an alliterative version of the Oath of Fëanor and was aborted after 150 lines; some brief fragments of a 'Lay of Eärendel'; 'Light as Leaf on Lindentree' (the alliterative version of the song of Beren and Lúthien); and, last but not least, 'The Lay of the Children of Húrin', begun in 1918 and abandoned long before it was finished. This is the first version of the story of Túrin Turambar, and like the other poems mentioned above, it is written in Old-English long-verse. There are actually two versions, plus some snippets which Tolkien eventually developed into a short, independent work. This lay is by far the longest alliterative text in the volume: the first version counts 2276 lines, the second 816 lines. As even the longer version covers less than half of the story as it is known from

---

36 The first quote is from Hanna Filler, but Rosendorfer does not give a source.

the posthumously published texts, these numbers should give an idea of the original scope. In his foreword to *The Lays of Beleriand* Christopher Tolkien calls it 'the most sustained embodiment of his abiding love of the resonance and richness of sound that might be achieved in the ancient English metre' (*The Lays of Beleriand*, 1).

Even so, though smooth enough in places, this early work is not without flaws, as the following lines (the beginning of the first version) should make clear:

> 'Lo! The **g**olden dragon of the **G**od of Hell,
> the **g**loom of the **w**oods of the **w**orld now gone,
> the **w**oes of Men, and **w**eeping of Elves
> **f**ading **f**aintly down **f**orest pathways,
> is **n**ow to tell, and the **n**ame most tearful
> of **N**íniel the sorrowful, and the **n**ame most sad
> of **Th**alion's son Túrin o'er**th**rown by fate.'

A rather inauspicious beginning, and not just because the verse is metrically and stylistically weak (how does 'fading faintly' work?). Later it gets better and Rosebury thinks that the work as a whole has an 'impressive narrative urgency'. Even so, it

> suffers in the end from the unadaptableness of modern English to the metrical and assonantal idiom of Beowulf: diction and syntax are too often, and too obviously, constrained by the demands of the medium. [...] The effect is of a resourceful pastiche. (Rosebury, 97)

'In general, the impression it makes on me is one of strain', comments Shippey in a survey of Tolkien's development as an alliterative poet (Shippey, 'Tolkien's Development', 2009, 67). The author is struggling visibly to do what Rosebury believes cannot be done: adapt modern English to the ancient verse-form. Among other things, the metrical variety is limited: of the five possible types of half-lines, two are used considerably more often than the other three. The otherwise common A-type, two lifts, each followed by a dip (e.g.: KNIGHTS in ARMour) poses difficulties in modern English with its lack of endings, and its occurrence in the Túrin lays is relatively rare.

In later poems, like *King Sheave*[37] and the two *Legend* poems – whose main metre, Norse *fornyrðislag*, uses the same five types of half-lines – Tolkien managed to solve this problem by taking recourse to the gerund form. An illustration from the preliminary part of 'The New Lay of the Völsungs', *Upphaf*:

> 'The **GU**ESTS were **MA**Ny:
> **GR**IM their **SING**ing
> **BO**AR'S flesh **EAT**ing
> **BEA**Kers **DRAIN**ing;
> **MIGH**Ty ones of **EAR**TH
> **MAIL**clad **SIT**ting
> for **O**NE they **WAI**Ted
> the **WORLD**'S **CHOS**en.

This stanza has no less than four half-lines of the A type using the gerund form (which may look like the other extreme, except that the fragment was picked for this reason).[38]

For a discussion of the alliterative poem *The Homecoming of Beorhtnoth, Beorthelm's son*, which is tricky to date correctly but precedes *The Lord of the Rings*, I refer to Shippey's article. The poem is rather colloquial and loosely written; the proof-readers of the Ballantine edition did not even notice it was poetry. But it represents another step forward.

Finally, we get to Tolkien's major opus. Most of the alliterative poetry in it belongs to the Rohirrim. There are seven examples of Rohirric alliterative verse: a scrap in *The Two Towers*, I, two longer poems and three scraps in *The Return of the King*, I, plus a fragment in II which is partly identical with one of the earlier ones. In addition, there are two non-Rohirric alliterative poems: Treebeard's 'Lore of Living Creatures' in *The Two Towers*, I, 4, to which Pippin later adds a line, and the prophecy of the seer Malbeth in *The Return of the King*, I, 2. None of these poems is strophic and they consist of long-lines of the Anglo-Saxon type: the number of dips is higher than in Eddaic poetry.

---

37 This is a poem of 153 lines, based on a semi-historical tale hinted at in the early part of *Beowulf*, and incorporated in Tolkien's story 'The Lost Road' (*The History of Middle-earth* V, 87-91). It was written in the 1930s, posibly around 1936, and therefore not much later than the *Legend* poems.
38 For the different types of halflines, see the *Legend*, 46. Tolkien uses four out of five types here: B, 3x A, E, A, B and C. Examples of D-type halflines are DWARF ANDvari, or DRINK SINfjötli, in 'Andvara-Gull' resp. 'The Death of Sinfjötli'.

A prime example is Éomer's epitaph over King Théoden from Chapter VI of *The Return of the King*:

> '**M**ourn not over**m**uch! **M**ighty was the fallen,
> **m**eet was his ending. When his **m**ound is raised,
> **w**omen then shall **w**eep. **W**ar now calls us!'

Another example is this verse from the end of the previous chapter; note that it contains two different instances of secondary alliteration (a b b a and a b a b):

> '**A**rise, **A**rise, **R**iders of Théoden!
> **F**ell deeds awake: **f**ire and slaughter!
> *Sp*ear shall be **sh**aken, **sh**ield be *sp*lintered,
> A *s*word-day, a **r**ed day, ere the *s*un **r**ises!'

That Tolkien used Anglo-Saxon poetry as a template for Rohirric poetry is logical: the Riders of Rohan speak Old English, or rather, the Old Mercian variety of it, as Shippey demonstrated (Shippey 1982, 92-3). They are Anglo-Saxons on horseback. And within the fiction that *The Hobbit* and *The Lord of the Rings* are translated from the so-called 'Red Book of Westmarch', the language of the Rohirrim stands to the Common Speech as Old English stands to Modern English. Interestingly, though, the last line above is reminiscent, not of an Old English poem but of an Icelandic one: the forty-fifth stanza (*Edda*, Neckel/Kuhn ed.) of the *Völuspá* contains the line: '*Vindöld, vargöld, aðr verold steypiz*' – 'A wind-age, a wolf-age, ere the world is wrecked.' An army of warriors whose culture is modelled on that of Anglo-Saxon England chants a battle-song reminiscent of a sentence from the *Poetic Edda*; it doesn't get more Tolkienish than that.

Why the 'Lore of Living Creatures' and the 'Prophecy of Malbeth' alliterate is difficult to say. From a formal point of view there are hardly any differences between these poems and those of the Rohirrim, though Treebeard's poem, containing only three half-lines of more than four syllables, has few enough dips to resemble an Eddaic poem (except that it is not strophic).

> '**L**earn now the **l**ore of **L**iving Creatures!
> **F**irst name the **f**our, the **f**ree peoples:
> **E**ldest of **a**ll, the **e**lf-children;
> **D**warf the **d**elver, **d**ark are his houses;
> **E**nt the **ea**rthborn, old as mountains;
> **M**an the **m**ortal, **m**aster of horses.' (*The Two Towers*, I, IV)

The alliterative poems in Tolkien's major opus are formal masterpieces, and not only because they conform to all the main rules. (In the poem in *The Two Towers*, I, III, he seems to have an a a / x a line: '**ea**st and **o**nward / rode the **E**orlingas'. In fact, the lifts in the off-verse are E- and -ling-, with 'rode' being a heavy first dip, as verbs sometimes are.) Of course they do: Tolkien taught Germanic metres in his university classes and wrote about them in his aforementioned introduction 'On Translating Beowulf'. In his ring epic he is obviously at ease with all the technicalities of this demanding metre, handling them in a sovereign way. He also manages to convey, sometimes subtly, sometimes with force, the spirit of original Anglo-Saxon verse, especially in the shorter Rohirric fragments like the first example given above. 'If anything shows what alliterative poetry can do in modern English, it is the eight examples of it to be found in that work.' (Shippey, 'Tolkien's Development', 2009, 71). Apparently Rosebury does not agree: he has no special praise for the poetry of the Rohirrim, and does not think that *The Homecoming of Beorhtnoth* is among Tolkien's more important works as a creative artist (Rosebury, 124). Still, the difference in quality, technical and stylistic, between these and the Túrin lays should be noticeable even to eyes not accustomed to reading this kind of verse.

One thing is remarkable: Tolkien apparently had a strong preference for the long-line. He used it in all his alliterative poetry, with the exception of the three bird verses in 'The New Lay of the Völsungs', which are written in *ljódahattr* (in his source the birds use both *ljódahattr* and *fornyrðislag*) and a number of poems in the Songs for the Philologists.[39] The metrical variety of the *Poetic Edda* is not reflected in the *Legend* poems, which predominantly use *fornyrðislag* lays. But it is also obvious that this metre, with its hammer strokes, was closest to his heart.

---

39 Only extant in a private edition of 1936. According to Humphrey Carpenter (271), Tolkien contributed thirteen poems, among them one in Gothic and seven in Old English. Four of these, including the Gothic poem, were reprinted in Shippey 1982.

12.2.5. Rhythm and patterns

It should be clear by now that any formal flaws in Tolkien's alliterative poetry have to do with the finesses – of which there are more than have been mentioned here - rather than with the basic alliteration rules of Germanic verse. And unlike Wagner, Tolkien did not transgress against these, except possibly in one crucial case in the *Legend* (IX, 4), as Shippey argued in his review of it. In '**oa**ths were remembered / **a**ll **u**nfulfilled', the alliteration pattern is a x / a a. This 'jarring discord', only discernible for 'ears attuned to the metre', comes at a crucial point of the story: Sigurd realises he has inadvertently betrayed his bride but is powerless to act, and the betrayal will lead to his death.[40]

To Tolkien, however, metre was a more important aspect of Old English and Norse poetry than alliteration. He even argued that alliteration is not fundamental to it and that the verse would retain its metrical character even if written 'blank' ('On Translating Beowulf', 66).[41] He actually did write blank verse according to the metrical patterns of Old English poetry, as was shown in an analysis of Tolkien's description of the river Withywindle in Chapter VI of *The Lord of the Rings* (Holmes 34f). A thorough search of the entire epic would probably yield many more examples.

Remarkably enough, for both the composer and the author it is the rhythm that is most important: both linked alliterative poetry to the natural rhythms of speech. Wagner did so in *Oper und Drama*, where he calls language a rhythmic melody and refers to 'the people' as the original, spontaneous poets and mythmakers, Tolkien in his introduction to the translation of *Beowulf*:

> The lifts and dips utilised in this metre are those occurring in any given sequence of words in natural (if formal) speech, irrespective of whether the passage is regarded as verse or prose. (*The Monsters and the Critics and Other Essays*, 63)

But in his famous Beowulf lecture, he notes that the lines of alliterative poetry

> do not go according to a tune. They are founded on a balance; an opposition between two halves of roughly equivalent phonetic weight, and significant

---

40 The German reviewer Freund believes Shippey was making too much of a mere slip – but he also lets Shippey say the opposite of what he actually said.
41 Gylfason disagrees. To him alliteration is 'the most important feature of Icelandic prosody. It is chiefly alliteration that makes the *Poetic Edda* verse as opposed to highly stylized prose' (79).

content, which are more often rhythmically contrasted than similar. They are more like masonry than music. (*The Monsters and the Critics and Other Essays*, 30)

At first sight this seems to clash with the known fact that Germanic alliterative poetry, like most ancient poetry in whatever language, was usually sung rather than spoken. But Tolkien probably did not mean to say that it was unsingable, just that singing it was not just a matter of adding a tune. This might explain why Wagner's ring contains so few catchy songs and is constructed of so many *Leitmotive*. But the view of music as a linear tune and the opposite of a structure is rather narrow. Music is not limited to the monophony of a single melody; it can be highly architectural. In a footnote to *Oper und Drama* Wagner combines language, music and building, imagining 'speech to have sprung from melody not in chronological order, but in architectonic array' (II, VI, n. 2).[42]

Goethe called architecture 'frozen music'.[43] The *Ring* is a brilliant piece of liquid architecture, and so are some of Tolkien's alliterative poems, for that matter.

Whatever Tolkien may have meant here, the fact remains that he discusses metrical patterns and their variations in a concise, scholarly way, showing great dedication to alliterative poetry for its own sake. Wagner on the other hand theorises at (rather exhausting) length about the relationship between *Stabreim* and music and about the potentiality of alliterative verse to recover, by way of musical drama, the ancient unity of poetry and music he believed to have existed in the past. The former saw alliterative poetry as an end in itself, purely for the beauty that could be achieved with it, for the latter it was a means to an end. Though Wagner never stated it explicitly, he may have considered his own verses to be a return to a more original mode of speech than represented by the alliterative poetry of the various Germanic languages. If so, and if Tolkien had suspected this was the case, he would probably have rejected such an idea as bogus, perhaps not only as a philologist, but also as a poet. And he was a modern master in the art of writing Germanic alliterative poetry, while Wagner's true mastery lay elsewhere.

---

42 German: 'Ich denke mir die Entstehung der Sprache aus der Melodie nicht in einer chronologischen Folge, sondern in einer architektonischen Ordnung.' In 'Zukunftsmusik', however, where he discusses the unending melody, Wagner speaks of music as a stream of events overflowing into each other rather than as an architectural arrangement.
43 'Baukunst [ist] eine erstarrte Musik' (*Konversationen mit Eckermann*, 1836).

12.3. Proverbiality

Besides archaising language and alliteration, proverbiality is another trait Tolkien and Wagner share. *The Lord of the Rings* abounds with proverbs and wise sayings of various kinds, both traditional and coined by the author. Shippey made a list of about seventy of them, though he admits he cannot always tell what is a proverb and what is not (Shippey 2005, 281). Among the traditional ones are rather trite proverbs like: 'what's done can't be undone', 'every little helps', 'it's an ill wind that blows nobody any good', and 'live and learn'. Some characters are more proverbial than others: Gaffer Gamgee, Sam's father, seems to have a saying for each occasion, and Sam applies them liberally in the course of the story. (Which incidentally makes him resemble Sancho Panza of Don Quijote fame, who throws proverbs at everybody as a comical device.)[44]

The Gaffer is also able to use this proverbs creatively, like when he says: 'All's well that ends better'. Likewise, Éomer varies familiar proverbs: 'Need brooks no delay, yet late is better than never'. So does the Orc chief in *The Return of the King* who tells Frodo and Sam that 'where there's a whip, there's a will.' The traditional proverb underlying this piece of orcish wisdom also turns up at another occasion, translated into the Rohirric way of speaking: 'Where will wants not, a way opens,' says Éowyn – and she goes on to prove the truth of it by becoming Dernhelm and joining the Ride of the Rohirrim. Tolkien, says Shippey, makes it sound as though Éowyn's version is the ancestor of the modern English proverb. But unlike its modern counterpart this one alliterates like an Old-English long-line. So does Legolas's 'Rede oft is found at the rising of the sun', which is neither an Anglo-Saxon nor a modern English saying, but simply Tolkienian.

Bilbo turns around a traditional proverb in his verse about Aragorn, quoted during the Council of Elrond: instead of 'All that glitters is not gold', he states that 'All that is gold does not glitter'. In fact, proverbial sayings make up half of the verse (the other half looking more like a series of prophecies). Later, when the Fellowship is about to leave Rivendell, Elrond and Gimli have an Old-English

---

44 Pointed out to me by Pamina Fernandez Camacho. The name Sancho is also a hobbit name (Sancho Proudfoot is the hobbit who searches for treasure in the pantry of Bag End in *The Fellowship of the Ring* I, I), which suggests a deliberate Don Quijote link.

sounding exchange that is entirely proverbial, after Elrond has told the travellers that no one will have to go further than he wants to.

> Gimli: 'Faithless is he that says farewell when the road darkens.'
> Elrond: 'Maybe, but let him not vow to walk in the dark who has not seen the nightfall.'
> Gimli: 'Yet sworn word may strengthen quaking heart.'
> Elrond: 'Or break it[.]' (*The Fellowship of the Ring* II, 3)

In *The Two Towers*, Gandalf and Théoden have a similar exchange of sayings. In these cases the sayings are not traditional but coined by Tolkien, they flow from the story, like most of Gandalf's sayings do: 'Even the very wise cannot see all ends,' or 'Often does hatred hurt itself', or 'A treacherous weapon is ever a danger to the hand'. The same goes for sayings by characters like Legolas, Aragorn, Théoden, Galadriel, Pippin, and even Grishnákh – but what Grishnákh says: 'Little people should not meddle in affairs that are too big for them', is quite thoroughly disproved by the story.

Tolkien's works contain sayings and proverbs, too. In *The Hobbit*, we find Bilbo's 'Never laugh at live dragons' (with alliteration). 'The New Lay of the Völsungs' contains a number of proverbs in keeping with the proverbial style of the Eddaic lay *Hávamál*. Not surprisingly, all Tolkien's *Legend* proverbs alliterate. The most obvious examples are: 'Gold oft begrudgeth the greedy hand' (Hreidmar); 'Weak might hath woman for wisdom's load' (Signý); 'Stout heart is better than strongest sword' (Sigurd); 'Gifts oft are given to greedy hand' (Grímhild). 'Woe worth the words by women spoken!' exclaim Sigurd and later also Högni, creating the impression that this a traditional saying – and indeed the *Hávamál* contains a whole chapter full of similar misogynist proverbs. In contrast to the first *Legend* poem 'The New Lay of Gudrún' has few proverbs, while *The Silmarillion* material also largely lacks them, though it is strong in predictions. *The Children of Húrin* has 'An honest hand and a true heart may hew amiss', but this was added to the story in the 1950s. The elder Tolkien was decidedly more proverbial than the younger.

What Shippey did for Tolkien, Hans von Wolzogen – the man who drew up the first list of *Leitmotive* in the *Ring* - did for Wagner,[45] but far from counting seventy proverbs and sayings, he claims to have found a mere two, after which he spots an additional few that do not sound particularly proverbial. Von Wolzogen mentions Wotan's traditional 'Alles ist nach seiner Art' (Everything is after its own kind), which echoes the first chapter of Genesis, and 'Wandel und Wechsel liebt wer lebt' (Whoever lives, loves change and variety). Von Wolzogen's list also contains Brünnhilde's 'Selig in Lust und Leid lass die Liebe nur sein' (Blessed in joy and grief let love alone remain), one of several projected *Götterdämmerung* endings that did not make it to the final version.

He does not mention Wagner's use of 'Stock und Stein' (stock and stone) in *Das Rheingold* 2, literally a stock phrase,[46] nor his allusions to the traditional 'Undank ist des Welten Lohn' (The world's reward is ingratitude). The first of these allusions is Loge's remark in the second scene of *Das Rheingold*: 'Immer ist Undank Loges Lohn (Ever ingratitude is Loge's reward). Towards the end of the cycle, in *Götterdämmerung* II, 5, Brünnhilde alludes to it, be it in a non-proverbial manner: 'O Undank, schändlichster Lohn!' (O ingratitude, most shameful reward!). Also lacking is Erda's 'Alles was ist, endet' (All that is, ends), a variant of the traditional saying 'Alles hat ein Ende',[47] which may seem trite, but in its context has the quality of a warning prediction and becomes the turning point in Wotan's character arc. In *Das Rheingold* 1 the Rhinemaidens sing: 'Was nur lebt, will lieben' (All living things want to love), and their last sentence in this opera has a proverbial quality, too: 'Falsch und feig ist was dort oben sich freut' (False and faint-hearted is what revels above), even though it derives too much of its significance from the context to look like a real proverb. But Sieglinde's 'Feige nur fürchten den, der waffenlos einsam fahrt' (Only cowards fear him who travels alone unarmed) does sound like a proverb, and so does Hunding's

---

45 This study contains many examples of Wagner's lexical, grammatical and syntactic archaisms, not to mention his numerous verbal ideosyncrasies, and defends his use of them by pointing out that Goethe did it, too.
46 In *The Road to Middle-earth* Shippey spends a page on Tolkien's use of the phrase 'stock and stone' during Gandalf's last conversation with Treebeard (*The Return of the King* I, VI) as an echo of various texts from English literature from the Middle Ages to Wordsworth. (1992, 200) See also Vink, 52.
47 To which Germans often add: '*Nur die Wurst hat zwei.*' (There's an end to everything, only a sausage has two.)

unoriginal though characteristic 'Mit Waffen wehrt sich der Mann' (A man defends himself with arms). Likewise Fricka's 'Mit Unfreien streitet kein Edler / der Frevler straft nur der Freie' (A lord does not fight with thralls / only the free man punishes the evildoer).

Not quite proverbial are Wotan's words to Brünnhilde just before he locks her into sleep: 'Erwarte dein Los, wie sich's dir wirf' (Await your fate as it has fallen to you): he is adressing her alone, not making a general statement. Yet the meaning is not far removed from Völsung's terse utterance in the *Legend*: 'Fate none can flee'. Having killed Fafner, Siegfried says laconically: 'Zur Kunde taugt kein Toter' (The dead can bring no news), and the same kind of dismissive comments on women found in the *Hávamál* and, to a lesser degree, in the *Legend*, are also put in Siegfried's mouth after his encounter with the three Rhinemaidens in the final act of *Götterdämmerung*. To remain with these maidens, their 'Nur wer der Minne Macht entsagt / nur wer der Liebe Lust verjagt' (Only he who forswears love's power / only he who forfeits love's lust) has a strongly formulaic character thanks to the rhyme, combined with the alliterations.

It is possible to discern a pattern in Tolkien's, whereas no comparable pattern can be found in Wagner's. A limited, but significant number of wise sayings in *The Lord of the Rings* show the workings of Providence, as the following selection shows: 'Strange are the turns of fortune' (Gandalf), but while 'few can foresee whether their road will lead them, till they come to its end' (Legolas), 'things will go as they will' (Treebeard), and moreover, 'a traitor may betray himself and do good that he does not intend' (Gandalf again). These form the 'ideological core', as Shippey puts it (Shippey 2005, 285).

The proverbial statements in the *Ring* do not form such a core; it is the music that creates the patterns in the form of the musical motifs. When the motif of the Ring of Power transforms into the Walhalla motif, the listener intuitively recognises the link between the power of the ring and that of the gods, notably Wotan's, without identifying the similarity on an intellectual level. In the same way, when the ascending motif introduced in *Das Rheingold* 1 becomes a descending motif in the fourth, the end of the world that came into being in the opening bars is felt to be inevitable on a deeper level than only through Erda's words that 'all that is, ends'. The reason is that the second motif, when heard, is the logical consequence of the first. The *Ring* lacks a verbal 'ideological core'; the core it has is a musical one, summed up in the final motif of *Götterdämmerung*, whether this is labelled 'Compassionate Love', 'Glorification of Brünnhilde' (Wagner), 'Sacrifice', 'Redemption through Love', 'Renunciation of the World' or 'Phoenix' (Kitcher & Schacht, 183). There is a reason why Wagner struck out the final words he had put into Brünnhilde's mouth at various stages of the writing, leaving the last statement to the music.

Chapter 13

Narrative Elements

13.1. The Ring and the Legend – correspondences[48]

13.1.1. Introduction

Tolkien's 'The New Lay of the Völsungs' has even more narrative elements in common with Wagner's opera cycle than his ring epic. Here the use of common sources (the *Prose Edda*, the *Poetic Edda* and the *Völsunga saga*) does indeed explain most of the similarities between the two works. When they differ, it is mainly because Wagner changed, combined or invented elements or drew from medieval German texts, notably the *Nibelungenlied* and the late medieval ballad *Das Lied vom Hürnen Seyfrid*. Generally speaking Tolkien stuck more closely to the sources. It was only later, in *The Hobbit* and to an even greater extent in *The Lord of the Rings*, that he combined and interlaced a host of diverse and at times contradictory sources into a single, coherent whole that is on many counts more original than the plot of Wagner's *Ring*.

13.1.2. From the beginning to Ragnarök

As mentioned in II. 1, in his introduction to the *Legend* Christopher Tolkien remarks that the *Ring* cycle

> must be seen less as a continuation or development of the long-enduring heroic legend than as a new and independent work of art, to which in spirit and purpose *Völsungakviða en nýja* and *Guðrúnarkviða en nýja* bear little relation. (*Legend*, 10)

This is undoubtedly true: Wagner was not trying to guess what the lost pages of the *Poetic Edda* contained, or to prove that modern English was a suitable

---

48 A variant version (abridged in some parts, expanded in others) of this section of the book appeared as 'The Dying Sun' in *Hither Shore* 8 (2012).

vehicle for the *fornyrdislág* metre of medieval Norse poetry, while Tolkien's aim was not to compose a *Gesamtkunstwerk* or to create a model for the Artwork of the Future. Wagner was not in the first place interested in the 'theory of courage' that Tolkien considered so important in the ancient literature of the North; Tolkien was not occupied with the themes of Love versus Power and Nature versus the Law that form the core of Wagner's opera cycle. Even so, this does not mean both works have nothing in common except a number of elements from their common sources plus Germanic alliterative metres.

Both the *Legend* and the *Ring* tell the tale of the Dragonslayer, Sigurd or Siegfried, but they embed it in Norse mythology as a whole. In the Icelandic sources, the tale begins with a transgression by some gods. They rob a dwarf of his treasure to pay for a wrong committed against a third party. However, both Wagner and Tolkien use the creation of the world as their starting point. Tolkien follows the account of the *Völuspá* in the *Poetic Edda*, while Wagner combines elements from both Eddas with ideas of his own, adding the creation of the world from a single note of music.

Likewise, unlike the Icelandic poets, both end their stories with *ragnarök*. Wagner's version differs markedly from that of the *Völuspá*. There, gods and monsters fight each other in an apocalyptic battle. The old gods fall, the Sun turns black and the Earth sinks into the sea. But this is followed by a new beginning in a renewed world, in which the next generation of gods replaces the old ones. *Siegfried's Tod* ended with the renewal of Wotan's reign. But Wagner struck the renewed reign of the gods, possibly influenced by Ettmüller, who believed that the stanzas describing the reborn world were a late, Christian addition to an originally heathen poem (Ettmüller, 53). In the final version of *Götterdämmerung* the abode of the gods burns with all its denizens, and only human survivors are left.

As mentioned before, Tolkien generally follows the Icelandic sources more closely than Wagner does, both in the alliterative lays and in the rhyming *'Prophecy of the Sybil'*, Appendix B of the *Legend*. We have the Gods and the monsters – the legions from Hell – as well as the last battle and the renewed Earth in both poems. Yet there are also elements not found in the Eddaic sources, or not explicitly.

It has long been the object of debate whether the *Völuspá* is the work of a Christian poet recounting the beliefs of his pagan ancestors as he knew them or a Christian work using the pagan images of previous generations. As early as 1806 the enlightenment philosopher Adelung suggested that both the Eddas were written by Christian clerics. The historian Rühs concurred and wrote a discourse on the origins of Icelandic poetry (1813) in which he claimed that the Eddaic myths were derived from Anglo-Saxon sources. Their authors were Christians, and the myths contained no information about pagan Germanic beliefs (Williamson, 100f). In Denmark, N.F.S. Grundtvig postulated a higher god, Alfader – one of Odin's names – above the Eddaic pantheon, much like Ilúvatar stands above the Valar in Tolkien's *Silmarillion* (Agøy 1995).

These views were attacked by various scholars, most notably the Grimm brothers, and for a while the theory went underground. It re-emerged when the Norwegian theologian Bang (1879), and after him the philologist Bugge (1881), suggested that the myths in Old Icelandic literature and especially the Edda derived from Christian and classical concepts. Bugge was the editor of the *Hauksbók*, the second of the two surviving Edda manuscripts (the first being the *Codex Regius*), which contains a version of the *Völuspá* foreshadowing the coming of Christ: 'Then comes a ruler / to keep dominion, / a mighty lord / majestic over all.'[49]

Again the idea was rejected by the very influential German school of philology. The author of the *Hauksbók*, Haukr Erlendsson, died in 1334, long after the *Völuspá* was written, and the above verse is considered to be a later addition. But Tolkien most likely knew it and may have agreed with Bang and Bugge, an assumption not only based on his personal beliefs, but also on the fact that he translates *ragnarök* as 'day of Doom', a close equivalent of the Christian concept of Doomsday, and on his use of the figure of Sigurd.

In the first *Legend* poem, Sigurd is the hero who, having tasted death, dies no more but 'shall deathless stand' to prevent the Earth from perishing. The poem does not explain how he will achieve this, but only says that his participation

---

49 A later version of the *Hauksbók* expands on this with lines like 'Then comes one / who is greater than all / though never his name / do I dare to name.' An interesting online-article regarding this question is: http://www.dur.ac.uk/medieval.www/sagaconf/steinsland.htm.

in the great battle on the day of Doom is necessary to save the Earth. The Icelandic texts know nothing of this; various combatants are mentioned, but Sigurd Fáfnisbane, the 'serpent slayer', is not among them: Tolkien deviates from his medieval sources here. These sources do speak of a glorious figure who dies in the old world and returns to reign benevolently over the new Earth, but this figure is not Sigurd, nor does he take up arms at *ragnarök* or slay serpents. Curiously enough, he is conspicuous by his absence in the *Hauksbók*, but Tolkien mentions him in the final stanza of the Prophecy poem, which ends with the line: 'all ills be healed in Baldur's reign'.

13.1.3. Baldr

In Norse mythology Balder, or Baldr, as his name is in the Eddas, is a son of Odin. He is a flawless god associated with light, love and beauty. When he is killed through a trick of the ambiguous Loki, half god, half giant, the onset of *ragnarök* draws near. He is burned on a pyre together with his wife Nanna, who died of grief, and his horse. This story, told in the *Prose Edda*, has echoes in both the *Ring* and the *Legend*. At the end of the *Ring* Brünnhilde ascends Siegfried's pyre on horseback to be burned along with his body, while Brynhild, in the *Legend* as well as in the Icelandic sources, tells the Niflungs to put her and Sigurd on a pyre together with their horses, after which she throws herself on her sword and dies. It is also interesting to note that in the original story, one of the most famous rings from Norse myth, Draupnir, was laid on Balder's pyre; this ring multiplied wealth by dripping eight new rings on each ninth morning. In the *Ring* cycle, Brünnhilde takes Alberich's accursed ring with her to be cleansed by the flames, after which the Rhinemaidens recover it and take it back to the river. There is no equivalent for this in the *Legend*, as Andvaranaut disappears from the story before Sigurd's murder.

After his death, Balder had to remain in the underworld until after *ragnarök*. At that point, he would return, so the *Völuspá* suggests, to rule the new Earth together with other sons of the old gods. The last stanza of the Prophecy refers to this reign, but Tolkien only mentions Balder by name (*Legend*, 367).

According to Grimm's *Teutonic Mythology*, the name Balder possibly derives from the Baltic loan word *baltas*, meaning 'white, good'.[50] The Norse god Balder has often been compared to the dying vegetation gods of many mythologies and religions, especially of the oriental type, and not surprisingly, also with Jesus Christ. The fact that he was the son of the chief god Odin, and his Christ-like perfection, seem to support the idea that the Balder myth was influenced by the Gospel. That Balder does not rise from the dead and only returns after *ragnarök*, however, suggests a pre-Christian origin for the myth. Just as in the case of the *Völuspá*, the matter remains under debate. But even if the Balder myth was not influenced by Christianity, many newly converted Norsemen may have considered it a foreshadowing of the Gospel story,[51] and it is quite possible Tolkien held such a view as well.

Because the *Prose Edda* describes Balder as being 'so fair of feature and so bright, that light shines from him', it has been claimed that he was a sun-god. This would seem a logical conclusion, but in that case one would expect to find traces of a sun cult with Balder as the centre, and there is no evidence for the existence of such a cult in Norse mythology. In the Germanic languages, the sun is female (an aspect Tolkien transferred to his world of Arda, where the maiden Arien guides the vessel of the sun across the heavens). Nevertheless, if Balder is a god, he is one of light and day, both impossible without the sun. Balder's Anglo-Saxon name, Bældæg, contains the word for 'day'. That the god succumbs to the forces of darkness until the world is renewed fits into the rather dark worldview of Norse myth - the further North one comes, the longer darkness and winter last.

---

50 Grimm also identified the name with the Old High German name Paltar and with Old English B(e)aldor, meaning 'lord', 'prince' or 'king', which he traced back to a hypothetical Germanic word, *balþoz*, 'bold'. The name Baldor will ring a bell with readers of *The Lord of the Rings*. There, Baldor, son of Brego and grandson of Eorl, was a prince of Rohan who ventured inside the Dwimorberg after a vow spoken rashly at a feast. He never returned. It is probably his remains Aragorn, Legolas and Gimli find when they are about to take the Paths of the Dead. Baldor seems a suitable name for a bold prince who goes into darkness to remain there while the world lasts, though the rest of his story is rather different.
51 That the *Völuspá* alludes to Balder's death by calling it a 'bleeding offering', could mean that the poet was of this opinion (in which case it is likely that he was a Christian).

13.1.4. The solar hero and the Saviour

Like Balder, Sigurd has also been interpreted as a sun god or a solar hero. Among the scholars who viewed him as such was the 19th century philologist Max Müller. He was the proponent of the theory of solar mythology according to which gods were originally celestial phenomena and the application of their names to personifications of these phenomena – in other words, the making of myth – was a 'disease of language'; Tolkien rejected this notion in his well-known 1939 lecture 'On Fairy Stories'. Max Müller called Balder 'the divine prototype of Sigurd' (*Peasant Customs,* 103) and interpreted the stories about the dying god and the dragonslayer both as solar myths. Just like the sun goes down in the evening and summer makes way for autumn and winter, the fate of these heroes is inevitable. The powers of darkness overcome them, but they will rise again.

Despite his rejection of Müller's theory, Tolkien compares Sigurd to the sun in a way none of his sources do. 'The New Lay of the Völsungs' contains a number of passages associating Sigurd with light in general and with the sun in particular. This begins with his birth:

> 'Sigurd golden
> as a sun shining,
> forth came he fair
> in a far country.' (IV, 16)

Brynhild addresses him as 'bright and fair' (VI, 13). When he rides to war with the Niflungs, 'flamed all before / the fire of Sigurd' (VII, 21). On his wedding day we see 'golden Sigurd / glorious shining' (VIII, 7). At the wedding of Gunnar and Brynhild, 'in came Sigurd / as sun rising' (IX, 2). After Sigurd's death, Brynhild orders the Niflungs to prepare a pyre and

> '[i]n flames send forth
> that fairest lord
> now as sun setting
> who as sun did rise!' (IX, 75)

In the first stanza of *Guðrúnarkviða en nýja*, ('The New Lay of Gudrún'), the passing of Sigurd is also compared with the setting of the sun. None of this is found in the *Eddas* or the *Völsunga Saga*, Tolkien's main sources. This is all the more remarkable as Tolkien usually follows his sources quite closely, often even literally. Was he influenced by Müller's solar myth theory after all?

Probably not. In the aforementioned lecture 'On Fairy Stories', written about half a dozen years later, he dismisses the theory according to which gods were mere personifications of natural phenomena and the stories about them, the myths or mythical allegories as he called them, were originally accounts of elemental changes and processes of nature. He points out that it is the personality of Man that lends significance to these stories about natural objects.[52] The Norse god Thórr, for instance, may have a name meaning Thunder and a hammer called Lightning (Miöllnir), but he has a marked personality:

> ... it is asking a question without much meaning, if we inquire: Which came first, nature-allegories about personalized thunder in the mountains, splitting rocks and trees; or stories about an irascible, not very clever, red-beard farmer of a strength beyond common measure? [...] To a picture of such a man Thórr may be held to have 'dwindled', or from it the god may be held to have been enlarged. But I doubt whether either view is right – not by itself, not if you insist that one of these things must precede the other. It is more reasonable to suppose that the farmer popped up in the very moment when Thunder got a voice and face; that there was a distant growl of thunder in the hills every time a story-teller heard a farmer in a rage. ('On Fairy Stories' §§ 29-31)

It is highly unlikely that Sigurd is a personification of the sun: he has sun-like qualities, the way Thórr has thunder-like qualities, but he is a person, not an allegory. 'On Fairy Stories' was written about half a dozen years after the *Legend*, yet the character of Sigurd, though he is no god, seems well-suited to illustrate the theory Tolkien puts forward in his essay.

Tolkien may also have intended Sigurd to be a Christ-like figure. On first reading, the first *Legend* poem seems to suggest that Sigurd is an Odinic warrior. Though his name is not mentioned in the earlier stages of the poem, he is obviously the one chosen by Odin to die young and come to Valhöll (II, 14), to wait there for what can only be *ragnarök*, the 'day of Doom' mentioned in *Upphaf* 14. Yet Sigurd is more than just a warrior picked by Odin to add to the ranks of the *einherjar*, the warriors who have fallen in battle and who will fight

---

52 Wagner would have concurred. In *Oper und Drama*, he suggested that in order to find explanations for the various phenomena in the world around them, humans had imagined beings not unlike themselves: the gods. People wanted to recognise themselves in an admired or beloved object of representation (II, II). This idea was already present in his Wibelungen essay.

the forces of darkness at *ragnarök* shoulder to shoulder with the gods. He is 'the World's chosen' (*Upphaf* 20), the hero who shall rescue the world (*Upphaf* 15). In this first part of the poem this hero is not yet identified. Only when *Upphaf* 14 and the first half of 15 are repeated with significant modifications in IX 80 and the first half of 81, it becomes clear that the hero is Sigurd. But the lines

> 'In the day of Doom
> he shall deathless stand
> who death tasted
> and dies no more'

of IX, 80 have a strong Christian ring to them. Tolkien could not cast Balder in the part of the Chosen, for the god does not play a role on the day of Doom, nor does he fit the profile of a warrior. And having both Balder and Sigurd as light heroes would have been redundant. That Balder was present in Tolkien's thoughts about the ruin and renewal of the Earth is attested by the Prophecy, but he had no use for Balder in his lays.

However, as the first lay in Wagnerian fashion covered both the beginning and the end of the present world, Tolkien did need a saviour figure. After all, the monsters are vanquished in the *Völuspá*, the main source for the *ragnarök* account. That he consistently calls Sigurd the 'serpent-slayer' in the stanzas about the day of Doom also suggests that his hero is to fulfil the role of the god who slays the Miðgardsormr, the great World Serpent emerging from the sea to poison the sky at *ragnarök*. In the Icelandic sources, predominantly the *Völuspá*, it is Thor who slays the serpent and in his turn is killed by it. Tolkien does not actually show his hero taking the place of the god, but his choice of words is interesting, to say the least.

If Bang and Bugge were right in assuming that the account of *ragnarök* is the Norse version of the Christian Last Battle, the Armageddon (including the victory over the ancient serpent, the devil), why not go all the way and replace the victorious sons of the fallen gods mentioned in the *Völuspá* by a Christ-like hero of light? Or so Tolkien may have thought. This hero could only be Sigurd. 'The New Lay of the Völsungs' is all about him. He has Odin, the chief god of the Norse pantheon, for an ancestor and Tolkien makes him near-flawless, putting the blame for his death on other things: on Andvari's curse, on women

– Grímhild, Brynhild and Gudrún – and on Gunnar's weakness of character. He also points to Odin, who looks to 'ages after' and for that reason wants his hero in Valhöll. Sigurd foresees his own death but seems heroically resigned to it instead of actively trying to prevent it. In short, he fits the role.

The stag symbolism reinforces this. In Gudrún's dream in the *Völsunga saga*, Sigurd is represented by a stag. This is a traditional Christ symbol, and if Tolkien intended Sigurd to be a Christ-like figure and knew about this symbolism, this would explain why he retained the stag in the dream Gudrún has in the *Legend*, but got rid of the golden-feathered hawk which in the saga also plays a role in her dream.[53] That the motif of Sigurd slaying the Serpent is found in many Norwegian church portals, for instance on the doors of the stave church of Hylestad depicted on the cover of the UK paperback edition of the *Legend*, may also have contributed to the special role Tolkien gave his hero. Sigurd's killing of Fáfnir has often been considered to represent the victory of Christianity over the old, pagan religion. But this is allegory, which Tolkien said he disliked cordially.

Tolkien was not the first to turn the legendary dragonslayer into a saviour figure in post medieval times. Though he gave him the German version of the name, Siegfried, instead of the Norse version, Wagner had done the same more than eighty years previously. During his foray into German(ic) history, mythology and medieval literature in the 1840s he probably came across Mone's *Einleitung in das Nibelungenlied* (1818), which suggests that Balder and Siegfried are one and the same. Hauer argues that the composer, possibly basing himself on Mone, consciously linked Siegfried and Balder. Writing the first draft of what later would become *Siegfried* he inserted a reference to Balder's death as the event that brought on the end of the Gods. However, he deleted this at a later stage, after he had decided it would be Siegfried's death that would mark the onset of the Gods' downfall (Hauer 61).[54] The moment Siegfried became the dying solar hero of the *Ring*, references to Balder became redundant. Wotan's

---

53 The hawk came from the German tradition. The *Nibelungenlied* contains only one version of the dream: Chriemhilt's favourite hunting hawk is torn apart by eagles. Like the slaying of the stag, this symbolises the hero's death. This version of events is decidedly more elegant and less convoluted than the *Völsunga saga*.
54 Wagner's text: 'Um der Götter Ende sorgen die Götter seit Balder sank' (About the end of the gods the gods worry since Balder went down).

second and last encounter with the earth-goddess, Erda, is based on the Eddaic lay *Baldrs Draumar*, in which Balder's fate and the end of the world are being foretold by a sybil (*völva* in Old Norse, 'Wala' in the *Ring*, identical with Erda). Substituting the god with the human hero has been called a bold move on Wagner's part, but if he believed them to be basically one and the same it seems the most logical step, once he had chosen Siegfried for his protagonist.

Before he wrote his *Ring*, Wagner's study of Germanic history and myth had already resulted in a peculiar essay containing the first seed of what would become the *Ring*: *Die Wibelungen: Weltgeschichte aus der Sage* (1848, see also Part II). In this essay he muses about the way the people imagines its gods and heroes in a way presupposing a great deal more introspection than Tolkien did when he analysed the figure of Thor. Gods and heroes are the personifications, concrete and recognizable, of what the 'spirit of the people' imagines its own essence to be; though their personalities possess a remarkable individuality, what they embody could not be more universal and encompassing.

The essay further describes Siegfried as a sun-god in a way reminiscent of Müller's ideas (though the essay preceded Müller's writings on the subject). Defeating the dragon means vanquishing the monster of chaotic Night. 'This is the original meaning of Siegfried's fight with the dragon, a fight like Apollon fought against the dragon Python.'[55] Like day must give way to night and summer to winter, Siegfried was defeated in the end. This begs a comparison with the death of Balder, who, if not a traditional sun god, was a god of light. Wagner did not explicitly identify Siegfried with Balder; in his characteristic, idiosyncratic way he identified him with someone else: Siegfried is Jesus Christ. He is a son of God whom his kinsmen call Siegfried, but who is called Christ by the rest of humankind.[56] Wagner actually went as far as claiming that the Siegfried myth had existed in the Germanic world before Christianity was introduced, making it easier for the pagans to believe in a god who died and rose again.

The initial version of *Siegfrieds Tod* bears out this idea: after their immolation Brünnhilde and Siegfried ascend to Walhall to live happily ever after, assur-

---

55 German: Dies ist die ursprüngliche Bedeutung von Siegfrieds Drachenkampf, einem Kampfe, wie ihn Apollon gegen den Drachen Python stritt.
56 In the essay he is also the ancestor of Friedrich Barbarossa, King Arthur's once and future German counterpart, who sleeps under a mountain until the people of Germany will have need of him.

ing the Gods that their wrongs have been expiated since Siegfried has taken their fault upon himself. This is blatantly close to Christ expiating the sins of mankind. Furthermore, much like Balder in the *Völuspá*, Siegfried is destined to be Wotan's successor and the new ruler of the world, comparable to Christ reigning after the downfall of Satan. Later Wagner repeatedly changed the ending of the *Ring* under the influence of Feuerbach and Schopenhauer, and in the process he struck the passage in question. In *Oper und Drama* he suddenly contends that Germanic saga is the opposite of Christian myth (II, IV).

Yet not all traces of Siegfried as Christ have disappeared from the definitive version of his tetralogy. Towards the end of *Götterdämmerung* II, 5 Brünnhilde declares that Siegfried's death alone will serve as payment for the treason of all, and *Götterdämmerung* III, 2 Siegfried sings *Mich dürstet* ('I thirst'), one of the Words of Christ on the Cross.

It must be said here that the anti-Semite Wagner, though very interested in the Jesus-figure – he wrote the draft for an opera about him – rejected the Jewish ancestry of Jesus and, following Schopenhauer, declared him to be 'Aryan'. In 'Die Kunst und die Revolution' he equated Jesus with Apollo. As a devout Catholic Tolkien would have been horrified by this, as a philologist he would have rejected the concept of an 'Aryan race' as bogus (though in itself the idea of a hierarchy of races was not alien to his way of thinking; see for instance Faramir's account of the various races of Man in *The Two Towers* II, 5). However, given the relative obscurity of Wagner's theoretical writings it is unlikely that he ever read any of it.

Tolkien was not necessarily influenced by Wagner when he made Sigurd a Christ-like figure in the *Legend* with the help of sun imagery. In the Bible, Christ is compared to the sun without Norse sun gods or solar heroes as intermediaries. In the Old Testament, the prophet Malachi refers to the coming Messiah as the Sun of Righteousness (4:2). In the New, Jesus is called the daybreak or sunrise, depending on the translation (Luke 1:78). His face shines like the sun in Matthew 17:2 and Revelations 10:1. Christ is a serpent-slayer as well, vanquishing the 'ancient serpent' that first reared its head in Genesis 1. And whereas Tolkien gives us a Christ-figure who will be victorious in the end, poiting ahead to a future eucatastrophe, Wagner removes the victory from the final version of his cycle, leaving the audience with a dead sun that will rise nevermore. In the final version of *Götterdämmerung*, however one interprets the prospects of humanity, Siegfried does no longer enter Valhalla under applause like Sigurd does in the *Legend*. This is a fundamental difference.

On the Tolkien side, it must be noted that Tolkien never presented the sun as a divine symbol in his secondary world of Arda. There, it is a derivative source of light 'a second best thing, and "the light of the Sun" (the world under the sun) become terms for a fallen world and a dislocated imperfect vision' (*Letters*, 148). In the same way, Sigurd is a good man but not flawless.

Nonetheless it remains remarkable that both the *Ring* and the *Legend* are using so many light metaphors for the chief hero. References to the sun, fire, flames, light, radiance, etcetera abound in both works, but they tend to cluster around Sigurd/Siegfried. Examples from the *Legend* were given above; here are a few from the *Ring*. In the first version of *Siegfried* Brünnhilde greets the hero who awakens her with a quote from the Eddaic lay *Sigdrífomál*: '*Heil dir, Sonne! / Heil dir, Licht! / Heil dir, leuchtender Tag!*' ('Hail, o sun! / Hail, o light! / Hail, o radiant day!'). In the final version this greeting is no longer directed at Siegfried, after Wagner came to have doubts about using solar myth in his drama. Tolkien quotes the stanza from *Sigdrífomál* verbatim in 'The New Lay of the Völsungs', but here, Brynhild does not address her awakener but the world at large, and as in the original, she hails the night as well as the day. Wagner omits the greeting to the night (E. Magee, 149).

Despite Wagner's doubts, Brünnhilde still calls Siegfried *siegendes Licht* ('victorious light') no less than three times in the awakening scene on the mountain, and also *leuchtender Spross* ('radiant scion'). His star shines on her, she says, and at the end of *Götterdämmerung* II she speaks of his flashing eye that gleamed at her. Siegfried's nemesis Hagen refers to him as *der strahlende Held*, 'the shining hero'. The Rhinemaidens ask 'Lady Sun' to send them the hero who will return the Rhine gold to the waters, and at the end of the cycle Brünnhilde says that his light illuminates her *wie Sonne lauter*, 'clear like the sun'. By then Siegfried has already died, but to her he still radiates. Finally, Wagner's original stage directions prescribe a strong light on Siegfried whenever he appears; when he dies, the stage is darkened. He does not directly compare his hero to the sun as often as Tolkien does, though. This scarcity of direct comparisons could also be a result of his toning down of the solar symbolism at a later stage of composition.

It is less surprising to see Wagner, whose *Ring* is strongly and consistently symbolical, introduce a hero who symbolizes light, than to see Tolkien doing so. His lays are not symbolical throughout, and when they are, it is usually because his sources provide him with the symbols – except in the case of Sigurd. Sigurd's role as a solar hero with overtones of Christ is, in fact, the *Legend*'s major addition to the source material, and given the above it is a surprisingly Wagnerian addition. What Tolkien does not do, is connect Sigurd's death with *ragnarök*. In the sources it was Balder's death that brought it on and Tolkien's approach, though it allows for trimming, combining and unifying the different versions of the story, excludes the conflation of characters from two separate tales. All the same the prophecy about *ragnarök*, which he gives in *Upphaf*, is repeated affirmatively after the description of Sigurd's entry in Valhöll.

13.1.5. Odin and Wotan

'The New Lay of the Völsungs' contains another addition to the source material that must be mentioned here: the expansion of Odin's role.[57] In the Icelandic texts this manipulative god disappears after the slaying of the dragon. He begets a human dynasty, thrusts a sword into the tree in Siggeir's hall for his descendant Sigmund to pull out, causes the latter's death and provides Sigurd en passant with an heroic steed. Previously, at some unspecified moment, in a different source altogether, Odin had raised a wall of flames around a Valkyrie he had put to sleep after she had disobeyed his orders. Tolkien mentions all these scenes, except the one in which Odin provides Sigurd with advice regarding the slaying of Fáfnir. As Christopher Tolkien writes, his father probably considered this an intrusion modelled on other stories, which diminished Sigurd's achievement as a dragonslayer (*Legend*, 208).

---

57 Michael Papadopoulos of Leeds Trinity and All Saints College discussed the part of Odin in his paper for the 24th International Studies in Medievalism Conference 2010 in Groningen, 'Wagner's treatment of Óðinn in "Der Ring des Nibelungen" and his influence on Tolkien's Sigurd and Gudrun'. An abstract is found in this document: http://www.medievalism.net/conferences/abstracts.pdf, but when this book was being written, the full text was not available in print.

Once Sigurd has killed the dragon, the god vanishes from the saga, leaving the human characters to their own devices. In 'The New Lay of the Völsungs' Odin keeps showing up. He takes the body of Sinfjötli, Sigmund's son by his own sister, to Valhöll; he sends Sigurd from the vanquished Siggeir's hall back to Gjúki's court; and finally he raises a new wall of fire around Brynhild's hall once she has returned there.

All this is part of Odin's plan to bring about Sigurd's death and thereby assure himself of the hero's presence in Vallhall at the onslaught of *ragnarök*. Tom Shippey argues that even Grímhild's use of the potion that made Sigurd forget Brynhild was instigated by Odin, though it is rather unusual for the god to work this way. In Icelandic literature he has a tendency to withdraw his protection from his favourite heroes at some fatal point, allowing them to be killed. Then the valkyries can take them to Valhalla, where they will increase the ranks of the *einherjar*. Both in the *Völsunga saga* and in the *Legend* Odin breaks the elderly Sigmund's sword with his spear, causing the warrior's death (94-5). But he rarely acts through others, and Grímhild's decisions seem very much her own. Yet Shippey writes that

> the uncertain roots of human motivation are [...] a feature of Tolkien rather than his Old Norse sources. What put it into Grímhild's mind to attach Sigurd to her sons through marriage to Gudrún, and which made her prepare the potion of oblivion to blot Brynhild from his mind? Tolkien does not say, but her first whisper follows directly on Ódin's command quoted above. (Shippey 2010, 308)

In any case, the outcome is ultimately in Odin's favour.

A chief god manipulating events is familiar to the audience of Wagner's *Ring*. Wotan does some of the same things Odin does in the source texts and in Tolkien's poem. In *Die Walküre* he begets offspring on a human woman, leaves a sword in a tree trunk and causes Siegmund to be slain. He puts a disobedient Valkyrie to sleep, raising a fame wall around her. Wotan does not provide Siegfried with a horse – Grane is a gift from Brünnhilde – but just as in the *Legend*, he makes some appearances not mentioned in the source texts. However, by that time he has changed from a manipulative, powerful god into an ineffective Wanderer who is no longer capable of influencing the events. The one last time he tries, in *Siegfried* III, 2, he fails dismally.

His role in *Siegfried* is entirely Wagner's invention. In Act I the Wanderer (Wotan) challenges Mime to an Eddaic riddle contest, mostly to recapitulate the preceding installments of the *Ring* for the benefit of the audience. In Act II he briefly shows up before Siegfried slays the dragon, but not to give advice, for being a free hero Siegfried must act of his own accord. He does not even get to see the god; the Wanderer's role in this stage of the story is to keep an eye on Alberich, who must be prevented from regaining the accursed Ring. In the 3rd Act the Wanderer vainly tries to prevent Siegfried from approaching the sleeping Brünnhilde – again, Siegfried must prove himself a free hero. In *Götterdämmerung*, finally, the god prepares the conflagration of Walhall, but he does so off stage. At this point he does no longer interfere; his role has become entirely passive. After Fafner's demise, Wotan is simply incapable of influencing the cause of events anymore. In this respect Wagner remained more faithful to the sources than Tolkien, at least in a literal sense. The hero has asserted himself by slaying the dragon, and the god withdraws. As Wagner generally takes a fair amount of liberty towards his sources, it is surprising to see him follow those more closely here than the philologist Tolkien did.

Shippey suggests that Tolkien's choice has to do with the nature of the *Völsunga saga*. This is a combination of two radically different legends, and he decided to present the whole story as part of a divine plan. Originally in Norse myth the world of the gods and that of men were strictly separate. By the time the saga was written, around the middle of the 13th century, this distinction was no longer felt to be of importance. Therefore the author could combine the mythical with the heroic tale, but he did not fully smooth out the seams. Tolkien may have felt the sudden disappearance of Odin was a result of this and wanted to amend things (Shippey 2010, 306f).

He goes further: like his Sigurd became a Christ-figure, Odin, the *Aldaföðr* of Norse mythology, came to resemble God the Father. As such he is comparable to N.F.S. Grundtvig's Alfader and the forerunner of Ilúvatar in *The Silmarillion*, whose name is Quenya for 'Father of All'. Moreover, he is also comparable to Wagner's Wotan. According to the 'Wibelungen' essay the Germanic peoples could completely identify the biblical God with their highest god Wuotan (as

Wagner spelled his name at the time), or so he claims; it was only the outward trappings that needed to be changed.⁵⁸

Wagner wrote at a time when Germanic philology was still more or less in its infancy and had probably no idea about the history of the *Völsunga saga*. He had a different agenda for his expansion of Wotan's role. *Legend*-Odin mostly remains the remote and mysterious divinity he is in the *Völsunga saga*. Wotan is one of the main characters of the *Ring* cycle – *the* main character, according to some – and thoroughly 'human' despite the fact that he retains his original epithet Allfather, *Allvater* in German. As Wagner wrote to his friend Röckel (see page 53), Wotan resembles us in every way. So he could not simply disappear halfway. It is only when Brünnhilde takes over the role of main character that he disappears from the stage (at least according to Wagner's stage directions), though he keeps playing a role in the story.

Disregarding other sources of inspiration, we can conclude that Wagner's Siegfried and Tolkien's Sigurd have common traits they do not share with their Icelandic template. Both are being compared to the sun and both are each in his own way Christ-like figures. Add to this a consistent use of alliteration, centuries after Germanic alliterative verse went out of use; the embedding of the tale in Norse mythology as a whole; the substitution of the god Balder with the solar hero Sigurd/Siegfried, and the expanded role of Odin, and it becomes clear that the similarities between Wagner's *Ring* and Tolkien's *Legend* are not limited to their elementary subject matter.

As for correspondences on the textual level: Schreier mentions some in his essay on Wagner and the Inklings, for instance the announcement of Sigurd/Siegfried's birth (189). Tolkien has 'Thy womb shall wax / with the world's chosen' (*Legend*, 96), Wagner '*den hehrsten Helden der Welt / hegst du, o Weib / im schirmenden Schoß*' (the world's noblest hero / o woman, you shelter / in your protective womb', *Die Walküre*, III, 2). Apart from showing the contrast between Tolkien's terse and Wagner's more flowery styles, this is an obvious parallel not based on the source text, in this case the *Völsunga saga*. More exam-

---

58 Of course this fails to explain why many Germanic tribes put up such a fierce resistance against Christianity.

ples could no doubt be found,[59] but this would not add anything fundamental to the conclusion given above.

13.2. The Ring and the Legend – differences

13.2.1. Assorted differences

There are also many differences between the *Ring* and the *Legend*, or rather, 'The New Lay of the Völsungs'; 'The New Lay of Gudrún' deals with the fate of Gudrún and her brothers after Sigurd's death, and for Wagner this non-mythical part of the story held no particular interest. The *Ring* is mostly mythical whereas the *Legend* – as the title makes clear – is not. The *Ring* is ostentatiously and consistently symbolical, bordering on the allegorical, the *Legend* much less so. Wagner uses the sources to construct his own story, whereas Tolkien's version is, among other things, an attempt to reconstruct a missing part of an original Norse poem, and he follows the source texts quite faithfully. Wagner treats them more freely, making them say what he wants them to say, whereas Tolkien, though following his own interpretation, gives them a little more leeway to speak for themselves. He conscientiously picks and chooses from often contradicting material to create the most logical and likely version of the story, whereas Wagner synthesizes, welding often disparate elements together – in the way Siegfried remakes Nothung: the ancient stories are ground to splinters and forged into a new shape. The *Ring* becomes an extended metaphor for Wagner's views on art (among other things), while the *Legend* is more like a trial run of Tolkien's philology-inspired imagination.

These broad generalizations cover most of the differences between the two works. Many of these differences are trivial. Tolkien takes the name of Sigmund's sister Signý – who is not Sigurd's mother – from the *Völsunga saga*. Wagner takes the name of Siegmund's sister – who is Siegfried's mother – from the *Nibelungenlied*,

---

[59] Schreier gives two more. One of these is dubious: in the ransom scene the still visible hair of Freia/otter's whisker – to be covered with the ring – is not mentioned in direct speech in the source texts (Reginsmál, *Snorra Edda*); it is told rather than shown. However, the change from description to dialogue is inevitable in Wagner's dramatic work and occurs so often in Tolkien's poem that the presence of direct speech in both cases seems coincidence. Schreier's final example, the awakening scene on the mountain in which the Valkyrie explicitly asks who has woken her, is just wrong. Both Wagner and Tolkien quote the lay *Sigdrífomál* here.

where Sigelint is Sigemunds wife but not his sister.[60] In the sources and in the *Legend*, Fáfnir kills his father, in the *Ring* he kills his brother.

Some differences have to do with theatrical economy. Tolkien reduces the number of birds from *Fáfnismál* to two, Wagner decided one was enough. Tolkien retains the character of Gjúki, father of Gunnar, Högni and Gudrún: he is not important but the sources mention him, so he is in. Wagner omits Gibich, father of Gunther and Gutrune, precisely because he is not important.

Some differences are caused by the fact that Wagner uses a great deal of Eddaic material from lays not belonging to the Sigurd story, like the riddle-game between Mime and the Wanderer, or the exchange of the Wanderer and Erda. Sometimes, when a choice between conflicting sources is inevitable, they choose differently: Tolkien's Sigurd is murdered in his bed, as in the *Völsunga saga* and the 'Short Lay of Sigurd', while Siegfried meets his fate in the forest, the version found in the *Nibelungenlied* but also in the incomplete lay following the gap in the *Poetic Edda*, the *Brot af Sigurðarkviða*.

Occasionally, Tolkien and Wagner appear to be telling completely different stories. Tolkien's Niflungs are identical with the human Gjúkings (Wagner's Gibichungen), while the Nibelungen of the *Ring* are cave-dwelling dwarves. In the *Legend* it is Sigurd's foster-father, the smith, who reforges the broken sword, in the *Ring* it is Siegfried himself who reforges it, an act unprecedented in the sources, and it is with this self-made sword he hews the mighty spear asunder that broke it the first time around. No medieval Icelandic poet would have dreamed of letting any hero of whatever stature break Odin's spear and the notion would have been almost as alien to Tolkien's mind even if he had chosen to follow his sources less faithfully. And finally, the famous dictum 'both rings were round and there the resemblance ceases' is perfectly applicable to the ring Andvaranaut on the one hand, and Alberich's sinister piece of work on the other.

Tolkien tackles conflicting and/or confused sources the way one might expect from a philologist, for instance regarding Brynhild. Valkyries can be several things in Norse myth and saga. They can be female divinities granting or

---

60 Tolkien gave Sigurd's mother the name Sigrlinn, though the saga has Hjördis. In the *Poetic Edda*, Sigrlinn is the mother of Sigurd's half-brother Helgi, but the Commentary to the *Legend* suggests this was changed because 'a transference of the names took place' in the original texts (*Legend*, 201).

withholding victory in battle on Odin's command, choosing the slain worthy to enter Valhalla, serving the dead heroes. They can be family guardian spirits, seeresses protecting combatants with runic spells, or human women who have armed themselves to join the fray. They could serve as priestesses at rites where captives were put to death after battle (Ellis Davidson, 61).

In the story of Sigurd the Dragonslayer it seems that two traditions were conflated, one about a divine, magical valkyrie and another about a human warrior princess. According to the 'Note on Brynhild' (*Legend*, 241-245), Tolkien eventually came to the conclusion that the Brynhild of the Eddaic lays, and especially the fragmentary lay of Sigurd, was a humanized valkyrie, a 'semi-magical personage, ultimately derived from a Valkyrie legend' (242). The Brynhild from the *Völsunga saga* on the other hand was mortal, the daughter of Budli and the sister of Atli, living at the home of her foster father Heimir. The *Legend* leaves the character's exact status vague. Odin has punished her for granting victory to the wrong hero, but we are not told that she is a divine being stripped of her immortality. She seems to be a queen in her own right, living in a hall on this world, not somewhere among the dwellings of the gods. Unlike the *Völsunga saga* and the lay *Helreið Brynhildar* (Brynhild's Hell ride) Tolkien provides no further information concerning her background. As a result of all this, Brynhild remains rather enigmatic and remote. She is clearly mortal but she never becomes completely human, and one suspects that she is not Tolkien's favourite character.

Wagner felt no scholarly restraints. He simply combined the divine and the mortal woman by transforming one into the other in the course of the story. Brünnhilde is no enigma: we know who her parents are (Wotan and Erda) and what her relationship with her father is, we see her become human before she becomes a mortal woman, we witness both her moral failure and her ultimate moral victory. When a Wagner-hating lawyer using the pseudonym 'Ernst Von Pidde' subjected her to a fictive trial he ended up convicting her for life, among other things for arson (77), but it is obvious she has Wagner's full sympathy. Ultimately, though larger than life, she is anything but remote.

13.2.2. Characteristic choices

These are only a few examples. It would be pointless to give a systematic list of all instances in which the *Ring* cycle and the *Legend* differ. Because Tolkien closely follows the Icelandic source texts, such a list would for the most part coincide with a list of differences between the *Ring* and its various sources, which is not the purpose of this book.[61] Only a few will be discussed in more detail now to some shed light on the dissimilar ways in which the dramatist and the philologist would approach the same story elements, sometimes making opposite choices. This is where Christopher Tolkien's assertion that his father's lays bear little relation 'in spirit and purpose' to Wagner's opera cycle applies without reservation.

In this category fall the treatment of the hero's foster-father Regin/Mime, plus the way the incest theme is handled, both discussed earlier, and further the character of the chief god, Odin/Wotan (as opposed to his role), discussed in the previous section. In all these cases, Tolkien's Regin excepted, both add elements to the source material or change it in some way, Wagner usually more so than Tolkien. Another good example of their different treatment of a single scene taken from the *Völsunga saga* is the episode of the sword in the tree.

In the saga, a man enters the hall where the wedding feast of Siggeir and Signý takes place. No one knows him by appearance. The rim of his hat obscures his face, he is barefoot and clad in breeches of white linen. He appears to be old and grey and has only one eye. In his hand he has a sword which, to everyone's astonishment, he thrusts to the hilt into the bole of the big tree growing inside the hall! 'Whoever pulls this sword out may keep it as a gift,' he announces, 'and he himself will prove that he has never wielded a better blade.' Having said so, he strides out of the hall.

Tolkien omits the hat, the lack of footwear, the missing eye and the breeches of white linen. Instead a 'hoary-bearded', huge man enters the hall wearing a dark cloak, from which he pulls the sword he thrusts into the tree trunk; Tolkien does not mention how deeply. He turns the man's words into a challenging

---

61 Readers wanting to know more about this are referred to the books of Cooke and Björnsson. Both trace Wagner's sources meticulously. For Tolkien's treatment of his sources, see his son's commentary in the *Legend*.

invitation to heroic doom, leaves out the claim to the weapon's quality and – last but not least – makes the greybeard identify himself by applying one of the many names of Odin to himself: 'Who dares to draw / doom unfearing, / the gift of Grimnir / gleaming deadly?' By having him openly predict that the sword will bring doom, Tolkien removes the god's untrustworthiness, which in medieval Norse literature had been one of Odin's characteristics, from his version of the story.

Wagner describes the scene in *Die Walküre* by mouth of Sieglinde, who replaces Signý in his version. He, too, omits to mention that the man is barefoot and wearing white linen breeches, giving him the traditional blue robe of Odin instead. But precisely as in the saga, the man is described as a stranger, old and grey, and wearing a hat. This hat obscures 'one of his eyes'. The men in the hall are afraid of the 'ray of light' coming from the other, visible eye (a sun image added by Wagner, as the original held none). But Sieglinde is both teary-eyed and comforted when she sees it. The man swings a sword which he sticks into the tree to the hilt. He does not speak a single word, though.

Tolkien replaces the stranger's laconic and businesslike announcement, so typical of Icelandic saga literature, by a heroic challenge. He adds a trademark reference to doom and an equally trademark name.[62] Wagner presents a light effect, a sun image and various emotions. He also makes the stranger more mysterious by not giving him any text. Both lend the scene a characteristic flavour, one going for the heroic tone of voice and betraying a fondness for the concept of doom and for names, the other going for the theatrical effect, drawing attention to the symbolism and taking the psychological approach. It is in such details that the differences lie.

---

62 It has to be said, though, that Wagner outdoes Tolkien when it comes to attributing epithets to the chief god of the Norse, calling him Allvater, Siegvater, Heervater, Lichtsohn, Licht-Alberich, Wanderer, Allrauner, Weckrufer and Stürmebezwinger (Allfather, Victory-father, Father of Hosts, Son of Light, Light-Alberich, Wanderer, Universal Lore Whisperer, Wake-up Caller and Controller of Storms, and I may have overlooked a few). However, this is still a far cry from medieval Icelandic literature, where Óðin has dozens of names and epithets. Tolkien on his part remains truer to the sources in that he calls up a far more impressive, grim and mysterious image of the god than Wagner with his only-too-human Wotan.

13.2.3. Half-brother and full brothers

The character of Hagen provides an example of the way Tolkien and Wagner treated contradictory sources. In the *Nibelungenlied*, Hagen is not Gunther's relative but his vassal; the names of Gunther's brothers also start with G, and these identical initials denote close kinship. When the story migrated to Scandinavia and Gunther became Gunnar, Hagen, now called Högni, became his brother. According to the Eddas and the *Völsunga saga* their sister is called Gudrún (Chriemhilt in the *Nibelungenlied*, in the Norse texts the name of her mother, Grímhild) and a third, full brother is named Gotthorm. In the poem *Hyndluljóð*, however, this Gotthorm is the half-brother of Gunnar and Högni, a son of Grímhild but not of their father Gjúki, while Snorri makes him a stepbrother. In most Norse texts Gotthorm is the murderer of Sigurd, but according to the *Brot af Sigurðakviðo* the last part of the 'Old Lay of Sigurd' following the eight pages' gap in the *Poetic Edda*, Högni also has a hand in the hero's death: '*Sundr höfom Sigurð sverði högginn*' (We have hewn Sigurd asunder with a sword), he says (stanza 7, *Edda*, Neckel/Kuhn ed.). The last lay in the *Codex Regius*, the *Hamðismál*, also suggests his complicity.

Wagner adopted the notion that full siblings have identical initials, so Gunther's sister gets a Germanised form of her name in the Norse versions, Gutrune. Grimhild remains their mother. Like Gotthorm in some of the Norse sources, Hagen is the half-brother of Gunther and Gutrune, a son of Grimhild, in his case this is made clear by the different initial. In the *Ring*, he is sired by Alberich; that he had a non-human father was an idea Wagner took from the *Thidreks saga*. Like Gotthorm and unlike Gunther/Gunnar, Hagen has not sworn an oath of blood-brotherhood with Siegfried and is therefore free to kill him. This move enables Wagner to retain Hagen as the name of Siegfried's murderer according to the *Nibelungenlied* and possibly to the *Brot*, and also the evil motif behind the deed, which in the Norse tradition had become a necessary, though fatal revenge to preserve a ruler's honour. By making Hagen the son and intended[63] accomplice of Alberich, he combined the character's villainous nature with the motif of the cursed ring that inspires those who covet it to greed and evil. Wagner was a clever manipulator who managed to fuse contradictory tradi-

---

63 The intention is Alberich's; Hagen wants to keep the ring for himself.

tions, but as pointed out by Christopher Tolkien, in the end the story he tells is his own, not a retelling or reconstruction of his sources.

Tolkien chose to follow the *Hyndluljóð* and make Gotthorm a half brother. Högni is the instigator of the murder, but does not partake in it. Both he and Gunnar have sworn an oath of blood-brotherhood to Sigurd, the 'Short Lay of Sigurd', tells us. Gotthorm has not, but this is not stated explicitly; it is merely implied by the fact that he is identified as 'Grímhild's offspring' and a bastard, which suggests he was not worthy to swear the oath.

As Tolkien only used the Norse texts, there was no need for him to reconcile any of them with the Middle High German version. Högni, while being harsh and uncompromising, is not sinister; in the context of the story revenge is a duty to which you sacrifice your own blood, like Signý does when she avenges her father on her husband Siggeir. As a result, the originals shine through more clearly in his version, which was what Tolkien wanted them to do. Being a philologist, he wanted to make the ancient story speak for itself as best it could, weeding out what he considered to be impurities, straightening out what he considered to be distortions, while at times making small, but apparently necessary changes. The lays resulting from this tell us what *he* believed the sources to be saying, or to have said in the parts that are missing. Which is fortunate, for else these lays would have been redundant, except as an exercise in poetry.

The final example encompasses not only two fundamentally different takes on the source material, but also two different solutions to a complicated problem at the heart of the story of Sigurd/Siegfried and Brynhild/Brünnhilde.

13.3. Solving a conundrum: The ring at the core

13.3.1. The sources

One of the common elements in Wagner's *Ring* and Tolkien's *Legend* is the episode in which Sigurd wins Brynhild,[64] is tricked into forgetting her and goes on to win her once again, but now for Gunnar. On this second occasion

---

64 I use the original Norse names when referring to the common storyline.

he impersonates Gunnar, deceiving his beloved. He spends the night at her side, but puts a naked sword between them. Discovering the deceit Brynhild is furious. She accuses Sigurd of having slept with her and demands revenge, which ultimately leads to the hero's death.

This episode is found in the *Prose Edda*, the *Völsunga saga* and the *Thidreks saga*, all of them Icelandic sources Tolkien and Wagner have in common. Their remaining common source, the *Poetic Edda*, lacks this part of the story because of the gap in the manuscript, but the drama is implied in what follows and glimpses of it are found in other Eddaic lays. The Middle-High German *Nibelungenlied*, used only by Wagner, has a different version, but the deception and the deceived woman's fury are present here as well.

Most of the sources remain vague as to what happened between Sigurd and Brynhild. A ring changing hands greatly adds to the confusion, as it remains unclear who gave it to whom in what context and for what reason. Given the havoc it wreaks, it seems to prove something important, but what? Wagner and Tolkien both faced the challenge of unraveling this knot in order to come up with a logically consistent version of events. They had to make choices, and as it turns out both made rather different ones.

A survey of the sources shows the extent of the confusion. Two of the Icelandic texts agree that the main character, Sigurd, killed the dragon Fáfnir, gaining possession of a treasure that includes a cursed ring called Andvaranaut. (The ring's magical properties have no further relevance in the source texts.) He then meets Brynhild, a valkyrie and enters into some kind of relationship with her. In one of the source texts he gives her a ring, which later turns out to be Andvaranaut. Then he rides on to the court of the Gjúkings. According to one source he is fed a magic potion which makes him forget Brynhild, after which he is promised the hand of Gudrún if he helps her brother Gunnar to win Brynhild. He achieves this by changing shapes with Gunnar and jumping his horse across the ring of flames surrounding her. But after a crucial quarrel with Gudrún present in all the extant sources, Brynhild discovers the deceit, feels betrayed and demands revenge. This leads to Sigurd's murder.

Part Three: The Amateur and the Professional   247

How does this deceit come to light? Here the sources give confusing answers. We go back to the situation right after the slaying of Fáfnir.

1) In the *Prose Edda* Sigurd finds a sleeping valkyrie in a house on a mountaintop. He cuts away her hauberk. She wakes up 'and her name was Hild' ('battle' in Norse), 'she was called Brynhild', says the text. Sigurd leaves, arrives at the court of Gunnar, son of Gjúki, and marries Gunnar's sister Gudrún. Sigurd and Gunnar ride to the mountain to win Brynhild for Gunnar. A wavering fire, Norse *vafrlogi*, now burns around her house. Sigurd manages to leap across it on his horse Grani, after having changed shapes with Gunnar, whose horse shied before the flames and who could not get Grani to leap across them either. Sigurd

> wed Brynhild that evening. And when they went to bed, he drew the sword Gram from its sheath and put it between them. And in the morning, when he rose and dressed, he gave Brynhild as a *linen fee* the golden ring which Loki had taken from Andvari and took from her another ring as a remembrance.[65]

Later the women argue about who has the more valiant husband. Brynhild claims it is Gunnar, who crossed her wall of fire. Gudrun points to Andvaranaut on Brynhild's hand, remarking that it was not Gunnar who took it from Fáfnir. Also, she shows Brynhild the remembrance ring Sigurd gave her. Now Brynhild knows that the man who spent the night at her side after leaping across the fire must have been Sigurd. She is deeply insulted and this leads to Sigurd's murder. The crux of this version is that Brynhild receives Andvaranaut, the cursed dwarven ring, as a linen fee after the wedding night – and a linen fee is a morning gift in exchange for a newly married woman's virginity.

2) In the *Völsunga saga*, it is Gudrún who has Andvaranaut and triumphantly shows it to Brynhild, claiming that Sigurd took it from her, Brynhild's, finger after the wedding night, and that Sigurd was her husband before Gunnar. Which means that the man who crossed the *vafrlogi* was not Gunnar but Sigurd. This version has its own problems. Wearing Gunnar's shape, Sigurd spends three nights with Brynhild laying his sword between them, and then takes Andvaranaut from her in exchange for another ring. Previously in the

---

65 Icelandic: 'Þat kveld gekk han at brúðlaupi með Brynhildi. En er þau kvómu í sæing, þá dró hann sverðit Gram ór slíðrum ok lagði í milli þeira. En at morni þá er han stóð upp ok klæddi sik, þá gaf hann Brynhildi at *línfé* gullbauginn þann er Loki hafði tekit af Andvara en tók af henne annan baug til minia.' (Italics mine)

saga they had met and declared their love and he had given her a ring, but it is only in this scene we find out that it must have been Andvaranaut. Was it Brynhild's original morning gift? The saga does not tell of any wedding, yet Sigurd and she must have been together, for they have a daughter. This also means that Brynhild is quite well aware of the fact that it was Sigurd who took her virginity, which ought to take the sting out of Gudrúns's accusation – yet it doesn't. And why did Sigurd take back Andvaranaut? The author of the saga does not explain any of this.

3) The third Icelandic source, the *Thidreks saga*, is a translation of a low German version of the story. At some point, Sigurd has met the warrior-like Brynhild and promised to marry her. But he changes his mind when he meets Gunnars's sister Grímhild and helps Gunnar to win Brynhild in exchange for Grímhild's hand. Brynhild greatly resents this, reproaches Sigurd for his change of heart and refuses to share her bed with Gunnar, who is unable to subdue her because she is stronger than he is. He asks Sigurd to deflower her, which will make her lose her strength. Sigurd does this, disguised as Gunnar. Some time later, the two women quarrel over the right to sit in the high seat in the hall. When Brynhild claims it because Sigurd is hardly better than a vagabond, Grímhild bluntly tells her it was Sigurd who deflowered her, not her own husband. Brynhild denies this, until Grímhild shows her the ring Sigurd took from her in the wedding night. In itself, this somewhat crude version makes sense – except that just as in the *Nibelungenlied* the ring is not Andvaranaut, and the connection with Andvari's curse, which brings about the death of most of the people involved, has been lost. Sigurd comes across as the boor he also is in Wagner's *Ring* – much of his character and history there is indeed based on the *Thidreks saga*.

4) As mentioned, the *Poetic Edda* no longer contains a direct account of the episode, but the surviving fragment of the 'Old Lay of Sigurd' ends with a reference to the naked sword separating him from Brynhild, with the addition that the steel glistened with poison. The 'Short Lay of Sigurd' tells us that Sigurd granted Brynhild to Gunnar, though she was meant to be his. On his deathbed Sigurd stresses once again that he loved Brynhild, but kept his oath to Gunnar and never dishonoured him, not wanting to be called the lover of Gunnar's wife. In *Helreið Brynhildar*, a late poem, it is Brynhild herself who states that they lay side by side for eight nights as though Sigurd '*minn broðir um borin*

væri' (was born my brother, 12). Of all the sources, only the preserved lays of the *Poetic Edda* seem absolutely certain that nothing whatsoever transpired between the two at any point of the story.

5) In the Middle-High-German *Nibelungenlied* Brünhild is not a valkyrie but a 'Queen of Iceland', famous for her physical strength. She has had no prior relationship with Siegfried (the German equivalent of Sigurd), who helps Gunther to defeat her in an athletic contest while wearing the Tarnkappe, an invisibility cloak. When Gunther needs Siegfried to break her resistance in the wedding night – Brünhild will retain her strength unless and until she is deflowered – Siegfried subdues her, taking her ring and her girdle, which he then gives to his own bride Kriemhild. Now follows the famous quarrel, this time over the right to enter church first. Brünhilt claims precedence, as Kriemhild is married to her husband's vassal. Kriemhild then shows her ring and girdle, claiming that Siegfried has slept with Brünhild, which makes her his paramour. This ring is not Andvaranaut, nor is it cursed; just like the girdle, it only functions as a symbol of defloration. The text strongly implies that Siegfried did the deed, despite Gunther's request that he refrain from it, but the poet remains circumspect about it in this courtly epic.

13.3.2. The botched tradition

So, what really happened and what is the role of the ring used as proof? Is it a symbolic object bringing a wrong to light? Or is it a cursed object causing evil, which would explain why most characters involved meet a sticky end? Is it possible to arrive at a believable core version of the tale, one that contains no contradictions and leaves no questions unanswered?

These questions were raised by Shippey when he discussed the *Königsproblem* of 19th century Germanic philology, the tangled relations between all the different versions of the Nibelungen story, in the context of a comparison between Tolkien and Wagner. He did so on no less than three occasions. The first time[66] was a few years before the publication of the *Legend* in 'The Problem of the Rings: Tolkien and Wagner' (Shippey 2007, 97-114). In this paper Shippey purported

---

66 Before that, Shippey had briefly discussed the same problem in the 2nd, revised edition of *The Road to Middle-earth* (274-276), but without mentioning Wagner. He included a diagram showing the relations between the various textual versions of the story, including the hypothetical lost lays on which the surviving versions were based.

to show what choices the amateur-philologist Wagner had made when faced with all the contradictory versions of the tale and what solution he reached. The connection with Tolkien lay in Wagner's use of the cursed ring and in his loss of the heroism which played such a prominent role, both in ancient Germanic literature and in Tolkien's own works – according to Shippey a loss concomitant with the choices Wagner made.

At the time, Shippey knew of the existence of Tolkien's *Legend* poems, but as they were not available yet he could not compare the two most notable post-medieval versions of the story. He did so briefly in his review of the *Legend* in the *Times Literary Supplement* (Shippey 2009) and more thoroughly in a much longer review (2010).

In the essay, Shippey concludes that Wagner deals 'neatly and expediently' with the ring problem:

> Siegfried gave Brünnhilde the Ring when he woke her from her enchanted sleep, and they declared undying love. Hagen, son of Alberich, gave Siegfried the potion of forgetfulness, so that he forgot his love for Brünnhilde. He won her for Gunther, and Brünnhilde gave the Ring to the man who conquered her, whom she thought to be Gunther, perhaps as a sign of submission. She is then, in Act II scene 3 of *Götterdämmerung*, amazed to see it on Siegfried's finger. This is a good scene in every way. (Shippey, 2007, 108)

This summary is not entirely correct: Brünnhilde does not give the ring to the fake Gunther – he rips it from her finger (it is Hagen who falsely suggests it was a gift in order to make it more plausible that Sigurd betrayed Gunther's trust by sleeping with his bride). But as this makes for even better drama, it probably would not have affected Shippey's verdict. Yet there is a downside to Wagner's achievement: he loses the 'quarrel of the queens', present in all the medieval source texts, and with it the crucial role of Gunnar's sister: in *Götterdämmerung*, Gutrune is a reduced character, 'a pathetic and confused bystander', whereas she is a central figure in the medieval texts (108). Shippey also deplores the replacement of Gunnar's heroic brother Högni by an evil half-brother, Hagen (109). However, Högni's heroism only stands out in the part of the story Wagner did not use, so this seems not too great a loss. Moreover, the murder of Siegfried has nothing heroic at all and that Wagner actually did Högni a favour by not giving the murderer his name while at the same time omitting his later heroism.

The gist of Shippey's criticism is that 'Wagner in *Götterdämmerung* had botched the very kernel of the whole Norse/German heroic tradition', or that Tolkien must have thought so (109). If Wagner had tried to create an heroic epic in this tradition, such criticism would undoubtedly be to the point. It is true that he started out with the intention to compose an heroic opera about Siegfried's death. But somewhere along the road he realized that what he really wanted to create was a mythical drama, so the idea of the *Heldenoper* was abandoned. The most heroic of the four *Ring* operas is *Die Walküre*, but knowing that the wages of heroism was death, even there Wagner saw fit to counterpoise Siegmund's love-inspired heroism with the valkyries' cavalier attitude towards the dead heroes they carry to Walhall. Nor are the corpses hanging across their saddles particularly heroical. That Siegfried is not really a hero is hardly surprising, given the fact that most of the time he does not know fear – he never experienced it before he met Brünnhilde, and half an hour later he has forgotten it again. Being fearless does not make a hero; heroism is overcoming one's fear.

The feats described in the second part of the *Nibelungenlied* and in the two Eddaic lays *Atlakviða* and *Atlamál* never held much of Wagner's interest, so referring to characters from these heroic lays of the *Poetic Edda* to show where he went wrong seems beside the point. Maybe a reference to the *Völuspá* would have been more relevant: it was among his sources, it includes a last battle of gods against monsters, it has plenty of heroism in the face of certain defeat, and it is mythical. In the end, though, it lacks the tragic conflict that makes it good drama. (And of course it is impossible to put on stage. If he had been our contemporary, Wagner would perhaps have tried to use it in a film.)

There is something ironical about the idea that Tolkien handled the Norse/German heroic tradition better than Wagner did. It is Wagner who has always been accused of having inspired the national-socialist adulation of Germanic heroism with his *Ring*. The suggestion that it was not heroic enough appears to put Tolkien's own appreciation of Germanic heroism in a somewhat questionable light.[67] As Bachmann & Honegger point out, though condemning the national-socialist misuse of Germanic legend, he shows no awareness of

---

67 This is not to say that Tolkien was ideologically more shady than Wagner – on the contrary. But this aspect of his postulated criticism of the *Ring* would add weight to the argument that the Nazis misunderstood it.

any deeper lying parallels between their approach of it and his own (28-9). However, they mitigate this by pointing out that he was free of anti-Semitism (33f) and showed himself aware of the dangers of mythmaking in the 'Notion Club Papers' written 1945/6, where he points out how explosive myths and legends can be (36).

In his review of the *Legend* in the *Times Literary Supplement*, Shippey introduces a contest element to the Tolkien-Wagner comparison. Instead of only measuring the composer's work against Tolkien's philological expertise and his measuring rod of heroic courage, Shippey could now directly compare Wagner's solution to the aforementioned problem of the rings with the one Tolkien arrived at in the *Legend*. Again he outlines the problem, stressing the dilemma in which the contradicting source texts leave anyone who attempts to make the story internally plausible. The inevitable conclusion would be that either Sigurd behaved like a 'sexual predator' towards Brynhild, or that the story as it exists today, in several different versions but with the crucial episode missing from the *Poetic Edda*, is a mess that leaves everyone baffled, especially the author of the *Nibelungenlied* 'and Wagner after him'.

Everyone, that is, except Tolkien. His challenge was 'to cut to the heart of the story, make events psychologically plausible and do so without losing tragic force. This he has done,' claims Shippey – implying that Wagner had not and thereby more or less retracting his previous, more positive assessment of the way he had handled things in *Götterdämmerung*. What was a neat solution and good drama despite the loss of the queens' quarrel and the spirit of heroism, now paled into insignificance besides Tolkien's superior treatment of the subject. The professional English philologist had challenged the German amateur and defeated him. Unfortunately for the curious newspaper reader the *Times* review does not provide any details concerning either Wagner's bafflement or the precise nature of Tolkien's achievement. The latter would have been a spoiler, but in the case of the former this silence is a pity. It raises the question how solid the evidence is and adds to the impression that the author of the review was picking a bone with Wagner or at least with those of his admirers who use *The Ring of the Nibelung* to bash *The Lord of the Rings*.

13.3.3. The ring of fire

The lengthy review in the 2010 volume of *Tolkien Studies* is much more forthcoming with information. Once again, Shippey explains what the problem is, but this time he expands the ring-problem to incorporate the first meeting of Sigurd and Brynhild and the ring of flames surrounding the valkyrie, the *vafrlogi*.

The situation regarding the flame ring is indeed problematic, too. It is mentioned in all the Icelandic sources except the *Thidreks Saga*, which belongs to the German tradition. The lays of the *Poetic Edda* give conflicting information. *Sigrdrífomál* tells of a valkyrie punished by Odin for disobeying his command, and put to sleep on a mountain top. She is called Sigrdrífa, 'one who incites to victory'. Ascending the mountain Sigurd sees a great light, *svá sem eldr brynni, oc liómaði af til himins* ('which burned like fire and blazed up to the heavens'). Approaching it fearlessly, all he sees is a shield wall surrounding[68] the valkyrie; either the flames were not real or they subsided before he arrived there. The lay does not identify the valkyrie as Brynhild. In *Grípisspá*, essentially a biography of Sigurd told in the form of prophecies, the valkyrie on the mountain and Brynhild are different women as well. The late, syncretic *Helreið Brynhildar* does identify Sigrdrífa as Brynhild, while the *Prose Edda* names her both Hild and Brynhild and confirms her identity as a valkyrie.

As for the flame ring, the Hell Ride poem mentions both a shield wall and a fire, burning 'before' Brynhild's hall 'in the south' in two consecutive stanzas, coalescing the flame wall with the shield wall (Andersson, 115). *Grípisspá* has no flame wall at all. In *Fáfnismál* the *vafrlogi* surrounds the sleeping valkyrie on the mountain but she is not called Brynhild here. The *Prose Edda* mentions a ring of real fire around Brynhild's house on the mountain top, but not at the time Sigurd first finds (Bryn)Hild, only when he comes to woo her on Gunnar's behalf. Describing the first time Sigurd finds Brynhild (on the mountain) the

---

68 It is tempting to interpret the sources in which a ring of fire or a shield wall *surrounds* the valkyrie symbolically: crossing the ring means deflowering the maiden. But apparently the medieval authors did not see it this: either the deflowering is not combined with crossing the flame ring, or there is no ring, as in 'Brynhild's Hel Ride'. Wagner in his turn apparently failed to realize a woman can only be deflowered once, while Tolkien was prudish enough to shy away from the symbolism by keeping Brynhild a virgin on both occasions – unless he did not see it either. But perhaps sometimes a *vafrlogi* is just a *vafrlogi*.

Völsunga saga quotes the prose introduction to *Sígrdrifomál*; when he returns accompanied by Gunnar, the fire is real. Later the saga states that Sigurd braved the fire for Brynhild, whereas the sons of Gjúki did not.

So the sources disagree about the ring of fire as much as they do about Andvaranaut. Wagner and Tolkien both opt for a real fire which is there at the first meeting of the hero and the valkyrie, probably inspired by *Fáfnismál* and the identification of the sleeping valkyrie with Brynhild in the *Völsunga saga*. In his commentary to 'The New Lay of the Völsungs', Christopher Tolkien mentions that his father 'referred in other writing to Brynhild "having surrounded herself with a wall of flame"' (*Legend*, 218).

Shippey recounts Tolkien's version in full: Sigurd comes upon Brynhild inside a ring of fire, also described as a 'lightning fence'. They plight their troth. He leaves to win renown, because she has vowed to wed only the World's Chosen; she stays. He reaches the court of the Gjúkings, drinks the forgetfulness potion concocted by Gunnar's evil mother Grímhild and is promised Gudrún's hand in marriage if he helps win Brynhild for Gunnar. Arriving at Brynhild's ring of fire, Sigurd drives his horse across the flames in Gunnar's shape but puts his naked sword between himself and Brynhild during the night. The next morning he leaves while she is still asleep after having exchanged the ring on her finger for Andvaranaut. During the quarrel of the queens, Gudrun points out to Brynhild that this is the ring she is wearing on her finger, and that it was not Gunnar who won it from the dragon. Now Brynhild knows who it was that braved her flame wall the second time around, though he wore Gunnar's shape at the time. To exact revenge for Sigurd's 'betrayal' of their vows, she claims that '[m]y bed he entered, by my body laid him, betrayed thy trust' (*Legend*, 167). Tragedy ensues; only when it is too late and Sigurd is dead she mentions the sword lying between them.

One detail of this summary is incorrect: Brynhild does not stay inside the ring of fire. Though being a valkyrie, she is also a queen in her own right and 'a king shall wed' (*Legend*, 125), which Sigurd is not at that point. Once Sigurd has woken her up, she rides to her own court to await Sigurd's triumphant return as a king. While she is there, many suitors come to woo her but the poem implies she kills most of them. At last Odin arrives to kindle a new fire around her court to keep everyone out except the World's Chosen. Possibly Shippey conflated Tolkien's version with Wagner's, in which Brünnhilde does remain behind the flame wall until Siegfried returns. Sigurd, however, needs time to meet Brynhild's demand. In the mean time, she can hardly remain inside the ring of flames awake and well on the mountain top without any sustenance. Hence her return to her own court and Odin's renewed intervention. It looks as though this may be based on the Hell Ride poem, except that this does not have two rings of fire but one shield wall and one flame wall. Nowhere in the sources does Odin *re*kindle a firewall; this was Tolkien's interpretation, or invention.

As Christopher Tolkien points out, the *Völsunga saga* treats the valkyrie, Brynhild, in two incompatible ways (*Legend*, 220). Its author combines Sigrdrífa, the supernatural woman Odin put asleep on a mountain top by way of punishment with the human maiden Brynhild, in all probability the heroine of the lost 'Long Lay of Sigurd' (Andersson, 37) and a daughter of Budli,[69] who dwelled at her brother-in-law Heimir's court. Both plight their troth with Sigurd, which may have been the reason they came to be considered identical to begin with. The peculiar result of this authorial decision is that Sigurd meets Brynhild and swears oaths with her twice: once on the mountain, Hindarfjall, once at Heimir's court. On the mountain Sigurd sees the great, fire-like light; approaching he finds the shield wall. No flame wall surrounds Brynhild at Heimir's court when Sigurd first sees her. Later in the saga, when he arrives with Gunnar to woo her, there is a *vafrlogi* around her hall and he leaps his horse across it.

Tolkien repeatedly rejects the way the *Völsunga saga* treats the events (*Legend*, 220, 223, 225, 232), but he does retain both fires, though the first one apparently is not real. None of the sources has two flame walls and only the relatively late Hell Ride has Odin kindle the fire around Brynhild's hall. In the *Legend* the fires appear to be identical: both times Tolkien uses the word lightning, whereas the *Sigdrífomál* and the *Völsunga saga* both discern between a *liós mikit*, a great light, and a *vafrlogi*, a wavering fire, like the one mentioned in *Fáfnismál*

---

[69] In the saga, Budli is the father of Atli, whose name is the Norse cognate of Attila. But the Atli of the saga, the brother of Brynhild, has little to do with the historical Scourge of God. He is derived from the Atli of the Icelandic *Atlamál*, which is essentially an Icelandic family feud using names from the tale of Sigurd.

in connection with the nameless valkyrie on the mountain. Apparently Tolkien tried to fuse the two separate Brynhild traditions seamlessly where the author of the saga had left a visible seam. Whether he succeeded completely probably depends on the reader's prior knowledge of the story.

Wagner, writing a drama instead of an epic, reduces the time Siegfried is away to less than a day, using the forgetfulness potion to achieve theatrical economy in order to retain his original ring of fire.[70] In the initial version of *Götterdämmerung*, *Siegfried's Tod*, the fire is said to have died when the hero crossed it. Later it flares up again when Brünnhilde prays to Wotan, not knowing whether it is the returning Siegfried who approaches her or someone more sinister. Wagner changed this passage in the revision. In the final version the fire never wholly dies; on Siegfried's approach it just starts to burn more brightly again.

Both Wagner and Tolkien preferred to follow the *Sígrdrífomál* for the first meeting, replacing the illusionary blaze by the real fire of the *Fáfnismál*. To describe this fire Wagner uses the German translation of *vafrlogi*, *Waberlohe*, which he found in Grimm's *Deutsches Wörterbuch*. Tolkien retains the lightning effect from the original – a remarkable element, suggesting some kind of lightning storm on the mountain top.[71] This leaves a strong visual impression. Just like Wagner, he uses the valkyrie's awakening hymn from *Sigdrífomál* in this scene, though unlike Wagner he includes the greeting to the night – because his Brynhild is a less positive character than Wagner's? He also retains the shield-wall and the name of the mountain. For Wagner it is just the *Walkürenfels*, the Valkyrie Rock.

13.3.4. Did they do it?

According to the *Ring*, Siegfried and Brünnhilde unite in love, as they must have done in the *Völsunga saga*, given the fact that they have a daughter there, and Sigurd gives her the ring as a token of their love. Tolkien, critical as he was of the saga, considered this daughter a later addition and therefore omitted her. The *Prose Edda's* suggestive sentence about the linen fee is in keeping with

---

70 Wilberg argues that the magical mechanism of the potion fits the mythical experience of time according to which time is 'a quality of the condensed action' (Wilberg, 275).
71 As the fire on the mountain top is a specific trait of the Icelandic versions, the link with erupting volcanoes is obvious, as mentioned by Björnsson (124).

the fact that at the end of the story, Sigurd and Brynhild turn out to have a daughter as well, born 'at Heimir's'; in the *Völsunga saga* Heimir is Brynhild's brother-in-law and foster father, at whose court Brynhild dwells. Tolkien follows the *Poetic Edda*: in the *Legend* the two only plight their troth upon their first meeting on the mountain, and they do not lie with each other. Tolkien's religious convictions possibly excluded a situation in which Brynhild was a suitable marriage candidate for Gunnar while she was wed or betrothed to Sigurd. His version shows a general tendency towards desexualisation: he also retouches the indecent proposal Sigurd makes to Brynhild in the *Völsunga saga*, telling her he would like to share her bed and suggesting that she could have a relationship with both him and Gunnar. In Tolkien's version, he offers to slay Gunnar (*Legend*, 164); was murder less abhorrent to him than a love triangle? Did he decide this part of the saga was inauthentic? It was partly based on the 'Long Lay of Sigurd', *Sigurðarkviða in meiri*, one of the lost poems Tolkien was trying to reconstruct in the *Legend*; did he reject Sigurd's remark in the saga as a later interpolation? It is a pity that his son does not comment on this interesting change.

In any case, Wagner and Tolkien give different answers to the question whether the two had a physical relationship. Their opposite choices determine the further development of the story in each case. Once Sigurd has conquered the *vafrlogi* for the second time, now as Gunnar, and put his sword between himself and Brynhild during the wedding night, Tolkien closely follows the account in the *Prose Edda*. Sigurd exchanges rings with Brynhild, taking her ring and giving her Andvaranaut in return. Yet Tolkien made some important changes. As Shippey writes, Snorri's linen fee makes it 'dangerously plausible' that something happened between them during the night (2010, 304). He does not discuss the two Eddaic lays that unequivocally deny any carnal relationship between Sigurd and Brynhild, the 'Short Lay of Sigurd' and 'Brynhild's Hell Ride', but they obviously served as a foundation for the account in the *Legend*. Tolkien eliminates Snorri's suggestion of intercourse by omitting the linen fee. Also, he has the exchange of the rings take place while Brynhild sleeps. (This takes some suspension of disbelief: how many women will sleep through an exchange that involves prying a ring from a finger? But let us assume it is possible.)

The *Prose Edda* and the *Völsunga saga* then supplied the part missing from the *Poetic Edda*. Tolkien leaves no doubt whatsoever concerning Sigurd's innocence and good faith. His Christ-like hero, the World's Chosen, never betrayed his blood-brother Gunnar by sleeping with Gunnar's intended – not realising she was his own intended until it was too late. For that reason Tolkien took the ambiguity out of Snorri's account. (He retains another ambiguity found in all the originally Norse sources: when Brynhild demands revenge from her husband once the cat is out the bag in the form of Andvaranaut, she says: 'My bed he entered / by my body laid him,' accusing Sigurd ('The New Lay of the Völsungs', IX, 34); it is only after his death that she mentions the sword he put between them.)

This change is not unproblematic. Because of the forgetfulness potion, Brynhild was a stranger to Sigurd when he leaped across the fire wall. So why did he give her Andvaranaut, his great prize after slaying Fáfnir, if not as a linen fee? The *Legend* text says 'in token' (152), but in token of what? To be able to prove he had not been afraid of the flames, should anyone taunt him as a coward? Would it have been worse than being called a perjurer?

In the essay 'The Problem of the Rings', Shippey's objections to the *Prose Edda* were that a) it had two rings[72] and b) that Brynhild never noticed that she was wearing Andvaranaut until Gudrun told her that she did. But this is exactly what we find in the *Legend*: two rings and an unattentive Brynhild. That Brynhild would never notice that she is suddenly wearing a different ring sounds like something only male authors could have thought believable. That she would notice it without suspecting anything was wrong, makes sense if the exchange was made after the 'bridegroom' slept with his bride. Therefore, Snorri's version actually makes a little more sense than Tolkien's.

In the *Legend*, the quarrel of the queens closely resembles the version in the *Prose Edda*, except that Tolkien leaves out the linen fee once again. Gudrun points out to Brynhild that the ring she wears is Andvaranaut and that it was not her husband Gunnar who won it or rode the *vafrlogi*. She also shows her own ring and asks the other woman if it was Gunnar who took it from her. Exactly as

---

72 In *The Legend of Brynhild*, Andersson argues that this was also the case in the missing 'Long Lay of Sigurd', much of which can be reconstructed from the *Völsunga saga* (25).

in the *Prose Edda*, Brynhild now suddenly realizes she has Andvaranaut on her finger and demands revenge, which then leads to Sigurd's murder. So, though making a firm decision concerning Sigurd's sexual morals, Tolkien leaves some of the question Shippey asks in the essay unanswered. Obviously, he had his own problem with the cursed ring.

Discussing Wagner's version Shippey only notes that Wagner did not seem to know how to deal with the events during the much-discussed wedding night, for in *Götterdämmerung* II, 2 Siegfried 'assures Gutrune that he was faithful to her, but in II, 4 he seems quite unable to explain how he came by the ring [...] which we saw him take by force at the end of Act 1' (Shippey 2010, 305).

For Wagner, the union between Siegfried and Brünnhilde is the central concern, love versus power being the main theme of the *Ring* cycle. She truly becomes his wife in every meaning of the word, she loves him deeply and she cherishes the ring he gave her as a token of their love. In this context the quarrel of the queens would have struck a false note; too much emphasis would have been on the deceived woman's hurt pride and diminished status, neither of which interested Wagner as much as the betrayal of love did.

The central concern of the oldest Norse source was the disastrous betrayal of oaths – not just those of Sigurd towards the other characters, but also Brynhild's oath to wed the best of men. She is deceived into being untrue to herself and thwarted in her ambitions, and she makes everyone suffer for it. This concern is Tolkien's as well: it is no coincidence that the only line in the *Legend* that does not alliterate correctly, as Shippey points out in his reviews, speaks of oaths unfulfilled ('The New Lay of the Völsungs', IX, 4). Love does play a part in his version, but Brynhild calls herself 'vow-breaker', 'oath-breaker' and 'dishonoured' before complaining hat she is 'love-bereaved' (159). Though unfulfilled oaths also play a role in the *Ring*, Wagner's central concern in this part of the story is the cruel betrayal of love, romantic, passionate love. In this he was taking his cue from the *Völsunga saga*, where frustrated desire has taken the place of thwarted ambition.

The scene that replaces the Queens' Quarrel in *Götterdämmerung* II, 3 – the quarrel of Brünnhilde and Siegfried – is more powerful than the one in the

Norse texts. There the quarrel is about who has the right to wash her hair in river water not used by the other – almost a fight of the house-and-garden variety. It is the German poem that offers the grand image of two noble ladies having an altercation on the steps of Worms cathedral. Wagner's deviant take on this is as magnificent as the scene in the *Nibelungenlied* and it works well on the stage – yet it has a flaw. Siegfried can only be Brünnhilde's antagonist because he is clueless about their previous relationship. In most of the Icelandic source texts, and also in the *Legend*, Sigurd gradually remembers his troth-plighting with Brynhild when it is too late, but he does not mention it to anyone in order to avoid hurting people's pride and feelings. He just tries to make the best of it. This makes him a more mature character than Siegfried ever gets the chance to become. (On the other hand, if Wagner had decided to retain the women's quarrel, the final installment of the *Ring* would have needed to be even longer than it is now.)

Having replaced one of the queens with Siegfried, Wagner had to find a different way to let the deception come to light. Siegfried forcefully pulls the ring from Brünnhilde's finger when he abducts her in Gunther's shape. As he keeps it on his own finger, instead of giving it to Gutrune, Brynhild immediately discovers it when she sees him in Gunther's hall the day after. She is hurt and furious to see him at Gutrune's side and questions his ownership of the ring: if Gunther took it from her, how come Siegfried is wearing it now? When a bemused Gunther denies that Siegfried got the ring from him, she realises it must have been Siegfried who ripped it from her. She announces to the world that he made her his wife in the full sense of the word. And he did – only on a previous occasion.

Siegfried, who does not remember their first meeting due to the forgetfulness potion, rejects her accusation under oath: he has not slept with her. As he told Gutrune earlier, he put a blade between himself and Brünnhilde during the wedding night, as the end of the abduction scene has already made clear. So to his best knowledge he does not commit perjury. Yet when Brünnhilde promptly swears he has just done so, this is technically true, as she never specified *when* he made her his wife. In other words, Wagner also uses ambiguity by omission, just like Tolkien and some of the sources do. The difference is that Tolkien's Sigurd never bedded Brynhild, while Siegfried and Brünnhilde did make love. Most of the medieval sources, the Icelandic prose texts as well as the *Nibelungenlied*, either admit or strongly suggest that the latter was what had really happened. Only a couple of lays from the *Poetic Edda*, followed by Tolkien, deny it – possibly also the missing part of the 'Old Lay' (the oldest) and the entirely missing 'Great Lay of Sigurd', both very crucial texts. This is not entirely certain: the *Völsunga saga*, which is is based on both, does imply a sexual relationship. But as mentioned above Tolkien rejected the existence of Brynhild's and Sigurd's daughter Aslaug as a later addition. The *Legend* is his argument in favour of Sigurd's innocence, an argument both scholarly and poetical, but not entirely umproblematic.

The Wagner scene is strong, as Shippey wrote before he knew Tolkien's version of the tale, and the music makes it terrific. However, it has one catch, and it is this which may have led to Shippey's claim that the problem of the rings baffled Wagner, though he does not lay his finger on the precise spot.[73] Siegfried may have forgotten his love for Brünnhilde, but he took the ring back from her *after* drinking the potion. Yet he does not seem to remember this either, because he claims to have taken it from Fafner. So either he is lying or this must be a plothole. In one of his books about the *Ring*, Wapnewski calls Siegfried too straightforward to bend the truth in a believable manner (Wapnewski 1998, 271). Even so, he ought to have wondered how Brünnhilde came by the ring in the first place when he found her on the rock. Nothing in Wagner's opera suggests that he ever does.

When dealing with the problem of the ring Wagner consistently follows the *Völsunga saga*: there is a previous sexual relationship between Sigurd and Brynhild, and Sigurd takes Andvaranaut, or in his version Alberich's ring, back from her after crossing her flame wall to win her for Gunnar. There is something to be said for this scenario: the ring used to be in his possession before, and his memory of giving it to Brynhild when they first met was blocked by the potion (the saga avoids this problem altogether by never mentioning when Sigurd gave Brynhild the ring). Wagner's plothole, alternatively Siegfried's blockheadedness, is basically that of the saga: the hero never wonders how the valkyrie came by

---

[73] Shippey focuses on the wedding night, not on the moment when Siegfried forcefully took the ring back from Brünnhilde, but this is where the real problem originated.

the ring he recognised as his property after crossing the flame wall. Gudrún must have wondered about it at some point – and come to realize what had to be the answer. This made her taunt possible in the first place. As Wagner omits the quarrel of the queens, the plothole, if it is one, is more glaring in his version, which shifts the attention to the hero himself.

But what if Siegfried is lying deliberately? Shaw notes that he is 'manifestly puzzled' (Shaw, 256), so he apparently does not think this is the case. Wapnewski however, after first quoting the famous maxim that even Homer nods sometimes, explains Siegfried's response to Brünnhilde's accusation by accusing the ring. It is the cursed ring that has made him forget or even suppress his shameful and petty, but deathly deceit (Wapnewski 1988, 28). Kitcher and Schacht go even further. They point out how appropriate it is that Siegfried, who thoroughly profanes his and Brünnhilde's love in this scene, is wearing the ring that could only be forged after Alberich renounced love (Kitcher & Schacht, 172). Also, 'Siegfried's keenness to retain the Ring and to protest that it is his is [an] indication of the corruption of his character' (173), which started with his arrival at the court of the Gibichungs – that is, human society. They suggest, just like Shippey, that there is something fishy about his claim that he did not touch Brünnhilde and put his sword between them: why would she have followed Gunther home meekly, if not because his look-alike had convincingly played his role as a newlywed?[74] The difference is that they do not ascribe it to bafflement on Wagner's part, but consider it a part of Siegfried's corruption process (174).

True enough, both ring and curse motifs are heard when Siegfried pulls the ring from her finger and also when she sees it on his at the court of the Gibichungs. However, when he claims he did not get the ring from her or from Gunther, the orchestra plays a fragment of the ring motif (which is logical) and the forgetfulness motif, but not the curse motif. Nor does any ring-related motif sound when he swears a holy oath on Hagen's spear that he has remained faithful to his blood-brother Gunther. Even if Siegfried realizes he has, in fact, robbed the ring from Brünnhilde – which the audience, not being privy to his thoughts, never finds out – his oath to Gunther compels him to deny it.

---

74 Some of the sources, and Tolkien, avoid this problem by making the crossing of the flame wall the condition of Brynhild's surrender. Snorri avoids it by mentioning the linen-fee, thereby suggesting Sigurd consummated Gunnar's marriage for him.

On the other hand, music and story are often at variance in the *Ring*, and as Dahlhaus puts it, ambiguity is a central category of Wagner's aesthetics (1971, 109-110). So possibly the uncertainty regarding the nightly events on the Valkyrie Rock and Sigurd's denials in the court scene are intentional; Brünnhilde's words at the end of the cycle would confirm such a reading: '*Echter als er schwur keiner Eide [...] und doch, alle Eide [...] trog keiner wie er!*' (Truer than he none ever swore oaths [...] and yet none betrayed all oaths [...] like he did!'). If this is the case, the ambiguity is part of the message.

For Tolkien, exculpating Sigurd and keeping him as pure as possible was of the essence, as the alternative would have made him unfit to be the World's Chosen. He had the surviving lays of the *Poetic Edda* on his side, the poems whose form he imitated in the *Legend*. These were probably older than Snorri's prose version, though they were written down later. In his quest for authenticity, he probably saw no other option, quite apart from the fact that he would not have wanted it otherwise.

Yet even in this version, no one is entirely blameless. Even Tolkien cannot change the fact that Sigurd lends himself to an act of deception against a proud and ambiguous, but innocent woman and later betrays her secret by giving her ring to Gudrún. He may not be a sexual predator, but he is a man of his time, showing little regard for a woman's situation – until he realises she should have been his. Later, he rationalises his behaviour by claiming that Brynhild has nothing to complain about, because Gunnar is heroic, too – as though this would heal her hurt feelings. The attempt to turn him into an ideal hero feels somewhat contrived, though he remains a paragon of men compared to Siegfried, who started out as the shining hero who would redeem the gods but ended up as a shallow, brutish lout – something even Wagner himself came to realize in the end (Deathridge, 62f).

In addition, as mentioned before, Tolkien took recourse to a trick more reminiscent of the much-criticized *Völsunga saga* than of any Eddaic lays: using Odin as a deus ex-machina to rekindle the fire-wall around Brynhild, though even the *Völsunga saga* had moved beyond such superhuman intervention at that point of the story. In the *Poetic Edda*, mythical lays are separated from heroic lays; gods and men do not meet and meddle. In his reconstruction of the tale of Sigurd the Dragonslayer Tolkien disregards this rule when it comes to Odin. This is all the more remarkable in view of his strict adherence to the intricacies of the Eddaic metres. It seems probable that his Christian agenda has as much to do with this as Wagner's much more debated agenda influenced his changes to the story. In the end, and perhaps put a bit bluntly, it is through this and other additions and manipulations that the work becomes somewhat more than a pastiche.

In the end, both the *Ring* and the *Legend* were determined less by any attempts to solve the *Königsproblem* of 19th century Germanic philology, than by what their creators wanted the story to say.

Chapter 14

Conclusion

According to a frequently repeated claim, the professional philologist Tolkien must have been critical of the amateur Wagner for misrepresenting Norse myth in *Der Ring des Nibelungen*. However, Tolkien uttered his contempt for Wagner's work as a teenager, before he became a professional and most likely also before he acquired a more detailed knowledge of the *Ring* cycle, both text and music. It is possible that he came to realise later that Wagner had not even tried to represent his sources faithfully and that criticising him for failing to do so was beside the point. What must have annoyed him, though, was that the public at large took Wagner's cycle for the genuine article, believing it to be the best modern representation of the story of Sigurd the Dragonslayer. The poems of *The Legend of Sigurd and Gudrún* may have been an attempt to correct this erroneous idea, which still persists today. Another possible incentive was the ideological misuse of Northern myth in Germany, which was becoming apparent in the early thirties to those well-versed in Norse philology.

Meanwhile, though it was true that Wagner was a philological amateur, he was a well-informed one. He acquainted himself with virtually every German translation from the Old Norse that appeared in his day as well as with important studies like Grimm's *Deutsche Mythologie*, and he used a fair number of them for his *Ring* cycle. In addition, he may have had a basic knowledge of Old Norse. The text of his *Ring* shows a linguistic awareness and versatility not far behind what Tolkien displays in his writings, though occasional mistakes betray the fact that Wagner was self-taught. Both use lexical, grammatical and syntactical archaisms in abundance – and both earned ample criticism for it. Other common traits are a propensity for word-play and proverbiality, the occurrence of kennings (extended metaphors typical for Norse poetry), and last but not least, alliteration.

Wagner was the first to reuse Germanic and especially Norse stave rhyme consistently in post-medieval times: almost the entire *Ring* cycle is written in alliterative verse. Some of the basics seem to have escaped him, given the number of transgressions against the rules as laid down by Snorri Sturluson in the *Prose Edda*. Wagner's own writings about stave rhyme, however, suggest that following rules was hardly his concern and that he was more interested in using stave rhyme to create what he considered natural patterns of speech. The alliterations in his texts are congruent with the rhythm of the music.

The reintroduction of an ancient Germanic verse form to an audience unfamiliar with it gave rise to much criticism and many parodies, and occasionally people still complain about it. This is not the case with Tolkien's alliterative verses, which first reached the general public a hundred years after Wagner's revival of the genre, in the form of poems or fragments of poetry scattered throughout *The Lord of the Rings*. Alliteration abounds in his oeuvre, his prose works included, and some of his texts are entirely alliterative, notably the two *Legend* poems. Though his earlier alliterative poetry shows him wrestling with the metre in an attempt to adapt it to modern English, the later poems attest to his mastery of it. It is difficult to catch him at making mistakes, and in one case a seeming error appears to be a ploy to make a point for the perceptive reader. His dedication to the Germanic and Norse alliterative metres for their own sake, especially Norse *fornyrðislag*, contrasts with Wagner's adaptation of them as a means to an end, and a way to illustrate his theory about the origins of poetry and music.

Even if the *Legend* with its *fornyrðislag* verses was indeed written to 'correct' the idea that the *Ring* was a true representation of Norse mythology, 'The New Lay of the Völsungs' nonetheless shares some traits with Wagner's work. He and Tolkien both begin their Nibelungen story with the creation of the world. Though only the *Ring* actually ends with the downfall of the gods, this is predicted twice in the first *Legend* poem and determines much of what happens there. Sigurd and Siegfried are both heroes of light, comparable to the sun, and both are conceived as saviour figures. Odin's role is extended beyond anything found in the source texts Wagner and Tolkien have in common. It is even possible to find similarities on the textual level.

All the same on many levels the differences are greater. Wagner uses the source texts mainly as building blocks in a new construction, whereas Tolkien appears to be reconstructing the most likely version of the story, following the sources more faithfully. But he does not do so slavishly: subtle changes show that he, too, has an agenda of his own. His and Wagner's choices reflect their different backgrounds and purposes. When the sources are in conflict, Tolkien can often be seen to analyse and take his pick, whereas Wagner is more likely to combine, synthesise and remould. Faced with the major problem of 19th century Germanic philology, the various conflicting versions of the Nibelungen story, they come up with rather different solutions. Tolkien does so mostly by omitting things, desexualising the story and polishing up the image of the hero. Wagner by making radical alterations and recasting a central feature of all the original texts, the Quarrel of the Queens. Yet neither solution is entirely flawless: the wishes and needs of their creators had the last word.

Afterword

Afterword

This study mostly concentrates on the similarities between Wagner and Tolkien: their Rings of Power, their use of myth and archaic language, their interest in fairy tales, their defence of a nature endangered by those who attempt to dominate it in order to further their own ends, and the ambiguous endings of their ring stories, not to mention many minor correspondences. Though not all similarities are valid arguments in favour of Wagner's influence on Tolkien, it is very unlikely that the latter was not influenced by the *Ring* cycle at all. Both 'The New Lay of the Völsungs' and *The Lord of the Rings* can to a certain extent be considered products of his engagement with Wagner's work. Yet in all probability this influence was negative rather than positive, and to call Tolkien an imitator or an epigone would be missing the point.

In many respects, the two were very different people with very different aims. From Tolkien's viewpoint as a strict Roman Catholic, the German composer, who was an atheist for much of his life and an heretic when he leaned towards Christianity, must have stood out as someone with questionable political and religious ideas and dubious personal morals. That he allowed a cult to develop around himself must have appalled the man who believed that only God has the right to divine worship, and who built his mythology around this notion. That he dabbled in philology may have angered the professional linguist, however apt he proved at it. Whereas Wagner was in many respects a revolutionary, the conservative Tolkien was nothing of the kind, though he did not exactly swim with the stream either. He looked back towards a revered, ancient past, deploring its disappearance and bringing what he considered its most important values to the attention of a public that had largely forgotten them. With *Der Ring des Nibelungen*, Wagner looked forward and pointed ahead to a future which he hoped his art would help achieve, and for which it was necessary to destroy the old in order to create the new. Even though he mitigated his views in a later stage, this idea cannot have held much appeal for Tolkien, to put it mildly.

All the same, Tolkien's interest in Germanic myth in general and Norse mythology in particular almost inevitably brought him into a Wagnerian sphere of influence. *Der Ring des Nibelungen* cast a long shadow that was hard to circumnavigate. Tolkien actually moved into it when he embarked on his *Legend*, which can be seen as a first attempt to 'liberate' Norse myth from the grasp of the German composer and his – often racist – heirs and followers. Yet, though a formally brilliant retelling that remains much closer to the originals than Wagner's version, it is doubtful whether it could have been a match for the elaborate musical structure that is the *Ring*, even if it had reached the general public shortly after he wrote it. *The Lord of the Rings*, written against the dark backcloth of a world war displaying a distorted version of Wagner's myth, is much more original and creative than the earlier work, embedded as it is in a unique personal legendarium, and it has a far better chance of holding its own against the monumental *Ring* cycle.

In the end, though, it seems best to leave the idea of competition behind and to view Wagner and Tolkien as natural allies despite the things that divided them. Both were great mythmakers for their times and for times to come, both were enemies of absolute power and oppression, and it is perhaps less relevant where the resemblance ceases.

Bibliography

ADAMS, Robert M., "The Hobbit habit", In: *The New York Review of Books*, 24/19, 24.11.1977.

ADORNO, Theodor, *Versuch über Wagner*, Berlin/Frankfurt am Main: Suhrkamp, 1952.

AGØY, Nils Ivar, "'Quid Hinieldus cum Christo?' New Perspectives on Tolkien's Theological Dilemma and His Sub-Creation Theory", In: *Proceedings of the J.R.R. Tolkien Centenary Conference*, 31-38.

Mytenes mann. J.R.R. Tolkien og hans forfatterskap, Oslo: Tiden Norsk forlag, 2003.

AMERONGEN, Martin van, *De buikspreker van God: Richard Wagner*, Zwolle: De Arbeiderspers, 1983. (English: *Wagner, A Case History*, London: Dent, 1984).

AMON Hen. Bulletin of the Tolkien Society, 208 (11/2007); 210 (3/2008).

ANDERSSON, Theodore M., *The Legend of Brynhild*, Islandica XLIII, Ithaca & London: Cornell University Press, 1980.

ARVIDSSON, Stefan, "Slita dvärg. Om frånvaron av arbete i Nibelungentraditionen", In: C. Raudvere, A. Andrén, K. Jennbert (eds.), *Hedendomen i historiens spegel: bilder av det forkristna norden*, Lund: Nordic Academic Press, 2005, 97-132.

Draksjukan. Mytiska fantasier hos Tolkien, Wagner och de Vries, Lund: Nordic Academic Press, 2007.

"Hur Sigurd blev Frodo", In: *Dagens Nyheter*, 09.28.2009.

"Greed and the Nature of Evil", In: *The Journal of Religion and Popular Culture* 22 (2010). http://www.usask.ca/relst/jrpc/art22%282%29-tolkien_wagner.html (retr. date: 16.11.2010).

ATTEBERY, Brian, "What took them so long?", In: *The Sunday Times*, 8.4.2007.

BACHMANN, Dieter and Thomas Honegger, "Ein Mythos für das 20. Jahrhundert: Blut, Rasse und Erbgedächtnis bei Tolkien", In: *Hither Shore* 2 (2005), 13-41.

BAYREUTHER Blätter. Deutsche Zeitschrift im Geiste Richard Wagners, Hrsg. Hans von Wohlzogen, 22 (1899).

Berne, Peter, *Apokalypse. Weltuntergang und Welterneuerung in Richard Wagners 'Ring des Nibelungen'. Eine Werkeinführung für das Dritte Jahrtausend*, Worms: Wernersche Verlagsgesellschaft, 2006.

The Bible.

Bidlo, Oliver, "Mittelerde als Ausdruck Romantischer Kreativität und Sehnsucht", In: *Hither Shore* 7 (2010), 32-47.

Birzer, Bradley, "Both rings were round and there the resemblance ceases: Tolkien, Wagner, Nationalism and Modernity", ISI conference 'Modernist and Mist Dwellers', Seattle Opera House, 3.8.2001. http://www.isi.org/lectures/text/pdf/birzer.pdf (retr. date 27.08.2009).

Björnsson, Árni, *Island und der Ring des Nibelungen*, Reykjavík: Mál og Menning, 2003 (Original title: Wagner og Völsungar, 2000).

Blisset, William, "The Despots of the Rings", In: *South Atlantic Quarterly* 58 (1959), 448-456.

Bloom, Harold, *Modern Critical Interpretations. J.R.R. Tolkien's The Lord of the Rings*, New York: Chelsea House, 2000.

Bradley, Marion Zimmer, "Men, Halflings and Hero Worship", In: Neil D. Isaacs and Rose A. Zimbardo (eds.), *Tolkien and the Critics,* Notre Dame, Iowa: University of Notre Dame Press, 1968, 109-127.

Bragason, Úlfar (ed.), *Wagner's Ring and Its Icelandic Sources*, Reykjavik: Stofnun Sigurðar Nordals, 1995.

Bratman, David, "Liquid Tolkien: Music, Tolkien, Middle-earth and More Music", In: Eden, 140-170.

Brennan Croft, Janet (ed.), *Tolkien And Shakespeare: Essays on Shared Themes And Language*, Jefferson NC & London: McFarland, 2006.

Brljak, Vladimir, "The Book of Lost Tales: Tolkien as Metafictionist", In: *Tolkien Studies* 7 (2010), 1-34.

Bugge, Sophus, *Studier over de nordiske Gude- og Heltesagns Oprindelse*, Christiania [Oslo]: Alb. Cammermeyer, 1881.

Burns, Marjorie, *Perilous Realms, Celtic and Norse in Tolkien's Middle-earth*, Toronto: University of Toronto Press, 2005.

Byatt, A.S., *Ragnarok. The end of the Gods*, Edinburgh, London, New York, Melbourne: Cannongate, 2011.

Carnegy, Patrick, *Wagner and the Art of the Theatre*, New Haven: Yale University Press, 2006.

CARPENTER, Humphrey, *J.R.R. Tolkien: A Biography*, London: Allen & Unwin, 1977.

CARR, Jonathan, *The Wagner Clan. The Saga of Germany's Most Illustrious and Infamous Family*, London, New York: Atlantic Monthly Press, 2007.

CARTER, Lin, *Tolkien, A Look Behind the Lord of the Rings*, New York: Ballantine, 1969.

CHANCE, Jane (ed.), *Tolkien the Medievalist*, London: Routledge, 2003.

Tolkien and the Invention of Myth. A Reader, Lexington, Kentucky: University Press of Kentucky, 2004.

CHISM, Christine, "Middle-earth, the Middle Ages and the Aryan nation. Myth and history in World War II", In: Chance 2003, 63-92.

CICORA, Mary A, *Mythology as Metaphor. Romantic Irony, Critical Theory and Wagner's Ring*, Westport CT: Greenwood Press, 1998.

CLEASBY, R. and G. Vigfusson, *An Icelandic-English Dictionary*, London: Oxford University Press, 1874.

COOKE, Deryck, *I Saw the World End. A Study of Wagner's Ring*, London: Oxford University Press, 1979.

CULSHAW, John, *Reflections on Wagner's Ring*, London: Secker & Warburg, 1976.

CURRY, Patrick, *Defending Middle-earth: Tolkien, Myth and Modernity*, Edinburgh: Floris Books, 1997.

DAHLHAUS, Carl, *Wagners Konzeption des Musikalischen Dramas*, Regensburg: Gustav Bosse Verlag, 1971.

Richard Wagners Musikdramen, Ditzingen: Reklam, 1996.

DARCY, Warren, "'The World Belongs to Alberich!' Wagner's Changing Attitude towards the *Ring*", In: Spencer and Millington, 48-52.

DAVIDSON, H.R. Ellis, *Gods and Myths of Northern Europe*, Harmondsworth: Penguin Books, 1964.

DAVIS, James, "Showing Saruman as Faber: Tolkien and Peter Jackson", In: *Tolkien Studies* 5 (2008), 55-71.

DE LA MOTTE FOUQUÉ, Friedrich, *The Magic Ring*, Robert Pearse Gillies (transl.), Amy Sturgis (ed.), Kansas City: Valancourt Books, 2006.

DEATHRIDGE, John, *Wagner Beyond Good and Evil*, Berkely, Los Angeles, London: University of California Press, 2008.

DI GAETANI, John Louis, *Richard Wagner and the modern British novel*, London: Associated University Presses, 1978.

DIMOND, Andy, "The Twilight of the Elves. Ragnarök and the End of the Third Age", In: Chance 2004, 179-189.

DOKUMENTE *zur Entstehungsgeschichte des Bühnenfestspiels 'Der Ring des Nibelungen'*, W. Breig and H. Fladt (eds.), In: Richard Wagner, *Sämtliche Werke*, C. Dahlhaus (ed.), vol. XXIX/I, Mainz: Akademie der Wissenschaften und der Literatur, 1976.

DROUT, Michael, "A Mythology for Anglo-Saxon England", In: Chance 2004, 229-247.

"Tolkien's Prose Style and its Literary and Rhetorical Effects", In: *Tolkien Studies* 1 (2004), 137-162.

DUCHEN, Jessica, "The return of the original Ring lord", In: *The Independent*, 22 July 2005.

DZAMBA Sessa, Anne, "At Wagner's Shine: British and American Wagnerians", In: David C. Large and William Weber (eds.), *Wagnerism in European Culture and Politics*, Ithaca & London: Cornell University Press, 1984, 246-277.

DIE EDDA. *Die ältere und jüngere Edda und die mythischen Erzählungen der Skalden*, Übersetzt und mit Erläuterungen versehen von Karl Simrock, Stuttgart: Cotta, 1851.

EDDA. *Die Lieder des Codex Regius nebst verwandten Denkmälern*, Gustav Neckel (ed.), Vierte, umgearbeitete Auflage von Hans Kuhn, Heidelberg: Carl Winter Universitätsverlag, 1962.

EDEN, Bradford Lee (ed.), *Middle-earth Minstrel. Essays on Music in Tolkien*, Jefferson NC, London: McFarland, 2010.

ELLISON, John, "Tolkien, Wagner, and the End of the Romantic Age", In: I.R. Morus, M.J.L. Percival and C.S. Rosenthal (eds.), *Tolkien & Romanticism. Proceedings of the Cambridge Tolkien Workshop 1988,* Cambridge: The Tolkien Society, 1988, 14-20.

"Tolkien's Shire and Wagner's Nuremberg, a comparison", In: *Mallorn* 22 (1985), 13-16.

"Tolkien's world and Wagner's: the music of language and the language of music", In: *Mallorn* 36 (1998), 35-42.

"Tolkien's Mythology of England. The Shire as 'Local Community'", In: Richard Crawshaw (ed.), *Tolkien, A Mythology for England?* The 13th Tolkien Society Seminar, Telford, 2000, 59-70.

EMERICK, Laura, "Pop culture owes huge debt to Wagner", In: *Chicago Sun Times*, 27.3.2005.

ENNIS, Jane S., *A Comparison of Richard Wagner's ring and William Morris's Sigurd the Volsung*, Ph.D. thesis, University of Leeds, 1993. http://members.fortunecity.co.uk/leonora/ring1.html (retr. date: 26.11.2009).

ETTMÜLLER, Ludwig, *Die Lieder der Edda von den Nibelungen: Stabreimende Verdeutschung nebst Erläuterungen*, Zürich: Drell, Füssli und Compagnie, 1837. Repr. Whitefish, Montana: Kessinger Publishing, 2009.

FIMI, Dimitra, "'Mad Elves' and 'Elusive Beauty': Some Celtic Strands of Tolkien's Mythology", In: *Folklore*, 117/2 (2006), 156-170.

"Tolkien's 'Celtic' Type of Legends: Merging Traditions", In: *Tolkien Studies* 4 (2007), 51-71.

Tolkien, Race and Cultural History. From Fairies to Hobbits, Basingstoke, New York: Palgrave McMillan, 2009.

FISHER, Jason, (ed.), *Tolkien and the Study of His Sources. Critical Essays*, Jefferson NC: MacFarland & Company, 2011.

FLIEGER, Verlyn and Carl F. Hostetter (eds.), *Tolkien's Legendarium. Essays on The History of Middle-earth*, Westport CT, London: Greenwood Press, 2000.

FLIEGER, Verlyn, "'There would always be a fairy-tale': J.R.R. Tolkien and the folklore controversy", In: Chance 2003, 26-35.

"A Mythology for Finland. Tolkien and Lönnrot as Mythmakers", In: Chance 2004, 277-282.

"Do the Atlantis story and abandon Eriol Saga", *Tolkien Studies* 1 (2004), 43-68.

Interrupted Music. The Making of Tolkien's mythology, Kent, London: The Kent State University Press, 2005.

FORSTER, E.M., *Howards End*, London: Edward Arnold, 1910.

FREUND, Wieland, "Tolkien's Beziehungsanalyse von Wagners Nibelungen", In: *Die Welt*, 20.08.2010.

GARTH, John, *Tolkien and the Great War: The Threshold of Middle-earth*, London: HarperCollins, 2003.

GERMANIC Mythology. Texts, Translations, Scholarship. *The Manuscript Texts of Völuspá*. II -Hauksbók. http://www.germanicmythology.com/works/hauksbokvoluspa.html (retr. date: 14.05.2011).

GILLIVER, Peter, Jeremy Marshall and Edmund Weiner (eds.), *The Ring of Words: Tolkien and the Oxford English Dictionary*, Oxford: Oxford University Press, 2006.

GISBERT, Paul (pseud. von Pniower, P.), *Der Ring der nie gelungen, Cricrilogie äußerst frei nach R. Wagner's Der Ring des Nibelungen*, Berlin: Wedekind und Schwieger, 1877.

GREENMAN, David, "*The Silmarillion* as Aristotelian Epic-Tragedy", In: *Mythlore* 14/3 (1988), 20-5.

GREGOR-Dellin, Martin, *Das kleine Wagner-Buch,* Reinbek bei Hamburg: Rowohlt, 1982.

Wasser, Berge, Nibelungen. *Wagner, der Ring des Nibelungen. Vorabend: Rheingold*, Programmbuch der Oper Bonn, 1990.

Richard Wagner. Sein Leben, Sein Werk, Sein Jahrhundert, München, Wien: DTV, 1991.

GRIMM, Jakob, *Deutsche Mythologie*, Göttingen: Dietrichsche Buchhandlung, 1835.

GROOT, Ger, "Voor mijn dochter is Wagner weer de sprookjesverteller", In: *Trouw*, 27.1.2010, 27.

GRUSHETSKIY, Vladimir, "How Russians see Tolkien", In: *Proceedings of the J.R.R. Tolkien Centenary Conference*, 221-225.

GUTHKE, Karl S., "Arthur Schopenhauer reads Wagner", In: *Harvard Magazine* 99/1 (1996) http://harvardmagazine.com/1996/09/schopenhauer.2.html (retr. date: 9.6.2012).

GYLFASON, Þorsteinn, "Richard Wagner as a poet", In: Bragason, 77-86.

HAKKAART, Johanna M., *Reis door een partituur. Wagners Ring des Nibelungen,* Assen: Van Gorcum, 2000.

HALL, Robert jr, "Tolkien's Hobbit Tetralogy as 'Anti-Nibelungen'", In: *Western Humanities Review*, XXXII/1 (1978), 351-359.

HAMMOND, Wayne G. and Christina Scull, *J.R.R. Tolkien, Artist and Illustrator,* London: HarperCollins, 1995.

HAMMOND, Wayne, "A Continuing and Evolving Creation", In: Flieger and Hostetter, *Tolkien's Legendarium*, 19-30.

HANSEN, Léon, "Mann, Mulisch en de mythe", In: *Trouw*, 13.11.2010, 70-71.

HARVEY, David, "Tolkien's Ring and Der Ring des Nibelungen", *One Ring to Rule Them all. A Study of the History, Symbolism and Meaning of the One Ring in J.R.R. Tolkien's Middle-earth*, 1995, http://www.tolkienonline.de/etep/1ring5.html (retr. date: 27.8.2009).

HAUER, Stanley R., "Wagner and the Völospá", In: *19th Century Music* XV/1 (1991), 52-63.

HAYMES, Edward R. (transl.), *The saga of Thidrek of Bern*, New York: Garland, 1988.

"The Two Rings", Lecture held for the Wagner Society of New York, 14.01.2009. Available on CD-Rom via the Society.

Wagner's Ring in 1848, Rochester NY: Camden House, 2010.

HENNING, Reinhard, *Mythologie in Tolkiens Middle-Earth*, Facharbeit Englisch, Luisenburg-Gymnasium Wunsiedel, 2002. http://www.wikinger.org/pages/facharbeit.pdf (retr. date: 27.8.2009).

HIGGINS, Andrew, "Strange Ring Fellows", *Wotan's Musings* (weblog), http://wotanselvishmusings.blogspot.com/2011/01/wagner-and-tolkien-thread-strange-ring.html (retr. date: 3.1.2011).

HILLARD, Steve, *Mirkwood*, Austin: Cruel Rune Publications, 2010.

HODGART, Matthew, *James Joyce. A Student's Guide*, London: Routledge, 1978.

HOLMES, John, "'Inside a Song': Tolkien's Phonaestetics", In: Eden, 26-46.

HOMER, *The Iliad*.

HONEGGER, Thomas, "A Mythology for England? Looking a Gift Horse in the Mouth", In: E. Segura and T. Honegger (eds.), *Myth and Magic. Art According to the Inklings*, Zurich, Berne: Walking Tree Publishers, 2007, 109-129.

"The Rohirrim: 'Anglo-Saxons on Horseback'? An Inquiry into Tolkien's Use of Sources", In: Fisher, 116-132.

HOOKER, Mark, "Reading John Buchan in Search of Tolkien", In: Fisher, 162-192.

HOPPE, Uwe, *Her den Ring. Wagners Ring ganz durch*, Studiobühne Bayreuth, 2007.

HOSTETTER, Carl F. and Arden R. Smith, "A Mythology for England", In: *Proceedings of the J.R.R. Tolkien Centenary Conference*, 281-290.

HOVE, Ivo van, "Het moet niet groter dan groot", In: *De Standaard*, 7.7.2006.

INGENSCHAY-Goch, Dagmar, *Richard Wagners neu erfundener Mythos. Zur Rezeption und Reproduktion des germanischen Mythos in seinen Operntexten*, Bonn: Herbert Grundmann, 1982.

INGLIS, Fred, *The Promise of Happiness*, Cambridge: Cambridge University Press, 1981.

"Gentility and Powerlessness: Tolkien and the New Class", In: Robert Giddings (ed.), *J.R.R. Tolkien: This Far Land*, London: Vision Press, 1983, 25-41.

JENKINS, Richard, "Review of Shippey's J.R.R. Tolkien, Author of the Century", In: *The New Republic online*, 7.2.2002.

Jensma, Goffe, *De gemaskerde god. François Haverschmidt en het Oera Linda-boek,* Zutphen: Walburg Pers, 2004.

Joe, Jeongwon, "Why Wagner and Cinema? Tolkien Was Wrong", In: Jeongwon Joe and Sander L. Gilman (eds.), *Wagner and Cinema,* Bloomington, Indianapolis: Indiana University Press, 2010, 1-24.

Kalevala. Het epos der Finnen, Verzameld door Elias Lönnrot, in Nederlandse verzen gebracht door Mies le Nobel, Zeist: Uitgeverij Vrij Geestesleven, 1985.

Kasper, Hartmut, "Reitet, reitet, reitet für Gondor! oder: Wollen wir den totalen Ring? Lose Gedanken zur Frage, was Tolkien uns mit seinem Herrn der Ringe sagen wollte", In: Thomas le Blanc and Bettina Twrsnick (eds.), *Das Dritte Zeitalter. J.R.R. Tolkiens "Herr der Ringe",* Schriftenreihe und Materialen der Phantastischen Bibliothek Wetzlar 92 (2005), 281-290.

Kazimierczak, Karolina Agata, "Unfolding Tolkien's Linguistic Symphony. Relations between music and language in the narratives of J.R.R. Tolkien, and in compositions inspired by him", In: *Arda Philology,* 2 (2009), 56-79.

Keller, Gottfried, "Am Mythenstein", In: *Sämtliche Werke* 7, Berlin: Suhrkamp, 1996.

Kilby Clyde S. and Marjorie Lamp Mead, *Brothers and Friends: The Diaries of Major Warren Hamilton Lewis,* San Francisco, 1982.

Kilian, Crawford, "Homesick for Middle-earth. Tolkien's 'new' work proves a harsh prophecy", In: *The Tyee,* 26.4.2007.

Kitcher, Philip and Richard Schacht, *Finding an Ending. Reflections on Wagner's Ring,* Oxford: Oxford University Press, 2004.

Lachenicht, Susanne, "When Nationalism meets Cosmopolitanism. WagnerWorldWide", a lecture series held at the University of Bayreuth, Fall/Winter 2011, http://www.youtube.com/WagnerWorldWide#p/a/u/2/wnBCNg-gyS6g (retr. date 28.11.2011).

Lacon, Ruth, "To Illustrate or not to Illustrate, That is the Question...", http://www.tolkienlibrary.com/press/1026_To_Illustrate_or_Not_to_Illustrate.php (retr. date 15.1.2012).

Lee, Feng-Shu, *The Ending of Wagner's Ring,* Ph.D. thesis, University of Chicago, http://gradworks.umi.com/3460201.pdf (retr. date: 02.09.2011), TBP 2012.

Lee, Stuart D. and Elizabeth Solopova, *The Keys of Middle-earth. Discovering Medieval Literature through the Fiction of J.R.R. Tolkien,* Basingstoke, New York: Palgrave Macmillan, 2005.

Leech, Caroline, "The Battle of the Rings", In: *Western Mail,* 30.11.2006.

LeGuin, Ursula, "From Elfland to Poughkeepsie", In: Robert H. Boyer and Kenneth J. Zahorski (eds.), *Fantasists on Fantasy. A Collection of Critical Reflections by Eighteen Masters of the Art,* New York: Avon Books, 1984, 195-209.

Lindow, John, "Interpreting Baldr, the Dying God", Lecture at the University of Sidney, 4.9.1993, http://www.humanities.org.au/Resources/Downloads/Lectures/Triebel1993.pdf (retr. date: 11.1.2011).

Lönnrot, Lars, "The Nordic Sublime", In: Bragason, 31-41.

Lord of the Rings an Imitation of Wagner's 'Ring Cycle'? Philosophistry.com: http://philosophistry.com/archives/2004/01/lord-of-the-rings-an-imitation.html (retr. date: 27.8.2009).

Luke, Helen M., "The Ring", In: Helen M. Luke, *The Laughter at the Heart of Things,* New York: Morning Light Press, 2001, 10-36.

MacLachlan, Christopher, *Tolkien and Wagner: The Ring and Der Ring,* Zurich, Jena: Walking Tree Publishers, 2012.

Magee, Bryan, *Aspects of Wagner.,* Oxford: Oxford University Press, 1988.

Magee, Elizabeth, *Richard Wagner and the Nibelungs,* Oxford: Oxford University Press, 1991.

Magic Words, an interview with Amy Sturgis, by Joe Crowe. *Revolution SF,* July 15, 2006. http://www.revolutionsf.com/article.php?id=3246 (retr. date: 9.6.2012).

Makai, Péter Kristóf, "Faërian Cyberdrama: When Fantasy becomes Virtual Reality", In: *Tolkien Studies* 7 (2010), 35-55.

Martin, Gregory, "Music, Myth and Literary Depth in the 'Land ohne Musik'", In: Eden, 127-148.

Morris, William, *The Collected Works. Vol. 12. The Story of Sigurd the Volsung and the Fall of the Nibelungs,* London: 1911 facsimile reprint by Elibron, 2004.

Müller, Anja, "The Lords of the Rings: Wagner's *Ring* and Tolkien's 'Faerie'", In: *Musicorum. Le livret en question,* Tours: Université François Rabelais, 2006-2007, 343-360.

Nairn, Tom, "The Lord of the Rings: Ethnicity in your Dreams", In: *Open Democracy,* 27.2.2002.

Naveh, Reuven, "Tonality, Atonality and the Ainulindale", In: Steimel and Schneidewind, 29-51.

Das Nibelungenlied, Übersetzt von Karl Simrock. Leipzig: A. Schumann's Verlag, n.d.

NOAD, Charles, "On the Construction of 'The Silmarillion'", in: Flieger and Hostetter, 31-68.

O'DONOGHUE, Heather, *From Asgard to Valhalla. The Remarkable History of the Norse Myths,* London, New York: I.B. Tauris & Co Ltd., 2008.

OHLMARKS, Åke, *Sagan om Nibelungarna,* Stockholm: Gebers, 1973.

Tolkien och den svarta magin, Stockholm: Sjöstrands förlag, 1981.

ÓLASON, Vésteinn, "Early Icelandic Myth and Legend as Background for the Ring", In:. Bragason, 43-55.

PANAGL, Oswald, "'Vermählen wollte der Magen Sippe dem Mann ohne Minne die Maid'. Archaisches und Archaisierendes in der Sprache von Wagners 'Ring'", In: Ulrich Müller and Oswald Panagl (eds.), *Ring und Gral,* Würzburg: Königshausen & Neumann, 2002.

PANTLE, Christian, "Zähme wilde Männer", In: *Focus Online,* 21.12.2001.

PEOPLE in the News, *Associated Press,* 9.12.2001.

PEASANT Customs and Savage Myths, Selections from the British Folklorists, ed. Richard M. Dorson. London: Routledge and Kegan Paul, 1968. 'Max Müller', 67-199.

PIDDE, Ernst von, *Wagners Musikdrama der Ring des Nibelungen im Lichte des deutschen Strafrechts,* Frankfurt: Bärmeier & Nikel, 1968.

PINKERTON, James P., "Lets Not Forget Where the Ringworld Ends", In: *Newsday,* 12.5.2002.

PLATO, *Politeia* (The Republic).

Symposion.

PROCEEDINGS *of the J.R.R. Tolkien Centenary Conference, Keble College, Oxford, 1992,* Patricia Reynolds and Glen H. Goodknight (eds.), Altadena: Mythopoeic Press, 1995.

RASK, Rasmus, *Vejledning til det islandske eller gamle nordiske Sprog* (1811), København: Nabu Press, 2010.

RICHARD *Wagner Handbuch,* Alfred Kroener, Ulrich Müller and Peter Wapnewski (eds.), Stuttgart: Kröner, 1986.

RIDPATH, Michael, *Where the Shadows lie.* Ice and Fire, Book 1, London: Corvus, 2010.

THE RING *Goes Ever On: Proceedings of the Tolkien 2005 Conference: 50 Years of The Lord of the Rings,* Sarah Wells (ed.), Coventry: The Tolkien Society, 2008.

Rosebury, Brian, *Tolkien, A Critical Assessment*, Revised edition, Basingstoke, New York: Palgrave Mcmillan, 2002

Rosendorfer, Herbert, *Bayreuth für Anfänger*, München: DTV, 1984.

Rosenløv, Jesper M., "Det episke sind. Tolkiens forfatterskab og livssyn", In: *Tidskriftet Nomos*, 1/1 (2003), 83-121.

Ross, Alex, "The Ring and the Rings, Wagner/Tolkien", In: *The New Yorker*, 22.12 and 29.12.2003 (German: *Der Herr der Ringe* und *Der Ring des Nibelungen*. Tolkien und Wagner. *Wagnerspectrum*, 2/4 (2008), 97-103).

Rothstein, Edward, "Gandalf and the Sorcerer's Stone of Evil: On Fighting the Good Fight", In: *The New York Times*, 15.12.2001.

Rutledge, Fleming, *The Battle for Middle-earth: Tolkiens Divine Design in "The Lord of the Rings"*, Grand Rapids: Eerdmans, 2004.

Ryan, J.S., "German Mythology applied – the extension of the literary folk memory", In: *Folklore* 77 (1966), 45-59.

"Othin in England – Evidence from the Poetry for a Cult of Woden in Anglo-Saxon England", In: *Folklore* 74 (1963), 460-80.

The Saga of the Völsungs. The Norse Epic of Sigurd the Dragon Slayer, translated with an introduction, notes and glossary by Jesse L. Byock, London: Penguin Classics, 1999.

Schreier, Josef, "Moderne Mythologie. Richard Wagner und die Inklings", In: *Inklings–Jahrbuch für Literatur und Ästhetik*, 28 (2010), 185-203.

Schuler, John, *The Language of Richard Wagner's Ring Des Nibelungen*, Lancaster: Steinman Folz, 1909, repr. LaVergne, USA: General Books, 2009.

Schwarz, Guido, *Jungfrauen im Nachthemd, blonde Krieger aus dem Westen*, Würzburg: Königshausen & Neumann, 2003.

Scott Rohan, Michael, "'Which story, I wonder?' said Gandalf... Was Tolkien the real Ring thief?", In: *The Ring Goes Ever On*. Vol. 2, 147-155.

"What's Wrong with Wagner?", In: *BBC Music Magazine*, April 2010. Source: *Wagner After All*, the magazine of the Dutch Wagner Society, Volume 15/3 (2010), 40.

Scruton, Roger, "Man and superman", In: *The Guardian*, 12.4.2003.

Scull, Christina and Wayne G. Hammond, *The J.R.R. Tolkien Companion and Guide. II, Chronology*, London: HarperCollins, 2006.

See, Klaus von, *Germanische Verskunst*, Stuttgart: Metzler, 1967.

SHAW, G.B., *The Perfect Wagnerite. A Commentary on the Niblung's Ring*, Major Critical Essays, Harmondsworth: Penguin Books, 1986, 177-307.

SHIPPEY, Tom, *The Road to Middle-earth*, London: George Allen & Unwin, 1982.

The Road to Middle-earth, 2nd expanded edition, London: HarperCollins, 1992.

"'A Fund of Wise Sayings': Proverbiality in Tolkien", In: *The Ring Goes Ever On. Tolkien 2005,* Vol. 2, 279-286.

Roots and Branches. Selected Papers on Tolkien, Zürich, Jena: Walking Tree Publishers, 2007.

"Tolkien Out-Wagners Wagner", In: *Times Literary Supplement*, 6.5.2009. http://entertainment.timesonline.co.uk/tol/arts_and_entertainment/the_tls/article6232731.ece .

"Tolkien's Development as a writer of alliterative poetry in modern English", In: *Lembas Extra (2009), Tolkien in Poetry and Song*, ed. Cécile van Zon, 64-73.

"Review of The Legend of Sigurd and Gudrún", In: *Tolkien Studies* 7 (2010), 291-324.

SINEX, Margaret, "Monsterized Saracens", In: *Tolkien Studies* 7 (2010): 175-196.

SMITH, Ross, *Inside Language. Linguistic and Aesthetic Theory in Tolkien,* Zurich, Berne: Walking Tree Publishers, 2007.

SØRENSENS *Wagner. Villy Sørensens udvalgte artikler om og oversættleser af Richard Wagner,* forord, redaktion og efterskrift af Sylvester Roepstorf, København: Gyldendal, 2005.

SPEAR, John, "Wagner versus Tolkien. Who is the Real Lord of the Rings?" Talk held at the Burbank Public Libary and the Redondo Beach Library (CA) on 10.05.2010 and 11.05.2010.

SPENCER, Stewart, "Engi má við sköpum vinna: Wagner's Use of his Icelandic Sources", In: Bragason, 55-76.

SPENCER, Stewart and Barry Millington (eds.), *Wagner's Ring of the Nibelung. A Companion*, London: Thames & Hudson, 2000.

'SPENGLER' [David P. Goldman], "The Ring and the Remnants of the West", In: *Asia Times Online*, 1.11.2003, http://www.atimes.com/atimes/Front_Page/EA11Aa02.html (retr. date: 9.6.2012).

"Tolkien's Christianity and the pagan tragedy", In; *Asia Times Online*, 4.4.2007, http://www.atimes.com/atimes/Front_Page/ID24Aa01.html (retr. date: 9.6.2012).

St. Clair, Gloriana, *Tolkien's Cauldron: Northern Literature and The Lord of the Rings,* PhD Thesis, Pittsburgh, Pa, 2000, http://works.bepress.com/gloriana_stclair/17 (retr. date: 02.10.2009).

Steimel, Heidi and Friedhelm Schneidewind, (eds.), *Music in Middle-earth,* Zurich, Jena: Walking Tree Publishers, 2010.

Stenström, A., "A Mythology? For England?", In: *Proceedings of the J.R.R. Tolkien Centenary Conference,* 310-314.

Sturluson, Snorri, *Edda. Gylfaginning og Prosafortellingene av Skáldskaparmál,* Anne Holtsmark and Jón Helgason (eds.), Oslo: Oscar Andersens Boktrykkeri, 1971.

Sven Erik Bechtolf reads Wagner, Der Ring des Nibelungen (complete), 8 Audio CDs and one mp3 CD, Col legno, 2005.

Sypeck, Jeff, "The heroes rest upon the sighs…", *Quid Plura,* weblog, May 11, 2009. http://www.quidplura.com/?p=316 (retr. date: 17.05.2009).

Tappert, Wilhelm, *Richard Wagner im Spiegel der Kritik; Wörterbuch der Unhöflichkeit,* Leipzig: C.W.F. Siegelt Musikalienhandlung, 1903.

Tolkien, John Ronald Reuel, *The Hobbit,* London: George Allen & Unwin, 1937.

The Lord of the Rings: The Fellowship of the Ring, London: George Allen & Unwin, 1954.

The Lord of The Rings, The Two Towers, London: George Allen & Unwin, 1954.

The Lord of the Rings, The Return of the King, London: George Allen & Unwin, 1955.

The Adventures of Tom Bombadil and other verses from the Red Book, London: George Allen & Unwin, 1962.

"Guide to the Names in the Lord of the Rings", In: *A Tolkien Compass. Fascinating Studies and Interpretations of J.R.R. Tolkien's Most Popular Epic Fantasies*, Jared Lobdell (ed.), New York: Ballantine, 1975, 168-216.

The Homecoming of Beorhtnoth, Beorhthelm's son, London: Unwin Books, 1975. First published in *Essays and Studies by Members of the English Association* 6 (1953).

The Silmarillion, London: George Allen & Unwin, 1977.

Pictures by J.R.R. Tolkien, Foreword and Notes by Christopher Tolkien, London: George Allen & Unwin, 1979.

Unfinished Tales of Númenor and Middle-earth, London: George Allen & Unwin, 1980.

"J.R.R. Tolkien, An Interview", In: *News from Bree* (11/1974), 3-5. Transcript of a 1964 BBC radio interview with Denis Gueroult, published on audiocassette as *Tolkien and Basil Bunting*, BBC Cassettes, London, 1980.

Interview with J.R.R. Tolkien by John Izzard, broadcast 30 March 1968 on BBC Radio.

J.R.R. Tolkien, Artist & Illustrator, Wayne G. Hammond and Christina Scull (eds.), London: HarperCollins, 1995.

The Letters of J.R.R. Tolkien, Humprey Carpenter (ed., with the assistance of Christopher Tolkien), London: George Allen & Unwin, 1981.

The Monsters and the Critics and Other Essays, London: George Allen & Unwin, 1981.

The Book of Lost Tales I. The History of Middle-earth 1, Christopher Tolkien (ed.), London: George Allen & Unwin, 1983.

The Book of Lost Tales II. The History of Middle-earth 2, Christopher Tolkien (ed.), London: George Allen & Unwin, 1982.

The Lays of Beleriand. The History of Middle-earth 3, Christopher Tolkien (ed.), London: George Allen & Unwin, 1985.

The Lost Road. The History of Middle-earth 5, Christopher Tolkien (ed.), London: George Allen & Unwin, 1987.

The Return of the Shadow. The History of Middle-earth 6, Christopher Tolkien (ed.), London: Unwin Hyman, 1988.

Sauron Defeated. The History of Middle-earth 9, Christopher Tolkien (ed.), London: HarperCollins 1992.

Morgoth's Ring. The History of Middle-earth 10, Christopher Tolkien (ed.), London: HarperCollins 1993.

The Peoples of Middle-earth, The History of Middle-earth 12, Christopher Tolkien (ed.), London: Harper Collins 1995.

The Annotated Hobbit, Revised and expanded edition, annotated by Douglas A. Anderson, London: HarperCollins, 2002.

Finn and Hengest, the Fragment and the Episode, Alan Bliss (ed.), London: HarperCollins 2006.

Tolkien On Fairy Stories, Expanded edition, with commentary and notes, Verlyn Flieger and Douglas Anderson (eds.), London: HarperCollins, 2008.

The Legend of Sigurd and Gudrún, Christopher Tolkien (ed.), London: HarperCollins, 2009.

"The Story of Kullervo" and Essays on *Kalevala*, transcribed and edited by Verlyn Flieger, In: *Tolkien Studies* 7 (2010), 211-278.

ÜBER WAGNER. *Von Musikern, Dichtern und Liebhabern*. Eine Anthologie, herausgegeben von Niké Wagner, Stuttgart: Reclam, 1995.

HET VIERDE Leven. Gesprekken met Hella Haasse, *Het uur van de wolf,* NTR documentary, 12 March 2004, Dutch TV.

VILL, Susanne, "Wagners Visionen – Motive aus Werken Richard Wagners in Fantasyfilmen", In: *Wagnerspectrum* 2/4 (2008), 9-95.

VINK, Renée, "Het is rond en het begint met een R.", In: *Tolkien Herdenkingsnummer van Lembas,* 's Gravenhage: Sirius en Siderius, 1983, 41-56.

VISCHER, Friedrich Theodor, "Vorschlag zu einer Oper", In: *Kritische Gänge 2*, Tübingen, 1844.

VREDENDAAL, Jaap van, "Tussen fantasy en filologie. Tolkiens eigen Edda", In: *Filter - Tijdschrift over vertalen*, 17/8 (2010), 27-36.

VRIES, Jan de, "Der Mythos von Baldrs Tod", In: *Arkiv for Nordisk Filologi* 7 (1955), 41-60.

WAGNER, Cosima, *Tagebücher*. Eine Auswahl von Marion Linhardt und Thomas Streit, München & Zürich: Piper, 2005.

WAGNER, Richard, *Wie verhalten sich republikanische Bestrebungen dem Königtume gegenüber?* Abhandlung verlesen im Dresdner Vaterlandsverein, 1848.

Die Kunst und die Revolution, Leipzig, 1849.

Das Kunstwerk der Zukunft, Leipzig, 1849.

Die Wibelungen. Weltgeschichte aus der Sage, Leipzig, 1848.

Eine Mitteilung an meine Freunde, Leipzig, 1851.

Gesammelte Schriften und Dichtungen. Band IV, Leipzig: C.F.W. Siegel, 1871.

Oper und Drama, Leipzig, 1852.

Zukunftsmusik, Leipzig, 1861. (First published as 'La musique de l'avenir', 1860).

Über Staat und Religion, Leipzig, 1864.

Der Fliegende Holländer, Insel Bücherei 98, Leipzig: Insel Verlag, n.d.

Lohengrin, Insel Bücherei 104, Leipzig: Insel Verlag, n.d.

Der Ring des Nibelungen. Ein Bühnenfestspiel für drei Tage und einen Vorabend. Das Rheingold (DR), Die Walküre (DW), Siegfried (S), Götterdämmerung (G), Insel Bücherei 93-96, Leipzig: Insel Verlag, n.d.

Die Meistersinger von Nürnberg, Insel Bücherei 502, Leipzig: Insel Verlag, n.d.

Parsifal. Ein Bühnenweihfestspiel, Insel Bücherei 103, Leipzig: Insel Verlag, n.d.

Briefe 1813-1883, Gertrud Ströbel and Werner Wolf (eds.), Leipzig: Breitkopf & Härtel, 1967 ff.

WAPNEWSKI, Peter, *Der traurige Gott. Richard Wagner in seinen Helden*, München, DTV, 1982.

Liebestod und Götternot. Zum 'Tristan' und zum 'Ring des Nibelungen', Berlin: Siedler 1988.

Der Ring des Nibelungen. Richard Wagners Weltendrama, München, Zürich: Piper, 1998.

WAWN, Andrew, *The Vikings and the Victorians, Inventing the Old North in 19th century Britain*, Cambridge: D.S. Brewer, 2002.

WEINREICH, Frank, *Polyoinos*, http://www.polyoinos.de/tolkien.html (retr. date: 24.1.2010).

WESTERNHAGEN, Curt von, *Die Entstehung des "Ring", dargestellt an den Kompositionsskizzen Richard Wagners*, Zürich, Freiburg i.B.: Atlantis, 1973.

Richard Wagners Dresdener Bibliothek 1842-49, Wiesbaden: Brockhaus, 1966.

WHITE, Michael and Kevin Scott, *Wagner for Beginners*, Cambridge: Icon Books, 1995.

WHITE, Michael, *Tolkien: a Biography*, London: Little, Brown, 2001.

WIESSNER, Hermann, *Der Stabreimvers in Richard Wagners "Ring des Nibelungen"*, Berlin: E. Ebering, 1924, repr. 1967 by Kraus Reprint.

WILBERG, Petra-Hildegard, *Richard Wagners mythische Welt. Versuche wider den Historismus*, Freiburg i.B.: Rombach, 1996.

WILLIAMSON, George S., *The Longing for Myth in Germany*, Chicago, London: University of Chicago Press, 2004.

WILSON, A.N., "Tolkien was not a writer", In: *The Telegraph*, 24.11.2001.

WOLZOGEN, Hans von, *Die Sprache in Richard Wagners Dichtungen*, Leipzig: F. Reinboth, 1878.

YATES, Jessica, "Tolkien the Anti-totalitarian", In: *Proceedings of the J.R.R. Tolkien Centenary Conference*, 233-245.

ZETTERSTEN, Arne, *Tolkien. Min vän Ronald och hans världar*, Stockholm: Atlantis, 2008. (English: *J.R.R. Tolkien's Double Worlds and Creative Process: Language and Life*, Basingstoke: Palgrave Macmillan, 2011).

Index of fiction

A

Aegnor 19
Ælfwine 98-100, 102
Ainur 26f, 127, 153, 185
Alberich 15-18, 21-23, 26-29, 31f, 36, 44, 50, 55, 58f, 74, 78, 81, 83f, 87, 89-91, 97, 107, 133, 134, 136, 140, 145f, 148, 157, 159, 197, 199, 226, 237, 240, 244, 250, 261f
Amfortas 20
Ancalagon the Black 32
Andreth 19
Anduin 28
Andúril 18
Andvaranaut 32, 37, 226, 240, 246-249, 254, 257-259, 261
Andvari 3, 5, 32f, 37, 49, 201, 230, 247, 248
Apollo(n) 232f
Aragorn 20-22, 29, 32, 34, 56, 62, 89, 188, 197, 218f
Arda 26, 89, 94, 102, 118, 119, 127, 131, 154, 156f, 185, 227, 234
Arkenstone, the 28
Arwen 20f, 156
Atalantë 185
Atli (Atle, Etzel) 7, 65f, 198, 241
Aulë 127

B

Balder (Baldr, Baldur) 226-228, 230-233, 235, 238
Barad-dûr 62, 86, 134, 165
Bard the Bowman 15, 19, 31, 33
Barliman Butterbur 189
Battle of the Pelennor Fields, the 62, 65f
Beleriand 22, 198
Beorthnoth, Beorthelm's son 68
Beren 21, 27, 35, 119, 211
Bilbo 18, 24, 33, 46-48, 51f, 56, 76-78, 96, 100, 107, 114, 146, 150, 199, 218f
Birnam Wood 137
Bombur 193f
Boromir 19, 42, 56, 151
Brandywine 194
Bree 194
Brünnhilde 16, 18-21, 24f, 29, 34, 42, 44f, 52, 56, 59, 88, 97, 129, 136, 157-160, 194-196, 220-222, 226, 233f, 236-238, 241, 245, 250f, 255f, 259-263
Brynhild 3, 34, 50, 56, 226, 228, 231, 234, 236, 240f, 245-248, 252-261, 263

C

Carcharoth 28
Common Speech, the 187, 214
Crack of Doom, the 72, 194

D

Dark Lord, the 25, 44, 47, 133
Déagol 17f, 28, 32, 56, 78
Denethor 16, 19, 25, 34, 56, 187
Dernhelm 17, 218
Doom of Mandos 127
Dragonhelm of Dor-Lómin, the 17
Dwarves 3, 5, 15, 17, 24, 28, 32, 36f, 47, 52f, 61, 71f, 77, 127, 136, 138, 240
Dwimorberg, Dwimordene 188

E

Eärendil/Eärendel 32, 102, 185
Easterlings 62-66
Eldar 185, 194
Elendil 18, 22, 32
Elessar 156
Elrond 23, 56, 187, 218f
Elsa 136
Elves 18f, 25f, 29, 47, 50f, 61, 63, 69, 72f, 93, 97f, 100, 134, 138, 151, 154, 156, 185, 212
Ents 23, 4, 131-133, 137, 151, 197
Entwives 23, 133
Éomer 214, 218
Eorlingas 192, 215
Éowyn 17, 25, 34, 187f, 218
Erda 26, 90, 131, 148, 220f, 232, 240f
Eriol 98
Ermanrik (Ermanarich, Iormunrek) 7

F

Fafner 15-18, 26, 29, 51, 91, 136, 149, 197, 221, 237, 261,
Fáfnir 32, 198, 202, 231, 235, 240, 246f, 258
Fangorn 197
Faramir 16, 34, 56, 68, 233
Fasolt 17f, 29, 32, 87
Fëanor 89, 127, 153, 187, 211
Finrod 19
Flosshilde 58
Freia 17, 19, 91, 121, 199
Fricka 84, 87, 195, 221
Frodo 4, 16, 18f, 21, 25, 28f, 48, 51, 56, 72, 77, 85-90, 92f, 100, 114, 127, 142, 154, 194, 198f, 218

G

Galadriel 23, 56, 63
Gandalf 21, 23f, 26, 33f, 48, 56, 77, 85, 114, 143, 155, 187f, 197, 219, 221

Gibich, Gibichungen (Gibichungs) 240, 262
Gimli 218f
Gjúki 187, 236, 240, 244, 246f, 254
Glaurung 32
Goldberry 24, 131, 194
Gollum 16, 18f, 25, 29, 33, 46f, 51-53, 56, 58, 75-78, 87-89, 96, 107, 114, 197f
Gotthorm 244f
Grail 121
Grímhild 219, 231, 236, 244f, 248, 254
Grimnir 198, 243
Grishnákh 219
Gudrún 194, 198, 219, 228, 231, 236, 239f, 244, 246-248, 254, 262f, 265
Gutrune 194, 196, 240, 244, 250, 259f
Gunnar 228, 231, 240, 244-248, 250, 253-255, 257f, 261, 263
Gunther 19, 240, 244, 249f, 260, 262

H

Hagen 18f, 25, 31, 45, 87, 89, 159f, 171, 182f, 196, 234, 244, 250, 262
Hans Sachs 114
Haradrim 62, 64, 67
Helen of Troy 89
Heorrenda 98
Hild 247, 253
Hindarfell (Hindarfjall) 187, 255
Hobbits 5, 21, 23, 73, 77f, 85f, 100-103, 114, 127, 130, 133f, 146, 154, 189, 193f, 197f
Hreidmar 7, 32, 219
Huan 27f, 35
Hunding 27, 35, 148, 220
Húrin 187, 211

I

Idril 21, 185
Ilúvatar 26, 225, 237

Isengard 22, 89, 133f, 137, 164
Isildur 18f, 22, 56, 187

J
Jonaker 7

K
Kinslaying at Alqualondë 127
Kortirion 98
Kriemhild 249
Kullervo 13, 35f, 118

L
Laurelin 22
Legolas 150, 218f, 221
Licht-Alben 26
Loge 18f, 78, 129, 131, 140, 195, 197, 220
Lohengrin 41, 63f
Lonely Mountain, the 15, 146
(Loth)lórien 63, 151, 188
Lúthien Tinúviel 20f, 27, 35, 63, 119, 211

M
Melkor 26f, 133
Middle-earth 21, 26f, 29, 34, 44, 51, 64, 82, 90, 93f, 97f, 100f, 130, 133, 142, 153f, 156, 184, 187
Miðgardsormr 230
Mîm 28, 36, 50-53, 107
Mime 17f, 28, 31-33, 36, 50-53, 89, 107, 129, 136, 154, 197, 237, 240, 242
Minas Tirith 22, 151, 187
Morgoth 22, 28, 63, 86, 133f, 187
Mount Doom 24f, 51, 72, 88
Music of the Ainur 26, 27, 127, 153, 185

N
Narsil 18
Nazgûl King 187f
Nibelheim 134, 164, 199

Nibelungs 44, 133, 153, 157, 173, 182
Nienor 28, 118
Nothung/Notung 18, 84, 239
Númenor, Númenoreans 19, 22, 62, 98f, 133, 194

O
Oathbreakers, the 188
Odin 32-34, 36, 174, 192, 195, 199, 225-227, 229-231, 235-238, 240-243, 253-255, 263f, 266
Old Man Willow 131, 142
One Ring, the 4f, 15-18, 23, 25, 28, 44, 47f, 51, 56, 70, 72, 74, 85, 87, 91-94, 178f, 194
Orcs 18f, 40, 62, 66, 69, 133f, 197
Orthanc 197
Ortrud 121
Ottor Waefre 98, 191
Ossian (Oisin) 115

P
Paris (Iliad character) 89
Pippin 48, 132, 213, 219
Puss-in-Boots 139f, 144

Q
Quenya 13, 194, 237

R
Ragnarök 33f, 132, 153, 174, 176, 183, 195, 224-227, 229f, 235f
Rashbold, J.J. 194
Red Book of Westmarch, The 92, 100, 130, 214
Regin 50, 52f, 201, 242
Rerir 198
Rhinegold, the 12, 23, 26-28, 44f, 58, 81, 84, 193, 199, 209
Rhinemaidens (Rhinedaughters), the 21, 23-25, 27, 44f, 58, 84, 87, 131, 159, 195, 220f, 226, 234,
Ring of Power 3, 5, 16, 29f, 33, 36, 40 49, 55, 76, 78, 83, 87, 221

Ringwraiths 16, 19, 179
Rivendell 18, 47, 151, 218
Rohan 89, 100, 102, 197, 214
Rohirrim, Rohirric 25, 63, 100, 213-215, 218
Ruling Ring, the 47, 56, 83, 94

S

Sam Gamgee 23f, 56, 62, 86, 89f, 100, 127, 156, 198, 218
Saruman 21f, 24, 33f, 51, 89, 132-134, 173, 197
Sauron 7, 16, 18, 22, 25, 27, 29, 34f, 44, 58-60, 62-64, 68, 82f, 85f, 91, 96, 133, 149f, 156, 179, 193
Scatha the Worm 32
Shelob 89, 131
Shire, the 21f, 41, 90, 102, 114, 133f, 156, 193f
Siegfried 15f, 18f, 24, 28f, 31f, 40-42, 50-53, 55f, 72f, 84, 87f, 93, 96f, 103, 105, 107, 114, 120, 122f, 131f, 140, 147, 157-160174, 178, 180f, 195,-197, 199, 204, 221, 224, 231-234, 236-240, 244f, 249-251, 255f, 259-263, 266
Sieglinde 21, 28, 35, 52, 84, 148, 159, 193, 195, 220, 243,
Siegmund 18, 21, 25, 27f, 35, 52, 84, 148, 159, 192f, 195, 204, 236, 239, 251
Sigmund 32, 35, 54, 235f, 239
Signý 35, 54, 219, 239, 242f, 245
Sigurd 3, 7, 10, 31-36, 50, 52f, 172f, 178-181, 183f, 198, 202, 216, 219, 224-226, 228-231, 233-241, 244-250, 252-266
Silmarils 138
Sindarin 193
Sinfjötli 35, 236
Smaug 15, 31, 35, 146, 196f, 199
Sméagol 17f, 32, 51, 56, 58, 78, 197
Southrons 67

T

Tarnhelm, the 15, 17, 28, 78, 140, 145, 195
Tarnkappe, the 17, 249
Telperion 22
Théoden 89, 188, 214, 219
Thor (Thórr) 32, 230, 232
Tol Eressëa 98-100
Tom Bombadil 23f, 131, 154, 194, 197
Treebeard 114, 151, 213f, 221
Tuor 21, 28
Túrin Turambar 4, 27f, 32, 35f, 50-52, 107, 118, 138, 153, 211f, 215

U

Ulmo 157
'Underhill' 194
Undying Lands 26
Ungoliant 22, 133, 187

V

Vafrlogi 192, 247, 253, 255-258
Valar 19, 131, 138, 156, 225
Valinor 22, 26f, 35, 133, 211
Valhalla (Valhöll) 234, 236, 241
Valkyries 28, 33f, 69, 138, 148, 184, 236, 240, 251,
Völsung 3, 65, 173, 176, 184, 192, 198, 201, 213, 215, 219, 221, 223, 228, 230, 234-236, 239, 254, 258f, 266

W

Waberlohe 192, 256
Waldvogel, the 19, 33, 52
Walhall 22, 25f, 29, 52, 84, 129, 136, 148, 153, 157f, 221, 232, 237, 251,
Wälse, Wälsung 27, 35, 192, 194,
Walter von Stolzing 208
Waltraute 136, 209
Wanderer, the 18, 24, 33f, 236f, 240
Wellgunde 58

White Tree, the 22, 133
Wittig der Irming (Witege, Widia) /
Woglinde 58
Wolfe 27, 35
World Ash, the 22f, 33, 84, 87, 131f, 148, 174
Wotan (Wodan, Wuotan) 15, 18f, 21f, 24, 27, 29, 33f, 40, 42, 44, 53, 55f, 74, 78, 84, 87, 90, 121f, 126, 132, 148, 157, 192, 194f, 197-199, 220f, 224, 231, 233, 236-238, 241f, 256

Y
Yggdrasil 33, 132

Z
Zeus 54

General index

A
Acton, Lord 43
Aeschylus 137
'Ainulindalë' 27, 127
'Akkalabêth' 19, 62
Albert, Prince 11
Alvíssmál 32
Allegory 48, 64, 86, 93f, 142, 229, 231
Allen & Unwin 6, 79, 119
Amon Hen (magazine) 13
Anglo-Saxonism, Anglo-Saxons 5, 63, 98-102, 116-119, 198, 213-215, 218, 225, 227
Animal Farm 84
Appia, Adolphe 146
Arda Legendarium 119, 131, 156
Aristotle, Aristotelian Drama 136, 138, 164
'Athrabeth Finrod ah Andreth' 19
Atlakviða 65f, 251
Atlamál 65, 251
Atlantis 98f, 194
Attila the Hun 65f
Auden, W.H. 8

B
Bache Smith, Geoffrey 117
Baldrs draumar (see *Vegtamskviða*) 232
Baudelaire, Charles 10
Baynes, Pauline 142
Bayreuth 58, 75, 125, 128, 144, 146, 183
Beardsley, Aubrey 11
Beowulf (epic) 5, 9, 60, 67f, 98, 122, 186, 189f, 201, 212, 215f

Bible, The 233
Blok, Cor (10 – Alksandr), 142
Brecht, Berthold 141
Britain 11, 58, 62, 65, 98f, 101, 173, 197
Brot af Sigurðarkviða (Old Lay of Sigurd) 240
Buddhism, Buddhist 158f
Bugge, Sophus 225, 230
Bulwer-Lytton, Edward 11

C
Capitalism 82f, 86, 107, 134, 164
Carpenter, Humphrey 4, 6-9, 118, 130, 171, 188
Catalaunian Plains, Battle of the 65f
Celtic 101, 115, 117, 119
Chamberlain, Neville 47f
Chesterton, G.K. 4
Children of Húrin, The 4, 13, 28, 35, 50, 53, 107, 138, 188, 190, 219
Christ, Christian 21, 116, 120, 122f, 153f, 171, 181, 189, 224f, 227, 229-233, 235, 237f, 258, 264
Codex Regius 3, 225, 244
Communism 39f, 67, 82
Críst 102

D
Dasent, George Webbe 45
Degas, Edgar 11
Deutsche Heldensage, Die 191
Deutsche Mythologie 122, 182, 265
Deutsches Wörterbuch 123, 256
Doomsday 225
Don Quijote 218

Drama 10, 12, 23, 26, 42, 55, 57, 59, 96, 105, 126, 135-139, 141-149, 151-153, 164, 174-176, 179f, 187, 190, 193, 200, 207, 217, 234, 242, 246, 250-252, 256
'Drowning of Anadûnë, The' 99

E
Edda (see Poetic Edda, Prose Edda)
Eddaic 52, 65, 176, 180, 200f, 203-205, 207, 209, 213f, 219, 224f, 232, 234, 237, 240f, 246, 251, 257, 263f
Eddas 29, 31, 36f, 50, 178, 182, 224-226, 228, 244
Elliot, T.S. 11
England, English 11, 59, 66, 70, 78, 97-103, 108, 116-121, 130, 138, 146, 157, 163, 173, 178, 183, 188-192, 194, 200-202, 211f, 214f, 218, 252, 266
Ettmüller, Ludwig 182f, 191f, 202-205, 207, 224
Eucatastrophe 153, 161, 233

F
Faery, Faërian Drama 102f, 136, 138, 151f, 164
Fantasy 9, 12, 46, 65, 92-96, 125, 135f, 138f, 141-148, 150-153, 164, 189
Fascism, fascists 39, 63f, 66, 68-70, 72, 96, 105
Fáfnismál 33, 52, 240, 253-256
'Fall of Gondolin, The' 21, 179, 185
Feen, Die 20f, 136
Festspiele 58, 149
Feuerbach, Ludwig 158f, 233
Finland 13, 35, 115, 118
Finn and Hengest 192
Finnegan's Wake 60
Fliegende Holländer, Der 20
Fornyrðislag 173, 201, 205, 213, 215, 266

Forster, E.M. 11, 117, 119-121
Franco, General 39
Friedrich (Frederick) Barbarossa, Holy Roman Emperor 103, 123
Freischütz, Der 13, 147

G
Garden of Eden 39, 81
Gauguin, Paul 11
Germany, Germans 3f, 7f, 10, 12f, 17, 23, 30f, 36, 39, 41, 43, 47, 50, 54, 57f, 60-62, 64, 66f, 70, 73, 75, 78, 92, 95-98, 103, 105, 108, 114, 117, 120-126, 140, 163, 172f, 176-178, 180, 183, 190-196, 200, 202-205, 210, 223, 225, 231, 238, 244, 248, 250-253, 256, 260, 265
Gesamtkunstwerk 135, 151f, 164, 224
Gilson, Rob 117
Goethe, J.W. von 115, 121, 217
Gothic 7, 65f, 211
Götterdämmerung 24-27, 29, 39, 41, 44f, 49, 55, 69, 85, 97, 129, 136, 148, 157, 159-161
Grimm, Jakob 61, 121-123, 136, 140, 182, 225, 227, 256, 265
Grimm, Wilhelm 122, 182-184, 191, 208, 225, 227, 256, 265
Grimnismál 132
Grípisspá 253
Greek drama 125
Grundtvig, N.F.S. 115, 225, 237

H
Hamðismál 244
Hauksbók 225f
head-stave (*hofudstafr*) 200f, 204, 206
Heine, Heinrich 122
Heimskringla 182, 184
Held des Nordens, Der 179, 200
Helreið Brynhildar 34, 241, 248, 253
Hengist & Horsa 98

History of Middle-earth, The 86, 118f, 130, 211
Hitler, Adolf 5, 8, 43, 54, 61, 64, 68-70, 74, 92, 96f, 105, 177
Hobbit, The 4, 9, 15, 18f, 32f, 46-49, 51, 58, 71, 74, 76-78, 99, 101, 106f, 130, 186, 193, 196, 198f, 214, 219, 223
Holy Roman Empire, Holy Roman Emperors 108, 120, 123, 155
Homecoming of Beorthnoth, Beorthelm's son, The 68
Homer 89, 115, 262
Howards End 117, 119, 123
Huns 7, 65f

I

Iceland, Icelandic 3, 7, 9f, 32-34, 36, 49f, 52, 57, 65f, 78, 107, 116, 174-176, 178, 180f, 183f, 198f, 202f, 207, 214, 224-226, 230, 235f, 238, 240, 242f, 246, 248f, 253, 260f
Iliad, The 89

J

Jackson, Peter 58, 69f, 83, 128, 134, 142, 150f, 156
Jesus (see also Christ) 124, 227, 232f
Jordanes 65
Joyce, James 11, 60

K

Kalevala 13, 35, 115
Keller, Gottfried 190
Kepler 121
King Arthur 117
King Sheave 213
Kólbitar 175
Kullervo (symphonic poem) 13
'Kunst und die Revolution, Die' 41, 233
'Kunstwerk der Zukunft, Das' 41

L

Lawrence, D.H 11
'Lay of Leithian, The' 20
Leaf by Niggle 95
Legend of Sigurd and Gudrún, The 3, 26, 35, 52-54, 56, 58, 65f, 172f, 178, 184, 265
LeGuin, Ursula 189
Leitmotiv/Leitmotif 84, 26, 27, 132, 148, 197, 213, 220
Letters of J.R.R. Tolkien, The 6f, 27, 39f, 48, 53, 61f, 64, 66, 69, 73, 78, 86f, 89, 91f, 94, 97, 99, 102f, 117, 119, 126, 130, 133, 137-139, 146, 155, 172, 177, 189, 196, 234
Lewis, C.S. 8, 12f, 74, 98, 173, 175, 177, 196
Lied vom Hürnen Seyfrid, Das 223
Liszt, Franz 159, 174
Ljódahattr 201, 205, 215
'Long Lay of Sigurd' 255, 257
Lönnrot, Elias 115, 118f, 174
Looney 92
Lord of the Rings, The, passim 4, 6f, 13, 16-18, 20, 24, 26, 28f, 32, 34, 41, 44f, 47, 56, 58-61, 63f, 66, 68, 70-74, 77, 81, 84-87, 90, 92-94, 97-103, 105-108, 114, 119, 126-133, 138f, 142, 144, 150, 153, 155f, 161, 163, 165, 172, 178, 186-189, 194, 199, 211, 213f, 216, 218f, 221, 223, 252, 266
'Lost Road, The' 98f
Ludwig, King of Bavaria 64, 158
Luther, Martin 121

M

Macbeth 137f
MacDonald, George 178f
Madlener, Joseph 143
Málahattr 201
Mallarmé, Stephane 10
Mann, Thomas 11, 114, 126, 158

McKellen, Ian 143
Meistersinger von Nürnberg, Die 11, 41, 201
Middle High-German 3, 7, 17, 200, 249
Middle English 200
Mohammed 121
Mone, Franz 231
Mongols 66
Morris, William 9f, 29, 116, 120, 178f
Motte Fouqué, Friedrich de la 178f, 200
Müller, Anja 125, 143-146, 160
Müller, Max 228f, 232
myth (Mythos) 3, 5, 9, 12, 29-33, 39, 43, 54, 57, 59-62, 67, 69, 71, 81f, 91, 93-103, 105-108, 113f, 116, 121-131, 135-137, 143f, 155f, 163-165, 171-178, 180, 182, 192, 195, 198, 208, 216, 224-234, 237-240, 251f, 263, 265f
Mythopoeia 24, 92, 95
Mythopoeic/mythopoesis 57

N

Napoleonic Wars 120
Nazism, Nazis 6, 42f, 61-63, 68-73, 75, 82, 92, 95-97, 102, 105f, 108, 174f, 177
Nibelungenlied 3, 5-7, 17, 31, 34, 57, 65, 120, 178, 180f, 191, 223, 231, 239f, 244, 246, 248f, 251
Nietzsche, Friedrich 11, 92, 113
Norman Conquest 116
Norna Gests thattr 52
'Notion Club Papers, The' 99, 102, 194, 252

O

Ohlmarks, Åke 6-9
Old English 17, 100, 187f, 191, 193, 195-197, 200
Old High-German 200

Old Norse 172, 180-183, 192-195, 198, 200-202, 208, 232, 236, 265
Old Saxon 200
'On Fairy Stories' 12, 45, 92, 95, 119, 125, 135, 138f, 143, 147, 151, 153, 157, 161, 164, 228f
Oper und Drama 23, 41, 54, 135, 137, 145, 171, 208f, 216f, 233
Oresteia 137
Oxonmoot 128

P

Parsifal 10, 20, 51, 114, 124f, 144
'Part of the Tale of Aragorn and Arwen' 20, 156f
Pearl 9
Perrault, Charles 140
Philology 3, 50, 119, 121, 172f, 184, 225, 238f, 249, 264f, 267
Plato 4, 17, 54
Poetic Edda (*Elder Edda*) 3, 32, 106, 132, 172, 176, 178f, 181f, 190, 200, 202-204, 207, 210, 214f, 223f, 240, 244, 246, 248f, 251-253, 257f, 261, 263
Prose Edda (*Younger Edda*, *Snorra Edda*) 61, 106, 181f, 195, 201, 223, 226f, 246f, 253, 256-259, 266
Pullman, Philip 46

Q

Quenta Silmarillion 138, 157

R

Rackham, Arthur 11, 139, 175
Rask, Rasmus 202f
Return of the King, The 25, 46, 86, 150, 187, 213f, 218
Republic, The 17
Revolution of 1848 40, 88
Rheingold, Das 12, 16f, 34, 36, 74f, 78, 83f, 90f, 129, 131, 136, 140, 145, 159, 195, 205, 209, 220f

General Index

Rhine 21f, 24-26, 28f, 44, 49, 55, 131, 136, 181, 195, 199, 234
'Ride of the Valkyries' 148
Ring des Nibelungen, Der, passim 3-5, 7f, 10-20, 22, 24-31, 39, 41-46, 48-50, 52-54, 56-59, 61-63, 71-76, 78f, 81-84, 87f, 90, 92f, 96f, 102f, 105-108, 121-126, 128-133, 136-138, 140, 144, 146-149, 153, 155, 157, 160f, 163-165, 171-179, 181-184, 186, 190-192, 195-197, 199-205, 207, 209-211, 220-224, 226, 231-240, 242, 244f, 248, 251f, 256, 259-261, 263-266
Ring of Gyges, The 17
Röckel, August 53, 90, 124, 238
Romantic Age, Romanticism 6, 96, 113-115, 117, 120f, 178f, 210
Rosenberg, Alfred 96, 102

S

Saracens 67
Satan 86, 88, 233
Sauron Defeated 99, 156
Saxony 64
Scandinavia 33, 64, 174, 181, 200, 244
Schlegel, Friedrich von 121-123
Schopenhauer, Arthur 88, 114, 124, 158-161, 190, 233
Schumann, Robert 180
Scotland 116
Sea Bell, The 154
Secondary World 108, 113, 118, 138, 141, 151, 164, 194, 234
'Secret Vice, A' 24
Shakespeare, William 137f, 208
Shakespearian Drama 145
Shaw, G.B. 11, 262
Sibelius, Jean 13
Sieger, Die 124
Siegfried (opera) 13, 18f, 24, 28, 51-53, 84, 89, 124, 129, 131, 136, 149, 175, 180, 196, 231f, 234, 236f
Siegfried's Tod 41, 157, 202, 224, 256
Sigdrifumál 34
Sigurd der Schlangentödter/Sigurd the dragonslayer 7, 179, 241, 264f
Sigurðarqviða in scamma (Short Lay of Sigurd) 34, 240, 245, 248, 257
Silmarillion, The 6, 13, 17, 19f, 22, 26-28, 35, 58, 64, 86, 89, 94, 97, 100, 106, 119, 127, 129, 131, 153, 157, 187f, 219, 225, 237
Simrock, Karl 182, 192, 202f, 205
Sir Gawain and the Green Knight 9
Smith of Wootton Major 94f, 102
Soviet Union 7, 63f, 67
'Spengler' 29, 73f, 93
Spengler, Oswald 74f
Stabreim (stave rhyme) 207-209, 217
Stalin 7
Story of Sigurd the Volsung and the Fall of the Nibelungs, The 10
Sturluson, Snorri 181, 266
Sub-creator 91, 130, 144, 164
Symposium (Plato) 54

T

'Tale of Aragorn and Arwen, the' 20, 156f
TCBS 9, 117f
Thidreks saga 36, 176, 182, 244, 246, 248, 253
Tolkien, Christopher 47, 61f, 65, 73, 95, 99, 100, 150, 172, 184, 186, 212, 223, 235, 242, 245, 254f
Tolkien, J.R.R., *passim* 3-37, 39-79, 81-103, 105-108, 113f, 116-121, 123, 125-135, 137-157, 160f, 163-165, 171-173, 175-179, 181f, 184-199, 201, 210-221, 223-246, 249-267
Tolkien, Priscilla 12f
Tristan und Isolde 11, 124, 136, 158

U

Unfinished Tales 107, 157
United Kingdom 116
Unwin, Rayner 4, 77
Unwin, Stanley 4, 48, 99

V

Vafþrudnismál 32
Verlaine, Paul 10
Victoria, Queen 11, 70
Viking Age, Vikings 29, 67, 116
Vischer, Friedrich Theodor 180
Visigoths 65
Völsunga saga 5, 9f, 29, 31f, 34-37, 49f, 54, 65, 106, 116, 176, 179, 181f, 190, 223, 231, 236-242, 244, 246f, 254-259, 261, 263

W

Wagner, Adolf 479
Wagner (Liszt), Cosima 55, 147, 155, 183
Wagner, Friedelind 97
Wagner, Richard, *passim* 3-37, 39-79, 81-103, 105-108, 113f, 121-126, 128f, 131-138, 140, 143-153, 155, 157-161, 163-165, 171-184, 190-211, 216-218, 221-224, 230-246, 248-252, 254-257, 259-267
Wagner, Wieland 146f, 149
Waldman, Milton 91, 99, 119, 130
Wales, Welsh 59, 116f, 119
Walküre, Die 20f, 25, 27f, 35, 44, 52, 54, 84, 131, 136, 173, 190-196, 209, 236, 238, 243, 251
Weber, Carl Maria von 14, 147
West-Romans 65
Whistler, James 11
'Wibelungen, Die' 103, 123, 232, 237
Wilde, Oscar 11, 83
Wilhelm II, German Emperor 66
Wiseman, Christopher 9, 117, 171

Wood, Elijah 142f
World War I 9f, 54, 117-119, 125, 163, 173f, 211
World War II 8, 40, 54, 61, 64, 68, 70, 74, 77, 92f, 95f, 101, 108, 120, 125, 174f
Woolf, Virginia 11

Y

Yeats, W.B. 11

Z

Zauberring, Der (*The Magic Ring*) 29, 178f
Zimmerman, Morton Grady 139
'Zukunftsmusik' 124, 137

Walking Tree Publishers

Walking Tree Publishers was founded in 1997 as a forum for publication of material (books, videos, CDs, etc.) related to Tolkien and Middle-earth studies. Manuscripts and project proposals can be submitted to the board of editors (please include an SAE):

Walking Tree Publishers
CH-3052 Zollikofen
Switzerland
e-mail: info@walking-tree.org
http://www.walking-tree.org

Cormarë Series

The *Cormarë Series* has been the first series of studies dedicated exclusively to the exploration of Tolkien's work. Its focus is on papers and studies from a wide range of scholarly approaches. The series comprises monographs, thematic collections of essays, conference volumes, and reprints of important yet no longer (easily) accessible papers by leading scholars in the field. Manuscripts and project proposals are evaluated by members of an independent board of advisors who support the series editors in their endeavour to provide the readers with qualitatively superior yet accessible studies on Tolkien and his work.

News from the Shire and Beyond. Studies on Tolkien
Peter Buchs and Thomas Honegger (eds.), Zurich and Berne 2004, Reprint, First edition 1997 (Cormarë Series 1), ISBN 978-3-9521424-5-5

Root and Branch. Approaches Towards Understanding Tolkien
Thomas Honegger (ed.), Zurich and Berne 2005, Reprint, First edition 1999 (Cormarë Series 2), ISBN 978-3-905703-01-6

Richard Sturch, *Four Christian Fantasists. A Study of the Fantastic Writings of George MacDonald, Charles Williams, C.S. Lewis and J.R.R. Tolkien*
Zurich and Berne 2007, Reprint, First edition 2001 (Cormarë Series 3), ISBN 978-3-905703-04-7

Tolkien in Translation
Thomas Honegger (ed.), Zurich and Jena 2011, Reprint, First edition 2003 (Cormarë Series 4), ISBN 978-3-905703-15-3

Mark T. Hooker, *Tolkien Through Russian Eyes*
Zurich and Berne 2003 (Cormarë Series 5), ISBN 978-3-9521424-7-9

Translating Tolkien: Text and Film
Thomas Honegger (ed.), Zurich and Jena 2011, Reprint, First edition 2004 (Cormarë Series 6), ISBN 978-3-905703-16-0

Christopher Garbowski, *Recovery and Transcendence for the Contemporary Mythmaker. The Spiritual Dimension in the Works of J.R.R. Tolkien*
Zurich and Berne 2004, Reprint, First Edition by Marie Curie Sklodowska, University Press, Lublin 2000, (Cormarë Series 7), ISBN 978-3-9521424-8-6

Reconsidering Tolkien
Thomas Honegger (ed.), Zurich and Berne 2005 (Cormarë Series 8),
ISBN 978-3-905703-00-9

Tolkien and Modernity 1
Frank Weinreich and Thomas Honegger (eds.), Zurich and Berne 2006 (Cormarë Series 9), ISBN 978-3-905703-02-3

Tolkien and Modernity 2
Thomas Honegger and Frank Weinreich (eds.), Zurich and Berne 2006 (Cormarë Series 10), ISBN 978-3-905703-03-0

Tom Shippey, *Roots and Branches. Selected Papers on Tolkien by Tom Shippey*
Zurich and Berne 2007 (Cormarë Series 11), ISBN 978-3-905703-05-4

Ross Smith, *Inside Language. Linguistic and Aesthetic Theory in Tolkien*
Zurich and Jena 2011, Reprint, First edition 2007 (Cormarë Series 12),
ISBN 978-3-905703-20-7

How We Became Middle-earth. A Collection of Essays on The Lord of the Rings
Adam Lam and Nataliya Oryshchuk (eds.), Zurich and Berne 2007 (Cormarë Series 13), ISBN 978-3-905703-07-8

Myth and Magic. Art According to the Inklings
Eduardo Segura and Thomas Honegger (eds.), Zurich and Berne 2007 (Cormarë Series 14), ISBN 978-3-905703-08-5

The Silmarillion - Thirty Years On
Allan Turner (ed.), Zurich and Berne 2007 (Cormarë Series 15),
ISBN 978-3-905703-10-8

Martin Simonson, *The Lord of the Rings and the Western Narrative Tradition*
Zurich and Jena 2008 (Cormarë Series 16), ISBN 978-3-905703-09-2

Tolkien's Shorter Works. Proceedings of the 4th Seminar of the Deutsche Tolkien Gesellschaft & Walking Tree Publishers Decennial Conference
Margaret Hiley and Frank Weinreich (eds.), Zurich and Jena 2008 (Cormarë Series 17), ISBN 978-3-905703-11-5

Tolkien's The Lord of the Rings: Sources of Inspiration
Stratford Caldecott and Thomas Honegger (eds.), Zurich and Jena 2008 (Cormarë Series 18), ISBN 978-3-905703-12-2

J.S. Ryan, *Tolkien's View: Windows into his World*
Zurich and Jena 2009 (Cormarë Series 19), ISBN 978-3-905703-13-9

Music in Middle-earth
Heidi Steimel and Friedhelm Schneidewind (eds.), Zurich and Jena 2010 (Cormarë Series 20), ISBN 978-3-905703-14-6

Liam Campbell, *The Ecological Augury in the Works of JRR Tolkien*
Zurich and Jena 2011 (Cormarë Series 21), ISBN 978-3-905703-18-4

Margaret Hiley, *The Loss and the Silence. Aspects of Modernism in the Works of C.S. Lewis, J.R.R. Tolkien and Charles Williams*
Zurich and Jena 2011 (Cormarë Series 22), ISBN 978-3-905703-19-1

Rainer Nagel, *Hobbit Place-names. A Linguistic Excursion through the Shire*
Zurich and Jena 2012 (Cormarë Series 23), ISBN 978-3-905703-22-1

Christopher MacLachlan, *Tolkien and Wagner: The Ring and Der Ring*
Zurich and Jena 2012 (Cormarë Series 24), ISBN 978-3-905703-21-4

Renée Vink, *Wagner and Tolkien: Mythmakers*
Zurich and Jena 2012, (Cormarë Series 25), ISBN 978-3-905703-25-2

The Broken Scythe. Death and Immortality in the Works of J.R.R. Tolkien
Roberto Arduini and Claudio Antonio Testi (eds.), Zurich and Jena 2012 (Cormarë Series 26), ISBN 978-3-905703-26-9

Constructions of Authorship in and around the Works of J.R.R. Tolkien
Judith Klinger (ed.), Zurich and Jena, forthcoming

J.S. Ryan, *In the Nameless Wood* (working title)
Zurich and Jena, forthcoming

Tolkien's Poetry
Julian Morton Eilmann and Allan Turner (eds.), Zurich and Jena, forthcoming

Beowulf and the Dragon

The original Old English text of the 'Dragon Episode' of *Beowulf* is set in an authentic font and printed and bound in hardback creating a high quality art book. The text is illustrated by Anke Eissmann and accompanied by John Porter's translation. The introduction is by Tom Shippey. Limited first edition of 500 copies. 84 pages.
Selected pages can be previewed on:
www.walking-tree.org/beowulf
Beowulf and the Dragon
Zurich and Jena 2009, ISBN 978-3-905703-17-7

Tales of Yore Series

The *Tales of Yore Series* grew out of the desire to share Kay Woollard's whimsical stories and drawings with a wider audience. The series aims at providing a platform for qualitatively superior fiction with a clear link to Tolkien's world.

Kay Woollard, *The Terror of Tatty Walk. A Frightener*
CD and Booklet, Zurich and Berne 2000, ISBN 978-3-9521424-2-4

Kay Woollard, *Wilmot's Very Strange Stone or What came of building "snobbits"*
CD and booklet, Zurich and Berne 2001, ISBN 978-3-9521424-4-8

www.ingramcontent.com/pod-product-compliance
Lightning Source LLC
Chambersburg PA
CBHW070721160426
43192CB00009B/1274